GEOPOLITICS,
AND STRATEGY

Of Related Interest

Geoproperty: Foreign Affairs, National Security and Property Rights
Geoff Demarest

Boundaries, Territory and Postmodernity
David Newman

Military Power: Land Power in Theory and Practice
edited by Brian Holden Reid

Seapower: Theory and Practice
edited by Geoffrey Till

Airpower: Theory and Practice
edited by John Gooch

The National Security of Small States in a Changing World
edited by Efraim Inbar and Gabriel Sheffer

The Transformation of Security in the Asia/Pacific Region
edited by Desmond Ball

Security Challenges in the Mediterranean Region
edited by Roberto Aliboni, George Joffé and Tim Niblock

Regional Security in the Middle East: Past, Present and Future
edited by Zeev Maoz

Israeli Strategy after Desert Storm – Lessons of the Second Gulf War
by Aharon Levran

Geopolitics, Geography and Strategy

Editors

COLIN S. GRAY
(*Centre for Security Studies, University of Hull*)

GEOFFREY SLOAN
(*Britannia Royal Naval College*)

FRANK CASS
LONDON • PORTLAND, OR

First Published in 1999 in Great Britain by
FRANK CASS PUBLISHERS
Crown House, 47 Chase Side
London N14 5BP

and in the United States of America by
FRANK CASS PUBLISHERS
c/o ISBS, 5824 N.E. Hassalo Street
Portland, Oregon, 97213-3644

Website: www.frankcass.com

Reprinted 2003

British Library Cataloguing in Publication Data

Geopolitics, geography and strategy
1. Geopolitics 2. World politics – 1945–
I. Gray, Colin S. (Colin Spencer), 1943– II. Sloan, G. R.
(Geoffrey R.), 1955–
320.1`2
ISBN 0-7146-4990-2 (cloth)
ISBN 0-7146-8053-2 (paper)

Library of Congress Cataloging-in-Publication Data

Geopolitics, geography, and strategy / editors, Colin S. Gray, Geoffrey Sloan.
p. cm.
Includes bibliographical references and index.
ISBN 0-7146-4990-2. – ISBN 0-7146-8053-2
1. Geopolitics. I. Gray, Colin S. II. Sloan, G. R.
(Geoffrey R.)
JC319.G487 1999
320.1`2–dc21 99–38173
CIP

This group of studies first appeared in a double Special Issue on 'Geopolitics, Geography and Strategy' of *The Journal of Strategic Studies* (ISSN 0140 2390) 22/2-3 (June/September 1999) published by Frank Cass.

Printed in Great Britain by Antony Rowe Ltd

Contents

Sir Halford Mackinder aged 72 in a 1933 portrait by Sir William Rothenstein.

Frontispiece from *Mackinder* by W.H. Parker (Clarendon Press 1982) by permission of Oxford University Press and London School of Economics (where the original portrait hangs)

1

Why Geopolitics?

GEOFFREY SLOAN and COLIN S. GRAY

The popularity of geopolitical theory from 1945 to the present has been rather like the length of hemline on a woman's skirt; it has fallen and risen with the vagaries of fashion. The current vogue can be traced to 1979 when Henry Kissinger published the first volume of his memoirs titled *The White House Years*. It was significant that this book made continual use of the term 'geopolitics'. This was important for two reasons: first, Kissinger used it as a method of analysis to combat the American liberal policies of idealism; second, it was utilised as a means of presenting an alternative to the conservative policies of an ideological anti-Communism. Kissinger claimed for geopolitics a synonymity with global equilibrium and permanent national interests in the world balance of power. He defined geopolitics as follows: 'by geopolitical I mean an approach that pays attention to the requirements of equilibrium'.[1] The revival of the word 'geopolitics' by Kissinger resulted in two discernible paths of development. 'It led, by example and reaction, to further reflection on global strategy in the geopolitical tradition. Secondly, and perhaps in the end more significantly, it popularized the word geopolitics, which entered the language in a way which it never had before, though at the substantial price of ambiguity and confusion of meanings.'[2]

This special issue of the *Journal of Strategic Studies* has two related aims. First to make a contribution to dispelling the ambiguity and confusion that still surrounds the term geopolitics. Second, to illuminate the relationships between geopolitics, geography and strategy, and to show how the practice and study of strategy requires a continuing exchange between history and theory. In essence, geopolitics is an attempt to draw attention to the importance of certain geographical patterns in political history. It is a theory of spatial relationships and historical causation. From it explanations have been deduced which suggest the contemporary and future political relevance of various geographical concepts. Furthermore, it can be argued that geopolitics combines historical knowledge with a sophisticated capacity for theorising. The result has been a powerful analytical framework.

One of the aims of geopolitics is to emphasise that political predominance is a question not just of having power in the sense of human or material resources, but also of the geographical context within which that power is exercised: 'in nearly all international transactions involving some element of opposition, resistance, struggle or conflict, the factors of location, space and distance between the interacting parties have been significant variables. This significance is embodied in the maxim, "power is local". This is to say, political demands are projected through space from one location to another upon the earth's surface.'[3]

This is not to say that the geographical environment determines the objectives or strategies of the foreign or internal policies of a particular state. States do not find themselves in a geographical strait-jacket; instead, geography or geographical configurations present opportunities for policy-makers and politicians. This was recognised by one of the founders of modern geopolitical theory, Sir Halford Mackinder (1861–1947). Writing in 1890 he claimed that:

> the course of politics is the product of two sets of forces, impelling and guiding. The impetus is from the past, in the history embedded in a people's character and tradition. The present guides the movement by economic wants and geographical opportunities. Statesmen and diplomatists succeed and fail pretty much as they recognise the irresistible power of these forces.[4]

The extent to which geographical opportunities will be exploited depends on strategy. That is a concern with the deployment and use of armed forces to attain particular political objectives.

Political objectives are a consequence of choices made by policy-makers. It is from these choices that political and strategic importance is attached to geographical configurations and locations. It also reflects the nature of politics as a decision-making process. In this process the geographical factors which influence politics are a product of policy-makers selecting particular objectives and attempting to realise them by the conscious formulation of strategies. This relationship between the geographical environment and the decision-making process is a dynamic one; it is dependent upon changing levels of transport and weapons technology. This dynamic aspect is one of the most important links between geopolitical theory, geography and strategy. It illustrates the pivotal nature of the continuing exchange between theory and history.

Furthermore, geography can be described as the mother of strategy, in that the geographical configuration of land and sea, with respect to a state's strategic policy, or an alliance between states, can exercise a twofold strategic conditioning influence: on locations important for defence, and on the routes and geographical configurations which favour an attacking force, be it on land or sea. Geography, it is worth adding, is pertinent at the tactical, operational, and strategic levels of conflict, although its use or misuse by commanders at different levels can have very different consequences.

This special issue is divided into two parts. The first, comprising seven essays is designed to illustrate the way that geopolitical theory derives from interpretation of geographical configuration and historical experience. These studies address questions of methodology and approach: what reasonably might we expect geopolitical theory to achieve for illumination of the relationship between geography and strategy? The second part consists of a further five essays which offer a new focus on the relationship between geography and strategy, a relationship often ignored in the past.

Geoffrey Sloan explains the 1904, 1919, and 1943 versions of Mackinder's heartland theory in the context of the unique historical periods of their formulation. He then looks at the propositions which can be deduced to suggest future relevance for the heartland theory. Mackinder's view of geography is interpreted as a combination of a geographical *longue durée* and a theatre of military action. A good geopolitical analysis, Sloan suggests, must present a picture of the constellation of forces which exist at a particular time and within a particular geographical frame of reference. This approach makes Mackinder's geopolitical theories prominent among the most important of the twentieth century.

Jon Sumida breaks new ground with respect to the geopolitical theories of Rear Admiral Alfred Thayer Mahan (1840–1914). Mahan's work in the past has been judged negatively to have been cast unduly in a deterministic mould. Achievement of naval supremacy appeared directly linked to several immutable geographical conditions. Sumida explains why Mahan came to be associated with an absolutist approach to history. This was because of a set of physical and human geographical propositions whose use in connection with the explanation of major international political outcomes made it easy for many people to believe that Mahan argued that geography determined the course of history. Sumida's careful consideration of Mahan's work reveals that such a characterisation is faulty and seriously misleading. What emerges is a view of Mahan that has not been seen before. It is one where human affairs are complicated and outcomes dependent upon complex interactions and contingent forces. Mahan's view of the utility of history illuminating geography and strategy considers a range of possibilities, including contradictory or even mutually exclusive ones.

Ben Lambeth considers air power from two innovative perspectives. The first is what air power has become, particularly in the context and wake of Operation 'Desert Storm' in 1991. The thesis is that it has now become transformative in its effects and can produce strategic results in joint warfare; space surveillance and communications are a large part of what has given airpower the value-added clout it offers to joint force commanders today. The second perspective is in many ways the antithesis of the first. As early as 1919 Mackinder claimed that air power had an advantage over land mobility, but it had a boomerang nature since it proceeds from and to a land base after flight, and those land bases can be captured by land power. Lambeth also maintains that carrier-borne aircraft cannot conduct a sustained an air campaign. Therefore the great challenge for the future will be whether countries such as the United States can build partnerships and otherwise plan ahead for access in many parts of the world. This, Lambeth argues, will be critical if air power is to meet its promise in future conflicts.

Everett Dollman's is perhaps the most ambitious of the essays on geopolitical theory. For the first time an attempt has been made to discern the geopolitical dimensions of space. This has led to the coining of the adjective 'astropolitical'. Dollman uses Mackinder's heartland theory as his geopolitical template. He argues that the vast resources of solar space represent the heartland of the astropolitical model. Earth space, like Eastern Europe in Mackinder's design, is the most critical arena for astropolitics. Control of earth space not only guarantees long-term control of the outer reaches of space, it provides a near-term advantage on the terrestrial battlefield. From early warning and detection of missile and force movements, to target planning and battle damage assessment, space-based intelligence gathering assets, Dollman argues, already have proved themselves as legitimate force multipliers.

There is also a pertinent Mahanian geopolitical analogy. Mahan argued that control of certain bodies of water were particularly important for economic and military reasons. Space, Dollman argues, like the sea, can be traversed potentially in any direction, but because of gravity wells and the forbidding cost of lifting weight into orbit, over time space-faring nations will develop specific pathways for the heaviest traffic. Indeed, space highways and 'chokepoints' are clearly discernible already.

For much of the post-1945 period geopolitics has been something of an intellectual pariah. It is worth noting that between the 1940s and the publication of Colin Gray's *The Geopolitics of the Nuclear Era* in 1977 (with the exception of Sen's *Basic Principles of Geopolitics and History*, published in India in 1975) no book title in English used the term geopolitics. The effect of this condition of neglect was compounded by the advent of critical theory and postmodernism which emerged in International Relations in the 1980s.

The emergence of these approaches was a reaction to two things: first to the perceived dominance of neorealist and neoliberal perspectives; second to the disintegration of the Marxist 'dependency' critique of orthodox thinking on the subject. This approach has generated different 'critical studies' that have been applied to subject areas in International Relations. Geopolitics has not been excepted from this trend. However, it is important to understand just what this approach is attempting: 'what justified the label "critical", is a concern with human emancipation – the goal in each case is to re-orient their sub-discipline towards this goal, and to refuse to accept accounts of the subject area that do not privilege emancipation'.[5]

Gearóid Ó Tuathail, on critical geopolitics, argues that geopolitics has a self image as an instrumental form of knowledge and rationality. It takes the existing power structure for granted and works within it to provide advice to foreign policy makers. Ó Tuathail claims that its dominant modes of narration are declarative (this is how the world is) and imperative (this is what we must do). Critical geopolitics, it can be argued, is different in two important respects: first it is a problematising theoretical project that places the existing structure of power and knowledge in question; second it critiques the superficial and self-interested ways in which orthodox geopolitics reads the world political map by projecting its own cultural and political assumptions upon it while concealing these same assumptions.

In addition to these two perspectives Ó Tuathail suggests that geopolitics is mythic because it promises uncanny clarity and insight in a complex world. This claim of clarity is sustained by the use of such binaries from the geopolitical tradition as heartland/rimland, land power/sea power, and East/West. In short, critical geopolitics aims to persuade strategic thinkers to acknowledge the power of ethnocentric cultural constraints in their perception of places and the dramas occurring within them.

The last look at geopolitical theory is also an attempt to break new ground. David Lonsdale assesses the implications of information technology. Specifically, he argues that the defining characteristic which identifies the 'infosphere' as a dimension of strategy is the manner in which strategic power can be projected through and within this unique environment. He draws an important analogy with both sea power and air power. In both these environments the dominant operational concept is to gain command of a particular geographical dimension of strategy. Yet Lonsdale argues persuasively that use of the infosphere has its own challenges. The key being to ensure your own use, yet deny your adversary the same facility. He reminds us of the requirement for some functioning enemy information infrastructure if deception operations are to be effected. The primary characteristics of information power are flexibility and accessibility.

What has this to do with geopolitics? Lonsdale argues convincingly that information power is unlikely to become transformative in its effects and produce strategic results independently. Instead it will develop its own geopolitical logic and will supplement and enable success in the other existing environments of strategy. In short, in its own unique way it will become territorialised.

The aim of the second part of this Special Issue is to explore the relationship between geography and strategy and to draw geopolitical conclusions from it. Colin Gray sets out in a comprehensive manner the relationship between geography and strategy. He argues that geography cannot be an optional extra for consideration by the strategic theorist or planner, because it drives the character and potential contemporary reach of tactical, hence operational, prowess.

What is innovative about Gray's approach is that he first fixes the nature of strategy as the dialogue between policy and military power. He argues that in reconciling political objectives with military ones, the strategist must deal with a realm of great complexity and uncertainty. Policy, in a sense, must be more important than strategy, just as strategy must be superior to operations and tactics. Strategy would be literally senseless in the absence of policy. Having located strategy in the hierarchy between policy and military power, the geographical dimension of strategy is then elucidated. He argues that strategy is inherently geographical and that even when other dimensions are examined they are each subject to the influence of what can be termed fairly as geographical influence. In no sense is this a claim for geography as the 'master dimension' of strategy. Gray's argument simply is that geography always matters for strategic experience, and on occasion it will matter hugely.

Perhaps the most innovative aspect of this approach is the way in which geography and strategy are related to geopolitical theory. Gray argues that the principal glory of the 'grand narrative' of geopolitical theory is the ability to tie apparently disparate phenomena together in meaningful ways. He suggests that it is exactly the meaningful character of geopolitical theories that renders them so controversial.

Another important focus is what Clausewitz called the relationship between a logic of policy and a grammar of war. Gray underlines the point that the grammar of strategy literally and inalienably is dictated by the distinctive requirements of physical geography. Furthermore, he argues that to plan and act globally, rather than regionally or locally, is not to transcend geography, let alone geopolitics, in fact quite the reverse. A global perspective is simply to plan and behave for a more extensive domain. Strategy and politics must be 'done' within geography. Gray's thesis is that geography is inescapable.

Nicholas Rodger sheds new light on the subtle relationship between geography and strategic policy, a combination of conditioning influence and the changing meaning of geographical conditions. What he illustrates in an engaging manner is the profound influence that geographical configuration and weather had on naval operations prior to the advent of steam propulsion. Just moving your naval force from its base to where you wished it to fight was an exercise often fraught with danger. There were few safe landfalls and prevailing winds often prevented a naval commander from taking what appeared to be the most direct route. For example, in the eighteenth century the quickest passage normally available from Jamaica to Barbados (a distance of just over 1,000 miles by steamer) was via London or New York! Changes in transport and weapon technology were to have a profound impact on the relationship between geography and naval power. Technology was, and remains, a key dynamic factor in the relationship between the geographical environment and the decision-making process.

This point is also well exploited by Ewan Anderson on boundaries. The idea of a boundary is very much a product of nineteenth century developments in cartography, which is to say in changes in the technology of map making. The geopolitical implications of this have been profound, especially with respect to the political claims that states would make in the twentieth century. Anderson succinctly sums up the difference between frontiers and boundaries. Frontiers have a spatial extent whereas boundaries have no horizontal dimension. The crucial dimension of boundaries occurs in the vertical plane, enabling states to claim air space and subterranean space (though generally not overhead, extra-terrestrial space).

Significantly, he also identifies a crucial geopolitical challenge for the future. This is the issue of trans-boundary movements. It is an area where international law is still in an early stage of development. Perhaps the most important geographical issue concerning trans-boundary movements in the early twenty-first century will be the transportation route of oil and natural gas from the Caspian Sea basin. Since all the producer states are landlocked, transportation will require both pipeline and tanker. Thus the concept of boundaries will face a new challenge which will bind certain countries in this area closer together than they are at present.

Williamson Murray's focus is the relationship between geography and war from a historical perspective. Important changes occur when geography is interpreted as a theatre of military action. First, it becomes more abstract, certainly simplified and schematised. The military strategist or commander will perceive only those geographical features relevant to the military objectives he is attempting to achieve. This perspective of geography as a theatre of military action has a lineage traceable to antiquity.

This aspect of the military art is examined from the tactical, operational and strategic levels. At the tactical level, geography becomes terrain, a crucial component in war. Murray shows that for war in the twentieth century an ability to use terrain remained crucial. He cites the example of the lack of British tactical proficiency in World War II when they were consistently surprised to find that the Germans had sited their positions on reverse slope positions throughout the Normandy campaign. Also he argues convincingly that air power, despite claims to the contrary, is a prisoner of terrain in that air bases are the tactical framework within which an air force wages campaigns.

At the operational level, it is in the realm of logistics and intelligence that an appreciation of geography and distance is most vital. The finest understanding of the role of geography at the operational level, it is suggested, is given by the US Navy in its drive through the Central Pacific in 1943 and 1944. This superior operational performance was a product of 20 years of wargames and study at the Naval War College in Newport, Rhode Island.

Murray shows convincingly that it is at the strategic level that geography has exercised its greatest influence. The reason for this is rarely noticed. Mistakes at the tactical and operational level often can be corrected promptly. At the strategic level, however, mistakes tend to live forever – or at least until the war changes in two respects: first, the coalition of the participants; second, by radical change in war aims. An example of this is the fall of France in June 1940, and the inability of the Royal Navy to use naval bases in the south of Ireland. This created a crisis with grave potential strategic consequences which was only averted by America's entry into the war in December 1941.

One aspect of the relationship between geography and strategy still clouded in extraordinary controversy, is the impact of the German school of geopolitics on the statecraft and strategy of Nazi Germany. The founder of the German school, Major General Karl Haushofer (1869–1946), left a confusing legacy for future scholars to unravel. At the heart of the German school was the assertion of a dynamic relationship between the concept of a natural boundary and the idea of continuous geographical expansion. Geopolitics, wrote Haushofer 'shall and must become the geographic conscience of the state'.[6] As early as 1913 he advocated 'a transcontinental route free of Anglo-Saxons', which would link Germany with Russia and Japan.

After the Second World War both Karl Haushofer – until his suicide in 1946 – and his surviving son, Heinz, claimed that after 1938 Haushofer had worked for the Nazis only under duress. Yet Holger Herwig manages with the use of new primary sources to reveal another reality in which Haushofer used German geopolitics as a tool of political propaganda. For example, one month after the launch of Operation 'Barbarossa' in June 1941 Haushofer maintained that this operation constituted the greatest task of geopolitics, the rejuvenation of space in the 'Old World'. Furthermore, it constituted a bold attempt: ' positively and creatively to turn the task of forging Eurasia and Eurafrica into reality'.

These statements contributed greatly to the tendency, since 1945, for writers to perceive all geopolitical theory as synonymous with German geopolitics. However, two features made German geopolitics unique: first the subordination of all facts of political knowledge to the primacy of geography; second, the assertion that the German Reich was a superior polity whose destiny was quite separate from that of any other European state. As a result of these characteristics the shadows were cast long. Geopolitical theory became an intellectual pariah for the best part of 35 years.

In the final contribution to this Special Issue, John Erickson gives a compelling account of the phoenix-like rise of geopolitics in a country that formerly was in the forefront of demonising it. The former Soviet Union currently manifests an obsessive preoccupation with geopolitics. Erickson maintains that with the collapse of Communism Russia suffered a huge crisis of identity and a challenge to its security requirements of truly historic dimensions. The withdrawal from the centre of Europe, from Prague to Smolensk, has reduced Russia in Europe to the geostrategic condition that obtained three centuries ago. To deal with this revolutionary situation there has been a recourse to geopolitical thinking. In particular, Erickson shows how there has been a restitution of the geopolitical approach coupled with the introduction of the term national security. For the Russians national security embraces the idea of the state as a tool assuring 'the best possible conditions' for the individual, for society, and for the state itself, as conditioned by the entire spectrum of active geopolitical factors.

In post-Soviet Russia geopolitics also has been subject to an astonishing process of institutionalisation. The Section of Geopolitics and Security of the Russian Academy of Natural Sciences was established for all practical purposes by the Russian General Staff on 22 November 1991, its membership composed of senior Russian officers associated with the General Staff. This new institutional prominence is fused, as Erickson points out, with a radical revision in appreciation of Russian strategic capabilities, replacing previous parity with the United States by an emphasis on strategic stability. Yet it is also pointed out that the most important factors in Russia's 'geopolitical security' are internal conditions rather than external parameters.

In conclusion this special issue is one of the very few attempts to bring together recent theoretical advances in geopolitical writing with strategic analysis from a historical perspective. The resulting synthesis furthers the debate about geopolitical theory and, more broadly, about the role of geography in explaining the development of strategic thinking in the past and its possible evolution in the future.

Three points emerge most prominently about the nature of geopolitical theory: first, is its dynamic nature, a dynamism heavily attributable to the changes in transport and weapons technology; second, is identification of the main roles that geopolitical theory can play. First, it can fulfil an interpretative role. It suggests a view of international politics and strategic history which is shaped by the geographical configuration of land and sea and the political development of particular states. Second, geopolitics can function as a policy science. For goals to be secured certain geopolitical perspectives have to be taken into consideration. Geopolitics can help explain the structure of security problems. Third, geopolitics can be an instrument of political warfare.

Furthermore, geopolitical ideas can be a convenient vehicle for justification of political decisions taken on other grounds. The intended effect is to give coherence to certain political aims. In the case of strategic policy, political objectives are achieved through attention to the geographical configuration of land and sea.

Finally, these different roles raise the question of the future utility of geopolitical theory for those who will make strategy and policy. Sir Halford

Mackinder, writing in 1942, provided a synthesis of the qualities that policy makers will still find relevant in the twenty-first century:

> They must have a global outlook and a quick readiness to meet emergencies, for it was never more true than in this newly 'closed' world that 'our stability is but balance, and wisdom lies in the masterful administration of the unforeseen'; they must also have a trained power of judging values and be capable of long views in framing policies for the future; and they will, of course, still need an understanding of the momentum with which both Man and his environment come to the present from the past.[7]

Above all else, Mackinder underlined the point that geopolitics, geography, and strategy serve together.

NOTES

1. H. Kissinger, *The White House Years* (Boston: Little Brown 1979) p.914.
2. L.W. Hepple, 'The Revival of Geopolitics', *Political Geography Quarterly* 5/4 (Oct. 1986) p.522.
3. H. and M. Sprout, 'Geography and International Relations in an Era of Revolutionary Change', *Journal of Conflict Resolution* 6/1 (March 1960) p.145.
4. H.J. Mackinder, 'The Physical Basis of Political Geography', *Scottish Geographical Magazine* 6 (1890) p.84.
5. C. Brown, *Understanding International Relations* (Basingstoke: Macmillan Press 1997) p.53.
6. K. Haushofer, 'Pflight und Anspruch der Geopolitik als Wissenschaft', *Zeitschrift für Geopolitk* 12 (1935) p.443.
7. H.J. Mackinder, 'Geography, an Art and a Philosophy', *Geography* 27 (1942) pp.129–30.

PART I

GEOPOLITICAL THEORY AND STRATEGY: THE WORDS AND THE HISTORY OF IDEAS

2

Sir Halford J. Mackinder: The Heartland Theory Then and Now

GEOFFREY SLOAN

Sir Halford John Mackinder (1861–1947) was that rare beast in British twentieth century public life – a polymath. His career was diverse and breathtaking. It could have constituted the careers of at least five men, not one. It covered the fields of higher education, service education, diplomacy, politics, exploration and public service.[1] Mackinder himself recognised that his career had not been one of linear progression: 'There is another kind of career I will describe as erratic and such a career has been mine, a long succession of adventures and resignations. I do not admit to having been a rolling stone, because I have generally known where I was going – but I have certainly gathered no moss.'[2] Apart from a very small group of academics, few people today have knowledge of or interest in the history of this fascinating career that included serving as Liberal Unionist MP for the Camlachie Division of Glasgow (1910–22), Chairman of the Imperial Shipping Committee (1920–39), British High Commissioner to South Russia (1919–20), the creation of the University of Reading from 1892, Director of the London School of Economics (1903–8) and the initiation of the National Savings Movement (1915), and last but not least founding the School of Geography at Oxford University in 1899. Despite these notable achievements what have endured has been his strategic concepts. These can be encapsulated by the heartland theory. The three versions published in 1904, 1919 and 1943 constitute his most important legacy in terms of strategic thought.

It is the aim of this article to assess and explain the origins, development and importance of the heartland theory. Before this can be done it is important to establish the nature of the relationship between geography and international relations. This relationship can be viewed in three different ways. First it can be seen as an objective of policy, a prize in a conflict between two or more states. As a state exercises control over territory, any part of that territory can be a source of conflict with another state. It follows from this proposition that one of the primary functions of any state is to defend successfully its delineated borders from external attack. Yet, conversely, a portion of a state's population can, by violent or peaceful means, secede and create a new state, and consequently change the geographic scope of a state's political authority.

This is the most common view of geography held by international relations writers. Although the geographical scope of some states' political authority may change, in essence geography is one of the bedrocks of international politics, like the board of a chess game.

> The hundred and seventy or so states which engage in International Relations have several characteristics in common. Perhaps the most fundamental is that they are all territorially based. Each of them represents a physical sector of the land mass of the globe, and (subject to a few very minor exceptions) at the international level represents it exclusively. The same piece of territory is not the responsibility of more than one state. Then the world may be imagined as divided into states by frontiers rather as a farm is into fields by fences and walls.[3]

The wide coinage enjoyed by this view is a consequence partly of the historical evolution of the idea of sovereignty.[4]

The second view of territory is that of an environment. This perspective is both natural and historical. It includes 'all the features which specialists in fauna, flora, terrain and climate are in a position to discern'.[5] In addition, there is a historical view of the geographical environment, which constitutes a *longue dureé* or long duration. This perspective was developed by the French historian Braudel in his now classic work on the Mediterranean.[6] It was a mechanism he developed to deal with the physical geography of the Mediterranean and the restrictions and the opportunities it afforded for human development. In essence, the *longue durée* is a structure, an architectural outline that time alters little. It is also important to stress that this long duration is only one of three types of duration which all exist simultaneously. The effects of the geographical environment are the most persistent and unchanging:

> long-range duration at a quasi-immobility level of structures and traditions, with the ponderous action of the cosmos, geography, biology, collective psychology and sociology; level of middle-range

> duration of conjunctions or periodic cycles of varying lengthy but rarely exceeding second generations; a level of short duration of events, at which almost every action is boom, bang, flash, gnash, mess and noise, but often exerts only a temporary impact.[7]

A view of geography as both an environment and part of a *longue durée* means, to paraphrase Braudel, becoming used to a slower tempo, which sometimes almost borders on the motionless. Yet despite this slowness of pace, this approach helps to facilitate a study of men and society through territory.[8]

Third, geography can be interpreted as a theatre of military action. When geography is perceived in this way important changes take place which distinguish this approach from the previous two. First, it becomes more abstract, simplified and schematised. The flora and fauna no longer have the same relevance. There is no slow-moving *longue durée* which facilitates an understanding of society through territory. The military strategist or commander will perceive only those geographical features that are relevant to the military objectives that he is attempting to achieve. The same could be said of a policy-maker attempting to decide priorities in strategic policy.

This perspective of geography as a theatre of military action has a lineage which goes back to antiquity. Sun Tzu writing in the period 400–320 BC developed a typology by which a general could classify geography according to its utility in battle. 'Ground may be classified according to its nature as accessible, entrapping, intrusive, constricted, precipitous, and distant.'[9] This typology of Sun Tzu's illustrates well the view of geography as a theatre of military action which has become both simplified and schematised as a consequence of being utilised in this manner.

Sun Tzu also attempted to elucidate how geography was pertinent with respect to the battlefield objectives of the military commander:

> Conformation[10] of the ground is of the greatest assistance in battle. Therefore, to estimate the enemy's situation and to calculate distances and the degree of difficulty of the terrain so as to control victory are virtues of the superior general. He who fights with full knowledge of these factors is certain to win; he who does not will surely be defeated.[11]

At the tactical level, geography was also seen as important for the successful deployment of troops.[12]

Having examined the three ways that geography can be interpreted, it is important to ask what is the relevance of these perspectives to the heartland theory? The relevance, it will be argued, comes from interpreting Mackinder's most important concept as a synthesis of the second and third views of territory, a combination of a geographical *longue durée* and a theatre of military action. This view of the heartland theory is one that has been absent from recent attempts to put Mackinder's geopolitical ideas in context where an assessment can take place.[13] This interpretation of Mackinder's heartland theory raises a further question. How important is it to understand all three versions of the heartland theory in the context of a unique historical period? Finally, what explanations, if any, can be deduced which suggest the present and future political and strategic relevance of the heartland theory at the dawn of the second millennium?

Given the subsequent fame and some would say notoriety that the heartland theory achieved (for example, it was cited in 1978 as one of the 29 most important texts ever written[14]), it is important to place the 1904 version in its historical context. When Halford Mackinder rose on the evening of 25 January 1904 to address the Royal Geographical Society he was delivering a paper which was both in tune with national concerns and out of tune with international events. In terms of national concerns Mackinder's paper 'The Geographical Pivot of History' was delivered on a groundswell of anxiety about geography and the security of Britain and the Empire. The end of the Boer War in 1902 had produced a real concern about Britain's future role in the world. A Royal Commission had been set up in September 1902 to examine specifically Britain's shortcomings in that conflict, and had reported in July 1903. One of the identified weaknesses was the geographic and cartographic ignorance of British Army staff officers during the conflict.[15]

Seven months after publication of 'The Geographical Pivot of History' the Military Correspondent of *The Times*, Lieutenant-Colonel Charles A'Court Repington, wrote an essay called 'Geography and War'. In it Repington made very clear the link between geography and military operations: 'We have suffered and we shall continue to suffer, in the conduct of military operations because the teaching of geography has not assumed its proper place in national education. … The interest of the army in this matter is solid with politics, commerce and finance.'[16]

This article and subsequent exchanges in *The Times* correspondence columns underlined the point that the 'New Geography' which Mackinder had outlined as early as 1887 was different from what had preceded it. Furthermore, it was now beginning to play an important part in national concerns, and was needed if Britain's global preponderance was to be sustained. The innovative dimension of Mackinder's 'New Geography' was that it had a holistic approach. In a geographical sense one of the organising concepts was that of the region: 'The difference between my effort and those which preceded it was that they made use of the improved maps to illustrate single distributions, e.g. geological, historical etc, whereas I "attempted" a complete geographical "synthesis" … the regional idea was implicit in the paper on the "Scope and Methods of Geography" which I read at the beginning of 1887 before the Royal Geographical Society'.[17] The contemporary relevance of Mackinder's paper was borne out by the first comment that was made by Spencer Wilkinson,[18] after Mackinder had finished delivering his paper: 'As I was listening to the paper, I looked with regret on some of the space that is unoccupied here, and I much regret that a portion of it was not occupied by members of the Cabinet.'[19]

If Mackinder was riding a wave in a national sense, especially in terms of the public debate which both preceded and followed the publication of his paper, the opposite was true in the international environment. The heartland theory stressed the unassailable power of a land based state – Russia occupying the 'heartland' of the Eurasian continent. However, within a fortnight of his lecture, the Japanese Navy attacked Port Arthur in the first engagement of the Russo-Japanese War. Furthermore, the Japanese defeated the Russians in a naval battle off Port Arthur in August 1904. The final blow was the Battle of Tsushima Straits in May 1905 where the Japanese won a decisive sea battle. This battle effectively ended the conflict and Russian land power had lost this war.

The newspaper coverage of Mackinder's 1904 version of the heartland theory was brief. Mackinder offered a view that, while reflecting national anxieties concerning geography, war and Britain's security, was largely ignored. To enable an assessment to be made of this assertion it is important to examine the main ideas formulated in the 1904 address. The starting point for understanding Mackinder is the interplay between geography and military power, and the political and strategic consequences of this interplay. Military power, in 1904, consisted of land power and sea power. The interaction between these two mediums was, for Mackinder, one of the fundamental patterns of international politics. The boldly conceived paper 'The Geographical Pivot of History' offered a view that was contrary to the accepted wisdom of the day. The first assertion was that the last 400 years (roughly from 1500 to 1900) could be described as the Columbian epoch. The epoch was coming to an end, and the impact on international politics would be immense. The 'post-Columbian' age would, Mackinder asserted, have radically different characteristics. Their impact on international politics and strategic considerations could not be ignored. The first would be a closed political system:

> From the present time forth, in the post-Columbian age, we shall again have to deal with a closed political system, and none the less that it will be one of world-wide scope. Every explosion of social forces, instead of being dissipated in a surrounding circuit of unknown space and barbaric chaos, will be sharply re-echoed from the far side of the globe, and weak elements in the political and economic organism of the world will be shattered in consequence.[21]

His aim was to explain human history as part of the life of the world organism. He is also aware of the subtle relationship between geography and the evolution of policy decisions. In that the geographical environment does not define the choices of policy-makers, it none the less provides an important, if not crucial, conditioning influence: 'Man and not nature initiates, but nature in large measure controls.'[22]

The second assertion is the importance of the geographical configurations and location within which political power is exercised. In particular Mackinder underlined the changing political relevance of a state's geographical location. The main factors in bringing this change about were those that occurred in transport and weapons technology. Combining the two factors which had been discussed, Mackinder develops a synthesis between the patterns of physical geography and political history and a strong use is also made of analogy: 'A repellent personality performs a valuable social function in uniting his enemies and it was under the pressure of external barbarism that Europe achieved her civilisation. I ask you, therefore, for a moment to look upon Europe and European history as subordinate to Asia and Asiatic history, for European civilisation is, in a very real sense, the outcome of the secular struggle against Asiatic invasion.'[23]

This struggle against Asiatic invasion provides the logic for Mackinder to draw attention to the vital importance to the world of the modern expansion of Russia: 'The most remarkable contrast in the political map of modern Europe is that presented by the vast area of Russia occupying half the Continent and the group of smaller territories tenanted by the Western Powers.'[24]

This geographical configuration was then assessed by interpreting it as a combination of a geographical *longue durée* and a theatre of military action. This innovative geopolitical perspective facilitated an understanding of Russia's strategic importance *vis-à-vis* Europe in the past, and how it would be affected in the future by changes in transport and weapons. The historical starting point is the thirteenth century when the Mongol invasion of Europe began. However, Mackinder points out that this westward invasion, which affected Poland, Siberia, Moravia, Hungary, Croatia and Serbia was but one of three strategic thrusts made by the Mongols of Genghis Khan and his successors. The other two being south-west between the Caspian Sea and the Hindu Kush into modern day Iran, Iraq and Syria and the third one into Northern China.

This ability to strike in three directions was a product of a central geographical location fused with horse and camel mobility over open steppe land. Mackinder notes that the sixteenth century, the Tudor Century as he called it, saw two important yet unconnected strategic events:

> The Tudor Century, which saw the expansion of Western Europe over the sea, also saw Russian power carried from Moscow through Siberia. The eastward swoop of the horsemen across Asia was an event almost as pregnant with political consequences as the rounding of the Cape, although the two movements long remained apart.[25]

If the historical understanding was insightful it was Mackinder's comments about the future and the strategic and political consequences of changes in transport technology that were to give the concept of the geographical pivot of history a dynamic that was to propel it through the twentieth century. The specific transport technology that he was referring to was railways:

> trans-continental railways are now transmuting the conditions of land-power, and nowhere can they have such effect as in the closed heartland of Euro-Asia, in vast areas of which neither timber nor accessible stone was available for road-making. Railways work the greater wonders in the steppe because they directly replace horse and camel mobility, the road stage of development having here been omitted.[26]

Mackinder astutely also appreciated the strategic implication of the new technology for the interplay between geography and military power. In particular the confrontation between seapower and landpower. 'The Russian Army in Manchuria is as significant evidence of mobile land-power as the British Army in South Africa was of sea-power. True, that the Trans-Siberian railway is still a single and precarious line of communication, but the century will not be old before all Asia is covered with railways.'[27]

The great strength of Mackinder's heartland theory, evident in all versions, is the blending together of an understanding of the political implications of new technology with the persistence of certain geographical patterns of political history. This combination enabled him to put forward an explanation of how a technology-induced change in favour of land power would have profound political consequences for those states which were located in the Rimland area of the Eurasian landmass: 'the oversetting of the balance of power in favour of the pivot state, resulting in its expansion over the marginal lands of Euro-Asia, would permit of the use of vast continental resources for fleet-building, and the empire of the world would then be in sight.'[28]

FIGURE 1
THE NATURAL SEATS OF POWER

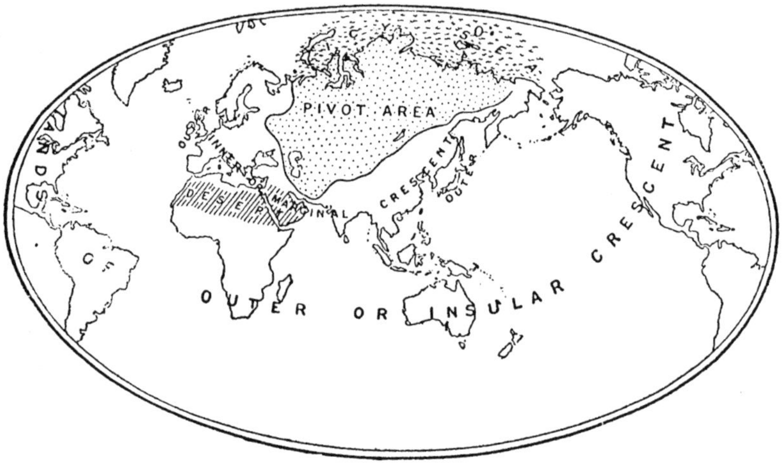

Source: H.J. Mackinder, 'The Geographical Pivot of History', *Geographical Journal* 23/4 (April 1904) p.435.

This assertion of Mackinder's was in many ways revolutionary as he was outlining at the beginning of the twentieth century what had been impossible at the beginning of the nineteenth – the evolution of a closed international political system, where the idea of world domination was, for the first time, a viable political aim. However, it has been claimed that Mackinder and the American frontier historian Frederick Jackson Turner (1861–1932) were essentially reflecting, in both a domestic and international context, what had been happening to scientific debate in the latter half of the nineteenth century: biology had taken over from philology and geology as the evolutionary science *par excellence*. The consequence of this was that geography was interpreted in a twofold manner:

'First, space must be seen as an important requirement of the social organism and second, space must be at a premium. This ensured that there would be a struggle for space analogous to the competition of species and the survival of the fittest. The easiest way to this was to argue that the available space was already filled up, which frustrated the natural tendency of societies to grow or expand spatially. This is exactly what Turner and Mackinder did.'[29] This revolutionary aspect of 'The Geographical Pivot of History' was something that was to have a growing pertinence as Mackinder developed the heartland theory in the two subsequent versions. It has been argued that this concept of a closed international political system was to convey succinctly the contemporary political message that both Mackinder and Turner wished to make due to its three main components: 'their conception of the role of environment in history; their understanding of the motor behind progressive sequential change in history; and their isolation of fundamental breaks in this historical process'.[30]

The second point that has to be made concerning the 1904 version of the heartland theory was that Mackinder made a plea at the end of his address against the seductive forces of geographical determinism, something that geopolitics was to become associated with in the post-1945 period: 'The actual balance of political power at any given time is, of course, the product on the one hand of geograpical conditions, both economic and strategic, on the other hand, of the relative number, virility, equipment, and organisation of the competing peoples.'[31] Mackinder distilled this perspective down to the subtle relationship between geography and strategic and political policy. As stated earlier the geographical environment does not define the choices of policy-makers, it none the less provides an important, if not crucial, conditioning influence: 'The social movements of all times have played around essentially the same physical features.'[32] Taken together these points mark out the 1904 version of the heartland theory to be both bold and innovative in its conception.

When the First World War began in August 1914, Mackinder who had been an MP since 1910 entered fully into public life to support the war effort. His first contribution was to boost recruiting for the British Army in Scotland. This had come about through his friend Lord Haldane bringing his name to the attention of Lord Kitchener, the War Minister. In just three days Mackinder organised 700 recruiting stations all over Scotland. In 1915 he was responsible for setting up the National Savings Movement. Yet he did not gain access to a Cabinet level job. While he had a patron in the War Cabinet, Lord Milner, he lacked the strong political base from which to achieve office. Despite the lack of promotion to Cabinet rank he continued to make an impact in the House of Commons. 'During the war Mackinder widened his speaking brief in the House to include almost every subject that come under discussion e.g. the availability of ploughmen, the housing of the working classes, margarine and the price of coal. He showed an anxious concern for the economic and social condition of Britain after the war, being one of the few who saw that even victory would leave the economy dislocated and the fabric of society damaged.'[33]

The concern for the post-war world was to have a geopolitical manifestation as well. It culminated in 1919 with the publication of *Democratic Ideals and Reality: A Study in the Politics of Reconstruction*. Its genesis can be traced back to December 1914. In that month Professor Lyde addressed the Royal Geographical Society on the subject of: 'Types of Political Frontiers in Europe'. He argued that there were three *a priori* conditions which in the future would be important for the fixing of frontiers to facilitate lasting peace. These were listed as first, the social unit should, as far as possible coincide with a geographical unit; second in the exercise of political sovereignty over new geographical areas the capability to assimilate new populations should be paramount; third, that frontiers should incorporate features where different populations naturally meet. It should not include waterdivides and mountain crests.[34]

In the subsequent discussion Mackinder, who was present at the address, gave a completely different interpretation. He argued that frontiers are fixed by a process of political bargaining:

> I think you will find that the old idea of balance of power will assert itself again in any congress of Europe, and that means that you will fix boundaries by the old process of bargaining ... Just consider what the end of this war may be. You are not going to crush out the German nationality. That is impossible; nor would it be desirable, if it were possible. You have 61- or 62-million in the German Empire, and you have to add to them, I suppose, some eight or ten million German Austrians. A nationality of 70 million in the centre of Europe, with an intensely national character, will have to be dealt with. It will still be so strong a power that I question whether there will be very much of ideal map-making. If you conquer that power, the object will be to clip its wings for the future.[35]

From these prescient comments that were made by Mackinder in December 1914 a trail of evolving geopolitical thought can be traced. The first element was the geographical location and demographic size of the German nation.

The second element of his thinking during the First World War underlined the importance of insuring the emergence of smaller states in the area of Eastern Europe. By 1916 Mackinder had helped to found the Serbian Society. This was an organisation that promoted the idea of the state that was to be called Yugoslavia. In a newspaper article in September 1916[36] he argued that Serbia would incorporate Bosnia, Herzegovina, Slovenia and Croatia. During this period he was drawn into the New Europe Group which contained the historian R. W. Seaton-Watson and the academic and future political leader Tomas G. Masaryk. Seaton-Watson's contribution was to set up in October 1916 a weekly paper entitled *The New Europe*. Mackinder by 1917 was a supporter of national aspirations in the geographical area, and in July 1918 he is listed as one of the collaborators on *The New Europe*.[37]

The crystallisation of the two elements that have been described was brought about with the publication of *Democratic Ideals and Reality* in 1919. This work was to represent Mackinder's most important contribution to the development of the heartland theory. Furthermore, its influence was to have a dramatic impact on his career. The key strategic concept behind the geographic pivot of history which Mackinder outlined in 1904 had been the development, for the first time in world history, of a closed international political system where world domination was, for the first time, a viable political aim. In Mackinder's 1919 version important changes and insights were made. First the geographical scope of the pivot of history was expanded, and given a new name – the heartland:

> the heartland for the purposes of strategical thinking includes the Baltic Sea, the navigable Middle and Lower Danube, the Black Sea, Asia Minor, Armenia, Persia, Tibet and Mongolia. Within it, therefore were Brandenburg-Prussia, and Austria-Hungary as well as Russia – a vast triple base of manpower, which was lacking to the horse-riders of history. The heartland is the region to which under modern conditions, sea-power can be refused access.[38]

The second was the real strategic impact that changes in transport and weapons technology would have on the heartland as it emerged from the facts of geography and history:

> today armies have at their disposal not only the trans-continental railway but also the motor car. They have, too, the aeroplane, which is of a boomerang nature, a weapon of land-power as against sea-power … In short, a great military power in possession of the heartland, and of Arabia could take easy possession of the crossways of the world at Suez.[39]

FIGURE 2
MACKINDER AND E. EUROPE/CAUCASUS, 1920

Source: B. W. Blouet, *Halford Mackinder: A Biography* (College Station: Texas A & M UP 1987) p.175.

Another insight that Mackinder provided was the importance of the threat that land power could pose to sea power, in the twentieth century. 'We have defeated the danger on this occasion, but the facts of geography remain, and offer ever-increasing strategical opportunities to land-power as against sea-power.'[40] Two of the reasons listed for the emergence of this threat were manpower[41] and organisation. Mackinder argued that it had only been in the last hundred years (i.e. since 1819) that a sufficient base of man-power existed able to threaten the liberty of the world from within citadel of the World-Island. Closely linked to a numerical sufficiency was organisation:

> Manpower – the power of men – is also, and in these modern days very greatly dependent on organisation, or, in other words, on the 'growing concern', the social organisation. German *Kultur*, the 'ways and means' philosophy, has been dangerous to the outer world because it recognises both realities, geographical and economic, and thinks only in terms of them.[42]

The real difference between the 1904 version and the 1919 version, apart from the three which have been outlined, was the focus on Central Europe as the future fulcrum of the balance of power in a confrontation between sea power and land power. Furthermore, Mackinder's second version was prescriptive in a manner that the 1904 version was not. It did what Mackinder had called for geography to do, as early as 1914: 'to give judgement in practical conduct'.[43] This approach was used to great effect in the second version of the heartland theory. 'Unless you would lay up trouble for the future, you cannot now accept any outcome of the War that does not finally dispose of the issue between German and Slav in East Europe. You must have a balance between German and Slav, and true independence of each … A victorious Roman general, when he entered the city, amid all the head turning splendour of a "triumph", had behind him on the chariot a slave who whispered into his ear that he was mortal. When our statesmen are in conversation with the defeated enemy, some airy cherub should whisper to them from time to time this saying:

> Who rules East Europe controls the heartland:
> Who rules the heartland commands the World-Island:
> Who rules the World-Island commands the World.[44]

This geopolitical jingle of Mackinder's was eventually to gain wide coinage. The antidote to this scenario was the end of the German-Russian two-state system in Eastern Europe and the emergence there of several middle-tier states supported by the League of Nations.

The irony was that the book was not widely reviewed,[45] and despite such insightful comments as 'if we accept anything less than a complete solution of the Eastern Question in its longest sense we shall merely have gained a respite, and our descendants will find themselves under the necessity of marshalling their power afresh for the siege of the heartland',[46] it is hard to find any historical evidence showing a direct connection between any aspect of British policy during this period and Mackinder's second version of the heartland theory.

However, there was one important consequence in terms of Mackinder's own career. In October 1919 Mackinder's friend Lord Curzon was appointed Foreign Secretary. As a result of this appointment Mackinder was asked by Curzon if he would accept the post as British High Commissioner to South Russia and to co-ordinate measures in that area to help General Denikin who was leading White Russian forces against the Bolsheviks. Mackinder's mission was short-lived, yet in terms of his influence on British policy we are presented with a painful paradox of a clear geopolitical vision yet ultimate policy failure. Mackinder's report which was written in the cruiser HMS *Centaur*, off Marseilles in January 1920, presented the British government with a coherent overall plan for defeating the threat of Bolshevism. It advocated a further sub-division of Eastern Europe and the Caucasus (see Map 2, p.26) into a series of states which ran from north to south. This buffer zone would consist of: White Russia, the Ukraine, South Russia, Georgia, Armenia, Azerbaijan, and Daghestan.

In addition the policy of giving stores and war material to the various White Russian armies was pronounced a failure by Mackinder despite the large expenditure that this had incurred. For example, between November 1918 and October 1919 Lloyd George's government spent £17.3 million on cash payments and the supply of marketable stores to the White Russian armies. This was on top of the £27.1 million that was spent on the deployment of army, naval and air force contingents.[47]

By contrast Mackinder's strategic vision was clear: 'it is now obvious that the Denikin Government alone cannot defeat Bolshevism, and that the method of mere military adventure associated with the names of [Admiral] Koltchak [Kolchak], Yechenitch [Yudenich] and Denikin must be abandoned. There must be substituted a system of alliances and of steady organisation *pari passu* with limited military allowances'.[48] Mackinder was also able to elucidate a clear geographical threat that would emerge if Bolshevism was not channelled and contained between two barriers. These barriers were both political and geographical. An alliance of newly independent states in the west, and the Caspian Sea and Caucasian mountains in the East.

Yet Mackinder also recognised that the last element had a temporary quality to it:

> it is only by strong immediate measures taken before the thawing of the Volga ice that the advance of Bolshevism, sweeping forward like a prairie fire, can be limited, and kept away from India and Lower Asia, pending the outcome of Poland and the Odessa. It must be remembered, moreover, that the very success of that Polish and South

> Russian advance, on a line extending from the Gulf of Finland to the Sea of Azoff, would tend to drive the Bolsheviks into Asia, and, it is essential, therefore, to regard the Caspian and Caucasian barrier as a part of the larger policy. But I cannot look upon a Caucasian barrier as more than a temporary expedient of a not very substantial character: the only final remedy is to kill Bolshevism at the source.[49]

It is also interesting to note that Mackinder's mission to South Russia, it can be suggested, had a liaison function with Britain's foreign intelligence service (SIS). This can be seen from a letter Mackinder wrote to Curzon on 23 November 1919, defending the size of his personal staff. In particular the decision to take a doctor for so small a mission:

> I have reason to know that the YMCA are preparing a considerable humanitarian Mission to South Russia, which I am told is to be backed by a large sum of money. The most experienced Anglo-Russian – men here like Bagge, Reilly, and Dukes[50] – assure me that this charitable mission will probably do more to increase British influence among the Russian masses than anything else. My idea is that my Doctor would act as liaison officer in this respect.[51]

It is also important to stress that by November 1919 when Mackinder met these three intelligence officers all SIS operations in Russia had been uncovered by the *Cheka* – the Soviet secret police. Consequently there was an enormous gap in terms of accurate information concerning conditions in Soviet Russia. This is reflected in a Cabinet memorandum dated October 1919: 'No authoritative statement has ever been made about conditions in Soviet Russia and there is no question upon which people differ more widely.' Perhaps more importantly it was reflected in the supplementary instructions that Lord Curzon sent to Mackinder in December 1919:

> the Cabinet particularly desired that they (Mackinder's instructions) should be supplemented in one respect. The information about many of these areas is so conflicting and so little is known with certainty about the condition and feeling in those parts of Southern Russia which have passed into Denikin's hands in the course of his advance, further his actual policy towards the states both in front of and behind him is in some cases so obscure – that before embarking upon any fresh policy for the future HMG would like to receive a report from you on the entire situation in its various aspects ... This will be of the greatest value to the Government not only in enabling them to understand the present situation, but in helping them to formulate a policy for the future.[52]

Mackinder's report on the situation in South Russia can be interpreted as being a hybrid of an intelligence report and a geographical construct for the future stability in the relationship between Eastern Europe and the heartland. Eight days after submitting the report Mackinder was introduced to the British Cabinet and was questioned by its members on the report.[53] What comes across in this Cabinet meeting is his sustained defence of a 'whole policy' which was embedded in the geographical parameters of the heartland theory. It was geography interpreted as a synthesis of a theatre of military action and a geographical *longue durée*. Its main emphasis was to commend to the British Cabinet of 1920 a view of events in Bolshevik Russia which could be shaped to Britain's and indeed Europe's advantage by taking into account the geographical configuration of land and sea and political developments:

> he would range up all the anti-Bolshevist States, from Finland to the Caucasus, giving them a certain amount of support. Denikin should be re-equipped for defensive purposes but on a more modest scale than before. We must be prepared to hold the Baku–Batum line and to take control of Denikin's fleet on the Caspian. Any policy of support to individual states merely involved waste of money without anything effective being done. It was necessary to adopt the whole policy or to do nothing.[54]

To consolidate Britain's position in Russia, Mackinder had proposed the following immediate practical steps. These had been included in his original report of 21 January 1920. What these proposals illustrate is the way Mackinder appreciated the importance of a favourable geographical field in which to exercise military and economic power. Furthermore, the need to ensure that his 'whole policy' was not jeopardised by an increase in geographical vulnerability due to the wrong choices being made by British policy makers or the action of the Bolshevik regime:

> a firm declaration by Britain especially that she will not make peace with Bolshevism should be issued, it is she, not France, which is suspect; it is her support and not that of France which is valued, it is Mr Lloyd George's definite promise and not that of M. Clemenceau which is desired, and ardently desired. Timely assistance should be given in naval and technical ways for the holding of the Isthmus of Perikop [entrance to the Crimea] and the defended areas of Odessa and Novorossisk. Help in the way of loans should be provided to the Poles provided they ally themselves with Denikin on proper terms in

regard to their eastern frontier. The Denikin Government should be recognised as *de facto*, provided that its bases be broadened.[55]

Unfortunately for Mackinder's geopolitical construct political events conspired against him. There was the correct perception by policy-makers that people in Britain and Europe were tired of war and foreign interventions and that the best way of dealing with the Bolshevik regime was to isolate it from the rest of the international community. Consequently his policy of creating a series of buffer states, consisting of White Russia, the Ukraine, South Russia, Georgia, Armenia, Azerbaijan and Daghestan, failed to gain support. The abandonment of this policy, Mackinder maintained would increase the chances of Russia becoming a great heartland power.

The Cabinet's lack of commitment to the policy that Mackinder had outlined was now clear. After Mackinder had reported to them on 29 January 1920, a short discussion then took place in regard to British Policy towards Russia: 'the immediate steps proposed in Sir Halford Mackinder's Report (Appendix II) did not meet with any support. The Cabinet agreed that the question of Sir Halford Mackinder's return to South Russia should be kept in suspense pending further developments of, and decisions regarding the policy of the Allies in Russia.'[56] It can be said that Mackinder's attempt to use his second version of the heartland theory to give judgement in practical conduct failed primarily due to the fact that decision-makers sensed a lack of public support for sustained foreign intervention in the aftermath of a war that had cost Britain one million war dead.

With the demise of the Soviet Union in 1991 there emerged 12 independent states which ranged from Estonia in the north to Azerbaijan and Kazakstan in the south. Furthermore, a new geopolitical construct has emerged. It has a close congruence to the plan Mackinder presented to the British Cabinet in January 1920. The aim of Mackinder's 'whole policy', was to create a favourable geographical field in which the ideological threat of Bolshevist rule could be contained, and prevent the emergence of a centralised military power that he described as a 'Jacobin Czardom'.[57]

Today these threats no longer exist. However, what has replaced it are the huge oil reserves that are supposed to exist in the Caspian region: 'estimates of proven and possible reserves across the entire area run to 200 billion barrels of oil product. This includes about 30 billion barrels of discovered reserves approximately equal to those of the North Sea.'[58] There have been claims that 'Central Asia is once more a key to the security of all

Eurasia.'[59] What has not emerged yet from the main Western Powers is a coherent geopolitical analysis that elucidates the constellation of economic and political forces which exist at present and the geopolitical field within which strategic and economic leverage can be exercised. The details of this problem are examined in John Erickson's essay in this special issue.

The third version of the heartland theory did not appear until the Second World War. By 1943 Mackinder was 82 years old and writing in the midst of the confusion of another conflict. Yet despite old age and the diffuse and global nature of the war he was living through, a clear geopolitical vision was presented. The 'Heartland', a phrase used only once in the 1904 paper, is given prominence by Mackinder. It moves from being a descriptive to a technical term: 'the Heartland provides a sufficient physical basis for strategical thinking'.[60] He also asserts that its utility is greater in 1943 than it has been in the past: 'I have described my concept of the Heartland, which I have no hesitation in saying is more valid and useful today than it was either 20 or 40 years ago.'[61]

When Mackinder identified the 'pivotal area' in his 1904 version, it was largely undeveloped economically. Yet by 1943 his prophecy concerning the ongoing organisational ability of the Bolsheviks, fused with a favourable geographical location, was on the way to being realised:

> the vast potentialities of the Heartland, however, to say nothing of the natural reserves in Lenaland [Mackinder's term for a huge Far Eastern part of the USSR beyond the River Yenisei], are strategically well placed. Industries are growing rapidly in such localities as the southern Urals, in the very pivot of the pivot areas, and in the rich Kuznetsk core basin in the lee of the great natural barrier east of the upper Yenisei River. In 1938 Russia produced more of the following foodstuffs than any other country in the world. Wheat, Barley, Oats, Rye and Beet. More Manganese was produced in Russia than in any other country. It was bracketed with the United States in the first place as regards Iron, and it stood second place in production of Petroleum.[62]

Mackinder saw not one but two threats to the dominance of the maritime powers. The first was Germany. This country was presented as a channel that has to be cleansed and controlled in the future by a combination of land power and sea power: 'the polluted channel might be swept clear very effectively if it were controlled by strong embankments of power on either hand – land power to the east, in the Heartland, and sea power to the west, in the North Atlantic basin. Face the German mind with an enduring

FIGURE 3
THE WORLD ACCORDING TO MACKINDER (1943)

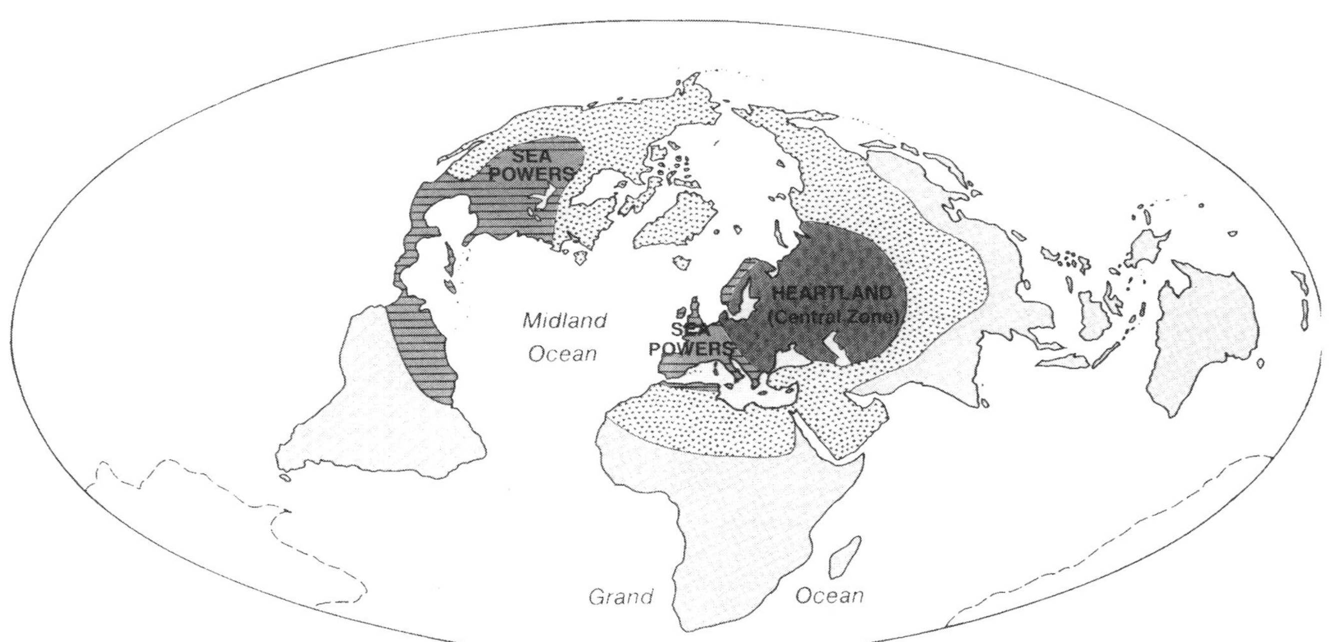

Source: B.W. Blouet, *Halford Mackinder: A Biography* (College Station: Texas A & M UP 1987).

certainty that any war fought by Germany must be a war on two unshakeable fronts and the Germans themselves will solve the problem.'[63] The other threat was the Soviet Union. If she was to emerge the conqueror of Germany, she would rank as the greatest land power in the world: 'the Heartland is the greatest natural fortress on earth. For the first time in history it is manned by a garrison sufficient both in number and quality.'[64]

Paradoxically Mackinder developed his most important concept after the heartland as a riposte to the threat of a resurgent Germany *not* the Soviet Union. Its essence was amphibiosity; the idea was that sea power in the final resort must be able to project power ashore to balance the threat from land power. The concept was given the name of the Midland Ocean. Its geographical scope was the North Atlantic and its dependant seas and river basins. Furthermore, it was made up of three elements: 'a bridgehead in France, a moated aerodrome in Britain, and a reserve of trained manpower, agriculture and industries in the eastern United States and Canada'.[65] This trinity of amphibiosity and the location of the three elements meant that the fulcrum of power had moved west yet again. He also traced with great prescience the geopolitical structure of the NATO alliance when it was formed in 1949.

There are two points that can be made about the Midland Ocean. First as far as Mackinder's writing is concerned it was not new. It had appeared in embryonic form as early as 1924:

> Western Europe and North America now constitute for many purposes a single community of nations. That fact was first fully revealed when American and Canadian armies crossed the Atlantic to fight in France during the Great War… In the United States the most abundant rainfall and the most productive coalfields are to be found in the east, but in Europe they are in the west. Thus the west of Europe and the east of North America are physical complements to one another and are rapidly becoming the balanced halves of a single great community.[66]

The second important point was that Mackinder's third version appears in the middle of a war that saw amphibiosity come of age and enacted on a global scale which had been inconceivable 20 years previously. Throughout the Second World War there were a total of 600 amphibious landings, or an average of one every 3½ days. In addition, nearly all these landings were successful. It can be suggested that in the third version he showed an appreciation of the relevance of sea power in relation to land power. In other words, it matters only insofar as it affects a state's ability to control and protect the land in both war and peace.

Having examined the three versions of Mackinder's heartland theory in their historical context, what can be deduced to suggest its present and future relevance on the eve of the twenty-first century? In one sense it can be argued that the heartland theory has no more utility. Although it became the dominant geopolitical paradigm of the Cold War and was of particular importance to the United States' policy of containment towards the Soviet Union,[67] it is important to note Mackinder himself argued that: 'every century has its own geographical perspective'.[68] As we move into the twenty-first century, new geographical perspectives will emerge that may be different from the geographical perspective of the twentieth century.

However, it can be suggested that there are three analytical aspects of Mackinder's heartland theory which will have relevance in the twenty-first century. First Mackinder identified the existence of a closed international state system where the idea of world domination was for the first time, a viable political aim. This type of system will sustain itself in the twenty-first century and continuing changes in transport and weapon technology will make inter-state relations even more intensive and complex than they have been in this century. Second, Mackinder through the heartland theory has left a theoretical legacy which can be utilised to outline the geographical perspective of the twenty-first century. He was concerned to draw attention to geographical patterns of political history.

> For the first time we can perceive something of the real proportion of features and events on the stage of the world, and may seek a formula which shall express certain aspects at any rate of geographical causation in universal history. If we are fortunate, that formula should have a practical value as on setting into perspective some of the competing forces in international politics.[69]

This statement was made when the twentieth century was four years old. Furthermore, it has much in common with the views on the theory of international relations put forward by writers today: 'Theory is used in international relations not only to define concepts and categories but used to draw concepts together so as to outline perspectives or build up "maps" of the international area.'[70]

Finally, Mackinder's ideas have often been associated with environmental determination. This was mainly a product of the use the German school of geopolitics made of his ideas from 1933 to 1945. Yet he was at pains to point out in the 1919 version of the heartland theory that geographical location alone was not what made a country a 'going concern'. Just as important were political organisation and the availability of manpower. By manpower he meant their numbers, efficiency, skill and health. In short, another aspect of the legacy for the future is that although the geographical environment does not define the choices of policy-makers, it nonetheless provides an important, if not crucial, conditioning influence. Thus the geopolitical perspective that Mackinder did so much to develop over a period of 39 years is not an inflexible imperialist paradigm, but like all good geopolitical analysis, represented a picture of the constellation of forces which existed at a particular time and within a particular geographical frame of reference.

Furthermore, Mackinder realised that the process of explanation and understanding required constant adaption to shifting conditions and circumstances in a world where chance, uncertainty and ambiguity were always present. This geopolitical view was one that he proclaimed as early as 1915. His words are indeed a fitting tribute to the future relevance and modernity of his approach: 'If we try to obtain laws from our human geography and especially laws which guide our action politically, we are attempting that which I believe is doomed to failure. We shall cause both the scientific men and the historians to throw stones at geography.'[71]

NOTES

1. The two biographies of Mackinder are W.H. Parker, *Mackinder: Geography as an Aid to Statecraft* (Oxford: Clarendon Press 1982); B.W. Blouet, *Halford Mackinder: A Biography* (College Station: Texas A&M UP 1987).
2. Dinner speech given by Sir Halford Mackinder at the Imperial Economic Committee, 13 May 1931. Mackinder Papers, School of Geography, Oxford University.
3. A. James, *Sovereign Statehood* (London: Allen and Unwin 1986) p.13.
4. For a discussion of the historical development of the idea of sovereign territory, see F.H. Hinsley, *Sovereignty* (Cambridge: CUP 2nd ed. 1986) pp.130–7.
5. R. Aron, *Peace and War: A Theory of International Relations* (London: Weidenfeld 1996) p.182.
6. F. Braudel, *The Mediterranean and the Mediterranean World in the Age of Philip II*, rev. edn, trans. by S. Reynolds (London: Collins 1972).
7. T. Stoinovich, *The French Historical Method: The Annales* (Ithaca NY: Cornell UP 1976) pp.1–9.
8. For a more detailed account of this perspective see F. Braudel, *On History* (U. of Chicago Press 1980) pp.105–110.
9. Sun Tzu, *The Art of War*, trans by S.B. Griffith (Oxford: OUP 1963) Ch.10, Verse I. 1971, pp.127–8.
10. This phrase can be interpreted as meaning topography of the ground.
11. Sun Tzu (note 9).
12. Chapter 11 is devoted entirely to the outlining of nine geographical conditions that affect the employment of troops.
13. One of the most recent attempts at assessing Mackinder omits any reference to the relationship between Geography and International Relations. See G.Ó Tuathail, 'Putting Mackinder in his Place', *Political Geography* 11/1 (Jan. 1992) pp.100–18.
14. See R.B. Downs, *Books that Changed the World* (Chicago American Library Assoc. 1978).

15. 'Lord Roberts was often struck with their (the staff officers') inability to read maps well or to explain quickly and intelligently about the contours and elevations', Sir George Gouldie, 'Geographical Ideals', *Geographical Journal* 29/1 (Jan 1907) p.9.
16. *The Times*, 19 Nov. 1904.
17. Mackinder to Gilbert, 23 April 1944. Mackinder Papers, School of Geography, Oxford University.
18. Spencer Wilkinson was a military historian and journalist. From 1909 to 1923 he was the first Chichele Professor of the History of War at Oxford University.
19. H.J. Mackinder, 'The Geographical Pivot of History', *Geographical Journal* 23/4 (April 1904) p.437.
20. On 26 Jan.1904 *The Times*, *Glasgow Herald* and the *National Geographic* made reference to Mackinder's address. On 30 Jan. 1904 the *Spectator* ran an article on it.
21. Mackinder (note 19) p.422.
22. Ibid. p.422.
23. Ibid. p.423.
24. Ibid.
25. Ibid., p.433.
26. Ibid., p.434.
27. Ibid.
28. Ibid. p.436.
29. G. Kearns, 'Closed Space and Political Practice: Frederick Jackson Turner and Halford Mackinder. Environment and Planning', *Society and Space* 1 (1984) p.27.
30. Ibid.
31. Mackinder (note 19) p.437.
32. Ibid.
33. Parker, *Mackinder* (note 1) p.43.
34. See L.W. Lyde, 'Types of Political Frontiers in Europe', *Geographical Journal* 45 (1915) p.128.
35. Ibid. p.142.
36. See *Glasgow Herald*, 30 Sept. 1916.
37. See H.L.C. Seaton-Watson, *The Making of a New Europe* (London: Methuen 1981) p.439.
38. H.J. Mackinder, *Democratic Ideals and Reality: A Study in the Politics of Reconstruction* [1919] (Suffolk: Penguin Books 1944) p.86.
39. Ibid. p.87.
40. Ibid.
41. This is a phrase that Mackinder was responsible for coining.
42. Mackinder, *Democratic Ideals* (note 38) p.106.
43. See Lyde (note 34) p.143.
44. Mackinder, *Democratic Ideals* (note 38) p.194.
45. The two most prominent reviews were *The Spectator*, 27 Sept. 1919, p.408 and the *American Historical Review* 25 (1920) p.258.
46. Mackinder, *Democratic Ideals* (note 38) p.116.
47. See *Cost of Naval and Military Operations in Russia from the date of the Armistice to the 31st Oct 1919*. CMD 395 (HMSO 1919).
48. Report by Sir H. Mackinder in the Situation in South Russia, 21 Jan. 1920: *From Documents on Foreign Policy 1919–1939*, First Series, *Volume III, 1919* (London: HMSO 1949) pp.768–87.
49. Ibid. pp.783–4.
50. Sidney Reilly and Paul Dukes were two of the best SIS officers operating in the Soviet Union between 1917 and 1919. See C. Andrew, *Secret Service* (London: Heinemann 1986) pp.319–24.
51. R.H. Ullman, *Anglo-Soviet Relations, 1917–21*, Vol II (London: HMSO 1961–72) pp.173–4.
52. Lord Curzon to Sir Halford Mackinder, 2 Dec. 1919, F0 800/251, PRO, Kew.
53. A summary of the supplementary points Mackinder made at the Cabinet meeting can be found in F0 800/251, PRO, Kew.
54. Notes of points, supplementary to his memo of 21 Jan. 1920, made by Sir H.J. Mackinder in

reply to questions put to him at the Cabinet Meeting held on Thursday, 29 Jan. 1920, at 11.30am. PRO, F0 800/251.

55. Report by Sir H. Mackinder (note 48) p.786.
56. Cabinet minutes, 29 Jan. 1920, CAB 23/30.
57. See Parliamentary Debate, House of Commons, *Hansard*, Vol.129. Col.1717, 20 May 1920 (London: IISS/OUP 1996).
58. R. Forsythe, *The Politics of Oil in the Caucasus and Central Asia, Adelphi Paper* 300 (London: IISS/OUP 1996) p.11.
59. A.S.F. Starr, 'Making Eurasia Stable Foreign Affairs', *Foreign Affairs* 75/1 (Jan.–Feb. 1996) pp.80–92.
60. H.J. Mackinder, 'The Round World and the Winning of the Peace', *Foreign Affairs* 21/4 (July 1943) p.598.
61. Ibid. p.603.
62. Ibid. p.600.
63. Ibid. p.601.
64. Ibid.
65. Ibid. p.604.
66. H.J. Mackinder, *The Nations of the Modern World: An Elementary Study in Geography and History* (London: George Philip 1924) pp.251–2.
67. For a detailed treatment of this point see G.R. Sloan, *Geopolitics in United States Strategic Policy 1890–1987* (Brighton: Wheatsheaf Books 1988).
68. H. J. Mackinder, *Democratic Ideals and Reality* (London: Constable 1919) p.39.
69. Mackinder, 'The Geographical Pivot of History' (note 19) p.25.
70. N. Woods, *Explaining International Relations Since 1945* (Oxford: OUP 1996) p.13.
71. See Lyde, 'Types of Political Frontier in Europe' (note 34) p.143.

3

Alfred Thayer Mahan, Geopolitician

JON SUMIDA

In the late nineteenth and early twentieth centuries, Rear Admiral Alfred Thayer Mahan (1840–1914) of the US Navy wrote books and articles that established his reputation as the leading naval historian and strategist of his generation. Mahan owed his fame to the appeal of his major propositions about navies and international relations. The first was that maritime commerce was essential to the economic prosperity of a great power. The second was that the best means of protecting one's own trade while interdicting the enemy's was to deploy a fleet of battleships capable of maintaining naval supremacy, the corollary of which was that a commerce-raiding strategy executed by cruisers was incapable of inflicting decisive injury. The third was that a nation with naval supremacy could defeat a country that was militarily pre-eminent. Many interpreted these arguments as tantamount to the contention that naval supremacy was the prerequisite to ascendancy in the world political order.

Mahan's ideas about sea power, which among other things dealt with the inter-connectedness of force, economics, and geography, have prompted considerable discussion of the relationship of his work to geopolitics. These inquiries, however, have been based on the assumption that Mahan's views were simple and thus easy to understand. Consensus about Mahan's thought was embodied in substantial scholarly monographs, whose conclusions seemed to be consistent with impressions that could be derived from the reading of both small and large samples of his writing. Confidence in the validity of the standard view was virtually absolute. Recent comprehensive and systematic examination of Mahan's many books, however, has revealed that his ideas about navies and nations were far more complex and sophisticated than had been thought to be the case. Indeed, what Mahan actually wrote about some important things was practically the opposite of what he was believed to have written.

The revisionist case was presented by the author of the present piece in *Inventing Grand Strategy and Teaching Command: The Classic Works of Alfred Thayer Mahan Reconsidered*, a monograph published in 1997.[1] The primary purpose of this essay is to examine the question of Mahan and geopolitics in light of certain findings of this book. It will thus survey previous studies of Mahan and geopolitics, provide a summary of the latest revisionist analysis of relevant portions of Mahan's work, and consider the implications of the new scholarship.

The main arguments are that Mahan's views on the importance of good political and naval leadership counter-balanced his remarks on the significance of geography, his unit of political analysis in so far as sea power in the twentieth century was concerned was a trans-national consortium rather than the single nation state, his economic ideal was free trade rather than autarchy, and his recognition of the influence of geography on strategy was tempered by a strong appreciation of the power of contingency to affect outcomes.

Prior to 1914, the popularity of Mahan's ideas about sea power and national greatness was in large part attributable to the widespread belief that the historical arguments that supported them were sound. During the First World War, however, encounters between groups of surface capital ships were few and indecisive, while submarine attacks on maritime communications brought Britain to the brink of defeat, which seemed to refute Mahan's argument that battlefleet action and not commerce raiding should be the basis of naval strategy. In addition, the enormous scale and intensity of land combat as compared with the relative inactivity of major naval forces, and the near victory of Germany as a result of military success on the continent, raised doubts about the validity of Mahan's contention that sea power was superior to land power. But although the persuasiveness of his particular analysis was diminished, the example of its grand strategic breadth, together with the work of Halford Mackinder, influenced Karl Haushofer.

In the concluding paragraphs of her essay on Mahan in the classic anthology *Makers of Modern Strategy* of 1941, Margaret Tuttle Sprout[2] maintained that 'no estimate of the influence of Mahan on military thought could be complete without mention of the part played by Mahan's theories in the development of German *Geopolitik*'. German geopoliticians, she noted, 'frequently expressed their admiration for Mahan, whose global philosophy was built on a scale more grandiose and more audacious than any European expansionist theories of his day'.[3] Sprout furthermore observed that the 'new German approach to statecraft comprises a theory of state power and growth built on expanding land power, roughly analogous to Mahan's philosophy of growing sea power'.[4] She then quoted the US political scientist Robert Strausz-Hupé's contention that the teachings of Haushofer, the leading German geopolitical theorist, had been prompted as a reaction to Mahan, being 'the most extreme negation of Mahan's theories'.[5]

William E. Livezey, in his literary biography of Mahan published in 1947, devoted a great deal of attention to the connections between Mahan and geopolitics. 'As expositor of sea power', he observed,

> Mahan was a geopolitical thinker long before that expression was coined; as espouser of sea power, Mahan was the precursor of Halford Mackinder, analyst exceptional of the forthcoming role of land power; as exponent of sea power, Mahan was the preceptor of Karl Haushofer, advocate extraordinary of depth in space, *lebensraum*, and land empire.

Livezey then provided a list of the specific aspects of Mahan's thought that were related to the central concerns of geopolitics. 'Mahan's sea-power doctrine', he maintained

> polarized a set of historical data concerning the role of the sea in its relation to national well-being. As he viewed the constituent elements affecting power on the sea, he discussed geographical position, physical conformation, extent of territory, number of population, character of people, and character of government. In the creation of national greatness as connected with sea power, he saw industry, markets, [merchant] marine, navy, and bases closely related and theoretically, at least, in that sequence.[6]

For Livezey, the association of Mahan and the proponents of geopolitics was pejorative. The unprecedented misery inflicted by the Second World War and the prospects of even worse to follow, he believed, invalidated any body of work that advocated or even accepted the necessity of national expansion through resort to force of arms. 'The doctrines of power and empire as enunciated by Mahan and his school of thought', Livezey declared

> have not proved sound as a basis for international action. The adherents of power politics have led the world to the brink of disaster;

> the proponents of unrestricted national sovereignty have brought civilisation to near destruction; the exponents of empire, whether their concept be that of master race or white man's burden, have half the world seething in revolt.[7]

The characterisation of Mahan and Mackinder as the major proponents of geopolitics was the theme of an entire chapter in Harold and Margaret Sprout's *Foundations of International Politics*, which was published in 1962. The couple conceded that Mahan never provided 'any neat exposition' of his geopolitical ideas and that to identify them required a reconstruction based upon 'bits and pieces, plucked from hastily written books and articles'.[8] 'Four geopolitical concepts underlie Mahan's thinking about international politics', they maintained, which were

(1) a continuous and unbroken ocean and connecting seas;
(2) a vast transcontinental, nearly landlocked state, the Russian Empire, extending without a break from the ice-bound Arctic to the rugged desert-mountain belt of inner Asia, and from eastern Europe to a point farther eastward than Japan;
(3) the maritime states of continental Europe and maritime borderlands of southern and eastern Asia; and
(4) the insular states, Great Britain and Japan, with which he also grouped the United States, all wholly disconnected from the mainland of Eurasia.[9]

The Sprouts believed that the forms of geopolitical analysis practiced by Mahan and Mackinder were 'built upon pretty much the same set of geographic features',[10] and that in particular, Mahan's arguments of 1900 about the dangers posed by an expansionist Russia 'clearly anticipated Mackinder's concept of the Eurasian "Heartland"'.[11] As did Livezey before them, the couple criticised both men and their followers for assuming that 'military wars determine, in the final reckoning, the ordering of influence and deference in the Society of Nations'.[12]

The condemnation of Mahan and Mackinder on essentially anti-militarist grounds was a reaction to the devastation of the Second World War and the belief that geopolitical modes of thought had been in part responsible for the aggressive policies of National Socialist Germany and Imperial Japan. Haushofer and his followers, whose ties to the Hitler regime were direct, were consigned to oblivion after 1945. The German school of geopolitics was the subject of an entire chapter in *Makers of Modern Strategy*,[14] but in the almost completely revised edition of this work of 1986, it was not only omitted, but no mention is made anywhere in the volume of Haushofer or even Mackinder. Mahan was not directly tainted by the war and was too important a figure to be ignored, but the new chapter on his writing did not discuss the relationship of the American naval strategic theorist to geopolitics.[15]

Livezey and the Sprouts, while recognizing that there were major differences between Mahan and Mackinder, emphasized the importance of areas of agreement. For Mahan's work, the consequence of this approach was damage by way of association with a pariah field. An alternative treatment was to portray the ideas of Mahan and Mackinder as being diametrically opposed, a mode of discourse, however, that exposed Mahan's reputation to perils of another sort. In the Wiles Lectures of 1964, G. S. Graham characterised the views of the two men on the relative value of sea and land power as opposite, although only briefly and in passing.[16] A decade later, the contrast between Mahan and Mackinder was the main theme of a long essay by Paul Kennedy published by the German military history journal *Militärgeschichtliche Mitteilungen*.[17] Kennedy then expanded this provocative piece into his seminal book *The Rise and Fall of British Naval Mastery*, which appeared in 1976.[18]

Kennedy did not put forward new interpretations of either Mahan or Mackinder. What he did do was compare what were generally believed to be the salient arguments of the two writers with respect to the relative value of sea and land power, and evaluate their applicability to the history of Britain in the twentieth century. For Kennedy, Mahan was a proponent of sea power as an independent variable, that is, naval supremacy was the source of economic preeminence, which meant that so long as Britain ruled the waves, wealth greater than that of any other nation would follow. The essence of Mackinder, according to Kennedy, was that sea power was a dependent variable of declining significance, which he expressed in the form of two propositions: 'Britain's naval power, rooted in her economic strength, would no longer remain supreme when other nations with greater resources and manpower overhauled her previous industrial lead' and 'sea power itself was waning in relation to land power'.[19] The naval and economic decline of Britain over the twentieth century in spite of her position of naval pre-eminence at the beginning enabled Kennedy to conclude that Mackinder's analysis, from the standpoint of prediction, had been proven correct, while that of Mahan discredited.

The force of Kennedy's reasoning was persuasive and its effect considerable and far-reaching. The classic status of Mahan's books had given simple-minded navalism a degree of intellectual respectability, an effect that evaporated when exposed to the heat of Kennedy's clear and vigorous exposition. Kennedy's approach expanded the discussion of national policy and strategy by addressing questions related to the economic underpinnings of modern military and naval institutions, and the geographical context of strategy, as well as force structure and their deployment. In particular, industrial policy and state finance emerged as critical variables, and because relatively little was known about their particulars and larger effects, Kennedy's work prompted many to undertake the study of these subjects, the result of which is a large and still growing body of scholarship that has transformed the study of foreign policy and war.

But if the earlier repudiation of geopolitical discourse after the Second World War had damaged Mahan's standing, exacerbating injury inflicted already by the First World War, Kennedy's rehabilitation of geopolitics by way of championing Mackinder's assessment of the role of geography in international relations still left Mahan at the margins of serious discussion. Tainted by connections to a suspect body of thought before, he remained condemned even after geopolitics had been exonerated because unfavorable evaluation of what was believed to be his basic concept had been used as a means of securing the exculpation. Both forms of injury, that is, guilt by association with wrongheadedness or guilt by wrongheadedness alone of a different sort, were based upon the conventional view of Mahan as an essentially narrow and inflexible determinist whose main analytical focus had been upon the rise of British sea power. Consideration of how this mistaken set of ideas became accepted is a necessary preliminary to the examination of Mahan's actual thoughts on sea power and twentieth century international relations.

The conflation of separate arguments that to Mahan were related but still different in important ways was probably the original source of major misunderstanding of his work. Mahan's serious historical writing was concerned with, among other things, the development of British naval supremacy in the later years of the age of sail, while many of his occasional short pieces, as well as the serious histories, called for the construction of a large American battlefleet and overseas territorial expansion. Readers who combined these juxtaposed themes could easily conclude that Mahan believed the achievement of naval supremacy was the prerequisite to international preeminence in the twentieth century, and furthermore that this was his goal for the United States.

Mahan was not only concerned with grand strategy, but also the nature of command. His considerations of both subjects were interweaved in his texts, and thus discussions of 'principle conditions' of geography or 'immutable principles' of strategy, though in fact distinct lines of inquiry that were handled with nuance and care for exception, were taken as indicators of a generally absolutist and determinist approach to history.

Correcting misunderstandings generated by casual or incomplete engagement with Mahan's writing by comprehensive and careful study, however, posed a formidable challenge because of the volume, difficulty, diversity, and changeableness of his output. Between 1883 and 1913, Mahan wrote 19 books, three of which were two volume sets; to read them all, allowing for differences in page size and fonts, requires the negotiation of some 5,000 pages of fine print. Mahan's desire to achieve precision through close reasoning and careful qualification meant that his presentation of argument was often convoluted and hard to follow. Eight of Mahan's books were anthologies of periodical articles or lectures, which had covered a wide range of subjects in order to meet the demands of the reading and listening public. And not surprisingly, during a serious and prolific writing career of nearly a quarter of a century, he changed his mind or inadvertently contradicted himself.

The task of producing a satisfactory overview of Mahan's writing defied even the efforts of the author. His *Naval Strategy* (1911), an attempt in old age to write a coherent analytical summary of his ideas, exhausted his body and depressed his spirit. It was, in Mahan's own opinion, the worst book he ever wrote,[20] his infirmity compromising complete and profound knowledge of his own works. Subsequent writers wrote in their prime, but either approached their subject with less than complete reading of Mahan's publications, inadequate methodology, or strong agendas. The essays in both editions of *The Makers of Modern Strategy* are supported by citations from no more than half of Mahan's books, while the Sprout essay in the *Foundations of International Politics* drew from only a fifth of the total. Mahan's main biographers, W. D. Puleston,[21] Livezey, and Robert Seager,[22] appear to have read all the books, but split their attention, simultaneously addressing the questions of text, context, and their relationship, an approach that in all three cases worked to the disadvantage of rigorous engagement with the form and substance of the writing. Seager's account, in addition, while highly informative, is suffused with personal *animus* against Mahan, which affected his judgments of his subject's work.

In 1989, Colin Gray argued that 'a reconsideration of Mahan is overdue'.[23] During 1995 and 1996, the author of the present essay, under the auspices of the Woodrow Wilson International Center for Scholars in Washington DC, was able to devote a full year to a systematic reconsideration of all of Mahan's books, prompted by his own misgivings about the basic accuracy of the existing interpretation of Mahan's writing, and knowledge that these doubts were shared by others. The goal of the inquiry was to answer two fundamental questions: did Mahan's books at any level represent a coherent body of thought, and if so, what was its nature?

To accomplish this, the descriptive analysis of *Inventing Grand Strategy and Teaching Command* was limited to Mahan's consideration of the two large phenomenon mentioned in the title, excluding for the most part his commentary on secondary matters such as racism, imperialism, militarism, Social Darwinism, diplomacy, and international law. The examination of Mahan and geopolitics does not require discussion of command, making it possible to deal with grand strategy alone, which is of central importance to the matter at hand, without recourse to the formal analytical apparatus used in the book.

The core of Mahan's literary output consisted of the four-part history of naval warfare from 1660 to 1815, the 'Influence of Sea Power' series, after the title of the first installment, *The Influence of Sea Power upon History, 1660–1783*, which was published in 1890. Mahan's lesser books consisted of shorter histories of particular conflicts (the American Revolution, part of the American Civil War, the Boer War); monographs on strategy, international relations, or theology; one biography; an autobiography; and eight collections of his articles and lectures. Two aspects of the 'Influence of Sea Power' series have been the main concern of previous examinations of Mahan and geopolitics: the discussion of the extent to which geography determined the sea power potential of a country in the first chapter of the first volume, and the focus of the entire series on the rise of British naval supremacy, which was connected to Britain's subsequent achievement of international economic and political primacy.

The first chapter of *The Influence of Sea Power upon History*, named 'Discussion of the Elements of Sea Power', was the longest in the book. It was a quickly composed, last moment addition to his manuscript that had been intended by the author to make the academic history of his main text more palatable to general readers. Inclusion of an extended discussion of American maritime interests and naval requirements was prompted by current vigorous public debate about these issues. Mahan's description of 'principal conditions affecting the sea power of nations' appears to have been derived in large part from a prize-essay by W. G. David published in 1882 by the United States Naval Institute.[24] Mahan's factors were geographical position, physical conformation (which included natural resources and climate), extent of territory, population size, national character, and political structure.

As a marketing device, the combination of topicality and already audience-tested material was a success. It was the first chapter, in the words of Mahan's latest biographer, that 'generated the greatest comment and speculation among American and British readers',[25] not the main body of the book. Many of Mahan's reviewers, indeed, 'seem not to have read past the controversial "Elements of Sea Power" or to have done much more than scan the chapter headings of the remainder of the volume'.[26] Five of the six elements, in combination with Mahan's contention that transport over water had been and would continue to be cheaper than carriage over land, constituted a set of physical and human geographical propositions whose use in connection to explanations of major international political outcomes made it easy for many readers to believe that Mahan argued that geography determined the course of history. Careful consideration of Mahan's text and more importantly the context, however, reveals that such a characterisation is faulty and seriously misleading.

Mahan's views on geographical position may be summarized as follows. First, an insular state was more likely to concentrate its resources on maritime development and overseas territorial extension than a continental one. Second, geographical factors could either 'promote a concentration, or to necessitate a dispersion, of naval forces' with large effects on a country's naval strategic circumstances.[27] Third, geographical position *vis-à-vis* other powers could confer 'the further strategic advantage of a central position and a good base for hostile operations against probable enemies' in terms not only of attack on territory but also on important trade routes.[28] And fourth, Mahan noted that control of certain bodies of water were particularly important for economic and military reasons.

For Mahan, physical conformation had several characteristics. Contour of the coast, by which he meant not only the length of seaboard but the number and quality of harbors, determined ease of access to oceanic trade, which was the fundamental issue. An important modifying factor was the physical attributes that affected economic activity on land, which if favorable discouraged maritime enterprise, while if unfavorable served as an incentive to such. A second important modifying factor was insularity or near insularity (as in the case of a peninsula), or the division of a polity by bodies of water as in the case of a country spread over an archipelago, which encouraged the development of sea forces as the most effective means of defence against seaborne invasion and protection of essential communications between important centers of politics and commerce.[30]

Extent of territory and number of population were related and somewhat misleading categories. For Mahan, the former was concerned not simply with the physical size of a country, but also population density. A small population situated in a large territory with a significant seaboard was more vulnerable to the effects of naval blockade than a much larger population in similar circumstances, the latter being more capable of generating effective military and naval forces. In so far as number of population was concerned, what mattered to Mahan was not the overall total, but the number who followed 'callings related to the sea' who could be counted as the potential effective personnel of a navy.[31] And by national character, Mahan referred primarily to 'aptitude for commercial pursuits'.[32]

Mahan's views on the relative costs of land and water transport were based upon several assumptions. He was not unaware that the invention of railroads had greatly improved the efficiency of land transport. But besides the fact that ships were still essential for transoceanic commerce, Mahan knew that overseas trade was large and highly productive of wealth, and he had good reason to believe that it would grow and become even more important as an economic activity for all maritime countries in the foreseeable future. In addition, he almost certainly realized that the efficiency gains that accompanied the advent of railroads were to some degree counterbalanced by the comparable application of industrial technology to the design and construction of ships, which reduced the costs of marine carriage significantly.[33]

Mahan's confidence in the continued critical importance of long-haul shipping was reasoned and not merely a projection of the economic conditions of the pre-industrial past into the industrial present and future, while his descriptions of the geographical factors that made up the 'Elements of Sea Power' were derivative and unexceptionable, a collection of platitudes rather than a breakthrough geopolitical manifesto. More important, Mahan stated explicitly that there was another major nongeographical influence on national maritime and naval policy. Before doing so he did note that 'the history of seaboard nations has been less determined by the shrewdness and foresight of governments than by conditions of position, extent, configuration, number and character of their people, – by what are called, in a word, natural conditions'.[34] But there was little meat on this geographical determinist bone, for in the next sentence Mahan observed that

> It must be admitted, and will be seen, that the wise or unwise action of individual men has at certain periods had a great modifying influence upon the growth of sea power in the broad sense, which included not only the military strength afloat, that rules the sea or any

> part of it by force of arms, but also the peaceful commerce and shipping from which alone a military fleet naturally and healthfully springs, and on which it securely rests.[35]

This passage prefaced Mahan's discussion of the six principal conditions, and it was on the non-geographical sixth condition, 'Character of the government,' that he devoted the most attention, in fact as many pages of text as that given to the five previous conditions combined. The first general lesson was given as

> The government by its policy can favor the natural growth of a people's industries and its tendencies to seek adventure and gain by way of the sea; or it can try to develop such industries and such sea-going bent, when they do not naturally exist; or, on the other hand, the government may by mistaken action check and fetter the progress which the people left to themselves would make.[36]

The second was the 'influence of the government will be felt in its most legitimate manner in maintaining an armed navy, of a size commensurate with the growth of its shipping and the importance of the interests connected with it', with the added observation that this included adequate provision for the 'healthful spirit and activity' of the navy as an institution and rapid shipbuilding and trained reserves.[37]

Mahan emphasised the governmental factor because he was convinced that historically the distribution of geographical favor had been such that more than one country possessed the potential to achieve naval supremacy, which meant that the final outcome had not been geographically determined but decided by human action. British naval policy in the eighteenth and early nineteenth centuries, Mahan believed, had been practically preordained by geographical circumstances, but its ultimate triumph over France was not. While Mahan recognized that the continental position of France required her to maintain substantial military forces that were superfluous to insular Britain, he thought that her economic strength and geographical advantages were sufficient to have provided for a fleet capable of winning naval supremacy had the government chosen to do so. Instead, France forfeited the opportunity to crush Britain while it was relatively weak through excessive concentration on land campaigns during the late seventeenth century and much of the eighteenth. This same continental strategy prevented France from developing the commercial empire that could have been the basis of much greater economic and military power than she actually achieved.

In the closing pages of his first chapter, Mahan addressed his main practical concern. His great fear at this time was that the isolationist sentiments of the electorate would prevent the American state from encouraging the expansion of the merchant marine and the building of a strong navy that he believed was essential to protect vital territorial and economic interests in a world in which competition between powerful nations was beginning to increase. His goal was to stimulate decisive government action that would produce a fleet 'which, if not capable of reaching distant countries, shall at least be able to keep clear the chief approaches to its own'.[38] For Mahan, the history of French naval policy in the eighteenth century was particularly relevant to the American situation in the late nineteenth century. 'The profound humiliation of France', he observed

> which reached its depths between 1760 and 1763, at which latter date she made peace, has an instructive lesson for the United States in this our period of commercial and naval decadence. We have been spared her humiliation; let us hope to profit by her subsequent example.[39]

The illustrative case to which Mahan referred was French naval success during the American Revolution. Mahan's account of this subject, which was the climax of *The Influence of Sea Power upon History*, consumed no less than six of his fourteen chapters. Put another way, some 40 per cent of the text was allocated to cover four per cent of the chronology. In this conflict, according to Mahan, a France undistracted by having to field armies against a continental European great power, and animated by an offensive naval strategy, used her battlefleet from 1778 to compromise Britain's position in North America. The aggressive campaigns of 1781–83 conducted by the brilliant French naval commander-in-chief in the Indian Ocean, Vice Admiral de Suffren, while ultimately checked, nonetheless demonstrated what the French Navy might have accomplished if led properly. And Mahan blamed France's failure to obtain even 'more substantial results' than it did on its unwillingness to press relentlessly for decisive action at sea, which could have destroyed British naval power when conditions were propitious.[40]

In the two-volume sequel *The Influence of Sea Power upon the French Revolution and Empire, 1793–1812*, which was published in 1892, Mahan could not work the period in terms of faulty or correct French grand strategy as he had done previously, because the disruption of French naval leadership and administration by political upheaval precluded operational success regardless of deployment. Instead, Mahan replaced the consideration of optimal policy choices for states with major maritime assets with an examination of whether a country supreme at sea was capable of defeating its opposite, a country supreme on land. The focus of Mahan's analysis was thus switched to Britain, and specifically to her grand strategy of economic attrition. Even so, Mahan maintained that because the balance of forces was so even, the final outcome was not predetermined, but hinged upon the actions of individual statesmen, and commanders at sea and in the field. Britain's victory in the end, according to Mahan, was in large part attributable to Vice-Admiral Lord Nelson's unrelenting pursuit of decisive naval engagement, an attitude that led to striking naval victories that had important larger consequences.

The theme of the critical importance of admiralship at sea was elaborated in the third installment of the 'Influence of Sea Power' series, a two-volume biography of Nelson entitled *The Life of Nelson: The Embodiment of the Sea Power of Great Britain*, which was published in 1897.[41] The concluding fourth work, *Sea Power in Its Relations to the War of 1812*, yet another two-volume effort that appeared in 1905, examined the disastrous consequences to the United States of naval unpreparedness, in effect dealing with the inverse form of his earlier main argument about the benefits of naval strength. American naval weakness, Mahan maintained, was the cause of an unnecessary war and exposed maritime commerce to British attacks that did serious harm to the economy and government finance. For Mahan, the lesson for the United States was not the need to build the world's largest navy, but rather the sufficiency of a modest fleet that could, when geographical and other circumstances were taken into account, deter even the world's leading sea power from settling outstanding differences through recourse to war.[42]

To sum up, the 'Influence of Sea Power' quartet was not unified around the theme of the rise of British naval supremacy. The principal concern of the first volume in the series was the French failure to fulfill her potential as a sea power. In the second book of the series, the main argument was that a grand strategy of economic attrition and protracted war based on naval supremacy enabled Britain to survive a Napoleonic onslaught that she might otherwise have lost. In the third book, Mahan focused on the necessity of having extraordinary operational leadership in order to convert naval superiority into naval supremacy. And finally, the leading contention of the concluding work was that a relatively small investment by the American state in a larger navy would have averted disaster, which was to say that British naval supremacy could have been neutralized in the Western Hemisphere, under the prevailing circumstances of a major war in Europe that had reached the point of crisis, by a more potent but still small US Navy.

It is true that Mahan, in an article published in 1902 in the *National Review*, in effect repudiated the central argument of *The Influence of Sea Power upon History* by asserting that 'history has conclusively demonstrated the inability of a state with even a single continental frontier to compete in naval development with one that is insular, although of smaller population and resources'.[43] Mahan's change of mind was probably the result of his writing about the wars of the French Revolution and Empire, which unlike the first volume of the 'Influence upon Sea Power' series chronicled a succession of major British naval victories that climaxed in the virtual annihilation of the combined French and Spanish battlefleets at Trafalgar. This tilt towards geographical determinism, however, was tempered by two major Mahanian propositions about the nature of sea power that disassociated it from the historical fortunes of Britain alone.

In the first place, Mahan was convinced that naval supremacy in the industrial age would have to be the product of co-operation between two or more powers. 'The circumstances of naval war', he maintained in the first chapter of *The Influence of Sea Power upon History*, 'have changed so much within the last hundred years, that it may be doubted whether such disastrous effects on the one hand, or such brilliant prosperity on the other, as were seen in the wars between England and France, could now recur'.[44] Mahan repeated this view and advanced related arguments in many of his lesser works, which henceforward will be identified in the text by date of original publication, with full citation reserved for the notes. In 1894, Mahan observed that it was 'improbable that control [over the seas] ever again will be exercised, as once it was, by a single nation'.[45] In 1907, he noted it was 'not likely, indeed, that we shall again see so predominant a naval power as Great Britain' during the Napoleonic Wars.[46]

As for the Britain of his own day, Mahan believed that it lacked the strength to maintain naval supremacy, the term meaning not just possession of the world's largest navy, but a degree of preponderance sufficient to control all major waters vital to her military and economic security. As early as in 1894, Mahan argued that 'Great Britain's sea power, though still superior, has declined relatively to that of other states, and is no longer supreme'.[47] In 1910, in response to the decisions that Britain's Liberal administration had made the year before to extend social welfare programs and in the face of a rapidly expanding German navy, Mahan warned that 'the British navy is declining, relatively, owing to the debility of a government which in the way of expenditure has assumed obligations in seeming excess of its power to meet by sound financial methods'.[48]

For Mahan, the fundamental problem for Britain, and also the United States, was the propensity of representative governments to economize when it came to expenditure on armed forces. 'Popular governments', he observed in the first chapter of *The Influence of Sea Power upon History*, 'are not generally favorable to military expenditure, however necessary'.[49] In 1897, Mahan argued that the governments of Britain and the United States lacked the capacity to make adequate financial provision for 'a complete scheme of national military policy, whether for offense or defense',[50] and that the 'instincts' of an insular state (a term which he believed described the United States as well as Britain[51]), with its 'extensive commercial relations', were 'naturally for peace, because it has so much at stake outside its shores'.[52] 'To prepare for war in time of peace', Mahan maintained in 1911, 'is impracticable to commercial representative nations, because the people in general will not give sufficient heed to military necessities, or to international problems, to feel the pressure which induces readiness.'[53]

Mahan preferred democratic to monarchical rule, and his solution, therefore, to the problem just described was transnational co-operation. 'Each man and each state', he wrote in 1900, 'is independent just so far as there is strength to go alone, and no farther. When this limit is reached, if farther steps must be made, co-operation must be accepted.'[54] Political and cultural affinity combined with the absence of major conflicting interests and the existence of strong common ones convinced Mahan that Britain and the United States had good reason to act in concert. Mahan was not an advocate of a conventional alliance, but rather an informal but nonetheless conscious coordination of efforts that produced a preponderance of force sufficient to achieve the benefits of naval supremacy realized by Britain alone a century before. 'To Great Britain and the United States', he wrote in 1894, '… is intrusted a maritime interest … which demands, as one of the conditions of its exercise and its safety, the organized force adequate to control the general course of events at sea'.[55]

Mahan's Anglo-American naval consortium was not to be a relationship of naval equals. America, Mahan wrote in 1912, could 'properly cede superiority, because to the British Islands naval power is vital in a sense in which it is not to the United States'.[56] But this view was contingent upon Britain maintaining her preeminent naval position. Mahan believed that the surpassing of Britain by Germany as the world's leading sea power was a real possibility, was distressed by reductions in American naval building that accompanied the anti-big ship Democratic take-over of the House of

Representatives in 1910, and troubled by the prospect that Japanese immigration to the West Coast would ultimately lead to a clash with Japan over the ownership of continental American territory.

These fears prompted Mahan in late 1912 to call for America to maintain a 'preponderant navy',[57] which, however, was in his mind still inferior to one that conferred 'paramountcy'.[58] The purposes of such a force, moreover, were regional and defensive, protection of American interests in the Caribbean and preservation of American sovereignty on the Pacific coast of the continental United States, not global and offensive as in the securing of worldwide naval supremacy.

The second major proposition that worked against the drawing of geographical determinist conclusions with respect to particular nation states and naval supremacy was Mahan's contention that sea power itself was a transnational phenomenon. It is true that in the introduction to *The Influence of Sea Power upon History*, Mahan defined sea power largely in terms of national commercial and naval rivalry directed by governments.[59] But in *The Influence of Sea Power upon the French Revolution and Empire*, sea power was separated from the nation state. Mahan noted that during the great wars of the late eighteenth and early nineteenth centuries, Great Britain wielded sea power 'as absolute mistress' because of the 'circumstances of the time'.[60] But he then observed that naval and commercial activity combined constituted 'a wonderful and mysterious Power' that could be 'seen to be a complex organism, endued [*sic*] with a life of its own, receiving and imparting countless impulses, moving in a thousand currents which twine in and around one another in infinite flexibility … throughout all it lives and it grows'.[61]

Even in *The Influence of Sea Power upon History*, which covered an era in which the commercial policies of great states were based upon mercantilist theory, Mahan found opportunities to praise the virtues of peace and free trade. The French East India Company's monopoly of commerce between major home and Indian ports was compared to 'the traffic throughout the Indian seas', which was 'open to private enterprise and grew more rapidly'.[62] The tripling in the size of the French merchant marine within 20 years of the end of the War of the Spanish Succession (1701–14), Mahan argued, was attributable to 'peace and the removal of restrictions, and not due in any sense to government protection'.[63] Mahan expressed his opposition to protective tariffs and favor of free trade for the US in his own time in an article published in 1890. He likened protection to 'the activities of a modern ironclad that has heavy armor, but inferior engines and guns; mighty for defence, weak for offence', and then observed that

> the temperament of the American people is essentially alien to such a sluggish attitude. Independently of all bias for or against protection, it is safe to predict that, when the opportunities for gain abroad are understood, the course of American enterprise will cleave a channel by which to reach them.[64]

The idea that sea power was not merely a desirable policy option for a particular state, but a self-sustaining supra-national system whose existence and development depended upon the actions of corporate institutions both public and private, and individuals, around the world, was the subject of further discussion in Mahan's other lesser works in later years. 'The unmolested course of commerce, reacting upon itself', Mahan observed in 1902,

> has contributed also to its own rapid development, a result furthered by the prevalence of a purely economical conception of national greatness during the larger part of the century. This, with the vast increase in rapidity of communication, has multiplied and strengthened the bonds knitting the interests of nations to one another, till the whole now forms an articulated system, not only of prodigious size and activity, but of an excessive sensitiveness, unequaled in former ages.[65]

'War has ceased to be the natural, or even normal condition of nations', Mahan argued in a separate piece written a month later, 'and military considerations are simply accessory and subordinate to the other greater interests, economical and commercial, which they assure and so subserve'.[66] Mahan then declared that 'as for economical rivalry, let it be confined to its own methods, eschewing force'.[67]

Although Mahan believed that the maritime commercial component of sea power on the whole favored peace rather than war, he was equally convinced that there were other factors that made major armed conflict a serious possibility. For Mahan, the three general threats to amicability were competition between European great powers for control over Asian and Africa territories that were coveted for their potential economic value; the susceptibility of governments to public opinion, which when inflamed could bring about war even if it were ill-advised; and the emergence of an Asia armed with industrial weaponry that would challenge Western Civilization for world dominion. In particular, Mahan feared the expansionist designs of militarist monarchical powers, which included Russia, the German empire, and Japan.

His concept of an Anglo-American naval consortium was thus intended to deter aggression and impose international order to facilitate the political and economic development of backward regions in peace, and to provide security to the bulk of the world's overseas trading activity and a bulwark against invasion to allow time for Britain and the United States to mobilize their economies for a protracted war of attrition in the event of hostilities.[68]

In 1900, Mahan declared that he believed in the existence of 'determinative conditions' whose effect was to 'shape and govern the whole range of incidents, often in themselves apparently chaotic in combination, and devoid of guidance by any adequate controlling forces'. He considered the tasks of identifying those forces and comprehending their dynamics, however, to be difficult ones when dealing with the past, and even more so when contemplating the future. 'In history entirely past', Mahan went on to observe,

> where an issue has been reached sufficiently definite to show that one period has ended and another begun, it is possible for a careful observer to detect, and with some precision to formulate, the leading causes, and to trace the interaction which has produced the result. It is obviously much less easy to discover the character and to fix the interrelation of the elements acting in the present; and still more to indicate the direction of their individual movement, from which conjecture may form some conception as to what shall issue as the resultant of forces. There is here all the difference between history and prophecy.[69]

For Mahan, in other words, even sound history could not serve as the guarantor of accurate prognostication because human affairs were complicated and outcomes dependent upon complex interactions and contingent forces. An intellect informed by history, on the other hand, might usefully consider a range of possibilities, including contradictory or even mutually exclusive ones. For example, in a collection of articles published in 1900, Mahan described the containment of Russia, whose power he recognized was derived from central position and control of extensive continental territory, by means of an informal coalition of Germany, Great Britain, Japan, and the United States, and also contemplated not only a collision of Europe and Asia in cataclysmic war because of cultural differences but the development of a World culture that reconciled east and west. Exposure of Russian weakness in the Russo-Japanese War and the rapid growth of the German and Japanese navies later prompted Mahan to issue warnings about the immediate dangers posed to the United States by a militant Germany or Japan, which were issued in spite of his continued anxiety about Russia in the long run.[70]

In light of the foregoing, it should be clear that Mahan viewed the naval component of sea power as a major influence in several possible widely varying sets of circumstances that might or might not involve war, not as the controlling force in the inevitable struggle by a single state for world mastery. Put another way, Mahan's writing about future international relations was contemplative rather than prescriptive, an engagement with multiple separate premises, each one explored with vigor but always with an awareness of other equally valid points of departure with a potentially conflicting or even opposite ultimate outcome. For Mahan, to take such an approach was not a confession of intellectual weakness or moral cowardice, but an appreciation of the limits of the intellect when confronted by the unpredictable nature of mankind's affairs. The 'philosophy of life', he wrote in 1900, 'is best expressed in paradox. It is by frank acceptance of contrary truths, embracing both without effort to blend them, that we can best direct our course, as individuals or as nations, to successful issues.'[71]

In the preface to his first collection of articles, Mahan wrote 'if such unity perchance be found in these it will not be due to antecedent purpose, but to the fact that they embody the thought of an individual mind, consecutive in the line of its main conceptions, but adjusting itself continually to changing conditions, which the progress of events entails'.[72] These words may be applied to all of his writing that concerned the events of his own day and the future. Mahan did not construct a system of thought that was used to process mechanistically current and prospective problems of twentieth century statecraft, but combined and re-combined principles and history in differing proportion depending upon circumstances to serve as the basis of judgment of particular cases. The geopolitical identity of Mahan is thus not to be found in samples drawn indiscriminately from a protean body of observations and conclusions, but through engagement with the coherent sensibility that produced them. Once this task is accomplished, effective criticism may begin.

Four revisionist propositions are especially relevant to the consideration of Mahan and geopolitics. First, Mahan's main concern in the 'Influence of Sea Power' series was the critical importance of decision making by statesmen and admirals, not the power of geographical factors to determine the course of history. Second, Mahan was convinced that naval supremacy in his own day and in the near future would most likely be exercised by a transnational consortium made up of Great Britain and the United States because neither power possessed the resources to maintain a large enough navy to do the job on its own, while both had large and growing seaborne commercial interests that needed strong protection in the event of war.

Third, Mahan's economic ideal was global free trade, a system that was an integral part of his concept of sea power and which, he was convinced, favored peace rather than war. And fourth, Mahan, did not have a single vision of the future, and while he was certain that sea power was bound by the nature of things to play an important role in international affairs, he did not hold that it would necessarily define its terms or dictate its outcomes.

The question of Mahan's influence on later practitioners of geopolitics is an inherently difficult one. Besides varying degrees of borrowing ranging from grand theft to pilfering, there are alternative possibilities including unconscious usurpation, faulty assimilation, or even independent invention. Mahan's concept of the threat posed by the enormous territorial mass of Russia anticipated Mackinder's 'heartland' theory in many ways, but whether or to what extent the latter author was affected has not yet been determined.[73] As for the German school of geopolitics, it is probable that the impression made by Mahan was created by incomplete reading, and therefore the product of distorted understanding, but in any case was a matter of general approach rather than particular argument. In so far as the intellectual indebtedness of Mackinder and Haushofer to Mahan is concerned, the new scholarship on the work of the American has little to offer. On the other hand, it does provide the basis for a useful reconsideration of Mahan's ideas in comparison to those of Mackinder.

Mahan believed that good strategy and effective operational command mattered a very great deal. Mackinder, whose own country was less populous and less well-endowed with resources, was more concerned with the efficient utilisation of national and imperial assets in the long term, and perhaps, after the experience of the First World War, much more conscious of the dangers and likelihood of unsatisfactory civilian and military leadership.[74] Mahan, aware of his own country's reluctance to spend on defence and cognizant of Britain's relative economic and naval decline, was a consistent proponent of Anglo-American naval cooperation as the basis of naval supremacy in the twentieth century. Mackinder flirted with the idea in 1905, 1909, and after the First World War,[75] but his main interest was the maintenance of an efficiently-integrated British Empire.[76] Mahan, confident of his own country's economic prowess and capacity to compete in a global market, embraced free trade and the vision of a world commonwealth.[77] Mackinder, fearful of British commercial vulnerability to more efficient foreign competitors, was a proponent of protection and in essence the division of the world (or even countries) into autarchic zones.[78]

From the standpoint of predicting the future, Mahan and Mackinder engaged a similar range of options, which may serve as a testament to essential agreement of outlook on the general terms that defined the relationship between geography and politics. Mahan thought of a transnational naval consortium as the executor of naval supremacy and the possible basis for the containment of an expansionist Russia by a coalition of peripheral maritime powers, a formulation that Mackinder also explored, though with less enthusiasm and confidence in an outcome favorable to the latter. Mahan's vision of the opposition of European civilisation against that of Asia was also entertained by Mackinder.[79] And both men feared the military threat posed by Germany in the shorter run.[80] Where Mahan and Mackinder differed most was not in their subject matter or conclusions but the format of inquiry. Mahan was an historian and essentially a humanist. Mackinder was a political geographer and at bottom a social scientist. In this important sense, they are not opposed but complementary.

Paul Kennedy's presentation of the approaches of Mahan and Mackinder to the question of sea power versus land power as opposites served a useful and important purpose by redirecting and restructuring the historical study of international relations. And at the level of the fortunes of a particular nation-state, Kennedy's assessment of the course of British history in the twentieth century is, if not beyond challenge,[81] still a very strong contender. Kennedy's presumption, however, that Mahan's view of the twentieth century was no more than an extension of the story of the rise of British sea power in the age of sail is not correct. The application of Mahan's actual concept of a transnational naval consortium as the basis for naval supremacy, moreover, transforms the story of British relative decline globally into one of her subsumption into a politically and economically preeminent conglomerate of associated states. Britain's status within this combination was ultimately reduced from a senior to a junior partnership with the United States, but its economic condition has remained generally prosperous and political influence significant.

Mahan has often been caricatured as little more than a prophet of national aggrandizement through command of the sea, remembered for the influence rather than the substance of his thought, and relegated to a side corridor in the pantheon of discredited thinkers.[82] But Mahan's recognition of the fundamental importance of patterns of sea transport and trade, examination of the relationship of continental and insular land structures, and the connection of these subjects to national policy set within a transnational perspective unshackled by commitment to a single future, were the manifestations of a penetrating and flexible intelligence. His concerns have remained central issues for current students of geopolitics, and his later exercises in prediction seem in hindsight remarkably sound:

containment of the Germans, then the Russians, with the question of conflict between Asian and Western civilisation explored if left undecided; and the emergence of a global free-trade economy based on shipping. Mahan's intellectual heirs may with good reason decline to read his large and difficult work in its entirety, but acquaintance with the quality of the mind and appreciation of the substance of its accomplishment are worthy projects, and for serious students of geopolitics, perhaps obligatory ones.

NOTES

1. Jon (Tetsuro) Sumida, *Inventing Grand Strategy and Teaching Command: The Classic Works of Alfred Thayer Mahan Reconsidered* (Washington DC: Woodrow Wilson Center Press/Baltimore: Johns Hopkins UP 1997).
2. Margaret Tuttle Sprout, 'Mahan: Evangelist of Sea Power', in Edward Mead Earle (ed.) *Makers of Modern Strategy: Military Thought from Machiavelli to Hitler* (NY: Atheneum 1966; first pub. by Princeton UP 1941) p.444.
3. Ibid. p.445.
4. Ibid. p.444.
5. Ibid.
6. William E. Livezey, *Mahan on Sea Power* (rev. ed.) (Norman, OK: U. of Oklahoma Press 1981; first pub. 1947) p.316.
7. Livezey (note 6) p.332.
8. Harold and Margaret Sprout, *Foundations of International Politics* (Princeton, NJ: D. Van Nostrand 1962) p.319.
9. Ibid. p.320.
10. Ibid. pp.217–8.
11. Ibid. p.325.
12. Ibid. pp.338–9.
13. W.H. Parker, *Mackinder: Geography as an Aid to Statecraft* (Oxford: Clarendon 1982) pp.178–82.
14. Derwent Whittlesey, 'Haushoffer: the Geopoliticians', in Earle (note 2) ch.16, pp.388–411.
15. Philip A. Crowl, 'Alfred Thayer Mahan: The Naval Historian', in Peter Paret (ed.) *Makers of Modern Strategy from Machiavelli to the Nuclear Age* (Princeton UP 1986) Ch.16, pp.444–77.
16. G.S. Graham, *The Politics of Naval Supremacy. The Wiles Lectures 1963–4* (Cambridge: CUP 1965) pp.29–30, 124–5.
17. Paul Kennedy, 'Mahan versus Mackinder: Two Interpretations of British Sea Power', in idem, *Strategy and Diplomacy 1870–1945: Eight Studies* (London: Allen & Unwin 1983) pp.41–85.
18. Paul Kennedy, *The Rise and Fall of British Naval Mastery* (NY: Scribner's 1976).
19. Kennedy (note 17) p.48.
20. Robert Seager II, *Alfred Thayer Mahan: The Man and His Letters* (Annapolis, MD: Naval Inst. Press 1977) p.546.
21. W.D. Puleston, *Mahan: The Life and Work of Captain Alfred Thayer Mahan* (New Haven, CT: Yale UP 1939).
22. Seager (note 20).
23. Colin S. Gray and Roger W. Barnett (eds.) *Seapower and Strategy* (London: Tri-Service Press 1989) p.7.
24. Seager (note 20) p.200.
25. Ibid. p.205.
26. Ibid. p.211.

27. Alfred Thayer Mahan, *The Influence of Sea Power upon History, 1660–1783* (Boston: Little, Brown 1890) p.29.
28. Ibid. p.30.
29. Ibid. pp.30–5.
30. Ibid. pp.35–42.
31. Ibid. pp.42–9.
32. Ibid. pp.50–8.
33. Ibid. pp.25–6.
34. Ibid. p.28.
35. Ibid.
36. Ibid. p.82.
37. Ibid.
38. Ibid. p.87.
39. Ibid. p.76.
40. Ibid. p.538.
41. Capt. A.T. Mahan, *The Life of Nelson: The Embodiment of the Sea Power of Great Britain*, 2 vols (Boston: Little, Brown 1897).
42. Capt. A.T. Mahan, *Sea Power in Its Relations to the War of 1812*, 2 vols (Boston: Little, Brown 1905).
43. A.T. Mahan, 'Considerations Governing the Disposition of Navies', *National Review* (July 1902), repr. in idem, *Retrospect and Prospect: Studies in International Relations Naval and Political* (London: Sampson Low, Marston 1902) p.169.
44. Mahan, *Influence of Sea Power* (note 27) p.84.
45. A.T. Mahan, 'Possibilities of an Anglo-American Reunion', *North American Review* (Nov. 1894) repr. in idem, *The Interest of America in Sea Power, Present and Future* (Boston: Little, Brown 1897) p.125.
46. Capt. A.T. Mahan, *Some Neglected Aspects of War* (Boston: Little, Brown 1907) p.168.
47. Mahan, 'Possibilities of an Anglo-American Reunion', *Interest of America in Sea Power* (note 45) p.130.
48. A.T. Mahan, *The Interest of America in International Conditions* (Boston: Little, Brown 1910) p.150.
49. Mahan, *Influence of Sea Power* (note 27) p.67.
50. A.T. Mahan, 'Preparedness for Naval War', *Harper's New Monthly Magazine* (Sept. 1897), repr. in idem, *Interest of America* (note 45) p.175.
51. For a full discussion of this complex issue, see Sumida (note 1) p.82.
52. Mahan, *Interest of America* (note 45) p.211.
53. A.T. Mahan, *Naval Strategy* (Boston: Little, Brown 1911) p.447.
54. 'Effect of Asiatic Conditions upon World Politics', *North American Review* (Nov. 1900), in A.T. Mahan, *The Problem of Asia and its Effects upon International Policies* (Boston: Little, Brown 1900) pp.177–8.
55. Mahan, 'Possibilities of an Anglo-American Reunion', *Interest of America* (note 45) p.111.
56. A.T. Mahan, *Armaments and Arbitration, or the Place of Force in the International Relations of States* (NY: Harper 1912) p.180.
57. A.T. Mahan, *The Major Operations of the Navies in the War of American Independence* (Boston: Little, Brown 1913) p.4. W.D. Puleston's contention that Mahan's goal for the US was absolute naval supremacy, which has been accepted by others, appears to be based upon an overdetermined reading of this passage, for which see Puleston (note 21) pp.324, 336.
58. For the distinction between the terms 'preponderance' and 'paramountcy', see A.T. Mahan, 'The Monroe Doctrine: A Consistent Development', *National Review* (Feb. 1902), repr. in Capt. A.T. Mahan, *Naval Administration and Warfare: Some General Principles with Other Essays* (Boston: Little, Brown 1908) pp.396–7.
59. Mahan, *Influence of Sea Power* (note 27) p.1.
60. Mahan, *Influence of Sea Power upon the French Revolution and Empire, 1793–1812*, 2 vols. (Boston: Little, Brown 1892) ii: p.372.
61. Ibid. ii: pp.372–3.
62. Mahan, *Influence of Sea Power* (note 27) p.243.

63. Ibid.
64. A.T. Mahan, 'The United States Looking Outward', *Atlantic Monthly* (Dec. 1890), in Mahan, *Interest of America* (note 45) pp.4–5.
65. A.T. Mahan, 'Considerations Governing the Disposition of Navies', *National Review* (July 1902), repr. in idem, *Retrospect and Prospect* (note 43) pp.143–4.
66. A.T. Mahan, 'The Persian Gulf and International Relations,' *National Review* (Sept. 1902), in idem, *Retrospect and Prospect* (note 43) p.246.
67. Ibid. p.249.
68. For sources of the matters discussed in this paragraph, which are extensive, see Sumida (note 1) pp.88, 92–5.
69. Mahan, 'The Problem of Asia' (Preface), *Problem of Asia*, p.vi.
70. For sources of the matters discussed in this paragraph, which are extensive, see Sumida (note 1) pp.94–8, and Puleston (note 21) p.351.
71. Mahan, 'The Problem of Asia' (note 67) p.1.
72. Mahan, *Interest of America* (note 45) p.v.
73. Parker (note 13) p.161.
74. Ibid. Ch.3.
75. Ibid. pp.59, 66, 80, 175.
76. Ibid. pp.65–75, 79.
77. For discussion of the broader context of this attitude, see Akira Iriye, *From Nationalism to Internationalism: US Foreign Policy to 1914* (London: Routledge & Kegan Paul 1977) Ch.5.
78. Parker (note 13) Chs.3–4.
79. Ibid. pp.211–2.
80. Ibid. pp.41, 61, 163, 167.
81. Keith Neilson, '"Greatly Exaggerated": The Myth of the Decline of Great Britain before 1914', *International History Review* 13/4 (Nov. 1991) pp.661–880.
82. A recent exception is Colin S. Gray, *The Leverage of Sea Power: The Strategic Advantage of Navies in War* (NY: Free Press 1992).

4

Air Power, Space Power and Geography

BENJAMIN S. LAMBETH[1]

Throughout the Cold War, 'strategic' air power was associated in Western defense thinking almost exclusively with intercontinental-range bombers and nuclear weapons. As such, it was considered to be an important adjunct of nuclear deterrence and one whose sole reason for existence was not to be used in anger. Everything else short of 'strategic' air power, so defined and understood, was relegated to the category of 'theatre' or 'tactical' air power, whose sole rationale was seen as supporting armored and mechanized infantry formations in combined-arms *land* operations. Little consideration was given, even by airmen, let alone by defense specialists more generally, to the potential ability of conventional air power to produce strategic results independently of land forces in joint warfare.

That all began to change, however, during the late 1980s as some airmen came to realize that technological trends during the preceding decade may have imparted to conventional air power a qualitative improvement in its ability to achieve theater joint-force objectives directly.[2] In a resounding confirmation of that realization, the allied air campaign against Iraq in the 1991 Persian Gulf War bespoke a virtual transformation in the lethality and effectiveness of the air weapon since Vietnam. The prompt attainment of allied air control over Iraq during the opening night of Operation 'Desert Storm' and, more important, what that control allowed allied air assets to accomplish afterwards by way of enabling the rapid achievement of the coalition's objectives on the ground marked, in the view of many, the final coming of age of air power.

In the immediate aftermath of the war, the predominant tendency, not just among airmen, was to credit coalition air power with the bulk of responsibility for allowing such a surprisingly easy win in the land campaign. True enough, most observers were quick to acknowledge the important role played by *all* allied force elements in producing Iraq's military defeat. Nevertheless, the predominant view was summed up by retired RAF Air Vice-Marshal Tony Mason, who observed that 'the Gulf war marked the apotheosis of twentieth century air power'.[3] The only unsettled question, then as now, was whether, in the words of a USAF air power theorist, 'Desert Storm' symbolized not only the maturation of air power, but also 'the domination of air power and a new paradigm of warfare' presaging 'a fundamental shift in the way many wars will be conducted and the need for a new way of thinking about military operations'.[4]

It is not the intent of this essay to suggest that air power can win wars all by itself, as some of its more outspoken proponents have long argued. On the contrary, the spectrum of possible circumstances that could test a future joint force commander is so diverse that one cannot say for sure that *any* single force element will always dominate across the board. Recent developments in the instruments of air warfare have most assuredly increased the *relative* leverage of the air weapon in comparison to that of other force elements. However, air power has by no means become a universally applicable tool providing an answer to every conceivable challenge that might arise to confront a theatre commander.

That said, although success in major theater wars will, as before, continue to require the involvement of all force elements in appropriately integrated fashion, new air and space capabilities now permit joint force commanders to conduct operations against organized enemy forces more quickly and effectively than ever before. Properly applied, those capabilities enable the achievement of strategic effects in major wars directly, by offering commanders the promise of engaging and destroying or neutralizing enemy ground forces from stand-off ranges with virtual impunity, thus reducing a threat to friendly troops who might otherwise have to engage undegraded enemy ground forces directly and thus risk sustaining high casualties. Such a strategic air campaign will not bring the quick and easy victory that the air power visionaries of the early twentieth century seemed to promise. However, in the words of one observer, it will bring a victory 'that is quicker and easier than a war waged without one'.[5]

The discussion that follows will expand on this assertion by reviewing the signal accomplishment of allied air power in 'Desert Storm', consider what distinguishes today's air weapon from that of even a decade ago by way of its ability to contribute to the successful outcome of joint campaigns, examine recent developments in space power as an essential enabler of air power, and address geography as a continuing constraint on air power's applicability and combat value.

AIR POWER'S ACCOMPLISHMENT IN 'DESERT STORM'

War began for Iraq at 0238 local time on 17 January 1991. The opening shots were Hellfire missiles fired from US Army Apache helicopters against two Iraqi acquisition radar sites that provided early warning to Iraqi air and missile defenses. That opened a corridor enabling F-15Es to attack fixed Scud surface-to-surface missile sites at the same time as the first allied bombs were hitting Baghdad. Nine minutes prior to H-hour, a pair of F-117 stealth fighters (2 of 10 in this initial attack) destroyed the interceptor operations center some 160 miles southwest of Baghdad to which the two early warning posts reported. The F-117s proceeded thereafter to attack a second target, the Iraqi western-sector air operations center, some 20 minutes later. These F-117 attacks blinded Iraq's air defenses and crippled key control nodes to help ensure the success of follow-on attacks by nonstealthy aircraft.

The most pressing challenge facing the allied attackers on opening night was to neutralize Iraq's extensive network of lethal surface-to-air missiles (SAMs). These suppression of enemy air defence (SEAD) missions featured some of the most demanding air operations of the entire war. The F-4G with the AGM-88 High-Speed Anti-Radiation Missile (HARM) did most of the actual shooting, with jamming support provided by EF-111s, EC-130s, and EA-6Bs. Such attacks were further supported by BQM-74 jet-powered drones and tactical air-launched decoys to stimulate and confuse Iraq's acquisition and tracking radars, much as the Israelis had done over the Beka'a Valley of Lebanon against Syria's SA-6 SAMs in 1982. The underlying concept of operations was to use a combination of tactical surprise and deception (by means of the decoys and drones) from the opening moments of the war to force the largest possible number of Iraqi SAM batteries to disclose their positions to coalition HARM shooters by activating their radars.

The initial efforts of the allied defense suppression campaign focused on neutralizing Iraq's radar-directed medium- and high-altitude SAMs so as to open up a sanctuary for coalition aircraft above 10,000 ft.[6] At one point during these attacks, more than 200 HARMs were in flight simultaneously. During the first four hours of the war, nearly 100 Iraqi air defense radar emissions were logged by coalition sensors. That number later declined to

15 and became only 'sporadic' thereafter.[7] In all, more than 500 HARMs were fired during the first 24 hours of the war. Iraqi air defenders quickly learned that to activate their radars meant to invite a deadly attack.

In all, more than 100 coalition fighters flew defense suppression sorties during the first night. By the US government's estimate, the heart of the Iraqi air defense system was destroyed within the first hour. The coalition's stated goal was the effective neutralization of Iraq's command and control within 24 hours of the start of combat operations. It actually achieved that objective in the first eight hours. After the first night, individual air defense sectors were forced into autonomous operations, and Iraq's air defense network no longer functioned as an integrated system. Thanks to superior training, tactics, and equipment, the coalition's loss rate to Iraqi surface defenses by the end of 'Desert Storm' was only one aircraft per 1800 combat sorties, 14 times lower than the US loss rate to enemy defenses in Operation 'Linebacker II' against Hanoi during the Vietnam war a generation earlier.

To all intents and purposes, allied control of the air over Iraq was achieved during the opening moments of 'Desert Storm'. In stark contrast to the halting conduct of Operation 'Rolling Thunder' against North Vietnam from 1965 to 1968, virtually every target set in the master attack plan was hit on the first night, with the stress on simultaneity in attacking key targets so as to maximize the shock effect. Altogether, 812 combat (or 'shooter') sorties were flown in the first 24 hours. That made the opening round of 'Desert Storm' the largest single air offensive to have been conducted anywhere in the world since the end of World War II.

The effect of allied air control operations during the first few days of the Gulf War was quintessentially strategic, for they deprived Iraq of any defenses or situation awareness. They also meant that no ground campaign needed to be launched until coalition air attacks had beaten down enemy ground forces to the desired level at arm's length. Yet those achievements, impressive though they were in and of themselves, were not what accounted for the central role played by air power in determining the war's ultimate outcome. On the contrary, they only secured a necessary buy-in condition which enabled allied air power to demonstrate its *real* leverage of greatest note, namely, the ability to neutralize an enemy army wholesale, and with impunity, by means of precision standoff attacks.

Three factors coalesced to enable allied air power to reduce Iraqi forces to a point where once the ground offensive began, it could advance in the certain knowledge that it would be engaging a badly degraded opponent. The first was the freedom made possible by the SEAD and offensive counterair portions of the allied air campaign for coalition aircraft to operate at will in the medium-altitude environment, unmolested by Iraqi radar-guided SAMs or fighters. The second was the surprise ability made possible by the eleventh-hour introduction of a platform called the Joint Surveillance and Target Attack Radar System (J-STARS), to permit the coalition's Joint Force Air Component Commander (JFACC) to see fixed and moving objects on the battlefield clearly enough, and on a large enough scale, to make informed force commital decisions and execute lethal attacks against ground force targets day or night. The third was the discovery during the air campaign's battlefield preparation phase of the ability of aircraft equipped with infrared sensors and a capability of delivering laser-guided bombs (LGBs) to find and destroy dug-in enemy tanks one by one in large numbers.

These factors, in combination, gave air power an edge in joint warfare that it had never before possessed on such a pronounced scale. Along with the collateral psychological effect of the nonstop bombing of Iraqi troop positions by both allied fighters and B-52 bombers, they were largely responsible for enabling air power to deliver on the promise made by some of its more vocal proponents that once the time came for any allied ground push, it would essentially be a walk-in.[8]

On 29 January, Iraq launched a ground attack from southeastern Kuwait into Saudi Arabia aimed at the unprotected coastal town of Al Khafji. Iraqi troops occupied the town for a day, in the process trapping two US Marine reconnaissance teams, but coalition ground forces quickly evicted them.[9] Soon afterwards, allied sensors detected a second wave of Iraqi columns forming up to reinforce those that had initially attacked Al Khafji. Apparently Iraq's intent was to engage that part of the Arab Joint Forces Command that was deployed along the northern Saudi coast and force the coalition into a ground war, trying at a minimum for a gambit that would sufficiently bloody the nose of the United States to have a disproportionate political effect on the American home front.

Initially, the Tactical Air Control Center (TACC) did not react to these indicators of Iraqi forces on the move because its airborne sensors had been focused on areas to the west in search of Iraqi Scud mobile missiles and because the coalition's top commanders, despite the initial foray into Al Khafji, were not expecting Iraqi forces in Kuwait to launch a major move against Saudi Arabia. Once it became clear, however, that a sizable Iraqi ground advance was forming up on the night of 30 January, the senior officer in the TACC swung J-STARS to the east and began diverting coalition fighters to engage moving ground targets in Kuwait. Upon being apprised of the Iraqi troop activity, the allied JFACC, Lieutenant General Charles Horner, saw instantly an opportunity to engage the Iraqi column before it made contact with allied ground forces. Affirming the decision to divert coalition air power from its original tasking, he committed more than 140 aircraft against the advancing column, which consisted of the Iraqi 3rd Armored and 5th Mechanized Divisions.

The ensuing air attacks continued throughout the night and well into the following day before it was over. As a result of the timely diversion of coalition fighters, the Iraqi forces never had a chance to mass and attack. Once the dust settled, coalition air power had all but shredded the advancing Iraqi column, forcing the survivors to beat a ragged retreat. In all, 357 tanks, 147 APCs, and 89 mobile artillery pieces were destroyed in the precision air attacks, not counting additional items of equipment in Republican Guard units farther north. A captured Iraqi officer who had previously fought in the Iran–Iraq War later volunteered that his brigade had endured more punishment from allied air power in 15 minutes at Al Khafji than it had experienced in eight years of fighting against Iran.

Not long after the showdown at Al Khafji, US Air Force F-111Fs were swung to attacking enemy armor in the Kuwaiti Theater of Operations (KTO) using 500-lb GBU-12 laser-guided bombs. This attack tactic was neither preplanned nor even remotely a part of the F-111's original concept of operations. The idea for it first crystallized in December 1990, before the onset of 'Desert Storm', in an in-theatre workup exercise called Operation 'Night Camel'. Its training missions pitted US Air Force fighters equipped with infrared (IR) navigation and targeting pods in simulated attacks against armored forces of the US Army's VII Corps. Their goal was to determine whether IR-equipped aircraft could conduct night interdiction against enemy supply lines and deliver cluster munitions against enemy armor concentrations. A byproduct of these 'Night Camel' missions was the discovery that armored vehicles stood out distinctly on infrared displays between sunset and midnight because their rate of heat dissipation was slower than that of the surrounding desert sand. It also was determined that such aircraft could conduct successful night attacks against point targets from medium altitude.

Although further explored during the 'Desert Shield' buildup of forces, the tactic was never resorted to in combat until it became clear that because of problems of reliable battle-damage assessment (BDA), allied intelligence could not confirm the destruction of enemy ground forces at a fast enough rate to meet the timetable for launching the ground offensive set by the coalition's Commander-in-Chief, General H. Norman Schwarzkopf. A wartime operational evaluation on the night of 5 February proved so successful that 44 more sorties were scheduled the following night. From that point onward, 73 per cent of all assigned F-111F sorties in the air tasking order (ATO) were devoted to attacking enemy ground forces, with aircrews flying 664 sorties altogether against Iraqi tanks over a 23-day period. Because the tactic was so reminiscent of taking potshots at tin cans with air rifles, F-111 aircrews promptly dubbed it 'tank plinking'.

This entailed a fundamentally new mission for F-111F and F-15E aircrews which had never before appeared in any ground-attack tactics manual. For two snapshot indicators of its effectiveness, however, F-111Fs on the night of 6–7 February successfully dropped more than 140 laser-guided bombs on Republican Guard armor and artillery. The following week, on the night of 13–14 February, 46 F-111Fs dropped 184 GBU-12s and destroyed 132 armored fighting vehicles (AFVs) for an overall kill rate of 72 per cent. Throughout the war, F-111Fs destroyed some 920 Iraqi AFVs out of an estimated total of 6100.[10] As a measure of the tactic's effectiveness, all coalition aircraft engaged in 'tank plinking' were officially credited with a combined total of 1300 confirmed kills by 14 February.

The impact of this new attack tactic on classic ground force survival assumptions was profound. Hitherto, the Iraqis had thought they could endure the air campaign by digging in during the day and massing only at night. However, as two F-111 crew members summed it up afterwards, what the J-STARS precision engagement tactic and 'tank plinking' combination showed was that 'if armies dig in, they die. If they come out of their holes, they die sooner.'[11] The effect on enemy behavior was to heighten the individual soldier's sense of futility and hopelessness. Many vehicles were simply abandoned by their operators once it became apparent that they could turn into death traps at any moment without warning. Viewed at the individual shooter-to-target level, tank plinking may have seemed only 'tactical' to the casual observer. Yet as a concept of operations for defeating an enemy army, it was decidedly strategic in both character and consequence. The peak kill rate it enabled was well above 500 Iraqi AFVs per day, and it remained above that rate for several days in a row. In previous wars, such targets would have been relatively unthreatened by air attack. The novel effect it produced was 'paralysis through intimidation'.[12]

Viewed with the benefit of hindsight, the coalition's conduct of the 1991 Gulf War for the limited goal of evicting Iraqi forces from Kuwait has now come to be seen by most as having been considerably less than a towering policy success. Yet as a more narrow exercise in the application of air power, Operation 'Desert Storm' was anything but inconclusive. On the contrary, the ability of the coalition air campaign to achieve air dominance so promptly over a well-endowed opponent who knew a fight was coming and then to damage his fielded army to a point where coalition ground forces could consummate a virtually bloodless win in a mere 100 hours rather than the two weeks anticipated, represented a watershed achievement in the history of conventional air operations.

In particular, the combination of real-time surveillance and precision attack capability that was exercised to such telling effect against Iraqi ground forces at Al Khafji and afterwards heralded a new relationship between air- and surface-delivered firepower in modern war. A key aspect of this transformation involved the resulting synergy of that combination in permitting the defeat of an army through *functional* effects rather than through a more classic drawdown by way of attrition. Just as the earlier SEAD campaign was able to neutralize Iraqi radar-guided SAMs not by physically destroying them in detail but by intimidating their operators from turning on their radars, so the precision attacks made possible by J-STARS put potential enemy armies on notice that they can no longer expect a night sanctuary or any place to hide. At the same time, they served notice that any attempt to move will equally ensure a swift and lethal attack. In all, the events at Al Khafji confirmed a new role for air power in saving friendly lives by substituting precision air attacks for ground forces within reach of enemy fire.

WHAT IS NEW ABOUT AIR POWER?

The most important advance in recent military aviation technology has been the introduction of low observability to enemy radar and infrared sensors, more commonly known as 'stealth'. As incorporated in the F-117, it proved to be decisive in the early suppression of Iraqi air defenses that led to the prompt establishment of allied air control in 'Desert Storm'. It is the dominant characteristic as well of the USAF's new B-2 bomber which attained initial operational capability in 1997 and which made its combat debut in NATO's Operation 'Allied Force' against Yugoslavia in 1999. And it will be the principal distinguishing feature of the F-22 air dominance fighter and tri-service Joint Strike Fighter now expected to come on line during the first two decades of the twenty-first century.

In the crucial area of ground-attack operations, stealth has greatly increased the likelihood of unobserved and unmolested penetration to target by an approaching aircraft.[13] Indeed, the low radar cross-section of a stealthy air vehicle has increased the latter's survivability in enemy SAM envelopes to a point of making existing SAMs all but obsolete against it. Its ability to permit an aircraft to operate at medium altitudes and, within some constraints, to rove enemy airspace at will allows a substantial increase in the capacity of attacking aircraft to engage surface targets on the move both with impunity and surprise.

Equally important, stealth has obviated the need to amass large force packages for most applications of air power. A typical non-stealthy attack package in 'Desert Storm' required 38 allied combat and combat-support aircraft altogether in order to enable eight of those aircraft to deliver bombs on three aim-points. Yet at the same time, only 20 stealthy F-117s simultaneously attacked 37 aimpoints successfully in the face of a far more challenging Iraqi surface-to-air defensive threat. The difference was more than a 1200 per cent increase in target coverage with 47 per cent fewer aircraft.[14]

In attacks against enemy surface defenses and airfields during the critical opening hours of a high-intensity conflict, even modest numbers of stealthy aircraft can be pivotal in shaping the subsequent course and outcome of a conflict by allowing air control to be gained quickly, neutralizing SAM and fighter defenses and paving the way for nonstealthy aircraft armed with precision-guided weapons to continue most of the hard work against enemy ground targets. Such aircraft further offer the ability to carry an air control campaign deep into enemy territory from the outset of combat, something that was generally not possible in high-intensity wars prior to 'Desert Storm'. This ability of stealth, in combination with improved battlespace information and precision-attack capability, to help end a conflict rapidly reduces the likelihood of a more drawn-out operation that could result either in a stalement or in the intrusion of political forces that could lead to an unsatisfactory outcome.

Granted, stealth does not render a combat aircraft fully invisible along the lines of the fanciful 'Romulan cloaking device' of *Star Trek* fame. What it does is reduce substantially the range at which an enemy's radar and infrared sensors can detect a platform from various look angles and to complicate severely the tracking of any stealthy vehicle that may be momentarily detected by enemy sensors. The net effect is to narrow significantly any defender's window of opportunity for successfully engaging and downing an attacking stealth platform. Low observability to radar means that stealthy platforms can be operated in high-threat areas with less concern for surface defenses and can fly on headings and at altitudes aimed at maximizing opportunities for early target acquisition.

One cannot, of course, operate stealth aircraft with complete abandon. Even the most advanced stealth aircraft must be flown in specific attitudes to known threat radars to preclude their being detected in time to be put at risk, as the surprise downing of a USAF F-117 by an apparent Serbian SA-3 missile shot during the fourth night of Operation 'Allied Force' disturbingly indicated. That said, the arrival of stealth technology has imparted a fundamentally new edge to offensive air power, namely, the ability to make an unobserved approach to the most heavily-defended air and surface targets and all that implies in terms of enhanced survivability and mission effectiveness. Not only can smaller numbers of such aircraft produce strategically decisive results early in a war, they can increase the value of nonstealthy aircraft by providing the latter a safe envelope within which to operate over hostile terrain.

True enough, one can ask whether the outlook for stealth countermeasures may be promising enough over the longer run to render the next generation of combat aircraft merely a passing advantage. Throughout the ages, it has been an iron law of weapons development for new concepts to be negated eventually by offsetting countermeasures. Naturally, in the case of low observability to radar, one can assume that adequately-endowed adversaries will seek aggressively to unmask such aircraft either through more capable radars or through sensors based on other physical principles, such as infrared, visible light, and acoustics. Yet today's stealth technology has rendered existing engagement radars, as well as the weapons that depend on them, virtually useless. Until as-yet non-existent countermeasures are developed and made readily available to potential adversary states, low observability to enemy radar and other sensors and its ability to open the way for precision attacks on an opponent's core instruments of power will be the predominant new characteristics of joint warfare.

As 'Desert Storm' attested, air power has matured over the past two decades to a point where it has finally become truly strategic in its effects. That was not the case before the advent of stealth, the capability for consistently accurate target engagement, and the availability of substantially improved battlefield information. Earlier air campaigns were of limited effectiveness at the operational and strategic levels because it simply took too many aircraft at too high a loss rate over too long a period of time to achieve too few results. Today, in contrast, air power can make its presence felt quickly and can impose effects from the outset of combat that can have a governing influence on the subsequent course and outcome of a joint campaign.

Moreover, there is no longer a need to amass force as there was even in the recent past. Such advances as low observability to enemy radars and the ability to destroy or neutralize both fixed and moving targets with a single munition have obviated the need for the sort of cumbersome formations of strike and support aircraft that were typically required in Vietnam. The large force packages that the US Air Force and Navy routinely employed during the air war over North Vietnam offered the only way of ensuring that enough aircraft would make it to their assigned targets to deliver the number of bombs needed to achieve the desired outcome. Today, improved battlespace awareness, heightened aircraft survivability, and increased weapons accuracy have made possible the *effects* of massing without having to mass. As a result, air power can produce effects that were previously unattainable. The only question remaining, unlike in earlier eras of strategic bombing, is *when* those effects will be registered, not whether. That new capability of air power was encouragingly reaffirmed by the recently-concluded Operation 'Allied Force' over Yugoslavia.

In light of this confluence of developments, air power may yet succeed in meeting the goal of its early visionaries and obviate altogether any need for surface engagements, at least in some circumstances. However, Air Vice-Marshal Mason suggests that a more seemly goal of air power modernization should be to produce situations 'which can subsequently be exploited by ground forces in greatly reduced numbers, with greatly reduced casualties, and greatly reduced costs'.[15] By building on the results gained by surprise and producing the sort of paralysis by intimidation that was inflicted on Iraq's integrated air defenses and army units by the allied air campaign, air power can neutralize an opponent's ability to pursue his objectives by means of force or reduce it to a point where the opponent cannot resist a counteroffensive by friendly surface forces. Already, this newly-acquired leverage has unburdened ground commanders of any need to undertake a frontal assault in direct contact with enemy forces until the costs of such an assault can be made tolerable.

SPACE POWER AS AN ENABLER

Although military involvement in the exploitation of space can be traced back to the 1950s, it was only in the crucible of the Gulf War that the synergistic potential of air and space power first began to be fully appreciated. When Iraq invaded Kuwait on 2 August 1990, the first coalition assets to make their presence felt on scene were not air, naval, or land forces, but rather the allied space systems already on orbit high above the gathering storm. Although these assets played only a supporting role in the allied force buildup and combat operations that followed, they were indispensable in determining the course and outcome of the war. Allied force enhancement through the medium of space came in the form of navigation and positioning support, communications, the provision of terrain and environmental information, weather reporting, indications and warning, attack warning, and surveillance and reconnaissance. Each contribution was pivotal in ensuring the coalition's information dominance throughout the war.

On the first count, the Navstar Global Positioning System (GPS) came of age by providing real-time navigation and targeting updates to numerous weapons types employed by coalition forces.[16] It proved particularly useful because of the undifferentiated terrain of the Iraqi desert, which presented unusually severe challenges to navigation.[17] Aircrews in combat aircraft equipped only with inertial navigation systems used hand-held GPS terminals to augment their less accurate analog navigational aids. For example, GPS cues were used by special operations forces for aircraft positioning, with Pave Low helicopters relying on them entirely for both day and night nap-of-the-earth penetrations into Iraq and Kuwait.

Because the GPS satellite constellation had not been fully completed at the time the Gulf War began in January 1991, there were seven time windows of up to 40 minutes each day during which fewer than the required minimum of four satellites were simultaneously in view of a receiver. These GPS 'sad times,' as they came to be called, obliged allied combatants to fall back on less capable systems and techniques or rely on less accurate GPS data. Nevertheless, GPS had a revolutionary impact on coalition operations throughout the Gulf War, perhaps most notably in facilitating the 100-hour ground sweep across the flat and featureless Iraqi desert into the blind side of Iraqi troops hunkered down in the Kuwait Theater of Operations (KTO).

As for allied communications, three satellites of the Defense Satellite Communication System (DSCS) constellation enabled continuous high-capacity, high data-rate, worldwide secure voice communications. These DSCS satellites supported 128 tactical terminals throughout the war. One of these was moved from the Pacific Ocean to the Indian Ocean to augment coalition communications, in the first instance of a US military satellite having been repositioned to support combat operations. The data load was so heavy that commercial space systems capabilities were purchased to augment the dedicated military space capabilities. Ultimately, both these and the military's satellites provided the main conduit for 85 per cent of all intra-theatre and inter-theatre communications.

With respect to overhead surveillance and monitoring, satellites of the Defense Meteorological Support Program (DMSP) provided commanders and planners with near-real time weather information. Among other things, they enabled the remote analysis of desert soil moisture content to help determine the best routes for General Schwarzkopf's 'left hook' into Iraq and the KTO. As for combat intelligence and post-strike BDA, classified national space reconnaissance platforms, along with other allied capabilities, were key contributors toward obtaining multi-spectral images of the theater and electronic intelligence. The American Landsat and French SPOT commercial remote-sensing satellites were enlisted to provide additional imagery support for terrestrial observation, notably via broad-area views of sufficient resolution to enable the creation of tailor-made yet unclassified products for combat mission planning.[18]

A space surveillance system that proved to be crucial in the ultimately unsuccessful hunt for hidden Iraqi Scud theater-ballistic missiles was the Defense Support Program (DSP) constellation of infrared-sensing satellites, which were able to detect the heat of the Scud's rocket exhaust plume within 30 seconds of launch. Although not originally designed to detect the launch of short-range ballistic missiles, DSP nonetheless helped greatly in locating Scud launch sites and in providing F-15E crews with near-real time target coordinates. It also helped alert Patriot missile defense crews to an incoming attack. Thanks to the fortuitous conduct by the Iraqis of three practice Scud launches during the 'Desert Shield' buildup, DSP operators were able to exploit those windfall events to tweak the system for better operations in a quick-response mode.[19] The Scud's short time of flight from launch to impact (only seven minutes), however, limited the practical usefulness of such information, aside from its alerting value.

After the dust settled, the USAF chief of staff, General Merrill McPeak, described 'Desert Storm' as 'the first space war'.[20] Purists might demur on whether the strictly support functions performed by allied space assets in that war were enough to justify such a categorical description. There is no denying, however, that the Gulf War represented the first instance in which the entire panoply of allied space assets was employed in direct support of combat operations at all levels. That amply bore out the more telling point by a British defence leader that 'Desert Storm' 'taught us that space has changed the whole nature of warfare'.[21]

GEOGRAPHY AS A CONSTRAINT

In considerable part because of the limitations of geography, air power continues to be shackled in its ability to meet all conceivable demands of a joint force commander. For regional air arms without a requirement for strategic reach, geographic considerations make for less of a planning factor than they do for the USAF, whose stock in trade is global engagement. In most cases, regional air forces do not face anything like the broad spectrum of climatological and other operational settings that the USAF must be equipped and prepared to contend with. The highly-capable Israeli Air Force, for example, has the advantage of operating in a setting that is generally conducive to the effective employment of air power. Such is not always the case for the USAF and some NATO air forces.

Air Vice-Marshal Mason has graphically demonstrated this point via the device of a notional air power pendulum which swings from the clear-cut case of 'Desert Storm', where targets were accessible and significant, the desert topography open and unrestricted, the weather generally favorable, bases readily available, and political support both at home and abroad unquestioned to the more challenging 1995 Bosnian scenario, where targets were mobile and generally of low value, the topography wooded and mountainous, the weather often forbidding, and political support far more fragile. As for other cases of air power application, Mason found the Six Day War of 1967, the Yom Kippur War of 1973, and the Beka'a Valley operation of 1982 far closer to the 'Desert Storm' model in terms of air power's effectiveness and dominance, whereas Somalia and other recent peacekeeping operations aggregated much closer to the Bosnian case, where air power proved of more limited value in dealing with events on the ground, even though Operation 'Deliberate Force' did, in the end, help coerce the Bosnian Serbs to put down their arms and accede to a truce.[22]

Indeed, the geographic setting of the 1991 Gulf War was almost uniquely congenial to the effective employment of air power. From an operational viewpoint, the open desert environment offered an ideal force employment arena, although distances to target and recurrent foul weather added offsetting complications. Taking note of that, some suggested in the aftermath of 'Desert Storm' that the right bumper sticker for air power should read: 'We do deserts. We don't do mountains or jungles'. It will be important for future technology application to ensure that this assertion is proven wrong. Today, it still comes disturbingly close to the mark. Although tellingly effective when finally used properly and with determination, allied air power application in Bosnia in 1994 and 1995 and in the 1999 Kosovo conflict proved to be a greater challenge than it was against Iraq. And there will be more, not fewer, cases like Bosnia and Kosovo in the future. As former US Secretary of Defense William Perry rightly cautioned shortly after the Gulf War ended, 'no one should be deluded into believing that the military capability that can easily defeat an army with 4,000 tanks in a desert is going to be the decisive factor in a jungle or urban guerilla war'.[23]

There was also the important fact of no Soviet resupply of military hardware and other consumables to Iraq. The US fought North Vietnam for ten long years a generation earlier, in part because Hanoi enjoyed a nonstop source of arms replenishments from two Communist sanctuaries to the north. In contrast, the winding down of the Cold War and Soviet President Mikhail Gorbachev's desire for improved relations with Washington served to ensure that Moscow would not provide similar support to Iraq. Thanks to the international trade embargo and Moscow's compliance in halting its arms transfers to Baghdad, it was only a matter of time before Iraq would run out of weapons and fighting strength under the weight of allied bombing. Had the Soviet Union chosen to back Iraq militarily, General Schwarzkopf's strategy would not have worked and the Gulf crisis would have taken a less certain course.

The very different case of Korea makes for a sobering reminder to any air power proponent that the going will not be invariably as easy as it was in 'Desert Storm' in future showdowns in which friendly air power might be challenged. There is where the Gulf War analogy breaks down quickly and where the USAF and US Army have a powerful need for mutual respect because of their mutual dependency. Although air power will unquestionably be the key to success in any war that might erupt there, no such war would be fought with the comparative luxury of fewer than 200 US combat fatalities, as was the case in 'Desert Storm'. With more than 500,000 armed combatants on both sides poised for immediate action along the demilitarized zone, any such war would entail close ground combat from the very start.

True enough, air power would quickly establish allied ownership of the skies over North Korea following any outbreak of war on the peninsula and would reduce the incidence of friendly combat fatalities by blunting an armored attack, diminishing enemy theater missiles and artillery, and gaining situational control by forcing the enemy to remain underground. It could further engage in systematic 'bunker plinking', although many of North Korea's underground facilities are sufficiently secure from air attack that it would require allied ground forces to go in and dig them out. But without question, allied air power would not be able to halt a North Korean armored and mechanized infantry invasion alone.

Distance is yet another geographic constraint for air forces with global commitments. In 'Desert Storm', the United States and its allies enjoyed a regional basing infrastructure that left almost nothing to be desired, thanks largely to the military assistance that had been provided to Saudi Arabia by the United States over the preceding four decades. The US Army Corps of Engineers had been building bases ever since the end of World War II to Saudi orders for what was clearly more capacity than the Saudi Air Force, by itself, could ever use. The quality of the bases varied from full facilities (as at Khamis Mushait, to the far southwest, where the F-117s were stationed) to bare-base facilities (as at Al Kharj) which offered little more than runways, taxiways, and ramp space. But at least they provided the needed springboard from which to conduct an air campaign that could hardly help but win. Had the allied coalition been unable to base its aircraft within a reasonable operating radius from Iraq, the air war would have looked quite different and would have had a less assured outcome.

Indeed, thanks largely to geographic constraints, USAF leaders would be the first to concede that they cannot execute their 'halt phase' strategy solely by using bombers based in the continental US, notwithstanding all the recent claims that have been made on behalf of air power's potential for halting and repelling an enemy armored attack. The Air Force simply lacks a sufficient number of intercontinental-range combat aircraft with the required munitions capability and must necessarily depend on forward-deployed projection forces to stop enemy invasions.

Of course, the USAF now has the ability to fly from Barksdale AFB, Louisiana, with B-52s or from Whiteman AFB, Missouri, with its newly-operational B-2s and deliver precision ordnance anywhere in the world, as was demonstrated to telling effect on an almost nightly basis throughout the 78-day NATO 'Allied Force' air campaign against Yugoslavia. The USAF has little, however, by way of mass or persistence in this respect. A dozen or so stealthy B-2s suitably loaded with smart weapons, which is about what will be available to a joint force commander at any moment, once the aircraft becomes fully operational, might well be able to do the job of 100 or so conventional fighters in a classic strike package. However, merely a dozen B-2s cannot singlehandedly conduct a sustained air campaign half a globe away. This problem will be partly ameliorated when the more plentiful B-1 inventory is equipped to carry the GPS-guided Joint Direct-Attack Munition (JDAM) and Wind-Corrected Munitions Dispenser (WCMD), thereby giving it a through-the-weather attack capability against multiple aim points on a single mission. Until then, any argument that US air power can single-handedly halt a massive armored assault halfway around the world on short notice will be hard to sustain.

To make matters worse, the sharp decline in the number of permanent US overseas bases since the Cold War's end has made regional access more essential than ever to the effective use of American land-based air power worldwide. Yet assumptions of easy and ready access can be dangerous. For example, ten years from now the two Koreas may have reunited, leaving open the question of whether the new Korean government will be more or less amenable to the continued presence of American combat aircraft on the Korean peninsula. On top of that, Japan may not be willing to take on any more US aircraft. That spotlights the need for the United States to be working hard now to ensure future access wherever and whenever it may be needed.

To be sure, the United States will most likely retain for some time its most vital air bases in Europe and the Pacific that survived the initial post-Cold War reductions. Yet more and more operations against certain regions may have to be conducted from the continental United States because of inadequate or uncertain basing alternatives closer to the theatre. As a stopgap measure, the US Navy commands an advantage with its aircraft carriers for some plausible contingencies that could occur in littoral settings suitable for carrier air operations. However, neither the nation's bombers *nor* its carriers have the needed wherewithal to sustain a theater air operation of campaign proportions. Only land-based attack aircraft can do that. Accordingly, partnerships to ensure regional access by American and allied forces when global challenges require such access will be essential to air power's successful application in the twenty-first century.

Motivated by the success of the *ad hoc* 'provisional' wings that were cobbled together for specific combat needs in 'Desert Storm', the USAF has since moved to establish an 'Air Expeditionary Force' (AEF) which can be built out of pieces from various different units for deployment on short notice as required. The intent of the AEF concept is to provide a new force projection tool aimed at deterring and, if need be, halting aggression by blunting an enemy ground offensive that could be a prelude to a major theater war. The idea is, in a sense, a revival of the now all but forgotten Composite Air Strike Force, an almost identical concept developed and institutionalized in the US Tactical Air Command's 19th Air Force for a time during the mid-1950s to deal with so-called 'brush-fire wars'.

In essence, the AEF seeks to provide the USAF with a mid-way solution between fighting from permanent overseas bases, which are growing in increasingly short supply, and reliance on operating from the continental US. A typical AEF might be composed of 35–40 aircraft drawn from three or four wings worldwide, including 6 bombers (B-52s, B-1Bs, or B-2s), 12 air-to-air fighters (F-15Cs or F-16Cs), 12 air-to-ground aircraft (F-15Es or Block 40 F-16Cs), and 6 SEAD fighters (Block 50 F-16CJs equipped with HARM). Airlift, consisting of up to 14 C-141s or C-17s, would constitute an important part of the deployment package also. The overall strike capability offered by such an entity would be somewhat greater than that provided by a single carrier battle group. More important, it could establish a fighting presence in a threatened area far more quickly than a carrier. The envisaged goal is for an AEF to be ready to engage in combat within 24–48 hours of receiving an execute order and to continue surge operations for at least seven days followed by withdrawal or augmentation thereafter.

The AEF concept is still in its refinement stage and has yet to be proven in short-notice combat, although USAF air expeditionary squadrons did gain some useful deployment and operational-use experience during Operation 'Allied Force'. The cost-effectiveness of the concept also has yet to be fully determined, and numerous questions bearing on its practicality remain to be satisfactorily answered. The latter include the prerequisites for getting aircrews ready to deploy on short notice, securing overflight clearances, and putting bombs on target within a mere 24 hours of a deployment decision. Air base access presents yet another unsettled issue, as do the requirements for base preparation, unit reconstitution, logistics coordination, force protection upon arrival, and ensuring adequate command and control and ISR (intelligence, surveillance and reconnaissance) support. Even a 48-hour timeline will be demanding in the face of such challenges, along with assembling a unit's personnel and equipment promptly upon arrival in theater and configuring and generating aircraft for immediate combat employment. Normal crew rest rules may have to be waived to achieve such exacting deadlines.

If the AEF concept is to be of immediate use to a joint force commander, it will have to demonstrate its ability to blunt an enemy ground push short of the latter's objectives and hold the line during any ensuing buildup for more sustained combat operations. This, in turn, will require exploiting to the fullest recent advances in information availability and air-delivered firepower. It will further require acceptance by theater commanders of an approach to joint warfare in which an early 'close' battle between opposed ground forces is supplanted by the use of friendly ground forces *not* to engage their enemy counterparts directly, but rather to cause a 'heavying up' and consequent slowing down of enemy troops so they can be engaged in detail by air power, as was done during and after the Battle of Al Khafji in 'Desert Storm'.

The USAF has not yet mobilized the full wherewithal needed to accomplish this mission with high confidence, although its impending acquisition of wind-corrected Skeet submunitions dispensers promises to give the F-15E, F-16C, B-52H, and B-1B the ability to achieve upward of 12 armored kills per delivery pass.[25] Properly directed, such a capability will allow gradual attrition against a ground opponent much along the lines of what the coalition did to Iraqi ground forces in the early wake of the Battle of Al Khafji. Moreover, with the right weapons load, USAF bombers may be able to contribute to the halt phase directly from the continental United States while AEF units are being established in theater.

In all events, the latter will require prior achievement of local air control, as well as a negation of any nuclear or chemical weapons threats to rear-area air bases and air and naval ports of disembarkation. It also will require adequate information availability and cueing through such assets as J-STARS, along with lethal firepower in enough numbers to make a difference. Ultimately, AEF exercises will need to be conducted routinely in peacetime to institutionalize the requisite support, build confidence among the theater commanders in their potential, and demonstrate their deterrent and combat value. Over the longer haul, with smaller and smarter munitions entering the USAF's inventory, desired effects may be achieved with fewer sorties, thus reducing both combat aircraft and lift requirements.

NOTES

1. Although this essay was written and submitted before the start of the US-led Operation 'Allied Force' against Yugoslavia from late March to early June 1999, pertinent aspects of that ultimately successful 78-day NATO bombing campaign have been referenced throughout the discussion as appropriate.
2. Most prominent among them was Col. John A. Warden III, USAF, who was the first to codify this idea systematically in his *The Air Campaign: Planning for Combat* (Washington, DC: National Defense UP 1988).
3. Air Vice-Marshal R.A. Mason RAF (Ret.), 'The Air War in the Gulf,' *Survival* 33/3 (May/June 1991) p.225.
4. Col. Dennis Drew USAF (Ret.), 'Desert Storm as a Symbol', *Air Power Journal* (Fall 1992) pp.6, 13.
5. Richard P. King, 'The Case for Strategic Attack', unpublished manuscript, p.15.
6. John D. Morrocco, 'Allies Attack Iraqi Targets; Scuds Strike Israeli Cities', *Aviation Week and Space Technology*, 21 Jan. 1991, pp.20–2.
7. David M. North, 'Carrier-Based U.S. Aircraft Flying Third of Desert Storm Strikes', *Aviation Week and Space Technology*, 4 Feb. 1991, p.27.
8. For a detailed treatment of the impact of the allied bombing on Iraqi troop morale and combat cohesion, see Stephen T. Hosmer, *Psychological Effects of U.S. Air Operations in Four Wars,*

1941–1991: Lessons for U.S. Commanders (Santa Monica, CA: RAND, MR-576-AF, 1996) pp.141–75.

9. This occasioned one of the early misfortunes of the war when 11 Marines were killed in two light armored vehicles that were taken out by inadvertent friendly fire, one from a Maverick missile fired by an A-10 and the other to surface fire, after the Marines had called in air strikes on the Iraqi probes.
10. Roy Braybrook, 'On Target! A Review of Precision Air Attacks in the Gulf War', *Air International*, Oct. 1991, p.179.
11. Majors Michael J. Bodner and William W. Bruner III, 'Tank Plinking', *Air Force Magazine*, Oct. 1993, p.31.
12. Price Bingham, *The Battle of Al Khafji and the Future of Surveillance Precision Strike* (Arlington, VA: Aerospace Educational Fdn 1997) p.20.
13. For more on the operational significance of low observability, see Major General Jasper A. Welch Jr USAF (Ret.), 'Assessing the Value of Stealthy Aircraft and Cruise Missiles', *International Security* 24/2 (Fall 1989) pp.47–62.
14. Commission on Roles and Missions, *Future Bomber Force* (Arlington, VA: Aerospace Education Fdn, May 1995) p.2.
15. Air Vice-Marshal Tony Mason RAF (Ret.), 'The Future of Air Power', address to the Royal Netherlands Air Force, Netherlands Defence College, 19 April 1996, p.4.
16. See Sir Peter Anson and Gp. Capt. Dennis Cummings RAF (Ret.), 'The First Space War: The Contributions of Satellites to the Gulf War', *RUSI Journal* 136/4 (Winter 1991) pp.45–53.
17. At the time, the GPS constellation had only 16 satellites on orbit, 5 short of the number required for full global coverage and 8 shy of the complete network, including 3 planned spares. One of the 16 satellites experienced a failure that threatened to degrade severely the war-support capability of the overall system. It remained off-line only until USAF operators at Air Force Space Command's Falcon AFB developed the needed software to put it back in service. For a snapshot overview of the GPS system and how it works, see Peter Grier, 'GPS in Peace and War', *Air Force Magazine* (April 1996) pp.76–9.
18. Dana J. Johnson, Scott Pace, and C. Bryan Gabbard, *Space: Emerging Options for National Power* (Santa Monica, CA: RAND, MR-517-JS, 1997) p.25.
19. Curtis Peebles, *High Frontier: The United States Air Force and the Military Space Program* (Washington DC: Air Force History and Museums Program 1997) p.74.
20. Gen. Merrill A. McPeak, USAF, briefing on 'Desert Shield' and 'Desert Storm' to the National War College, 6 March 1991.
21. Anson and Cummings, 'The First Space War' (note 16) p.53.
22. Air Vice-Marshal Tony Mason RAF (Ret.), *Air Power: A Centennial Appraisal* (London: Brassey's 1994) p.xiii.
23. William J. Perry, 'Desert Storm and Deterrence', *Foreign Affairs* 70/3 (Fall 1991) p.81.
24. Paul Killingsworth, 'Enhancing the Effectiveness of Air Expeditionary Forces', briefing to Maj. Gen. Lee A. Downer, USAF (Ret.), RAND, Santa Monica, California, 18 Aug. 1997.
25. For more on this new capability and its operational implications for joint force commanders, see David A. Ochmanek, Edward R. Harshberger, David E. Thaler, and Glenn A. Kent, *To Find, and Not to Yield: How Advances in Information and Firepower Can Transform Theater Warfare* (Santa Monica, CA: RAND, MR-958-AF, 1998).

5

Geostrategy in the Space Age: An Astropolitical Analysis

EVERETT C. DOLMAN

The resurrection and rehabilitation of geopolitics requires at a minimum continuing political relevance. In this brief essay I attempt to capture the essential quality of classical geopolitics and extend its reach to the realm of outer space, a transition I call 'astropolitics'. If geopolitical theory developed for the Earth and its atmosphere can be transferred to outer space, then, *a fortiori*, the utility and value of its fundamental concepts and holistic design remain relevant, and are suitable for a set of revised or neoclassical geopolitical propositions. In this view, the incorporation of space technology is simply the latest innovation in the continuing process of refining geopolitical theory.

The focus here is on that variant of geopolitics called geostrategy, or the strategic application of new and emerging technologies within a framework of geographic, topographic, and positional knowledge. To be sure, outer space has a distinct and definable geography, and much of the following rests on an exposition of its geographic characteristics. The remaining task is to associate and extend existing geostrategic propositions to the described space model.

MODELING THE ASTROPOLITICAL ENVIRONMENT

Jean Gottman argued that if the world were featureless as a billiard ball, without terrain or topography, geopolitics could not have been posited.[1] Probably so, but with the perspective of scale gleaned from an outer space vantage, the Earth's terrain is relatively smoother than a billiard ball, and topographic features effectively disappear. The important features of any celestial body are simply its mass (for determinations of gravitational pull), orbit, and relation to other space phenomena. Astropolitics is in this view the purest form of geopolitical analysis, converging entirely on elements of space and scale.

This grandest of all perspectives reestablishes one of the great achievements of the modern geopolitical theorists, the recognition that the study of politics could not be nationally isolationist in its perspective. The Earth, to them, represented a conceptual unity. Without using systems terminology, they conceived of a single political arena. Each national unit was an integral part of the whole. State actions affected others, and states were in turn affected by the actions and reactions of those others. This holistic approach was a revelation in its day, and pushed the politico-geographic paradigm to lofty new heights.

Rather than reduce the importance of nation-states within the system, however, classical geopolitical theory has tended to amplify the centrality of national or regional rivalries. By manipulating knowledge of geopolitical characteristics, states could hope to gain an advantage over others. At the very least, states could hope to prevent another from gaining advantages by blocking their efforts at control. The vision of astropolitics presented here reinforces those notions. The logic is so compelling that states wishing to remain sovereign must at a minimum prevent other states from gaining vital control of strategic space locations, pathways, and chokepoints. Before identifying these critical elements of astropolitics, to ensure a common ground for discussion, it seems prudent to briefly describe the physical properties and operating characteristics of outer space.

A BRIEF LESSON IN ORBITS AND ORBITAL MECHANICS

What appears at first a featureless void is in fact a rich vista of gravitational mountains and valleys, oceans and rivers of resources and energy alternately dispersed and concentrated, broadly strewn danger zones of deadly radiation, and precisely placed peculiarities of astrodynamics. Without a full understanding of the motion of bodies in space, in essence a background in the mechanics of orbits, it is difficult to make sense of this panorama.[2]

An orbit is the path of a spacecraft or satellite caught in the grip of gravity. Knowledge of orbits and orbital mechanics is vital for one primary reason. Spacecraft in stable orbits expend no fuel. Thus the preferred flight path for all spacecraft (and natural satellites) will be a stable orbit, specifically limited to a precise operational trajectory. With this knowledge we can begin to see space as a demarcated and bounded domain.

An orbit is described first in terms of altitude and eccentricity, or variation in altitude. The highest and lowest points in an orbit are called the apogee and perigee, respectively (see Figure 1). Orbits are usually specified as circular, or of constant altitude with no differentiation of apogee and perigee, and elliptical, that is of varying altitude and eccentricity. Once these parameters are established the orbit of the spacecraft can be envisioned as part of a flat plane passing through the center of the orbited mass. The time it takes for a spacecraft to complete one orbit is called its period. Additional useful details can be found by determining the satellite's inclination, the angle measured as the difference between the satellite's orbital plane and the orbited body's equatorial plane. The inclination tells us the north and south latitude limits of the orbit. It is also useful to know the orbital plane's position relative to a fixed point on the rotating body of the orbited mass. For the Earth, this point is the vernal equinox, and the distance from it to the spacecraft's rising or ascending pass over the equator is called its right ascension.

FIGURE 1

ORBITAL CHARACTERISTICS

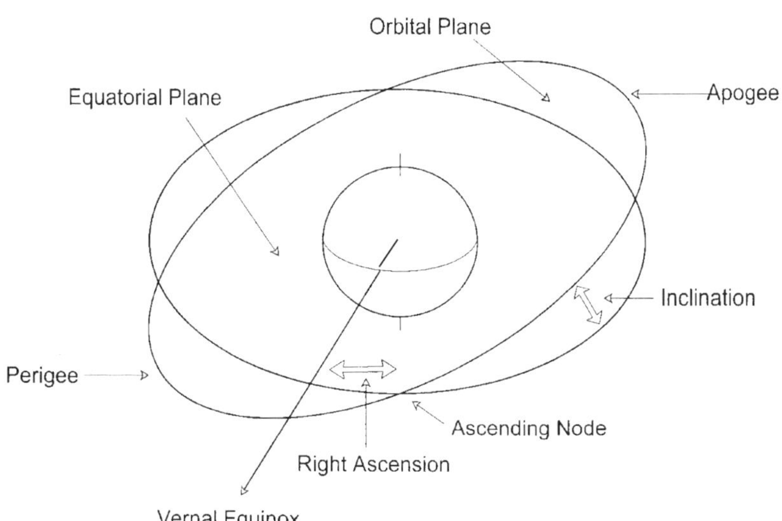

As a rule, the higher the altitude, the more stable the orbit, also, the *slower* the spacecraft travels relative to the body it orbits (orbital speed appears to increases as the spacecraft spirals down the gravity well of the orbited mass). Lower orbits are necessary if a close or detailed view of the Earth is desired, or a concentrated communications link is needed. Higher orbits provide a larger field of view, sacrificing detail for comprehension and offering wider electronic accessibility. Circular or constant altitude orbits are generally used for spacecraft that perform their missions continuously, over the entire course of the orbit, while eccentric orbits usually signify that missions are conducted at critical points in the orbit – usually at perigee or apogee.

The most vertical ascension orbit has a 90° inclination, perpendicular to the equatorial plane. This orbit is also called a polar orbit, meaning the spacecraft passes over the North and South Pole each complete orbit. The lowest inclination is 0°, which means the orbit is coincident with the equatorial plane. Inclinations below 90° are posigrade, which means they tend to drift eastward on each orbital pass, while inclinations above 90° are retrograde, tending to drift westward. If the spacecraft's altitude is constant at 36,000 km, the spacecraft will appear fixed relative to a point above the Earth. This is called a geostationary orbit, and is the only orbit that has this fixed-point capacity.

Orbits that are impacted by forces other than the constant gravitational mass of the orbited body have fluctuations in their natural movement. The orbit of an Earth satellite is never perfectly circular due to these fluctuations, called perturbations. The lower the altitude of a spacecraft, the more significant the friction caused by an encroaching atmosphere.[3] Orbits below about 160 km altitude (or an orbital period of 87.5 minutes) are theoretically possible, but not practically achievable due to accumulating atmospheric drag. Perturbations also come from the bulge at the Earth's equator caused by the centrifugal force of its over 1,000 mph rotation, which means the Earth's gravitational pull is not constant. The Earth is actually flattened slightly at the poles and distended at the equator, a phenomenon that also creates small deviations in the flight path of a ballistic missile. Other perturbations, increasingly significant as one moves away from the Earth, are the gravitational fields of the Sun, Moon, and other celestial bodies, and the effects of solar radiation including solar flares, and the impacts of meteors and debris that strike the satellite at hypervelocity. Thus, no orbit is perfect and all spacecraft must have some fuel to occasionally make corrections. The useful life of a spacecraft is, for the most part, a function of its fuel capacity and orbital stability.

Terrestrial orbits come in four generally recognized categories, based on altitude and mission utility (see Figure 2). The first encompasses *low altitude orbits*, between 150 to 800 km above the surface of the Earth. These are particularly useful for Earth reconnaissance (military observation and resource management) and manned flight missions. These altitudes allow for 14 to 16 complete orbits per day. Manned flights generally have low inclinations to maximize spacecraft to control center contact, while reconnaissance flights generally have high inclinations to maximize coverage of the Earth's surface. Low altitude orbits have the added advantage that satellites can be placed into them with cheaper and less sophisticated two-stage rockets. Orbits with a period in excess of 225 minutes (above 800 km) require at least a third stage boost to achieve final orbit.

FIGURE 2

TERRESTRIAL ORBITS

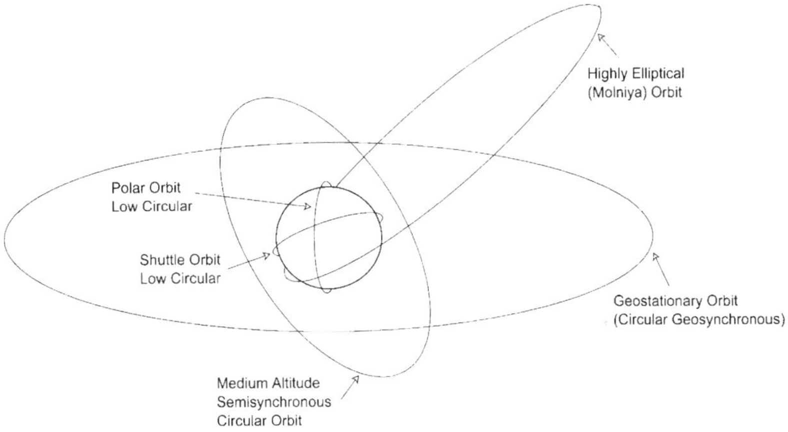

Medium altitude orbits allow 2 to 14 orbits per day, and range from 800 to 35,000 km in altitude. These are generally circular or low eccentricity orbits that support linked satellite networks (see Figure 3). Currently, navigational satellites that fix terrestrial positions through the triangulation of (at least) two or more satellites in view dominate this orbit, though increasingly high-speed global telecommunications networks are envisioned in operation here.

High altitude orbits, at least 35,000 km, provide maximum continuous

FIGURE 3

LINKED NETWORK (NAVSTAR/GPS)

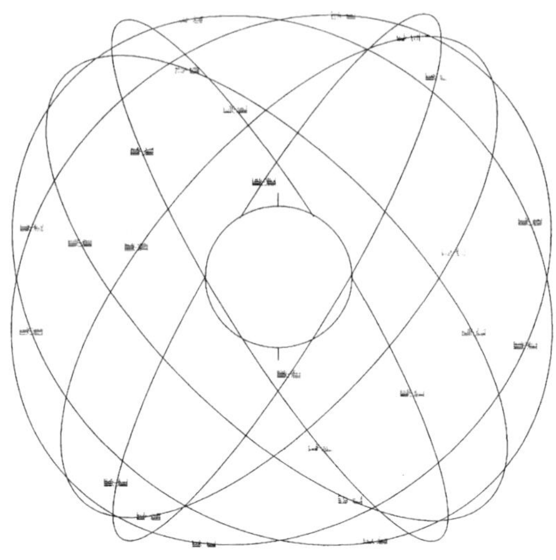

FIGURE 4

GEOSTATIONARY FIELDS OF VIEW

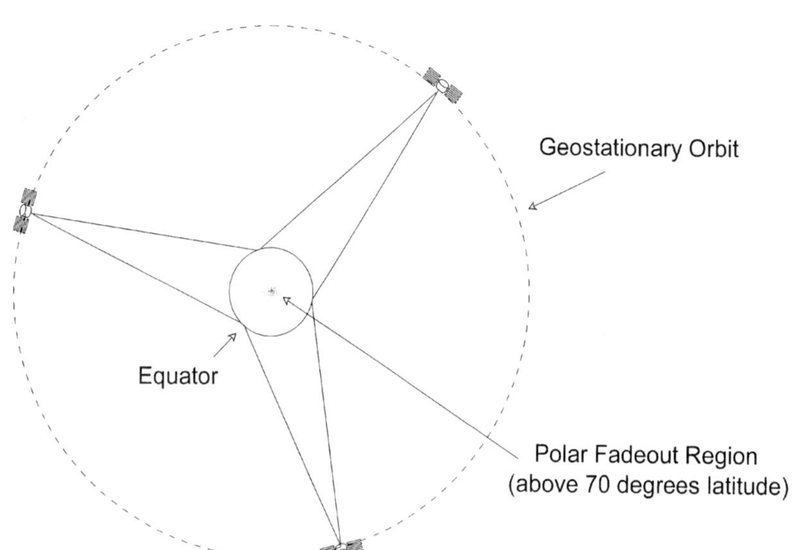

coverage of the Earth with a minimum of satellites in orbit. Satellites at high altitude orbit the Earth no more than once per day. When the orbital period is identical to one full rotation of the Earth, a *geosynchronous* orbit is achieved. A geosynchronous orbit with a 0° inclination (placed directly above the equator) appears fixed in the sky from any point on Earth. This is a *geostationary* orbit. Just three satellites at geostationary orbit, carefully placed equidistant from each other, can view the entire planet up to approximately 70° north or south latitude (see Figure 4, a satellite at geostationary orbit has a field of view of 28 per cent of the Earth's surface). Since the satellites do not appear to move, fixed antennae can easily and continuously access them. Global communications and weather satellites are typically placed in this orbit.

For those latitudes above 70°, the advantage of long dwell time over target provided by a geostationary orbit are absent. This is simply because the limb of the Earth is not functionally visible. One technique to overcome this deficiency is to use the fourth orbital category, the *highly elliptical orbit*. This orbit is described as highly eccentric with a perigee as low as 250 km and an apogee of up to 700,000 km.[4] Placed in a highly inclined orbit with apogee at 36,000–40,000 km, the satellite appears to dwell over the upper latitudes for several hours, making this a particularly useful orbit for communications satellites servicing arctic regions. This apparent pause occurs because the speed of the spacecraft at apogee is only about 3,000 mph while the speed at perigee is over 20,000 mph. When networked in the same orbit, one behind the other with equally spaced right ascensions, a minimum of three satellites can continuously access a single high latitude ground station. The Russians have made the greatest use of this semisynchronous 12-hour orbit, and associate it with the Molniya communications and weather spacecraft that use it. A highly elliptical orbit with apogee at over 700,000 km can have a period of more than a month, and is especially useful for scientific missions.

With this essential exposition of orbital definitions and mechanics out of the way, an analysis of the terrain of outer space and the interaction of classical geopolitical theories can begin.

THE FOUR REGIONS OF SPACE

Sir Halford Mackinder keyed his classic study of world power to the identification of distinct regions whose interactions defined the course of global history. History could be viewed as an alternating struggle between sea and land power, and nineteenth century naval dominance would eventually be overcome with the advent of the railroad. This emerging capacity would allow the efficient consolidation of the enormous Eurasian landmass, an area he referred to first as the *geographic pivot of history* and then as the world's *heartland*.[5] This huge potential state would form an impregnable land power that could not be defeated from the sea. In time, the vast natural resources of the heartland state would allow it to gain access to the sea and to construct a navy that, for sheer numbers alone, could overwhelm the peripheral sea powers. Inevitably, the world would be a single empire ruled from its natural core.

The key dynamic was the change in transportation technology, and the importance of military mobility. When the horse had been domesticated and bred to allow for the unnatural weight of a rider, the primacy of cavalry emerged and the medieval dominance of the central steppe 'hordes' was assured.[6] Grand improvements in sailing technologies allowed the seafaring states of Europe to encircle the central heartland and efficiently patrol its borders, shifting power as necessary to contain the mighty interior (the efficiency and speed of sea movement effectively canceling the advantage of interior lines, a direct analogy to the modern role of space power[7]). The advent of steam power initially accelerated this condition, as the first short-range railroads simply fed goods and supplies into oceanic commerce that were hitherto inaccessible.[8] As the railroads grew to transcontinental scope, however, the balance of power was shifting back again to the heartland.

Mackinder's world view divided the globe into three primary regions: the heartland or pivot area; the *inner crescent* comprised of the marginal lands around the heartland's periphery (including Western Europe, the Middle East, Indian subcontinent, and China); and the *outer crescent*, the great islands and island continents separated from the heartland and inner crescent by water (including the entire Western Hemisphere, Britain, Japan, and Australia). Crucial to Mackinder's strategy for Britain was the notion that if a state desired control but could not physically occupy the critical keys to geodetermined power, *then it must deny control of those areas to its adversaries*. So long as the peoples of the outer crescent could prevent any one state from uniting the heartland, their independence was assured, but should they fail to do so, the military juggernaut of a united heartland would be destined to rule the Earth.

The key to preventing such an outcome, according to Mackinder, was to ensure no inner crescent state gained control of Eastern Europe, the practical highway to the heartland. Mackinder cemented his theory and his fame with the dictum: '*Who rules East Europe Controls the Heartland. Who rules the Heartland commands the World Island. Who rules the World Island commands the World*'.[9]

Following Mackinder's lead, astropolitics begins with a demarcation of the geopolitical regions of outer space (see Figure 5). The resource potential of space, like the heartland, is so vast that should any one state gain effective control it could dictate the political, military, and economic fates of all terrestrial governments. The Moon, for example, is rich in aluminum, titanium, iron, calcium, and silicon. Iron is in virtually pure form, and could be used immediately. Titanium and aluminum are 'found in ores not commonly refined on Earth, [and would require] new methods of extraction'.[10] Silicon is necessary for the construction of photovoltaic solar cells, an impressive and needed source of cheap energy. Abundant oxygen for colonies and fuel can be extracted from the lunar soil simply by heating it. Water from impacting comets is presumed to have collected in the permanently shadowed edges of craters. This near-Earth resource can already be exploited given current technology. The potential of the asteroids, planets and their moons, comets and meteors, and the Sun can only be imagined. Access to these resources is possible only through the

FIGURE 5
FOUR REGIONS OF SPACE

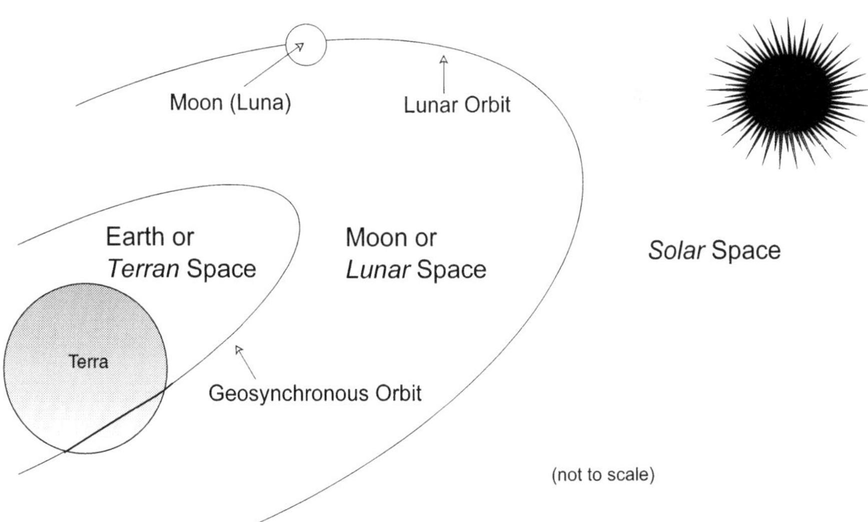

intervening regions between them and the Earth.

The four distinct astropolitical regions of space are described here on the basis of physical properties:

(1) *Terra* or *Earth*, including the atmosphere stretching from the surface to just below the lowest altitude capable of supporting unpowered orbit.[11] This is a critical concept for my model, and is a proper setting for space activities. Here the Earth and its atmosphere are the conceptual equivalents of a coastal area for outer space.[12] All objects entering from Earth into orbit and reentering from space must pass through it. It is on the surface of the Earth, Terra, that all current space launches, command and control, tracking, data downlink, research and development, production, antisatellite, and most servicing, repair, and storage operations are performed. Terra is the only region or model that is concerned with traditional topography (continental forms, oceans, etc., see terrestrial basing below) in the classic geopolitical sense, and is the transition region between geopolitics and astropolitics.

(2) *Terran* or *Earth Space*, from the lowest viable orbit to just beyond geostationary altitude (about 36,000 km). Earth Space is the operating medium for the military's most advanced reconnaissance and navigation satellites, and all current and planned space-based weaponry.[13] At its lower end, Earth Space is the region of post-thrust medium and long-range ballistic missile flight. At its opposite end, Earth Space includes the tremendously valuable geostationary belt, populated mostly by communications and weather satellites.

(3) *Lunar* or *Moon Space* is the region just beyond geostationary orbit to just beyond lunar orbit. The Earth's Moon is the only *visible* physical feature evident in the region, but it is only one of several strategic positions located there. Earth and Lunar Space encompass the four types of orbits described above, with the exception of the highly elliptical orbit with apogees beyond the orbit of the moon.

(4) *Solar Space* consists of everything in the solar system (that is, within the gravity well of the Sun) beyond the orbit of the Moon. The exploitation of solar space will be treated quite briefly, as expansion into this region using current technologies will be quite limited. Nonetheless, the exploration of solar space is the next major goal for manned missions and eventual permanent human colonization. The near planets (Mars and Venus), the Jovian and Saturnian moons, and the many large asteroids in the asteroid belt undoubtedly contain the

> raw materials necessary to ignite a neo-industrial age. From an antiquated *geopolitik* point of view, it also contains the *lebensraum* for a burgeoning population on Earth.[14]

The vast resources of Solar Space represent the heartland of the astropolitical model. Earth Space, like Eastern Europe in Mackinder's design, is the most critical arena for astropolitics. Control of Earth Space not only guarantees long-term control of the outer reaches of space, it provides a near-term advantage on the terrestrial battlefield. From early warning and detection of missile and force movements to target planning and battle damage assessment, space-based intelligence gathering assets have already proven themselves legitimate combat force multipliers. The most surprising and enduring contributions evident in the expanded military role of outer space technology, however, may have come from the previously under-appreciated value of navigation, communications, and weather prediction satellites.[15] With its performance in the Persian Gulf since 1990, space warfare has emerged from its embryonic stage and is now fully in its infancy.

All the industrially advanced states now recognize military space power as the apex of national security, and have tossed aside long-standing objections to military space programs as they eagerly pursue their own space infrastructures.[16] In future wars involving at least one *major* military power, space-support will be the decisive factor as nations rely ever more heavily on the force multiplying effect of 'the new high ground'.[17]

With the growing importance of space technology on the modern battlefield, control of space becomes increasingly vital. The geo/astropolitical mandates of space operations are now discussed in greater detail, beginning with Earth and Lunar Space associations and ending with terrestrial basing requirements.

ASTROPOLITICAL CONSIDERATIONS FOR EARTH AND LUNAR SPACE

American naval officer Alfred Thayer Mahan envisioned the sea as a 'wide common, over which men may pass in all directions, but on which some well-worn paths [emerge for] controlling reasons'.[18] These controlling reasons were predicated on the efficient movement of goods, and the geography of the Earth provided natural corridors of trade. The state that could control these corridors would realize such enormous commercial benefits that through its subsequent wealth it would dominate other states both militarily and politically. Outer Space, too, appears at first as a wide common over which spacecraft may pass in any direction, and to an extent this is so, but efficient travel in space requires adherence to specific and economically attractive lanes of movement, specific routes that are easy to project.

Gravity is the most important factor in the topography of space, and it dictates travel and strategic asset placement. The hills and valleys of space are more properly referred to as gravity wells. A two-dimensional representation is that of a weight sinking into a taughtly stretched sheet of rubber (see Figure 6). The more massive the body, the deeper the well. Travel or distance in space is less a function of distance than of effort expended to get from point to point. Travelling 35,000 km from the surface of the Earth, for example, requires 22 times as much effort as travelling a similar distance from the Moon, as the Earth's gravity well is 22 times deeper.[19]

FIGURE 6

TWO-DIMENSIONAL GRAVITY WELL COMPARISON

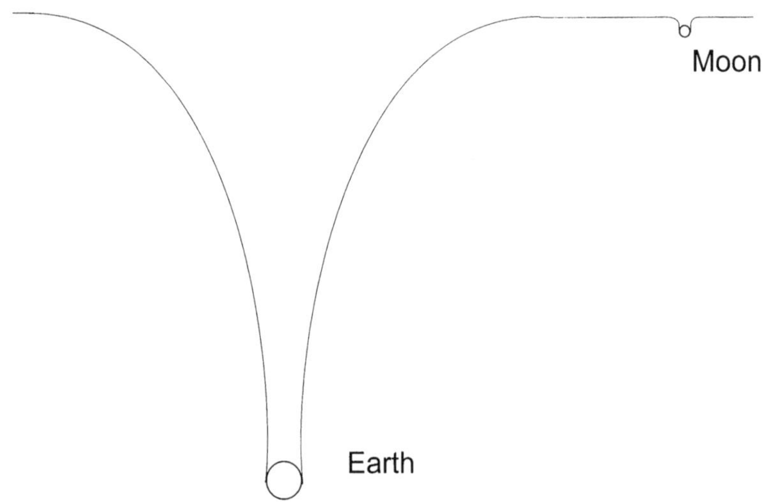

In spacefaring terms, the important measure is propulsive effort required to change a velocity vector, or the total velocity required to get from point A to point B. The total velocity effort (also called Δv or Delta V) is the key to understanding the reality of space travel and the efficient movement of goods. It is much cheaper, in terms of Δv, to propel a spacecraft from the Moon to Mars (56 million km at the closest orbital point) than to propel the same spacecraft from the Earth to the Moon (just 385,000 km).[20]

> Thus the Δv to go from low Earth orbit (an orbit just above the atmosphere) to lunar orbit is 4,100 m/s, which is only 300 m/s more than to go to geosynchronous [orbit, indeed] most of the effort of space travel near the Earth is spent in getting 100 km or so off the Earth, that is, into low Earth orbit. [More revealing,] to go from low Earth orbit to lunar orbit takes about 5 days, but requires less than half the effort needed to go from the Earth's surface to low orbit. [Thus,] certain points that are far apart in distance (and time) are quite close together in terms of the propulsive effort required to move from one to the other.[21]

The previous discussion of orbital mechanics has shown that a spacecraft in stable orbit expends no fuel, and is thus in the most advantageous Δv configuration. Efficient travel can be envisioned as a transfer from one stable orbit to another with the least expenditure of Δv. In space there are specific orbits and transit routes that because of their advantages in fuel efficiency create natural corridors of movement and commerce. Space, like the sea, can potentially be traversed in any direction, but because of gravity wells and the forbidding cost of getting fuel to orbit,

FIGURE 7

HOHMANN TRANSFER ORBIT

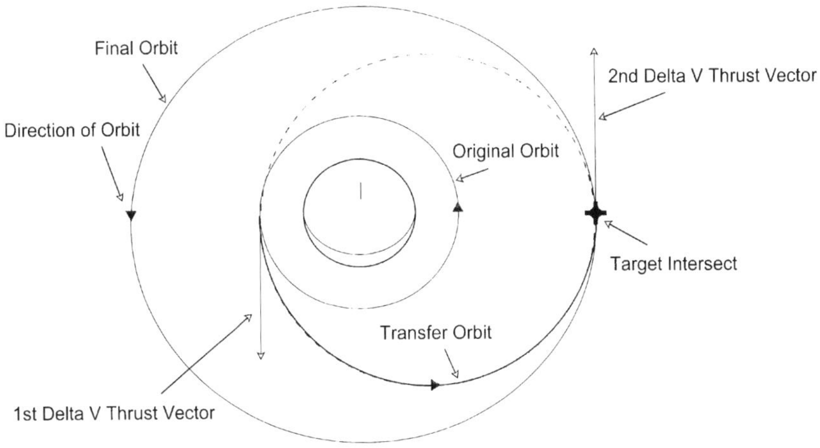

over time space-faring nations will develop specific pathways of heaviest traffic (see Figure 7).

Orbital maneuvers can be performed at any point, but in order to conserve fuel, there are certain points at which thrust ought to be applied. The most efficient way to get from orbit A to orbit B (the proper language of space travel) is the *Hohmann Transfer* (see Figure 7). This maneuver is a two-step change in Δv. Engines are first fired to accelerate the spacecraft into a higher elliptical orbit (or decelerate to a lower one). When the target orbit is intersected, the engines fire again to circularize and stabilize the final orbit. *The future lanes of commerce and military lines of communications in space will be the Hohmann transfer orbits between stable spaceports.*[22]

Britain's rise to power came, Mahan believed, because 'she had exploited her location across the sea routes' of Europe.[23] A modern astrostrategist can and should make similar arguments. Central to Mahan's theory was a discussion of *chokepoints*, globally strategic narrow waterways dominated by point locations. It is not necessary, Mahan argued, for a state to have control of every point on the sea to command it. In fact, such a strategy would be worse than useless. The military force required would drain every scintilla of profit from trade, not to mention every able-bodied seaman more usefully engaged in commerce. It is not even necessary to dominate the entirety of the lanes of commerce (or Hohmann transfer orbits just described). Instead, a smaller but highly trained and equipped force carefully deployed to control the bottlenecks of the major sea routes would suffice.[24] Control of these few geographically determined locations would guarantee dominance over military movement and world trade to the overseeing state.

Domination of space will come through efficient control of specific outer space strategic narrows, choke points, and lanes of commerce. The primary and first readily identifiable strategic narrow is low-Earth orbit itself. This tight band of operational space contains the bulk of mankind's satellites, a majority of which are military platforms or have military utility.[25] This is also the realm of current anti-satellite (ASAT) weapons technology and operations, including the US F-15 launched satellite interceptor and the massive Russian proximity blast co-orbital ASAT. Within this narrow belt are the current and projected permanently-manned space stations, and all space shuttle operations.

At the edge of Earth Space, beyond low-Earth orbit, lies the most obvious strategic narrow – the geostationary belt. This band about the equatorial waist of the Earth is the only natural orbit that allows for a stable position relative to a given point on the Earth. The geostationary belt has severe constraints on the number of satellites that can operate within it, due to the possibility of broadcast interference from adjacent platforms, however. This has caused it to be considered a scarce and precious *international* natural resource by *most* members of the international community. Nonetheless, in 1977, nine equatorial states asserted in the Bogota Declaration that national sovereignty extended upward, *ad just coloeum*, to geostationary altitude. The action is not unlike the attempts of several coastal states to extend the limit of territorial waters. In other words, the geostationary belt is considered the sovereign territory of those states directly beneath it, transforming an area routinely referred to as 'the common heritage of mankind' into a geopolitical conflict zone.

Mahan additionally advocated the establishment of naval bases at strategic locations, including Hawaii, the Philippines, and several Caribbean islands, to act as fueling and resupply stations for the seafaring state's navy. The range of ships and national interests of the state geographically determined their spacing. Without these bases, American war and trade ships would 'be like land birds, unable to fly far from their own shores'.[26] The notion is not fresh, and such staged basing is historically common, but its tendrils reach to outer space.

Giulio Douhet (1869–1930), an Italian general and the first of the air power geostrategists, also advocated a basing procedure predicated on new technology. He wrote extensively of the coming revolution in modern warfare due to the fact that aircraft were essentially unimpeded by the Earth's surface features (a critical change in the evolution toward astropolitics with the gradually decreasing importance of topography). Air power was limited in its operations, however, by critical *air operations routes*, which required precisely located takeoff and landing fields and effective maintenance and repair facilities at major centers.[27] US Army Air Corps Brigadier General Billy Mitchell (1879–1936) accepted Douhet's view that air bases represented vital centers of military operations, and believed his role was to extend theory into practice.[28] Mitchell professed that in the air age Alaska had surpassed Panama as a strategic focus for America, since aircraft based in this region could maximize their radius of action against potential foes.

Perhaps the most intriguing point locations in Earth–Moon Space are the gravitational anomalies known as Lagrange Libration Points, named after the eighteenth century French mathematician who first postulated their existence.[29] Lagrange calculated there were five specific points where the gravitational effects of the Earth and Moon would cancel each other out (see

Figure 8). An object fixed at one of these points (or more accurately, in tight orbit around one of these points) would remain permanently stable, with no expenditure of fuel. The enticing property of libration points is that they maintain a fixed relation with respect to the Earth and Moon. In practice, due to perturbations in the space environment including solar flares, orbital drift and wobble, and micrometeorites, only two of the Lagrange points are effectively stable – L4 and L5. The potential military and commercial value of a point in space that is virtually stable is highly speculative, but imaginatively immense. The occupation and control of these points is of such vital importance that an advocacy group called the L-5 Society was formed to influence national policymakers.[30]

FIGURE 8

LaGRANGE LIBRATION POINTS

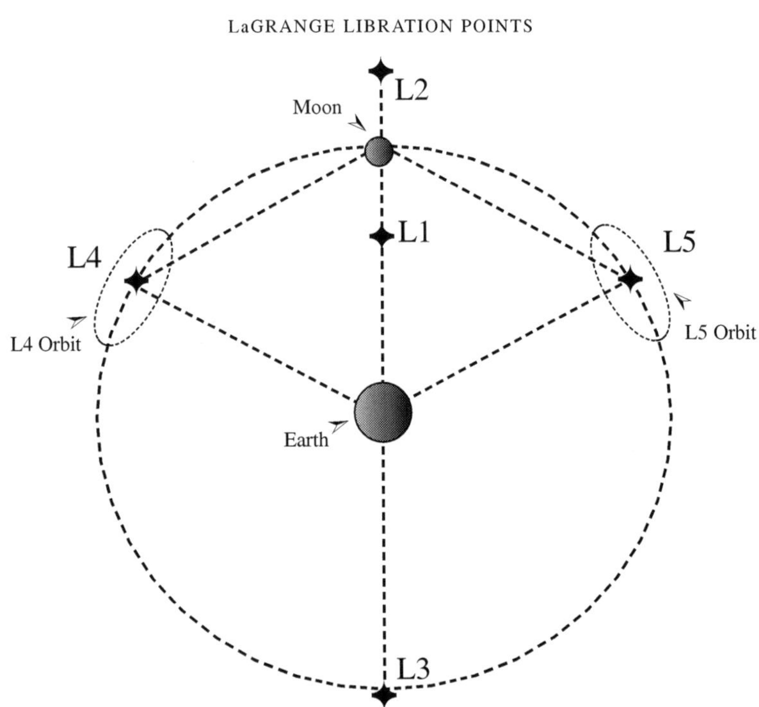

One final phenomenon of the region that requires mapping and understanding is the location and impact of the Van Allen radiation belts 'two donut-shaped regions circling the Earth inside the magnetosphere [that] trap charged particles and hold them. Spacecraft passing through the Van Allen belts are subject to damage. Astronauts passing through these areas risk [mortal injury]. Fortunately, they are well mapped and can be avoided.'[31] The inner belt first appears at about 400 to 1,200 km, dependent on latitude (see Figure 9). It extends outward to about 10,000 km with the deadliest concentration at 3,500 km. Anomalies in the belts put the lowest altitude at upper latitudes of the Southern Hemisphere, a particularly troublesome area for polar-orbiting satellites but easily avoidable by most manned flights. The second ring begins near 10,000 km and extends up to 84,000 km, with deadliest concentrations at 16,000 km. The edges of the belts are relatively benign, thus a safe operating channel is evident between the two belts from about 9,000–11,000 km altitude. Of note, the outer belt is flattened to about 59,500 km in sunshine, extending to its maximum altitude in the Earth's shadow.

FIGURE 9

VAN ALLEN RADIATION BELTS

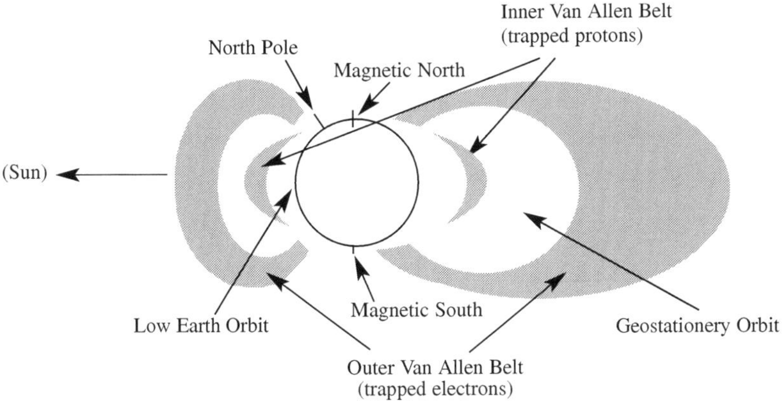

Astropolitics describes critical chokepoints in space as those stable areas including the planets, moons, libration points, and asteroids where future military and commercial enterprises will congregate. These are the coming ports of space, co-located with the valuable energy and mineral resources estimated to be there, or Mahan's, Douhet's, and Mitchell's weigh stations on the various Hohmann transfer routes to these resources.

ASTROPOLITICAL CONSIDERATIONS FOR TERRA

Earth is the current point of origin for all spacecraft and space support operations. Ultimately, efficiency and economy will dictate that all essential space operations, including construction and launch, tracking and control, and various forms of space commerce will take place in space. For now, however, all of these functions are earthbound. When the day comes that these functions are performed off world, the vast population that feeds off the bounty of outer space will remain, as will the governments that control space operations. The importance of Terra will not diminish, nor will the necessity of political control. The astropolitical question, given the current realities, is simply where on Earth are the vital centers most efficiently placed?

We begin with launch center location in part because of its intrinsic relationship with orbital efficiency. The originating launch site of a spacecraft has a significant impact on its orbit. The equator, for example, has particular value as a launch site location, especially into geostationary orbit. This is because the spin of the Earth can be used to assist in the attainment of orbital velocity, and the relative velocity of the Earth's motion decreases from 1,670 kph at the equator to no relative motion at the poles. Since the minimum velocity necessary to climb out of the Earth's gravity well is just over 28,000 kph, a launch vehicle would only have to achieve a speed of 26,400 kph relative to its launch point to achieve orbit. Conversely, a satellite launched due west along the equator would have to add 1,670 kph and thus would need to achieve a velocity of almost 29,700 kph relative to its start point to place a satellite into orbit, a 3,300 kph difference. The fuel/Δ)v impact is plainly significant. For example, a European rocket launched due east from the French Space Center at Kourou, French Guiane, just 5° north of the equator, receives a 17 per cent fuel efficiency advantage over an American rocket launched due east from Cape Canaveral, about 28.5° north of the equator. In perhaps a more powerful example, a Space Shuttle launched due east from Cape Canaveral has a cargo capacity of 13,600 kg. A Space Shuttle launched due west from roughly the same latitude (from the US Western Space Range at Vandenberg Air Force Base), can barely achieve orbit with its cargo bay empty.

Another factor of terrestrial launches is that the latitude of launch affects the inclination of the orbited spacecraft. Launches due east (90°) of Cape Canaveral will enter into low-Earth orbit at an inclination of 28.3° inclination. Indeed, launches due east from any site on the Earth will have an inclination exactly the same as the launch latitude, given a two-stage direct insertion launch.[32] Launches on *any other azimuth* will place a satellite into orbit at *greater* inclination than the latitude of the site. Thus the launch site determines the minimum inclination (with a launch due east). A launch due west allows for the maximum inclination (in the case of the

Cape, 151.7°, or 180° minus 28.3 °). Launching due north or south will result in a polar orbit, that is an inclination of 90° relative to the equator.

The polar, sun-synchronized orbit is in fact one of the most important for military reconnaissance and weather imaging. A spacecraft placed into polar orbit passes over both the North and South Poles. If placed in a slightly retrograde motion (greater than 90° inclination), this configuration allows satellites to eventually fly over every point on the Earth, and to *remain in the sunlight at all times* – extremely important for satellite cameras that work in the visible light spectrum and for satellites that require continuous solar access for power. To place a satellite into a polar orbit, the most efficient launch azimuth is due north or due south.

Thus a space launch center that can send rockets both due east and either due north or south has distinct orbital efficiency advantages. Because rockets eject lower stages, and occasionally destruct in flight, it is further necessary that the launch site has considerable downrange areas of open ocean or unpopulated landmass (at least 1,000 km). The optimum astropolitical launch points under these criteria are the northern coast of Brazil, the east coast of Kenya, and any of several Pacific islands east of New Guinea (see Figure 10). These locations are all sovereign national territory with astropolitical international importance.

There is at least one other critical feature for space launch centers that is based in astropolitical theory. Orbital perturbations degrade the stability of all but two Earth orbits, requiring regular expenditures of Δv to restabilize them. The highly stable orbits are inclined at 63.4° and 116.6° relative to the equatorial plane. This means a satellite in orbit at either of these inclinations will remain stable with minimal expenditures of fuel, greatly increasing their useful lifetimes. More importantly, satellites operating in networks will maintain their proper spacing without continual orbital corrections. Satellites launched due east (maximizing the earth's rotational effects) from a space center at 63.4° north or south latitude will efficiently enter a 63.4° inclined orbit with a minimum expenditure of on-board fuel. Geolocations at 63° north with sufficient downrange capacity include northern Siberia, the east coast of Greenland, far north Canada, and most of Alaska (see Figure 10). The 63° south latitude intersects the Antarctic landmass, a cost-inefficient terrestrial location for a major spaceport. The most accessible of these areas are Alaska and northwest Siberia. Russia's northern spaceport is efficiently located northeast of Moscow at Plesetsk, exactly 63.4° north latitude.

Finally, for the purposes of this essay, a brief discussion of satellite *fields of view* completes the terrestrial survey but does not exhaust the

FIGURE 10

OPTIMUM LAUNCH POINTS

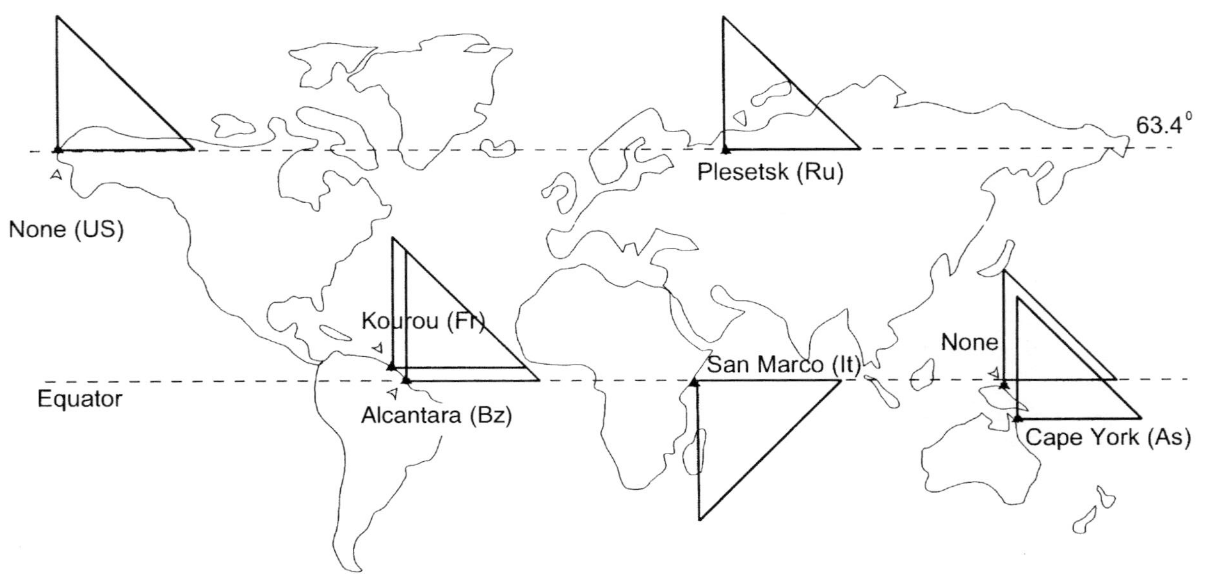

astropolitical ramifications of Earth-centered placement. The important point here is that in order to control satellites in space, or to control the Earth from space, a global network of terrestrial contact points *or* a global network of interlinked satellites, respectively, is required. Physical limitations of orbital mechanics dictate that the only position in space that allows a satellite to maintain a constant position relative to the surface of the Earth is the geostationary belt. In order to optimize Earth access from geostationary position, a network of at least three satellites is necessary to view any point on the Earth between 70° north and south latitude. Terrestrial areas above 70° latitude can not be reliably accessed, including much of Scandinavia, Russia, and Canada.

In order to provide truly global coverage of the Earth from space, including the polar regions, a minimum of four satellites is required. Placed in precise 63.4° inclined super-synchronous (greater than 24-hour) orbits, one satellite can be in view from any point on the Earth at any time. Because these satellites are not stable relative to the Earth's surface, terrestrial users need the ability to track and acquire satellites as they move in and out of view. Their use also entails practical encumbrances. Satellites at super-synchronous altitude require large, heavy, high output transmitters to communicate with terrestrial users (due to physical distance). They are further unsuitable for some missions, such as high-resolution Earth imaging (again due to distance). For these applications, some satellites must maintain orbits closer to the surface of the Earth.

Conversely, in order to guarantee continuous communications with a specific satellite from the Earth, at least three control stations spaced evenly around the Earth along the orbital plane are necessary for high Earth orbit and above altitude satellites and at least 16 stations for low-Earth orbit ones. This is why the US maintains deep-space tracking stations in Australia and Spain, and Russia has kept a fleet of space tracking and control ships deployed in international waters.

As satellite orbits decrease in altitude, and increase in practical value, more satellites are required to maintain continuous global coverage. The Global Positioning Satellite (GPS) navigation system, which has an operational requirement for four satellites to be in view of any one point on the Earth at any given time (for accurate geolocation), requires 21 satellites to be precisely spaced in inclined semisynchronous (12-hour) orbits at 24,000 km altitude. The planned Iridium commercial mobile communications network will employ a network of 66 satellites at 725 km altitude to ensure that at least one satellite is always in view.[33]

CONCLUSIONS

This brief descriptive has outlined a few of the more salient astropolitical concepts. It is not an exhaustive list. My purpose is to combine sophisticated astronomical concepts with political theory in a manner that is heuristic. As space technology progresses, many of the above assertions will become dubious or even moot. New hypotheses will surface that I have not yet considered. The astropolitical dictum that control of certain terrestrial and outer space locations will provide a distinct advantage in efficiency and will lead the controller to a dominant position in commercial and military power seems assured, however. Mahan recognized that control of the world's major chokepoints would not stop commerce in the nineteenth century – traders could simply 'sail the long way round' to avoid them – but in so doing the chokepoint controller would gain an undeniable edge. Astropolitics can project a parallel capacity. Control of these critical outer space locations may not deny another's access completely, but it will make access extremely cost-inefficient.

The foregoing is not meant to be an endorsement of the continued nationalist or conflictual exploitation of space inherent in an astropolitical analysis. It seems obvious that the maximum benefit to be gained from the riches of space will come as the result of a long-term globally cooperative effort. Nonetheless, so powerful is the lure of astropolitics that the *relative* gains anticipated for the state that successfully dominates space continues to provide a compelling incentive to act unilaterally. This incentive could in fact provide dramatic *short-term* impetus to space-based expansion that seems to be missing in the post-Cold War period.[34]

The analysis here is offered as an examination of optimal strategies and likely outcomes *given an assumption* of near-term continued nationalist military and economic competition (the assumption is made to set the geostrategic model in motion, it is not a prediction or a suggestion of probable or preferred outcomes). Within these analytic limitations, many classical geopolitical theories are fully compatible with, and prove remarkably applicable to, this dynamic realm of outer space.

NOTES

1. Jean Gottman (ed.) *Centre and Periphery* (Beverley Hills, CA: Sage 1980) p.1.
2. I am indebted to the many professionals at the Air Force Training Command's Joint Space Intelligence Operations Course (JSIOC) in Colorado Springs, who instructed me in orbital mechanics from 1986–90 when I took, and then had the opportunity to lecture in, their outstanding program.

3. The effects of atmospheric drag are significantly reduced as periods (altitudes) increase. Satellites in a circular orbit with a period of less than 93 minutes require large amounts of fuel to make orbital corrections due to atmospheric drag and other perturbations. Satellites in circular orbits with a period greater than 101 minutes are essentially unaffected by the atmosphere, and require relatively few attitude adjustments.
4. In theory, the Earth's gravitational pull extends about 900,000 km (one 166th the distance between the Earth and Sun, about twice the distance between the Earth and Moon). Beyond this distance Earth orbits are not possible, as a spacecraft will be drawn to another gravitational field.
5. H.J. MacKinder, 'The Geographical Pivot of History', *Geographical Journal* 23/4 (April 1904) pp.421–44, and idem, *Democratic Ideals and Reality: A Study in the Politics of Reconstruction* (NY: Henry Holt 1919).
6. 'Geographical Pivot' (note 5) p.430.
7. German economist Friedrich List (1789–1846) saw the coming power of the railroad as the cement of German unification, changing the strategic position of Germany from beleaguered battleground of Europe to a defensive bulwark operating with the advantages of interior lines (see Edward Meade Earle, 'Adam Smith, Alexander Hamilton, Friedrich List: The Economic Foundations of Military Power', in Peter Paret (ed.) *The Makers of Modern Strategy: From Machiavelli to the Nuclear Age* (Princeton UP 1986) pp.217–61). Rail power has no clear parallel to space power with the exception that as a new transportation and information technology, space asset deployment surely has the potential to alter the political and military relationships of the traditional world and regional powers. In the same manner as emerging rail power, control of a global space network gives the previous advantages of interior lines – quick redeployment of military assets, efficient monitoring of all fronts, and not insignificantly, a nationalistic sense of unification – from what has traditionally been seen as a classic exterior line position.
8. 'Geographic Pivot' (note 5) p.434.
9. *Democratic Ideals* (note 5) p.50.
10. Thomas Damon, *Introduction to Space: The Science of Spaceflight* (Malabar, FL: Orbit 1989) pp.180–2.
11. Also called the Karman primary jurisdiction line.
12. Barry Smernoff, 'A Bold, Two-Track Strategy for Space', in Uri Ra'anan and Robert Pfaltzgraf (eds.) *International Security Dimensions of Space* (Medfors, MA: Archon 1984) pp.17–31.
13. Paul Stares, *Space and National Security* (Washington DC: Brookings 1987) pp.13–18. See also idem, *The Militarization of Space: US Policy, 1954–984* (Ithaca, NY: Cornell 1985).
14. See Holger Herwig, 'Geopolitik: Haushofer, Hitler, and Lebensraum', in this issue.
15. Especially the case for Global Positioning Satellites, or Navstar/GPS. See Michael Ripp, 'How Navstar Became Indispensable', *Air Force Magazine* (Nov. 1993) pp.46–9.
16. Alastair McLean and Fraser Lovie, *Europe's Final Frontier: The Search for Security Through Space* (Commack, NY: Nova 1997).
17. Thomas Karras, *The New High Ground: Strategies and Weapons of Space Age Wars* (NY: Simon & Schuster 1983).
18. Alfred Thayer Mahan, *The Influence of Seapower Upon History: 1660–1783* (Boston: Little Brown 1890) p.25.
19. Marc Vaucher, 'Geographic Parameters for Military Doctrine in Space and the Defense of the Space-Based Enterprise', in Ra'anan and Pfaltzgraf, *International Security Dimensions of Space* (note 12) p.35. Vaucher's analysis comes very close to the type of astropolitical analysis I am attempting here, and his work deserves extraordinary praise.
20. Andrew Wilson (ed.) *Interavia Spaceflight Directory* (Geneva: Interavia SA 1989) p.600. Formerly *Jane's Spaceflight Directory*.
21. NASA Website, 'Two Kinds of Separation in Space: Metric Distance vs Total Velocity Change (Δv)', *Space Settlements: A Design Study* (HYPERLINK http://wwwsci.nas.nasa.gov/Services/Education/http://www-sci.nas.nasa.gov/Services/Education/SpaceSettlement/75SummerStudy/Table of Contents1.html, accessed 23 Nov. 1998).
22. 'Fast Transfers' are of course possible, but require a greater expenditure of fuel and will only be done if fuel is abundant or time is critical.

23. John Keegan, *The Price of Admiralty: The Evolution of Naval Warfare* (NY: Viking 1989) p.110.
24. These bottlenecks were easy to spot on a global map, and Mahan identified seven of them – the Straits of Dover, Gibraltar, and Malacca, the Cape of Good Hope, Malta, the Suez Canal, and the St Lawrence seaway.
25. See Wilson, *Spaceflight Directory* (note 20) for a representative catalog of spacecraft in orbit.
26. *Influence of Seapower* (note 18) p.83.
27. Giulio Douhet, *The Command of the Air* (1921) trans. by Dino Ferrari (NY: Coward, McCann 1942) pp.88–90.
28. Alfred Hurley, *Billy Mitchell: Crusader for Air Power* (U. of Indiana 1964) pp.81–3.
29. See Doug Beason, 'What are these Lagrange Points Anyway?', in Jerry Pournelle (ed.) *Cities in Space: The Endless Frontier,* Vol.III (NY: Ace 1991) pp.58–65. See also Vaucher.
30. The L-5 Society has since been absorbed into the National Space Society, where many of its former members are now primary officers.
31. Damon (note 10) p.40.
32. Spacecraft move from their original orbit, and in the process change their inclinations (this is how the Shuttle places payloads into geostationary orbit, releasing them with an attached upper stage or bus), but the transfer costs additional fuel, fuel that had to be placed on the launching rocket, ultimately limiting payload weight or spacecraft lifespan.
33. The Iridium constellation originally was to have 77 satellites, and was named after the 77th element on the Periodic Table. When the constellation was scaled back to 66 satellites at a slightly higher altitude, a name change to Dysprosium (Periodic Table element number 66) was not made, for commercial reasons.
34. The most spectacular growth in space development to date has arguably been the direct result of Cold War competition, see Walter McDougall "*... the Heavens and the Earth*" (NY: Basic Books 1985), Cass Schictle, *The National Space Program from the Fifties into the Eighties* (Washington DC: National Defense UP 1983), and Matthew von Bencke, *The Politics of Space: A History of US-Soviet/Russian Competition and Cooperation* (Boulder, CO: Westview 1997).

6

Understanding Critical Geopolitics: Geopolitics and Risk Society

GEARÓID Ó TUATHAIL

As we complete a century of geopolitics (the word was coined in 1899) it is both appropriate and necessary to reflect upon its history, meanings and use in a critically-minded manner. The critique of geopolitics is as old as geopolitics itself but as humanity grapples with the prevailing chaos, proliferating risks and pervasive disorder of a turn of a century condition, it is vital that we develop a critical perspective on the seductive simple-mindedness of geopolitics and its dangerous counter-modern tendencies.

Geopolitics can be described as problem-solving theory for the conceptualization and practice of statecraft. A convenient label for a variety of traditions and cultures of theory and practice, geopolitics sees itself as an instrumental form of knowledge and rationality. It takes the existing power structures for granted and works within these to provide conceptualization and advice to foreign policy decision-makers. Its dominant modes of narration are declarative ('this is how the world is') and then imperative ('this is what we must do'). 'Is' and 'we' mark its commitment to, on the one hand, a transparent and objectified world and, on the other hand, to a particular geographically bounded community and its cultural/political version of the truth of that world. Its enduring 'plot' is the global balance of power and the future of strategic advantage in an anarchic world.

Geopolitics is of the same ilk as political realism, distinguishing itself by its proclivity to find 'geography' as a singularly important element in foreign policy conceptualization and practice.

Critical geopolitics, by contrast, is a problematizing theoretical enterprise that places the existing structures of power and knowledge in question. Also a convenient label for a disparate set of literatures and tendencies that congealed in the 1980s into a developed critique of 'orthodox geopolitics' and the dangerous nostrums associated with it, critical geopolitics seek to recover the complexities of global political life and expose the power relationships that characterize knowledge about geopolitics concealed by orthodox geopolitics.[1] Eschewing explicit interest in providing 'advice to the prince', critical geopolitics critiques the superficial and self-interested ways in which orthodox geopolitics 'reads the world political map' by projecting its own cultural and political assumptions upon it while concealing these very assumptions.

Geopolitics, critical geopoliticians argue, operates with a 'view from nowhere', a seeing that refuses to see itself and the power relationships that make it possible. As an unreflexively eurocentric and narrowly rational cultural practice of 'experts' in powerful Western institutions (from universities to military bureaucracies to strategic 'think-tanks'), geopolitics is not about power politics: it is power politics!

Critical geopolitics strives to expose this power politics to scrutiny and public debate in the name of deepening democratic politics. For critical geopolitics, the notion of 'is' is always an essentially contested perspectival notion. Knowledge is always situated knowledge, articulating the perspective of certain cultures and subjects while marginalizing that of others. Its 'we' is a transnational community of citizens skeptical of the power concentrated in state and military bureaucracies, and committed to an open democratic debate about the meaning and politics of 'security'.

During the Cold War, the contrast between the orthodox geopolitics of both East and West and critical geopolitics was stark and clear. Orthodox Cold War geopolitics peddled dangerous simplifications about world politics while justifying the potentially catastrophic militarization of the European continent and other regions. The practical critical geopolitics of the European peace and environmental movements opposed the Manichean reasoning of both East and West, and the militarization of the planet it made possible.[2]

Since the end of the Cold War, the irredeemable complexity that critical geopolitics always asserted but orthodox geopolitics tried to repress has become even more undeniable. The contemporary geopolitical condition exceeds the 'either-or' reasoning of orthodox geopolitics, with its proclivity for us/them, inside/outside, domestic/foreign, near/far binaries and its reliance on mythic binaries from the geopolitical tradition like the heartland/rimland, land power/sea power and East/West. The old conceptual maps of geopolitics do not work in a world of speeding flows, instantaneous information, and proliferating techno-scientific risks.

Nevertheless, the urge to arrest this teeming complexity of our age by returning world politics to certain 'fundamental axes' or 'timeless truths' remains, merely the latest version of a long-standing countermodern impulse to (re)invent certainty in a world where the vertigious 'creative destruction' of transnational capitalist modernity dominates.

Ironically, the vertigo of our contemporary condition has rendered critical geopolitics more relevant to policy making than ever before while shifting political winds have brought some former peace movement figures to political power (Vaclav Havel in the Czech Republic and Joschka Fischer in Germany, for example). Critical geopolitics has long taken the dynamics of globalization, informationalization and 'risk society' seriously, recognizing that a new modernity of 'and' (ambivalence, multiplicity, simultaneity, globality, uncertainty, formlessness and borderlessness) is exploding in our inherited modernity of 'either-or' (calculability, singularity, linearity, nationality, certainty, dimensionality and [b]orders).[3] Like orthodox geopolitics, critical geopolitics is both a politically minded practice and a geopolitics, an explicitly political account of the contemporary geopolitical condition that seeks to influence politics. Unlike orthodox geopolitics, critical geopolitics has a much richer understanding of the problematic of 'geopolitics' and a better conceptual grasp, I wish to argue, of the problems facing states in conditions of advanced modernity.

This is a brief introduction to critical geopolitics. As an approach, critical geopolitics begins by arguing that 'geopolitics' is a much broader and more complex problematic than is acknowledged in orthodox understandings of the concept. To claim that geopolitics is the study of the influence of 'geography' on the practice of foreign policy by states is not to specify a narrow problematic for 'geography' has a multiplicity of different meanings. All states are territorial and all foreign policy strategizing and practice is conditioned by territoriality, shaped by geographical location, and informed by certain geographical understandings about the world. Geography is not a fixed substratum as some claim but an historical and social form of knowledge about the earth. To consult 'geography' historically was not to view raw physical landscape or 'nature' but to read a book. Though often forgotten today, 'geography' is not 'nature'. Rather, geography is an inescapably social and political *geo-graphing*, an 'earth writing'. It is a cultural and political writing of meanings about the world.[4] Similarly, geopolitics is a writing of the geographical meanings and politics of states.

For heuristic research purposes, critical geopolitics divides geopolitics into formal, practical, popular and structural geopolitics (see Table 1, p.111). Formal geopolitics refers to what is usually considered 'geopolitical thought' or 'the geopolitical tradition'. It is a problematic of intellectuals, institutions and the forces shaping geopolitical thought in particular places and contexts. Practical geopolitics is concerned with the geographical politics involved in the everyday practice of foreign policy. It addresses how common geographical understandings and perceptions enframe foreign policy conceptualization and decision making. A good recent example of this is how the geographical notion of 'the Balkans' helped condition how US foreign policy-makers approached, conceptualized and responded to the Bosnian Civil War, with damaging results for the region and for European security. Popular geopolitics refers to the geographical politics created and debated by the various media-shaping popular culture. It addresses the social construction and perpetuation of certain collective national and transnational understandings of places and peoples beyond one's own borders, what Dijkink refers to as 'national identity and geopolitical visions'.[5] Finally, structural geopolitics involves the study of the structural processes and tendencies that condition how all states practice foreign policy. Today, these processes include, as we have noted, globalization, informationalization and the proliferating risks unleashed by the successes of our techno-scientific civilization across the earth.

Combining practical and popular geopolitics, I will briefly discuss, first, how critical geopolitics has developed a revisionist historiography of certain prominent geopolitical figures and the 'geopolitical tradition', second, its critical analysis of practical and popular geopolitical reasoning in foreign policy and, third, its analysis of the contemporary geopolitical condition.

FORMAL GEOPOLITICS: DECONSTRUCTING THE GEOPOLITICAL TRADITION

The notion of 'the geopolitical tradition' is a somewhat arbitrary construct that has varied historical origins, central figures and key debates depending upon the definition and practical understanding of 'geopolitics'. To most strategists, geopolitics is a twentieth century tradition of thinking about statecraft that begins with Friedrich Ratzel, Alfred Mahan, Rudolf Kjellen and Halford Mackinder, develops in the interwar period with Karl Haushofer's German *Geopolitik* and Nicholas Spykman's 'rimland' theories, and finds expression today in the writings of contemporary figures like Henry Kissinger and Zbigniew Brzezinski.[6] This 'great man' specification of the tradition is idealist in its concentration on 'geopolitical

TABLE 1

THE TYPES OF GEOPOLITICS STUDIED BY CRITICAL GEOPOLITICS

Type of Geopolitics	Object of Investigation	Problematic	Research Example
Formal Geopolitics	Geopolitical thought and the geopolitical tradition	Intellectuals, institutions and their political and cultural context	Halford Mackinder, his geopolitical theories and imperialist context
Practical Geopolitics	The everyday practice of statecraft	Practical geopolitical reasoning in foreign policy conceptualiz-ation	'Balkanism' and its influence over US foreign policy towards Bosnia
Popular Geopolitics	Popular culture, mass media, and geographical understandings	National identity and the construction of images of other peoples and places.	The role of mass media in projecting images of Bosnia into Western livingrooms
Structural Geopolitics	The contemporary geopolitical condition	Global processes, tendencies and contradictions	How globalization, informationalization and risk society condition/transform geopolitical practices

thought' at the expense of geopolitical practice and practitioners (though the latter two were both). It also tends to be Eurocentric, neglecting Russian and Japanese geopolitical thought. Most importantly, it tends to elide fundamental questions concerning the specification of 'geopolitics' and the relationship of geopoliticians as intellectuals of statecraft to the power relationships characterizing their state, its national culture and its political economy.

While problematizing constructions of 'the geopolitical tradition', critical geopolitics nevertheless engages the intellectuals, institutions and texts of this tradition and its histories. In very broad terms, critical geopolitics seeks to contextualize geopolitical figures and unravel the textual strategies they use in their writings. It argues that orthodox geopolitical utilizations of classic geopolitical figures often neglect the context within which they lived, ignore the incoherences in their works, and ironically utilize their arguments to close off any openness to geographical difference. Critical geopolitics, in other words, seeks to recover the geography and geopolitics of 'geopolitical thought' while opposing any glib celebration of the so-called 'timeless insights' of certain geopolitical masters.

This approach is evident in a 'revisionist' literature on Sir Halford Mackinder, a widely celebrated 'founding father' of geopolitics (despite the fact that he never used the term in his writings and personally disliked it).[7] The Mackinder that appears in many orthodox accounts of geopolitics is a cardboard figure who is decontextualized from his imperialist context, defined by only a few texts and, in even cruder versions, by his sloganized version of strategy ('who controls..'. etc). The 'real' Mackinder is more complex and also more mundane, an ultimately minor figure in the history of strategic thinking. Halford Mackinder's life and work was conditioned by the structural geopolitics of British imperial decline. Mackinder's 'liberal imperialist' ideology was at attempt to modernize the organization and idea of the British Empire.[8] As an imperialist thinker and subsequent member of parliament, he stood for 'national efficiency' but the 'nation' he imagined was a nation of white male British gentlemen that were to be efficient in exploiting Britain's vast imperial possessions, maintaining white Anglo-Saxon supremacy, and subjugating the 'lesser races' and regions of the Empire. He envisioned the discipline of Geography as part of his overarching project of modernizing the British Empire. Geography was a discipline that should be used to teach British schoolchildren to 'think imperially'.[9] The techniques he sought to establish at its core, visualization, mapping and drawing, sparse description, were meant as practical skills for the 'man of action', the merchant, colonial administrator, and statesman.[10] The discipline of Geography as a whole, for Mackinder, was geopolitics.

The bulk of Mackinder's writings were devoted to geographical education. Mackinder's celebrated 'geopolitical texts' and his other writings are marked by the assumption that seeing is a naturalistic and objective activity. In asserting the innocence of 'visualization', Mackinder was merely naturalizing the political and ideological assumptions of his own culture and ideology. Mackinder's texts are marked by a blindspot that tries to deny interpretative activity while nevertheless relying upon it.[11]

Furthermore, the geopolitical 'insight' of these texts is vastly overrated. The 1904 'Geographical Pivot of History' address is remarkable in its neglect of the single most important power of the coming twentieth century, the United States, and the single most significant time-space compressing technology, the airplane. His geopolitical thesis about sea power, land power and transportation technology is historically simplistic, geographically determinist, and technologically unidimensional.[12] Mackinder's 1919 text *Democratic Ideals and Reality* is significant less for 'geopolitical insight' than as an illustration of the bizarre nature of Mackinder's organic conservatism and countermodern fantasies.

Mackinder's strategic ideas had understandably little influence over British foreign policy at the time and might well have sunk into obscurity if it were not for the historical accident of their 're-discovery' during World War II amid sensationalist and ill-informed media speculation about Karl Haushofer and German *Geopolitik*.

To understand the appeal of formal geopolitics to certain intellectuals, institutions and would be strategists, one has to appreciate the mythic qualities of geopolitics. Geopolitics is mythic because it promises uncanny clarity and insight in a complex world. It actively closes down an openness to the geographical diversity of the world and represses questioning and difference. The plurality of the world is reduced to certain 'transcendent truths' about strategy. Geopolitics is a narrow instrumental form of reason that is also a form of faith, a belief that there is a secret substratum and/or a permanent set of conflicts and interests that accounts for the course of world politics. It is fetishistically concerned with 'insight', and 'prophecy'.

Formal geopolitics appeals to those who yearn for the apparent certitude of 'timeless truths'. Historically, it is produced by and appeals to right wing countermoderns because it imposes a constructed certitude upon the unruly complexity of world politics, uncovering transcendent struggles between seemingly permanent opposites ('land power' versus 'sea power', 'oceanic' versus 'continental', 'East' versus 'West') and folding geographical difference into depluralized geopolitical categories like 'heartland', 'rimland', 'shatterbelt', and the like. Foreign policy complexity becomes simple(minded) strategic gaming.[13]

Such formal geopolitical reasoning is anti-geographical in its conceptualization and representation of the world. It is also a flawed foundation upon which to construct a foreign policy that needs to be sensitive to the particularity and diversity of the world's states, and to global processes and challenges that transcend state-centric reasoning.

PRACTICAL AND POPULAR GEOPOLITICS: GEOPOLITICAL REASONING IN THE PRACTICE OF STATECRAFT

Formal geopolitical reasoning is worth distinguishing from the practical geopolitical reasoning foreign policy decision-makers utilize in the everyday conduct of statecraft. In contrast to the formalized theories and grand strategic visions of geopolitical intellectuals, foreign policy decision-makers use practical and pragmatic geopolitical reasoning whenever they try to make spatial sense of the world, implicitly utilizing inherited forms of geographical knowledge to enframe particular questions and tacitly deploying cultural geographic discourses to explain certain dramas and events. Practical geopolitical reasoning is ordinary and informal everyday discourse. It is taught in educational establishments, part of the socialization of individuals into certain 'national' identities and geographical/historical consciousnesses.[14] Widely disseminated by the media in popular political culture, it has the significant quality of being unremarkable and can be described as 'common sense' geopolitics. It is also, in certain instances, an ethnocentric, stereotypical and formulaic form of knowledge about the world that produces bad foreign policy conceptualizations and practices. Common sense geopolitics does not necessarily make good sense geopolitics.

The power and significance of practical geopolitical reasoning can be illustrated by considering the power of 'Balkanism' in conditioning American foreign policy ambivalence towards the breakup of Yugoslavia and the Bosnian War. The section of the ABC News website devoted to the Balkans begins with the following observation:

> There are countless explanations for the volatility of the 'Balkan Powderkeg'. Historians variously blame disputes over resources, ancient hatreds or meddling by Great Powers intent on keeping the region unstable. But geography is also a powerful clue: Lying south of the Danube river, the Balkans region, like Afghanistan, is composed of scarce fertile valleys, separated by high mountains that fragment the area's ethnic groups, even though many have similar languages and origins.[15]

This description is part of the discourse of 'Balkanism' that helped define the Bosnian war in the American popular imagination. In this discourse, 'history' and 'geography' serve as *deus ex machina* explanations for the war. The Bosnian war happened because it was in 'the Balkans'. It was a product of 'ancient hatreds'. Geography helped make conflict inevitable. In her study of Balkanist discourse, Maria Todorova approaches 'the Balkans' in a manner inspired by Edward Said's approach to 'the Orient', that is as an historical geographical construct that reveals as much about the geopolitical consciousness of 'the West' as it does about the region it purports to describe.[16] Once a synonym for the mountain Haemus, the signifier 'Balkan' became a designator of the vast region between the Bay of Venice and the Black Sea in the construction 'Balkan peninsula', first used by the German geographer August Zeune in 1808 and subsequently by Robert Walsh, a British traveler in 1827. The reason for the inflation of the signifier seems to have been the persistence of an ancient Greek belief that Haemus was a majestic mountain chain linking the Adriatic to the Black

Sea.[17] The belief was erroneous but the term entered the vocabulary of travelers and scholars nevertheless though few had a precise idea of its exact meaning.

The transition of 'the Balkan peninsula' to 'the Balkans' and the remarkable emergence of the geographical category as a verb (to 'balkanize') was a consequence of the slow decline of the Ottoman Empire in the region and the violence of the Balkan wars and World War I. For most of the nineteenth century Todorova argues that 'there was no common Western stereotype of the Balkans', not because there were no common stereotypes but because 'there was no common West'.[18] The Balkan Wars and World War I, however, crystallized a dominant and thoroughly negative image of the region. The Balkans became an abstract symbol of the violence and instability that supposedly is a consequence of the mixture of heterogeneous nationalities in one region. Various discourses stressed racial and/or civilizational explanations for the ferocity and brutality of the violence. Discourses employing the concepts of 'southern Slavs', 'racial hybridity' and 'primitivism' abounded as did geographically determinist notions about the 'blood feuds' of mountainous peoples. 'The complex ethnic mixture was held responsible for the instability and disorder of the peninsula, which was diagnosed as afflicted by 'the handicap of heterogeneity.'[19]

In dominant Balkanist discourses, the Balkans were a location on the edge of Europe, territorially within Europe but not part of modern European space and time. The region was a homeland of essential and primitive nationalist passion, a liminal zone where European civilization ended and an 'other' non-European zone began. None of these discourses adequately described the political complexities of southeastern Europe and the key role of the geopolitical strategies of the great powers in fermenting violence in the region for their own ends. The Balkans served as a projection zone for European powers, a region which enabled them to see themselves as modern and advanced while they displaced their own nationalism and violence upon the region. As an 'other' to Europe, 'the Balkans' were ironically quintessentially European.

After World War II, the Balkan region was generally perceived as part of an 'Eastern Europe' defined by Communist Party domination and control. Elements within the Yugoslav state sought to overcome the historical legacy of 'the Balkans' by constructing a supra-ethnic civil nationalist identity 'Yugoslavian'. Flawed as it was by reliance on Tito's personality, Communist myth, and a rotational system of governance that ironically perpetuated ethnic identities, the Yugoslavian federal state was an historic effort to reject the myth of 'the Balkans'. Geography would not be historical destiny. An alternative universe of belonging and identity could be constructed. When the structures of Communist power came crumbling down in 'Eastern Europe' and this previously undifferentiated bloc was given the freedom to geographically differentiate itself, the key questions in Yugoslavia were whether the identity 'Yugoslavian' could survive the collapsed legitimacy of Communism or whether the federal state would succumb to 'Balkanization'.

The notion of 'southeast Europe' was always an alternative geographical identity for the Balkan region ever since it was first proposed in the late nineteenth century. Originally proposed as a neutral, non-political and non-ideological geographic designation, the term became associated with the geopolitical vision of the Nazis in the 1930s.[20] Yet the term was never essentially Nazi for it emerged independently in other linguistic traditions at the time. Used interchangeably with the classification 'the Balkans' ever since World War II, the term 'southeastern Europe' is nevertheless not without political and symbolic significance. Unlike 'the Balkans', the designation firmly and unambiguously locates the region within 'Europe' and thus within the same geographical and moral universe of 'European civilization'. Read as part of 'the Balkans', Bosnia is easily designated as beyond the West's universe of responsibility, as being located in a non-European zone of marginal strategic significance. Read as part of 'southeastern Europe', it is imaginatively closer to 'the West', part of 'our' domain of strategic responsibility. Securing its stability, consequently, was a much more urgent and pressing priority because it is part of 'Europe', part of 'us' as opposed to 'them'.

From a critical geopolitics standpoint what is important is the socially constructed nature of the categories of 'the Balkans' and 'Europe' and the power relations involved in their deployment and utilization as frameworks for understanding the Bosnian War. One can argue that the ambivalent positionality of Bosnia between the discourses of 'southeast Europe' and 'the Balkans' in the Western geo-political imagination helps accounts for the West's failure to intervene decisively to end the war until the summer of 1995. Within many European states, particularly those geographically close to and familiar with the former Yugoslavia, the discourse of 'southeast Europe' had greater resonance than it had within the United States where, with a political culture with little genuine geographical knowledge of the region, the imaginative geography of 'the Balkans' tended to be more dominant.

Discourses that persistently referred to the 'ancient origins' of the

Balkan war or the 'thousand year old hatreds' that characterized the region served to enframe the Bosnian War within Balkanist discourse. The genocide in Bosnia was *balkanized*, that is made meaningful within the terms of a flawed stereotype of the region and its history. This enabled certain policy analysts, most notably President George Bush, Secretary of State James Baker and General Colin Powell, to view the parties in the war as equivalent and to designate the whole region as a potential 'quagmire' for the United States rather than as a vital region of the European continent that required stabilization by NATO.[21] US foreign policy and NATO credibility suffered for four years because of the persistence of the flawed discourse of 'Balkanism', a hegemonic order of 'common sense' geopolitics that made the development of 'good sense' geopolitics more difficult.

Critical geopolitics is relevant to policy making in that it can help deconstruct the persistence of such stereotypical geopolitical conceptions and notions in popular and political culture. With its sensitivity to geographical difference and its critique of ethnocentrism, it forces strategic thinking to acknowledge the power of ethnocentric cultural constructs in our perception of places and the dramas occurring within them. Critical geopolitics is also cognizant of how technologies of time-space compression like global media networks transforms the strategic value of places in the global information age. Ostensibly marginal geopolitical locations like Bosnia can become symbolically strategic after a while if images of genocide and chaos are persistently projected from the region by Western television networks and media outlets. As I have argued elsewhere, this is precisely what happened with Bosnia and, I would add, is currently happening with Kosovo.[22]

STRUCTURAL GEOPOLITICS: UNDERSTANDING THE CONTEMPORARY GEOPOLITICAL CONDITION.

Even before the end of the Cold War, certain profound changes in the international system were underway that were transforming the spatiality and temporality of world politics. Globalization is the name given to a variety of different cultural and economic tendencies which are binding the world's largest economies closer together and dissolving the ability of any single state to full control and manage its own economic destiny.[23] Globalization is most pronounced in financial markets and the 'creative destruction' unleashed by unregulated transnational finance has created considerable volatility and instability in the international system.

Interestingly, the rhetoric of Cold War geopolitics is re-appearing with a new financial inflection as 'emerging market' become 'dominoes' tottering on the brink of failure and in need of financial bailouts by overstretched and underfunded regulatory institutions. The crises of globalization are initially financial but these can quickly become geopolitical and geo-strategic.

Facilitating the often dizzying pace at which these crises can develop is a second structural process, informationalization. Like globalization, this too is a buzz word for a multiple of related tendencies: the transformation of manufacturing and the service sector by information technologies, the creation of virtual built environments, the development of global telecommunicational systems, and the cultural experience of media saturation and information overload. But it too has transformed the spatiality and temporality of world politics. In a world where an infosphere of codes, flows and networks is the vital operational system for the technosphere of cities, states, economies and megamachinic bureaucracies, notions of 'here' and 'there', 'us' and 'them', 'domestic' and 'foreign', 'close' and 'far' are not what they used to be. Space appears to be displaced by pace while telemetricality appears more significant than territoriality. Geopolitics is becoming postmodern.[24]

A third structural transformation already unleashed well before the end of the Cold War was the qualitatively new world of risks created by the successes of advanced techno-scientific civilization. Since the explosion of the atomic bomb at the end of World War II, it has been evident that humanity was capable of inventing technologies that could radically alter the conditions of human life on the planet. The development of nuclear power, the widespread use of chemicals in all aspects of life after the war, and the more recent breakthroughs in genetic engineering have created a qualitatively new universe of risks for human kind. Environmental poisoning, ozone depletion and global warming are part of modernity's increasingly evident 'side effects' and boomerang processes. Informationalization has also created new dependencies and vulnerabilities, as the Y2K problem, communications mishaps, and network system crashes demonstrate.

These risks are diffuse and difficult to detect, risks that pervade everyday life in the advanced modern world. Unlike the 'natural' risks of the past, the risks of advanced techno-scientific civilization are manufactured and have potentially catastrophic consequences. Though rarely considered, many of these consequences are beyond conventional rational calculations, beyond the local and the personal, beyond even human lifetimes and the human species. In addition, catastrophic accidents, symbolized most dramatically by the Chernobyl nuclear disaster of 1986, are now not only possible but inevitable, predictable 'unanticipated consequences', for even the most unlikely event will occur in the long run.

For sociologists Anthony Giddens and Ulrich Beck, industrial modernity has been so successful that it has graduated to a new modernity, a reflexive modernity of 'risk society'.[25] Industrial society is a victim of its own success; 'high-powered industrial dynamism is skidding into a new society without a bang of a revolution, bypassing political debates and decisions in parliaments and governments'.[26] This new society is a society of generalized and globalized techno-scientific risks. Ignored or folded into the overarching East–West divide by the strategic community in the past, the full dimensions of this new global risk condition are only now being grasped by this community as it confronts problems of post-Cold War nuclear proliferation, chemical weapons production, bioterrorism and information warfare.[27]

Globalization, informationalization and proliferating techno-scientific risks have transformed the dimensionality and territoriality of geopolitics at the end of the twentieth century. Some have even suggested this marks 'the end of geopolitics' but such arguments have a narrow Cold War conception of geopolitics.[28] What can be said is that the problematic of 'national security' has itself become globalized, informationalized and, I would argue, is itself a threat to us if conceptualized in countermodern rather than reflexive ways. Adequately addressing the various dimensions, challenges and dangers of our contemporary geopolitical condition is not possible here, so I can do no more that briefly note three critical geopolitical arguments about this condition.

The first argument is that the problematic of 'national security' in the contemporary era is now global. While regional and state-centered threats are still significant security concerns, the most pressing security challenges, from terrorism to international organized crime and proliferating weapons of mass destruction, are now 'deterritorialized' and global. Most within the Western security community now recognize this and have a strong appreciation of the value of coordinated international diplomatic efforts through diplomacy, international assistance, arms control, and non-proliferation initiatives to shape the international geopolitical environment. However, two tendencies tend to undermine such efforts, the first a unilateralist and neo-isolationist reflex in states (like the US) which disparages international cooperative initiatives, the second an unwillingness on the part of Western states, alliances and economies to reflexively examine how they themselves may be contributing to global insecurity with their own narrow techno-scientific rationality, neoliberal nostrums, informational networks, profligate consumption, and export of deadly weapons and toxins.

This relates to the second argument made by critical geopolitics: that the institutions of Western modernity are experiencing a 'victory crisis'. Beck suggests that 'more and more often we find ourselves in situations which the prevailing institutions and concepts of politics can neither grasp nor adequately respond to'.[29] He describes an ironic legitimation crisis for the political institutions of the West at the end of the Cold War, as one world of risks passes and the new has not yet been fully grasped.[30] The institutions experiencing a 'victory crisis' include the free market, the welfare state, multiparty democracy, national sovereignty, and 'national security' bureaucracies. This 'victory crisis' is one of capability and rationality. Industrial society institutions cannot handle, manage and respond to the problems of risk society; our regulatory institutions cannot keep up with the global plurality of risks proliferating as we enter the second millennium. Furthermore their calculus of risk is suspect. Potentially catastrophic hazards have become normalized. Acceptable risks have become accepted risks. 'The inherent pluralization of risks … calls the rationality of risk calculation into question'.[31]

This 'victory crisis' is also one of lost historical foundations, as particularly 'national security' institutions designed to fight one type of threat now operate in a world where that threat has disappeared. Cold War era security institutions have a problematic existence in a world of transnational threats and global dangers. They promise security against a territorial threat but are struggling to respond to 'non-traditional' threats that often cannot be seen and have no agreed territorial source. Finally, the 'victory crisis' is one of contradiction. The new universe of global risks faced by 'national security' institutions are products of the success of these very institutions. Some of the most immediate threats now faced by the West, for example the threat of Iraqi weapons of mass destruction and the terrorism of fundamentalists based in Afghanistan, are threats the West had a hand in producing itself within its universities, its transnational chemical companies, its biological research labs and its intelligence services (the bases bombed by the US in August 1998 were originally established by the CIA to train Afghans to fight the Soviet invasion of their country). Contemporary geopolitics is characterized by many 'boomerang effects' with the institutions that are supposedly producing 'security' actually producing the opposite.[32]

The policy implications of this disjuncture between unreflexive Cold War institutions and the contemporary post-Cold War era of global risk society is the need for radical institutional reforms to create global systems of regulation and governance. Feeble movement in this direction has begun with the G7 attempt to overhaul the institutions regulating the global financial system. More radical structural reforms are needed to, among other things, re-cast NATO as a broad European security institution (with a 'no first use' nuclear policy), overhaul the United Nations Security Council, strengthen the Non-Proliferation Treaty, the Chemical Weapons and the Biological Weapons Conventions, and establish a permanent United Nations rapid reaction force.

The difficult politics of getting these reforms enacted brings us to the third argument made by critical geopolitics about the contemporary geopolitical condition: the dangers of countermodernity. Countermodernity is a persistent feature of modernity, a thoroughly modern restraining twin of the 'creative destruction' unleashed by modernization. The essence of countermodernity is its attempt to manage the chaos and upheaval caused by modernization. It does so by resorting to myth and violence, by inventing mythic traditions and communal fundamentalisms while drawing borders and organizing violence against those it designates as 'outsiders' to its naturalized community and 'chaotic' elements in its aesthetic visions of society. Finding expression in resurgent nationalism, religious fundamentalism and assertive unilateralism in the contemporary era, countermodernity is an aggressive creed of simplification, a political effort to discipline the chaos and uncertainties of living in a global world with 'timeless truths' and 'imagined essences'.

Historically, orthodox geopolitical discourse gave voice to such countermodern tendencies and inclinations. Today, this danger persists, particularly as institutions and intellectuals used to thinking in 'either-or' terms confront the uncertainties and unruliness of 'and'. As a largely conservative community, some within the 'national security' establishment persist in thinking about the problems of risk society using conceptual understandings wedded to simple modernization and Cold War rhetoric and rationality. They attempt to reduce the irredeemably global problems of risk society to an 'either-or' logic and represent risks as enemies, draw boundaries against this enemy, and then apply instrumental rationality to 'solve' the threat they pose.

One can find evidence of this countermodern tendency in certain contemporary geopolitical crises where global threats are territorialized as threats from 'rogue states'.[33] The problem of weapons of mass destruction, for example, becomes the problem of Saddam Hussein and what to do about Iraq. The problem of ballistic missiles becomes the problem of Iran, Iraq,

North Korea and China. Terrorism becomes the problem of 'rogue states' like Sudan and Afghanistan. Indeed, the Clinton administration's August 1998 cruise missile attacks against Sudan and Afghanistan illustrate the impulse to discipline 'and' by 'either-or' thinking. A formless transnational terrorist attack on US embassies in Africa demanded a resolute response. A weakened President and his inner circle decide, with debatable intelligence information, that a series of sites, former CIA bases in Afghanistan, a pharmaceutical plant outside Khartoum, are terrorist bases and facilities that present 'an immanent threat to the national security of the United States'.[34] Eighty cruise missiles are then sent to demonstrate 'a resolute response to international terrorism'. The world of 'and' is resimplified by the 'either-or' of state violence. The December 1998 bombing of Iraq is another example. The absurdity of bombing to stop certain states developing weapons of mass destruction illustrates the contemporary geopolitical condition, a world where either/or institutions are desperately trying to grapple with the risks and dangers of 'and'.

None of this is to suggest that so-called 'rogue states' are not threats that sometimes require resolute international response. Rather, it is to challenge the ways in which the threat is represented as a territorial threat 'out there' from 'non-Western others' rather than as a pervasive threat from our very own techno-scientific modernity. Behind the territorializing of global risks in 'rogue states' is a broader geopolitical question that is central to geopolitics today and likely to remain so into the twenty-first century: how does the West respond to the *inevitable* diffusion of weapons of mass destruction and ballistic missiles, techno-scientific capabilities pioneered by superpower military-industrial complexes, to developing states, to rogue states and even to failing states? Put differently, how is the Enlightenment West going to deal with the diffusion of its most deadly weapons, substances and delivery vehicles to the non-West? Whether the West responds by acknowledging that the problem is techno-scientific modernity as a whole – acknowledging that 'we (too) are the enemy', that 'our' laboratories, 'our' corporations and 'our' scientists first developed most of the weapons that now threaten us – or whether it responds by territorializing logics that view the problem as 'out there' with 'them' is a crucial question.

No state or national security complex has a monopoly on rationality and good sense. Acknowledging this and developing a critique of our own bureaucracies and techno-scientific rationality is part of the politics of critical geopolitics. This politics is conservative in that it opposes the 'creative destruction' of capitalist modernization and unfettered techno-scientific 'progress' for its own sake in the name of conserving human initiative, control and environmental quality. It is radical in that it critiques the persistence of our ethnocentric assumptions, the narrowness of our rationality (for it is not rational enough), the failings of our institutions, and the false solutions of our countermodern myths. The challenge of our contemporary geopolitical condition is to live with the ambivalence of global risk society and to strive for the construction of security at a global level. Whether this is possible in a world of clashing modernities, contradictory rationalities, competing states and dislocating change remains to be seen.

NOTES

1. Critical geopolitics varies from political economy analyses of world politics to largely textual analyses of foreign policy reasoning, inspired by Foucaultian discourse theory and Derridean deconstruction. For the former see John Agnew and Stuart Corbridge, *Mastering Space: Hegemony, Territory and International Political Economy* (London: Routledge 1995) and John Agnew, *Geopolitics* (London, Routledge 1998). For the latter see Gearóid Ó Tuathail, *Critical Geopolitics: The Political of Writing Global Political Space* (London: Routledge 1996). See also the special issues on 'Critical Geopolitics' in the journals *Environment and Planning D: Society and Space* 12/5 (1994) and *Political Geography* 15/6/7 (1996), Gearóid Ó Tuathail and Simon Dalby (eds.) *Rethinking Geopolitics* (London: Routledge 1998) and idem and Paul Routledge (eds.), *The Geopolitics Reader* (ibid. 1998).
2. See E.P. Thompson, *The Heavy Dancers* (NY: Pantheon 1985) and Mary Kaldor, *The Imaginary War: Understanding the East–West Conflict* (Cambridge: Blackwell 1990).
3. This contrast between 'either-or' and 'and' was first developed by Wassily Kandinsky in a 1927 essay. It is developed further in the works of the German sociologist Ulrich Beck. See his *Risk Society: Towards a New Modernity* (London: Sage 1992); *Ecological Politics in an Age of Risk* (Cambridge: Polity 1995); *The Reinvention of Politics* (ibid. 1997) and *Democracy Without Enemies* (Oxford: Blackwell 1998).
4. See Derek Gregory, *Geographical Imaginations* (Oxford: Blackwell 1994).
5. Gertjan Dijkink, *National Identity and Geopolitical Visions* (London: Routledge 1996). On popular geopolitics see Joanne Sharp, 'Hegemony, popular culture and geopolitics: the *Readers Digest* and the construction of danger', *Political Geography* 12 (1993) pp.491–503.
6. For a discussion of these figures see John O'Loughlin (ed.) *The Dictionary of Geopolitics* (Westport, CT: Greenwood 1994). For a consideration of traditions of geopolitics see Klaus Dodds and David Atkinson (eds.) *Geopolitical Traditions: Critical Histories of a Century of Geopolitical Thought* (London: Routledge 2000).
7. See, for example, Gerry Kearns, 'The imperial subject: geography and travel in the work of Mary Kingsley and Halford Mackinder', *Transactions, Institute of British Geographers* 22 (1997) pp.450–72 and James Ryan, 'Visualizing imperial geography: Halford Mackinder and the Colonial Office Visual Instruction Committee, 1902–11', *Ecumune* 1 (1994) pp.157–76.
8. Gearóid Ó Tuathail, 'Putting Mackinder in his place: Material transformations and myth', *Political Geography* 11 (1992) pp.100–18.
9. Halford Mackinder, 'On thinking imperially', in M.E. Sadler (ed.), *Lectures on Empire* (London: privately published 1907).
10. Marked not only by racial and imperialist discourses, geopolitics is also uncritically patriarchal in its assumptions, reasoning and heroic style. Geopolitics is a deeply masculinist practice that appeals to heroic public subjectivities.
11. This point is developed at length in Ch.3 of *Critical Geopolitics*. (note 1).
12. This argument is developed in *Geopolitics Reader* (note 1) pp.15–18.
13. For a contemporary example see Zbigniew Brzezinksi, *The Grand Chessboard* (NY: Basic

Books 1997), a book that manages to avoid some of the most pressing problematics of our time: globalization, informationalization, corruption, and deterritorialized threats.

14. For an excellent study of geopolitical consciousness see Anssi Paasi, *Territories, Boundaries and Consciousness: The Changing Geographies of the Finnish-Russian Border* (Chichester, John Wiley 1996).
15. See 'A Beginners Guide to the Balkans', ABCNews, at http://www.abcnews.com/sections/world/balkans_content/ [available Nov. 1998].
16. Maria Todorova *Imagining the Balkans* (NY: OUP 1997); Edward Said, *Orientalism* (NY: Vintage 1979).
17. Ibid. p.25.
18. Ibid. p.115.
19. Ibid. p.128.
20. Ibid. pp.27–8.
21. For a discussion of the 'quagmire' and the competing 'Holocaust' spatialization of the Bosnian War see Ó Tuathail, *Critical Geopolitics* (note 1) Ch.6.
22. Gearóid Ó Tuathail, 'A Strategic Sign: The Geopolitical Significance of Bosnia in U.S. Foreign Policy', *Environment and Planning D: Society and Space*, 17 forthcoming.
23. The extent and significance of globalization is deeply contested. For alternative views see Robert Reich, *The Work of Nations* (NY: Knopf 1991) and Paul Hirst and Grahame Thompson, *Globalization in Question* (Cambridge: Polity 1996). On the geographical dimensions of globalization see Kevin Cox (ed.) *Spaces of Globalization* (NY: Guilford 1997) and Andrew Herod, Gearóid Ó Tuathail, and Susan Roberts (eds.) *An Unruly World? Globalization, Governance and Geography* (London: Routledge 1998).
24. For a discussion of our contemporary geopolitical condition as 'postmodern geopolitics' see Gearóid Ó Tuathail , 'Postmodern Geopolitics? The Modern Geopolitical Imagination and Beyond', in *Rethinking Geopolitics* (note 1) pp.16–38, and Timothy Luke and Gearóid Ó Tuathail, 'Thinking Geopolitical Space: The Spatiality of War, Speed and Vision in the Work of Paul Virilio', in Mike Crang and Nigel Thrift (eds.) *Thinking Space* (London: Routledge 2000).
25. See note 3 and Anthony Giddens, *Beyond Left and Right: The Future of Radical Politics* (Stanford UP 1994).
26. Beck, *Reinvention of Politics* (note 3) p.26.
27. Richard Falkenrath, Robert Newman and Bradley Thayer, *America's Achilles Heel: Nuclear, Biological, and Chemical Terrorism and Covert Attack* (Cambridge, MA: MIT Press 1998); Leonard Cole, *The Eleventh Plague: The Politics of Biological and Chemical Warfare* (NY: W.H. Freeman 1996); John Arquilla, David F. Ronfeldt and Alvin Toffler (eds.) *In Athena's Camp: Preparing for Conflict in the Information Age* (Santa Monica, CA: Rand Corp. 1998); Gearóid Ó Tuathail , 'Deterritorialized Threats and Global Dangers: Geopolitics, Risk Society and Reflexive Modernization', *Geopolitics* 10, special issue on 'Postmodernity, Territory and Boundaries' (1999) forthcoming.
28. Gearóid Ó Tuathail, 'At the End of Geopolitics? Reflections on a Pluralizing Problematic at the Century's End', *Alternatives: Social Transformation and Humane Governance* 22 (1997) pp.35–55.
29. Beck, *Reinvention of Politics* (note 3) p.7.
30. Ibid. pp.12–13.
31. Ibid. p.32.
32. The Pentagon is one of the largest polluters in the United States. The weapons produced in the name of 'national security' at US military facilities across the country, such as the Hanford nuclear reservation in Richland, Washington, Rocky Flats in Colorado, have left a permanent legacy of toxicity. Producing nuclear 'national security' has long generated generational community insecurity, a 'side effect' of Cold War geopolitics that will be around for centuries. Lake Karachay near the former Soviet Union's 'secret' weapons complex at Chelyabinsk has been described as 'the most polluted spot on earth'. See Tom Athanasiou, *Divided Planet: The Ecology of Rich and Poor* (Athens: U. of Georgia Press 1996) p.120.
33. Michael Klare, *Rogue States and Nuclear Outlaws* (NY: Hill and Wang 1995).
34. On the ambiguous intelligence about the Khartoum plant see Seymour Hersh, 'The Guns of August', *The New Yorker*, 12 Oct. 1998.

7

Geopolitics: International Boundaries as Fighting Places

EWAN W. ANDERSON

The focus of geopolitics is upon the use of geography to illuminate politics and particularly political decision-making. Despite the increasing effects of globalization, the basic unit in the contemporary world political system is the state. It is an internationally recognized political and juridical entity which claims sovereignty over a specific area of land and possibly adjacent sea, the inhabitants of the area and the resources located therein. This area is delimited in the minds of individuals and groups owing allegiance to the state, in most cases on cartographic representations of the state and in some cases on the ground itself, by boundaries. Boundaries indicate the accepted territorial integrity of the state and the extent of government control. In the majority of cases boundaries are legally recognized by the states which share them and also by the international community.

However, partly at least as a result of the global geopolitical changes over the past decade, approximately one-quarter of the world's land boundaries can be classified as unstable. In addition, some two-thirds of the global maritime boundaries have yet to be settled.[1] Since the possession of agreed boundaries has a crucial bearing upon state security and is also of great political, economic and social significance, conflicts related to boundaries are likely to remain a key component of the international scene.

In the current global political system, the state is the highest level of political decision-making body. States have to agree to acquiesce in the decisions of supra-national bodies such as the United Nations (UN), the European Union (EU) and the International Court of Justice (ICJ). To be a member of such a super-national body therefore involves a certain loss of sovereignty. However, in contrast to the internal operation of a state, there is no set means of law enforcement. Sanctions or even political force may be brought to bear against a deviant state, but such occurrences appear to be highly selective. The occupation of parts of neighbouring states is tolerated in the case of Israel, but not in that of Iraq. Indonesian atrocities in East Timor attract relatively little attention in the West in contrast to those of Yugoslavia in Kosovo. Since boundaries are of such importance to the state, decision-making about their alignment is fundamental.

Furthermore, it is axiomatic that in any boundary settlement there must be the involvement of at least two states. Thus, given their significance in defining the territorial integrity and the limits of sovereignty of the state, it is hardly surprising that a high proportion of global flashpoints can be related to boundaries. The 1998 Chart of Armed Conflict[2] indicates 19 current international territorial and border conflicts. For example, Ethiopia has active conflicts on three of its five international boundaries, namely those with Sudan, Eritrea and the Somali republic.

The settlement of boundary disputes which can be effected in a variety of ways, requires geographical evidence and political will underpinned by international law. Each boundary is geographically unique and is therefore, in a measure, a special case. International law can provide guidelines, more explicit in the case of maritime than territorial boundaries. The current and past geography with a bearing on settlement involves a range of elements which can be broadly subsumed into the categories of physical and human geography.

It has been shown that states are the key component of the global political system and that boundaries are a major concern of their political decision-making. Each boundary is unique and the evidence of its settlement must focus upon geography. Therefore, the study of boundary settlement, involving the use of geography in decision-making, fits as closely as any subject to the definition of geopolitics. In examining the potential role of geographers, Prescott[3] distinguishes between the study of factors, the interaction between which characterizes a boundary and the study of the effects of a boundary, once established, upon the landscape. The former approach can be considered geopolitical, whereas the latter is part of political geography. Geopolitics contributes to the decision-making process on boundary delimitation.

As there are high and low politics, so geopolitics is not scale specific and there are high and low geopolitics.[4] Geopolitics developed as a study of the effect of physical geography and patterns of political history.[5] More recently, Cohen,[6] Child[7] and Kissinger[8] have adopted a far broader view of the contribution of geography and also of the scale on which it illuminates politics. Using the fundamental geographical elements of areas, lines and points, the variation in scale of geopolitical concern can be illustrated, using boundaries. It is probably true to say that most territorial disputes have some element of boundary conflict embedded in them. In many cases, such as that of Cyprus[9] the dispute is over territory but the emphasis is clearly on the boundary. Similarly, concerns over Abu Musa and the Tunbs Islands in the Persian-Arabian Gulf[10] centre on areas of land, but are essentially about the limits of sovereignty and therefore the boundaries of Iran and the United Arab Emirates (UAE).

As concerns over stretches of land may focus upon the actual boundary, so any boundary delimitation must involve gains and losses of territory. The boundary line is linear and theoretically without width, but even when it is a line within a relatively narrow waterway, there still may be gains and losses. For example, the boundary settlement between Kuwait and Iraq resulted in a change of location for the international boundary from the median line of Khor Zubair to the low water line (springs) on the Kuwaiti side. Thus, from having originally shared it, Iraq gained full access to the port of Umm Qasr.[11] Boundary issues may also involve disputes over a point. A clear example of this occurred with the demarcation of the Egypt-Israel boundary when there was a dispute over the southernmost point at a boundary marker at Taba. The area in contention measured 900 m^2.[12]

CHANGING SIGNIFICANCE OF BOUNDARIES

The chronology of international boundaries is a product of the spread of the state system globally over the last 350 years from its inception in Europe at the end of the Thirty Years War. The Treaty of Westphalia (1648) can be taken as a convenient point after which it was acknowledged that boundaries drawn around territory circumscribed a single political and legal unit over which the state had sovereignty. The idea of zonal frontiers between core areas of control was rejected and from then, individuals owed allegiance to a specific territory which linked them to those with sovereign control. This replaced the earlier feudal relationship in which allegiance existed on different levels. However, this change was not universal and today, in certain tribally-based societies, sovereignty is over people rather than place. This issue may therefore remain a concern over boundary disputes in places such as the Arabian Peninsula. Nonetheless, the general effect was that *de facto* frontiers were replaced by *de jure* boundaries up to which absolute sovereignty extended.

This change also highlights the main distinction between frontiers and boundaries. Frontiers have a spatial extent whereas boundaries have no horizontal dimension. The second dimension of boundaries occurs in the vertical plane, enabling the state to claim air space and subterranean space. The increasing domination of the boundary as a means of delimiting political and legal influence became virtually total with the closing of the world system at the beginning of the twentieth century.[13] The age of territorial imperialism in which stronger states tended to overstep the territorial jurisdiction of their weaker neighbours[14] only came to an end with the Second World War. Until that time, the economic and political developments which had produced the nation state system also set in motion the European subjugation of the rest of the world.[15] The majority of the boundaries of Africa, Asia and Latin America were drawn by Europeans, largely according to the interests of European nationalism. The geographical factors which would now be taken into account for boundary settlement were largely ignored in the face of the economic, strategic and diplomatic interests of the European states. In many cases the new states which emerged possessed territory, but were then required to build a nation. This process has become increasingly difficult in the light of the struggle for self-determination by minority groups on the one hand and the trends towards globalization on the other.

This was the period about which Lord Curzon[16] spoke: 'frontiers are indeed the razor's edge on which hang suspended the modern issues of war and peace, of life or death to nations'. In a similar vein, Holditch[17] noted: 'in the recent history of the world most of the important wars, and international quarrels to which wars seem to be the inevitable sequel, have risen over disputed boundaries'. This first extended period of boundary delimitation ended effectively in 1939. Following closely upon the end of the Second World War came the Cold War and the rise of the bipolar global political system. The rivalry of the two superpowers extended to every corner of the globe and effectively fossilized boundaries. Any change in the location of a boundary was resisted in case it attracted retaliatory action from the other superpower. There were of course boundary conflicts, but these were almost exclusively in what might be termed peripheral areas. For example, on three occasions there was conflict between Pakistan and India over the question of Kashmir and there was fighting between Libya and Chad over the Aozou Strip. Indeed prior to 1989, disputes over boundaries and territory were perceived to be characteristics predominantly limited to the developing world.

Since 1989, with the demise of the Warsaw Pact, the break up of the Soviet Union itself and the disintegration of Yugoslavia, the core region of

Europe and the neighbouring areas of Asia has become the focus of territorial instability. Kolossov and Krindach[18] identified some 160 current disputes over territory and boundaries within the former Soviet Union (FSU). Nevertheless, while they are now overshadowed, there remain major boundary problems, particularly in Africa, the Middle East, Latin America and Southeast Asia.

Moreover, dating principally from the 1958 Geneva Convention on the Territorial Sea and Contiguous Zone and on the Continental Shelf, a new dimension was added. With the recognition of the rights of a coastal state over its continental shelf, the number of potential disputes over boundaries has been greatly enhanced by maritime claims.

Not only are the likelihood and significance of boundary disputes now far greater than at any time since the start of the Second World War, but there are further dimensions of concern. In particular, the issue of transboundary movements, for which international law is still in an initial stage of formulation, is of growing importance. A major current example concerns the modes and routes of transportation by which oil and natural gas can be exported from the Caspian Sea basin. Since all the producer states are landlocked, transport must involve both pipeline and tanker. However, pipelines offer no guarantee of security and the Middle East is replete with damaged or closed pipelines. Sanctions against Iraq have been particularly effective because the main pipelines for export were under the control of Turkey and Saudi Arabia. Non-oil producers in the region stand to gain not only from the increasing prosperity generally, but also from transit dues. Therefore, in what is generally an underdeveloped area, disputes over pipeline routes are likely to continue.

A problem with some similarities is the division of water in internationally shared drainage basins. This is still dependent upon negotiation rather than accepted law, since no law is universally recognized. In many of the arid areas of the world, particularly the Middle East, water is such a sensitive issue that a new subdivision of geopolitics, hydropolitics, has been recognized.

Beyond these examples are many transboundary movements which are either undesirable or illegal or both, which form part of the macro-political agenda. This comprises those problems which are effectively global and well beyond the control of even the most powerful state. The transboundary movements of drugs, illegal arms, nuclear materials and weapons of mass destruction, refugees and terrorists are all examples which have further focused global attention upon boundaries.

This heightened awareness of international boundaries and particularly disputes over them are also taking into account postmodern discussion ranging from new approaches to territorial compartmentalization[19] to the role of cyberspace.[20] However, while land boundaries have been opened in Western Europe in particular,[21] it must be remembered that postmodernism in this context does not provide support for events in the remainder of the world. Even in Eastern Europe and the adjacent areas of Eurasia, the emergence of rejuvenated or entirely new states has commonly resulted in boundary disputes.

BOUNDARY CLASSIFICATION

A significant thread of research through boundary studies has been concerned with the effectiveness of boundaries. Initially, the emphasis was upon defensive characteristics, but as a more broadly based approach has been adopted, the potential functions of boundaries in the world-system tradition have been addressed.[22] The issue, however, remains much the same and is whether boundaries should be used to separate states or cultural groups, or to bring them together. Holditch (1916) believed that boundaries should fulfil the role of barriers and that the most effective were those that involved mountain chains, lakes or deserts. In contrast, 'bad' boundaries were exemplified by lines of latitude and longitude. From the standpoint of defence, straight lines were difficult to defend and since they were likely to cross a wide variety of terrain and required more specialist forces.

Lyde[23] believed that boundaries which were placed between people of similar ethnic and economic groups would lead to mutual cross-boundary exchange and thereby reduce the level of friction between adjacent states. By this reasoning, rivers were 'good' boundaries, since their use necessitated agreements on water extraction, irrigation, navigation and crossing points. History has shown that neither Holditch nor Lyde had revealed anything approaching universal truth. Modern means of warfare have largely negated the effects of natural features, while conflicts over the use of shared water abound.

Among morphological classifications, the commonly distinguished categories are: physiographic boundaries; geometrical boundaries; and anthropomorphic boundaries.[24] Physiographic boundaries are those which are drawn to follow some conspicuous feature of the landscape such as a mountain range or a river, or in some way related to a marsh, a forest or a desert. These are considered natural boundaries, but such terminology is incorrect in that all boundaries are manmade and therefore artificial.[25] In each case a specific line with, theoretically, no breadth, needs to be identified and this poses problems. For example, in the case of a river the boundary may be constructed to follow the bank, a median or middle line, a navigable channel or the *thalweg*, the line of deepest soundings. The First Gulf War between Iran and Iraq was fought over exactly where the boundary line should be with regard to the Shatt al Arab.

Geometrical boundaries are straight lines following lines of latitude or longitude or in some cases, drawn from fixed points. The boundaries of Gambia are fixed by arcs drawn from the centre of the river Gambia. Lines of latitude or longitude are common in Latin America and Africa and are characteristic of newly colonized areas. Since most were constructed before there was any detailed knowledge of the terrain or its resources and before anything other than sparse settlement had occurred, many have resulted in boundary conflict.

Boundaries drawn according to cultural elements such as language, religion or ethnology, are known as anthropomorphic. Among the best known of such boundaries are those between India and Pakistan and between India and Bangladesh.

It is clear that no such morphological classification is entirely satisfactory and no one category can be identified as particularly effective in reducing the likelihood of boundary conflict. Even along the highest mountain boundary in the world, that between China and India, there have been clashes.

In many ways a more appropriate classification in that it relates well to many of the boundary issues encountered, is that of Hartshorne.[26] This is a genetic classification in which four categories of boundary are recognized. Antecedent boundaries are those constructed before most of the elements of human geography were in place in the landscape. The straight line boundaries of the New World provide good examples. Subsequent boundaries are those delimited after the major components of the cultural landscape were in place. They may appear commonly therefore as anthropomorphic boundaries. Superimposed boundaries are similar to subsequent boundaries, except that they have been imposed by external powers and bear no relationship to the cultural landscape. Clearly these boundaries, typified by many of those drawn in Africa, are likely to be a potential source of friction. The fourth category, relict boundaries, are those, the functions of which have disappeared, but the effects of which can still be seen in the landscape. The most recent example of such a boundary is that between Hong Kong and mainland China.

Several other boundary classifications have been advanced, related in particular to the function of the state, but none allows any clear correlation with conflict prevention. Suffice it to record that the only general agreement appears to be that the more boundaries possessed by a state, greater is the likelihood of dispute.

BOUNDARY ACQUISITION

There are several ways in which boundaries may be acquired and Muir[27] has identified five. A boundary may be established at the limits of territorial expansion and this is legal if the territory claimed is considered to have been unadministered prior to the claim. Such territory is known as *terra nullius* or *res nullius*. In contrast, a boundary may be imposed by external powers such as a result of conquest or negotiation. From the historical perspective, a boundary may result from the contraction of a frontier zone between two states, or may be inherited from a period of colonial rule. In the case of the latter, the principle of *uti possidetis* may be applied. This means that the previous boundary, imposed by a colonial power is transferred to the newly-independent sovereign state. The principle is based upon the procedure adopted by Latin American states in the early nineteenth century[28] and was adopted by the Organization of African Unity (OAU). The fifth circumstance is by conquest over a sovereign state. This is now illegal, but certain states, notably Israel, have expanded their *de facto* boundaries in this fashion.

Of greater interest in any discussion on boundary conflict is that the acquisition of boundaries is the acquisition of territories. It is in the laying of claim to territory for strategic, political, economic or social reasons that disputes occur. Burghardt[29] identifies four modes of approaching territorial claims that are acceptable in international law and under which, therefore, sovereignty can be acquired. Since the entire territorial area of the globe, including Antarctica is now claimed, occupation and prescription are basically of historical concern, but can of course be used in current claims. Occupation implies the establishment of control over territory that was unadministered at the time of the claim or could be characterized as *terra nullius*. Prescription is achieved through the maintenance of effective control over the territory for a sufficiently long period. In any case based on prescription, there is clearly latitude for argument over terms such as 'effective control' and 'sufficiently long period'. Territory may also be acquired by cession, the transfer of sovereignty by treaty and by accretion or growth by some act of nature. Included under accretion would be an increase in area resulting from deposition or coral growth. Cession and accretion are both relatively clear cut, but effective control in the context of either occupation or prescription may well be difficult to prove. Nonetheless, it remains the basis for many claims in areas where boundaries have yet to be delimited.

In boundary cases the other major basis for a claim is territorial integrity. A foundation may be provided for this by the shape and relative location of a state. Such a claim may prevail in areas which were subject to division on the basis of physical features and is of definite relevance in the case of maritime boundaries and the adjacency of the state. The third main category of claim is based upon historical and cultural factors (Burghardt, 1973). Claims based on economic factors are rarely successful except in very specific circumstances when they are concerned with strategic lines of communication.

Claims like those set out by Burghardt have been advanced for arbitration. However, in boundary settlement there are many other approaches, largely based on diplomacy, ranging from negotiation to mediation and enquiry. While for judicial settlement, geography may be critical in providing evidence on territorial integrity, cultural factors and even government control, it is of even greater relevance to diplomatic approaches. The experience of the author in seven major cases has shown that current evidence of relevance to a boundary delimitation can be classified into: physical geography; human geography; geology; ecology; security; anthropology; and government.

This list, produced as a result of applied research compares well with those identified by Keegan and Wheatcroft:[30] physical, climatic, logistic, economic, military and political; Rama Krishna Rao and Sharma:[31] history, geography, ecology and security.

If agreement is reached and conflict is avoided, boundary settlement usually involves two or possibly three stages. First, drawing upon the geographical evidence agreed, the criteria for construction are identified and the approximate position of the boundary is allocated. Delimitation, which follows this process, necessitates the selection of a line on the ground and the construction of this line on a map. If the location of the boundary is not obviously indicated by, for example, the course of a river, there may be a demarcation stage in which boundary markers are established. A particular issue with maritime boundaries is that, of course, for the most part they cannot be demarcated. The boundaries of Saudi Arabia provide illustrations of all three stages. The boundary with Yemen has been allocated and the end points are known. The boundary with Qatar has been delimited and that with Kuwait has been demarcated. Indeed, in an effort to negate conflict, Saudi Arabia has agreed to more imaginative boundary settlements than any other state. These include in particular the use of porous boundaries and shared zones.

BOUNDARY CONFLICT

In considering warfare, it appears to be a truism that wars must almost always begin at borders. Claims over territory and the locational status of boundaries may not be solved peacefully and may involve the use of force. Some of these instances concern claims based on the factors identified, but many are the product of historical, cultural and economic factors. Even more are a mixture of several factors. For example, there are many incidents when conflict has occurred between Israel and its neighbours, affecting cultural, economic and ideological issues. Kocs[32] focused on the initial causes of military conflict in mapping interstate war between 1945 and 1987. He split state dyads into noncontiguous dyads, contiguous dyads where a never-resolved dispute existed over a contiguous boundary existed and contiguous dyads where no such dispute existed. As would be expected, he found that the probability of war is 40 times more likely between contiguous states if they are involved in an unresolved boundary dispute. The figure is reduced to 19 times higher if Israel were removed from the matrix.

It is generally accepted that the outcome of any boundary dispute is likely to hinge on five factors: the geographical importance of the dispute to each of the governments involved; the extent to which either of the states may derive some benefit; the relative strengths of the states involved; the world political climate, including the controls which can be exercised; and the merits of the arguments advanced by the contenders.

From the foregoing discussion, the great potential for boundary disputes is clear. Rather than attempt a global inventory, it appears preferable to provide as examples, those disputes which can be considered global flashpoints. These can then be categorized according to the major underlying cause for conflict.

Disputes throughout the Sahel and those involving many of the maritime boundaries can be attributed basically to physical geography. Boundary-related flashpoints such as the Gaza Strip, the Golan Heights, the West Bank, the Chagos archipelago, Ceuta and the Kola peninsula are primarily of political-strategic concern. Problems or potential problems over the

Hawar Islands, the Paracel Islands, Rockall, the Shatt al Arab and the Kuwait-Iraq boundary are dominated by economic geography. In contrast, while there are both physical and economic components, Bessarabia, East Timor, Kosovo, Kurdistan, Northern Ireland and Transylvania are primarily flashpoints as a result of social geography.

CONCLUSIONS

Considerations on the global strategic scale have long been accepted as part of the legitimate field of geopolitics. However, it is possible to make a strong case that geopolitics as a subject is not scale specific and that issues on what might be termed the 'tactical' scale are of geopolitical relevance. A field of study at the tactical level is that of boundary settlement and conflict. Furthermore, it is apparent that a high proportion of all current conflict is in some way related to boundaries. In the modern world, boundaries are as close as anything can be to fighting zones.

In boundary settlement and the analysis of boundary conflict, the approach is essentially geopolitical. The emphasis is upon the identification of evidence which will allow agreement, the resolution of any conflict and eventual boundary management. Within such evidence, geographical components predominate, whether of historical, strategic-political, economic or social geography. Thus, the study of boundary issues illustrates clearly the use of geography to illuminate political decision-making.

NOTES

1. E.W. Anderson, 'International Boundaries and the Law: Some Considerations', *Jane's Defence '96. The World in Conflict* (1996).
2. International Institute for Strategic Studies, *Chart of Armed Conflict* (London: IISS 1998).
3. J.R.V. Prescott, *Political Geography* (London: Methuen 1972).
4. C.E. Zoppo and C. Zorgbibe (eds.) *On Geopolitics: Classical and Nuclear* (Dordrecht: Martinus Nijhoff 1985).
5. H.J. Mackinder, 'The Geographical Pivot of History', *Geographical Journal* 23 (April 1904) pp.423–37.
6. S. Cohen, *Geography and Politics in a World Divided* (NY: OUP 1973).
7. J. Child, *Geopolitics and Conflict in South America* (NY: Praeger 1985).
8. H. Kissinger, *American Foreign Policy: A Global View* (Singapore: Inst. of SE Asian Studies 1982).
9. C. Grundy-Warr, 'Political Division and Peacekeeping in Cyprus' in G.H. Blake and R.N. Schofield (eds.) *Boundaries and State Territory in the Middle East and North Africa* (Wisbech: Middle East and North African Studies Press 1987) pp.70–97.
10. E.W. Anderson, *An Atlas of World Political Flashpoints* (London: Pinter 1993).
11. E.W. Anderson and J. Karam, 'The Kuwait-Iraq Border: A Reappraisal', *RUSI Journal* 139/3 (Autumn 1994) pp.47–50.

12. N. Kliot, 'The Development of the Egyptian-Israeli Boundaries: 1906–1986', in G.H. Blake and R.N. Schofield (eds.) *Boundaries and State Territory in the Middle East and North Africa* (Wisbech: Middle East and North African Studies Press 1987) pp.54–69.
13. P.J. Taylor, *Political Geography: World Economy, Nation-state and Locality* (London: Longman Scientific 1993).
14. R.D. Dikshit (ed.) *Developments in Political Geography: A Century of Progress* (New Delhi: Sage Publications 1997).
15. D. Downing, *An Atlas of Territorial and Border Disputes* (London: New English Library 1980).
16. Lord Curzon, 'Frontiers', *The Romanes Lecture* (Oxford: Clarendon Press 1907).
17. T.H. Holditch, *Political Frontiers and Boundary-making* (London: Macmillan 1916).
18. V.A. Kolossov and A. Krindach, 'The Emergence of New Political Boundaries in the Former Soviet Union: Some Actual Problems and the Case of the Russo-Ukranian Boundary in the Rostov Oblast', in W Gallusser (ed.) *Political Boundaries and Coexistence* (Berne: Peter Lang 1994) pp.65–76.
19. A. Paasi, 'The Changing Representations of the Finnish-Russian Boundary', in W.A. Gallusser (ed.) *Political Boundaries and Coexistence* (Berne: Peter Lang 1994) pp.103–11.
20. S.D. Brunn and J.A. Jones, 'Geopolitical Information and Communication in Shrinking and Expanding Worlds: 1900–2100', in G.J. Demko and W.B. Wood (eds.) *Reordering the World: Geopolitical Perspectives on the 21st Century* (Boulder, CO: Westview Press 1994) pp.301–21.
21. M. Anderson, *Territory and State Formation in a Modern World* (Cambridge: Polity Press 1996).
22. V.A. Kolossov and J. O'Loughlin, 'New Borders for New World Orders: Territorialities at the *Fin- de- Siecle*', *GeoJournal* 44/3 (1998) pp.259–73.
23. L.W. Lyde, *Some Frontiers for Tomorrow: An Aspiration for Europe* (London: A.C. Black 1915).
24. R.D. Dikshit, *Political Geography: A Contemporary Perspective* (New Delhi: Tata McGraw-Hill 1982).
25. J.O.M. Broek, 'The Problem of Natural Frontiers', *Frontiers of the Future Lectures* (Los Angeles: U. of California, 1940).
26. R. Hartshorne, 'Suggestions on the Terminology of Political Boundaries', *Annals of the Association of American Geographers* 26 (1936) pp.56–7.
27. R. Muir, *Modern Political Geography*, 2nd ed. (London: Macmillan 1981).
28. M.I. Glassner and H.J. de Blij, *Systematic Political Geography*, 4th ed. (NY: Wiley 1989).
29. A.F. Burghardt, 'The Bases of Territorial Claims', *Geographical Review* 63 (1973) pp.225–45.
30. J. Keegan and A. Wheatcroft, *Zones of Conflict: An Atlas of Future Wars* (London: Jonathan Cape 1986).
31. D.V.L.N. Rama Krishna Rao and R.C. Sharma, *India's Borders: Ecology and Security Perspectives* (New Delhi: Scholars' Publishing Forum 1991).
32. S.A. Kocs, 'Territorial Disputes and Interstate War 1945–1987', *Journal of Politics* 57 (1995) pp.159–75.

8

Information Power: Strategy, Geopolitics, and the Fifth Dimension

DAVID J. LONSDALE

> 'Now, as in revolutions past, technology is profoundly affecting the sovereignty of governments, the world economy, and military strategy.'[1]

The above quotation is illustrative of a growing literature which attributes revolutionary implications to the development and spread of Information Technology (IT). Typically these works predict the empowerment of small and/or non-state actors; the decline of the nation state; a decreasing relevance for the physical world and its relationships; and the rising importance of information in the strategic world at the expense of traditional physically-based military capabilities.[2]

Of course technological developments which facilitate a more effective exploitation of a particular dimension of strategy can have important consequences. For example, the utilisation of the air and space environments this century (the third and fourth dimensions respectively) have further complicated the strategic world, and have presented new vulnerabilities and opportunities. In response, many actors have had to develop an understanding of these environments and how to operate within them. Some technologies, such as nuclear-armed intercontinental ballistic missiles (ICBMs), may also have consequences for geopolitics and the continued relevance of geographical factors in international politics and strategy. Put simply, it matters that you can be hit by an ICBM in spite of geographical features which have traditionally acted as a form of defence, such as the Atlantic and Pacific oceans in the case of the United States.

In reference to the relationship between technology and geopolitics, it is important to remember that geopolitical theory has often rested on the premise that technology can help shape the geopolitical world. After all, Sir

Halford Mackinder regarded the development of railways as the key to unlocking the potential of the 'heartland', and thereby signalling the rise of continental powers at the expense of the maritime countries.[3] It is therefore not implausible that the continued development of IT could have significant consequences for strategy and geopolitics. However, we must not overplay the significance of the information revolution. To do so could lead to a form of technological determinism. Mackinder avoided this particular pitfall by suggesting in his later work that the heartland power could be offset by the Midland Ocean coalition.[4] This ability to offset technologically driven geopolitical change is a significant thought, to which this study will return.

Other theorists have been less restrained than Mackinder and have tended to overemphasise the significance of a new technology or dimension of strategy. This happened in the early years of air power during the interwar period. Most notable in this respect is the work of Giulio Douhet. This Italian general and theorist trumpeted air power as an independent means to victory.[5] Despite several comprehensive strategic bombing campaigns, most notably in World War II, Vietnam, and the 1991 Gulf War, the claims of Douhet have yet to be fully realised. Although, this does not mean that the third dimension is unimportant. Air power has for some time been regarded as the equal of the other forms of strategic power. In this respect a new technology or particular dimension of strategy may not become independently dominant, but may still attain a significant level of importance. With reference to IT, the fifth dimension is likely to become even more significant in the practice of strategy. But it would be a mistake to overlook the continued importance of physical geography and the military forces which operate in the traditional physical environment.

In light of these thoughts, the objective here is to provide a framework which promotes a better understanding of the role information activities can play in the 'means-ends' world of strategy.[6] To this end, it will be demonstrated that a fifth dimension (the infosphere) of strategy does exist. From this, the essay will explore the nature of this new dimension and analyse how this affects the practice of strategy within it. Analysing the advantages and limitations of 'information power' is crucial in any attempt to understand the long-term implications of the fifth dimension. It will be shown that these limitations suggest that physical expressions of strategic power, and the geography in which they operate, will remain salient. With these foundations in place we can begin to understand the significance the information revolution has for geopolitics.

Because the information age is still relatively young, the thoughts expressed in this work are inherently speculative, and are best regarded as preliminary thoughts, albeit ones that are based upon an understanding of the strategic past.

INFOSPHERE: THE FIFTH DIMENSION OF STRATEGY

As noted above, a considerable step in appreciating the significance of the information environment and its attendant power is to understand the nature of the fifth dimension. The other forms of strategic power: sea, land, air, and space, all have their own physical environments which have unique characteristics. The nature of each environment determines to a degree how the corresponding power can be utilised. Information power operates within an environment which is best defined as the 'infosphere'. Due to its ethereal nature the infosphere does not take easily to any concrete definition. In fact the infosphere is best thought of as a polymorphous entity where information exists and flows. Although clearly not a physical medium in the same vein as the other dimensions of strategy, an information dimension can be identified. Weapons, in the form of malicious software, can flow through the infosphere, and in this sense the fifth dimension acts as a medium for strategic power.

In a similar vein, a form of conflict can take place within the infosphere. Electronic warfare being perhaps one obvious example of this type of conflict. The World War II activities of the Royal Air Force's No.80 (Signals) Wing, the so-called 'Beam Benders', is just one interesting case.[7]

Like the sea, one of the functions of the infosphere is to act as a highway, through which information and weapons can flow. The sea is also a place where large deposits of natural resources are to be found. Having secure access to the sea helps ensure the ability to exploit these resources. Likewise, deposits of information reside within the infosphere. In an age in which information is increasingly regarded as vital to the effective functioning of society,[8] ensuring access to this resource will be critical. These characteristics seem to imply that the infosphere does indeed constitute a medium of strategy, and has enormous economic, social, political, and military relevance. Ultimately, the defining characteristic which identifies the infosphere as a dimension of strategy, is that various forms of strategic power can be projected through and within this distinct environment.

The above description of the infosphere requires some important qualifications. Parts of the infosphere are physically real in a strict sense. This applies substantially to the many physical assets which form part of the infosphere, such as satellites, cables, and computers. In this way, there exists a significant overlap between the fifth dimension and the physical world. Martin Libicki describes cyberspace (an important part of the infosphere) as being characterised by 'placelessness'.[9] This point is generally true, although not entirely, and may become less true as time progresses. Increasingly parts of cyberspace, and indeed information itself, are being territorialised, in that they are being claimed by businesses, individuals, and states. There is a sense that this is 'our' information, or these are 'our' computers, and we will choose whether to let you in or not. Of course with the right skills, access can be gained to some restricted systems and information. But it should not be concluded that boundaries in cyberspace are an illusion simply because computer systems and information can be accessed by unauthorised users. The fact that people can gain illegal access across a state's borders does not invalidate the geopolitical reality of nation states. These thoughts have important implications for those who claim that a new geopolitical reality is on the horizon because the infosphere is without boundaries. As Robert O. Keohane and Joseph S. Nye Jr note, '... information does not flow in a vacuum but in political space already occupied'.[10]

Whether or not the infosphere is strictly speaking a physical reality, is perhaps no more than a problem of definition with little real importance. In the practical world of strategy what really matters is perceiving the infosphere as a place that exists, understanding the nature of it, and regarding it as something which can be manipulated and used.

As noted, the nature of the infosphere has important implications for those operating within it. One of the most prominent characteristics of the fifth dimension, is that relative to the other dimensions of strategy it can be expanded or contracted far more easily, and to a much greater degree, by man's actions.[11] The fifth dimension is malleable, to some extent it can be moulded and shaped. For example, the launch of a new satellite or the connection of a computer to the Internet, are but two ways of expanding the fifth dimension. A new satellite produces new information, or a new conduit through which information can flow, and thereby the infosphere is expanded. The converse methods to achieve contraction should be obvious. Thus we have a situation in which some assets of information power (satellites, computers etc.) are also simultaneously elements of the infosphere. The infosphere can also be manipulated through the art of deception.

As is the case in the other dimensions of strategy, the relationship between those wishing to protect their information activities and those attempting to undermine them, will invariably be characterised by dynamism. Protecting and securing information flow and integrity will require constant vigilance.[12] This is an important point to note. There are few absolutes in the infosphere. As elsewhere in the strategic world, you are dealing with intelligent foes who will attempt to counter your information power activities. Again, this reality affects the degree of revolutionary change which the fifth dimension might produce. If information power is offset or abated, its strategic efficacy is likewise diminished.

Terms other than the 'infosphere' may be put forward to describe the fifth dimension. Another candidate which may be championed is 'cyberspace'. However, cyberspace connotes a modern construction. To cite Martin Libicki's definition, cyberspace is 'the sum of the globe's communications links and computational nodes'.[13] Cyberspace is only part of the infosphere. Like information warfare itself, the infosphere is an ancient component of strategy. Napoleon's use of a cavalry screen to hide the movement of forces is a classic example of information warfare.[14] By definition, Napoleon was also manipulating the infosphere. Consequently, Napoleon can also be said to have been exercising information power. In this example Napoleon was not using assets which are more readily associated with information power. In this sense the assets of information power need not be high-tech, nor dedicated solely to information tasks. A simple hilltop represents an asset of information power. The significance of physical high ground as an asset of information power has many historical examples. The battle for the Falkland Islands in 1982 presents one relatively modern case. The capture of Mount Kent by British forces established a useful observation post over Port Stanley, and prevented the Argentinians using the mountain to rain down observed artillery fire on 3 Commando Brigade.[15]

When considering the fifth dimension, a reasonable question to ask is why existence of the infosphere, and the concept of information power, have not been noted until recently. The most compelling response to this is that the information age has raised our awareness of information. Consequently we are adopting a mind-set which sees information as a tangible resource. It should be noted that long-established beliefs can be reassessed. For much of history it was taken for granted that time was absolute. It now transpires that time in fact is relative.[16] As the information age develops, and with it the growing significance of information, the infosphere may be attaining a greater prominence in many sectors of our economic, social, cultural, and military life. It is the developing salience of information that has raised the profile of the infosphere.

Of course mankind has always been aware of the existence and value of information. Information has always been an important resource. In warfare, knowledge of the whereabouts and disposition of enemy forces has always been important. Field-Marshal Slim was acutely aware of the value of information support during his campaign in Burma. He noted that a major difference between the Allies and Japanese during the early period of Japanese success, was that the Japanese had ample information, whereas 'It is no exaggeration to say that we had practically no useful or reliable information of the enemy strength, movements, or intentions.'[17]

An appreciation of information goes back even further into strategic history. One of the most prominent expositions of this is Sun Tzu's *The Art of War*, written in fourth century BC China.[18] But information may now become more directly important in war. Once foot soldiers of the Roman Republic joined battle, the outcome would be decided more by their fighting skills, morale, and leadership, than directly by their access to information, aside from the rudimentary information collected by their organic senses. The same can still be said about the infantryman of today. However, many of the weapon systems of the information age rely more directly on information to function effectively. The most obvious examples are munitions which rely upon the Global Positioning System (GPS) for their guidance. Better information gives many of these weapons the edge.

Increasingly, operations in warfare gradually may be determined more by access to information. The central role of information in warfare has been advocated strongly by Martin Libicki, who argues that as a result of the development of information technology, warfare will cease to be a force-on-force experience, and will increasingly be characterised by hide-and-seek, with the seekers having the edge. Information is also central to many current operational developments, including concepts such as the US Navy's 'Network-Centric Warfare', and the broader drive towards the digitisation of forces.[19]

To conclude, the greater exploitation of the infosphere is analogous to the exploitation of the air dimension this century. The third dimension has always played a role in warfare, mainly through the transmission of vocal or percussion commands, or as the medium through which projectiles travel. However, it took the invention of heavier-than-air machines to lead to a far greater exploitation of this dimension of strategy. Similarly, it may have taken the broader exploitation of the electromagnetic spectrum, and in particular the emergence of cyberspace, to realise fully the potential of information power.

CONTROL OF THE INFOSPHERE

A dominant operational concept in the air and sea environments is gaining command of the particular dimension of strategy. Douhet defines command of the air as: '[To] have the ability to fly against an enemy so as to injure him, while he has been deprived of the power to do likewise'.[20] Most of the air power theorists stress that command of the air is a vital prerequisite to other operations. Douhet theorised that complete command could be obtained through the destruction of enemy air assets, preferably whilst they were still on the ground.[21] Gaining 'total' command of the global infosphere, *à la* Douhet, is a highly unlikely prospect. To reach such a state, all potential enemies would have to be denied the use of all their information assets. Whereas an enemy air power has a relatively limited quantity of physical assets upon which his air power is based, the assets required to operate a form of information power are numerous. Also, because some of these assets come under the ownership of the civilian sector, and many are shared, excluding an adversary from the global infosphere is extremely difficult. The connections underlying the Internet are a prime example of how some information power assets are shared.

In line with Sir Julian Corbett's theory of sea power, at the global level the infosphere will commonly remain in an uncommanded state.[22] In fact it may prove disadvantageous to deny completely an enemy the use of his information assets. Certain information power activities require the existence of a functioning enemy information infrastructure. The more insidious acts of information power, such as cultural warfare, semantic attacks (which degrade the integrity of enemy information), intelligence gathering, and deception, all require a functioning enemy information infrastructure. The same applies to various acts of Strategic Information Warfare (SIW). In this sense, to facilitate an effective information power campaign for oneself, and deny the same to the adversary, an actor may want selectively to destroy some of the enemy's assets, or none at all. Such considerations are of course circumstantial and depend upon the campaign's objectives. Even on the battlefield, certain actions – such as deception – will require the existence of some enemy information assets. In this way, an information campaign is less about attaining command through the destruction of enemy assets, and is more about *control* of the infosphere. Control of the infosphere can be defined as *the ability to use the infosphere for the furtherance of strategic objectives, and the ability to prevent the enemy from doing the same (in an effective manner).* The qualification in brackets refers to the difficulties of completely preventing the enemy from utilising his information assets. In this respect the best that can be hoped for is to limit the strategic efficacy of his information power. 'Control of the infosphere' denotes a situation in which an actor is able to control information and its flow, and bend the infosphere to serve his strategic objectives. In this vein, one may not wish to destroy an enemy's information assets, but rather control what information can flow through, from, or into them.

With the difficulties of securing global command of the infosphere in mind, it is useful to look to the work of Corbett and John Warden III. Both of these theorists refine the concept of command. They both recognise that command does not have to be either 'total' or 'permanent'.[23] As already noted, to achieve command of the global infosphere will prove difficult, even on a temporary basis. However, command of the infosphere may be more possible at the local battlefield level, although 'control' is still a more appropriate term even in this context.[24] This level of control may be slightly qualified in the future by cellphones, computers with direct satellite links, and civilian information sources (SPOT satellite images can be acquired from the Internet).[25] Although, of course, being able to report back enemy positions via a cellphone is a far less potent use of information power than a real-time sensor-to-shooter relationship. As Joseph S. Nye Jr, and William A. Owens postulate 'some kinds of information, the accurate, timely, and comprehensive sort, are more valuable than others'. Having an information edge can matter.[26] In this sense, an actor operating with the more potent form of information power should be able to get inside the enemy's decision-making cycle, and thereby hold the advantage.

The 1991 Gulf War illustrates the value of having 'control' of the fifth dimension. The coalition forces possessed information dominance, and were able to wage acts of political and psychological warfare, as well as acts of deception against the Iraqis. The coalition forces selectively destroyed Iraqi communications architecture, leaving some nodes intact. As the Republican Guard forces began to move, and their land line communications became less useful, the Iraqis resorted to transmitting through radio communications. This latter form of communication is far easier to intercept. Leaving some enemy information assets intact paid dividends for the coalition.[27] The unqualified level of military victory for the coalition forces emphasises that an asymmetry of information power can be decisive, particularly if it results in control of the infosphere.[28]

The most important point to come from the above discussion is that the term 'command' is perhaps inappropriate to describe strategic relationships within the infosphere. The complexities of ensuring one's own use of the infosphere and denying the same to an adversary, allied to the requirement of a functioning enemy information infrastructure to facilitate certain information operations, suggests that *control* of the infosphere may be a more appropriate concept. Of course like command, control of the infosphere is never likely to be either total or permanent. But as already noted by Nye and Owens, having an information edge can confer significant advantages.

THE ACCESSIBILITY OF INFORMATION POWER

Information power is simply that form of strategic power that operates in or through the infosphere. The primary characteristics of information power are its flexibility and accessibility. The combination of these two characteristics endows information power with plenty of potential in the strategic world. Information power can be used in the following operations: Intelligence gathering; terrorism; strategic warfare; symbolic raids; small wars; political and cultural warfare; economic warfare; Operations Other Than War (OOTW); logistic support; interdiction; and in the direct support of conventional military operations.

The accessibility of information power is predominately the result of the very low entry costs required to engage in certain activities within the infosphere. These low costs enable small actors to operate reasonably effectively in the fifth dimension. This is not an entirely unique characteristic. Smaller actors can also operate significantly in the other dimensions of strategy. Terrorists or insurgents can of course operate with varying degrees of success in the physical world. Furthermore, relatively smaller powers can also employ sea power. As Colin S. Gray notes, a *guerre de course* can make a mockery of maritime surface command.[29] It is worth noting that groups such as the Tamil Tigers have been able to utilise sea power.[30] However, it is generally fair to say that a smaller actor exercising information power effectively can exert leverage more potently than is often the case in the other dimensions. Two recent events provide vivid examples of this. In 1996 the US General Accounting Office (GAO) released details of how attackers had temporarily seized control of computer systems that support US logistics.[31] In a similar vein, in the June 1997 exercise 'Eligible Receiver', National Security Agency computer specialists attacked their own country's computer systems, and allegedly could have shut down the command and control structure of Pacific Command as well as the entire electrical infrastructure of the United States.[32]

There are non-state actors who are defined and exist as strategic actors almost entirely due to cyberspace. Often these groups can only function effectively within the realms of the infosphere. Certain hacking groups fall into this category. Groups such as these operate predominantly in the Global Information Environment (GIE). However, the interaction between the GIE and the Military Information Environment (MIE) is such, that they could potentially influence matters on the battlefield to some degree. An important point to note is that *a little information power goes a long way*. This maxim emanates from the level of global interconnections in cyberspace, and the dependence of some actors upon these connections and the information flow they facilitate. This means that a small actor using information power has both global reach and the opportunity to engage in various kinds of information power activities, including political warfare, interdiction, and economic warfare, to name just three. The information age produces a reach and power almost unparalleled for sub-state actors.

Importantly, these smaller actors do not possess many of the assets specific to an information campaign in the MIE. It is important to distinguish between those who operate and are competent in the GIE, and those powers who are also competent in the MIE. And yet, the use of information power in the MIE is not restricted to powers such as the United States. General Muhammad Aideed's forces in Somalia were noted to have displayed a high degree of competence in using information assets (including cellphones), which kept them appraised of the movement of US forces. The American experience in Somalia reveals that although having a plethora of advanced information assets is generally a good thing, successful strategic performance relies on far more than just this.

THE ADVANTAGES AND LIMITATIONS OF INFORMATION POWER

Like the other forms of strategic power, operating in the fifth dimension has both advantages and limitations. When assessing the significance of information power for geopolitics and the fate of the physical dimensions, it is important to note the advantages and limitations of this form of power. The overall significance of information power is directly related to its strategic efficacy.

Information power presents several advantages for the user. First, some of the assets required to engage in acts of information power are relatively cheap to acquire. Internet ready computers are a case in point. Computers are not only inexpensive, they are also multi-role items in information power. They can be used for a range of operations including information denial; interdiction; economic warfare; semantic attacks; political and cultural warfare; intelligence gathering; SIW; and cyberterror. Information power can also be projected globally far more easily than other forms of power. Information power is also particularly good for covert activities.

Information power acts as a force multiplier across the spectrum of military activities. It has evolved into an essential companion to modern combat forces. Securing some level of control of the infosphere will help enable fast and effective command and control of forces; accurate and timely logistics; good reconnaissance of the battlefield; and in a more direct relationship, information power can vastly enhance the effectiveness of firepower, with real-time target information and precision strikes. By degrading an enemy's information power to a point where information dominance is achieved, offensive information operations can give friendly forces a war-winning edge. Control also paves the way for acts of political and psychological warfare, and acts of deception.

For an actor facing a conventionally superior force, information power may provide the means to engage in asymmetrical strategies. These strategies may include information denial; political warfare campaigns; or cyberterror. Even for a very significant military actor, information power offers a host of less-lethal and less-direct options which could prove less contentious in certain contingencies. In this context information power could take the form of information aid to an ally, as an alternative to sending military forces. This could prove useful in a counter-insurgency operation, and also suits the requirements for post-heroic warfare. In those circumstances in which military force is required, information power could provide greater accuracy and therefore less collateral damage, and consequently less controversy.[33] In essence, possessing information power endows an actor with greater flexibility and an increased range of instruments through which to pursue strategic objectives.

However, information power offers no panacea. Its limitations must be kept in mind. For instance, some of the assets of modern information power are vulnerable. Recent wargames have highlighted the possible future vulnerability of US space systems.[34] Some commentators have also noted the potential future vulnerability of large platform sensors such as the Airborne Warning and Control System (AWACS) and the Joint Surveillance and Targeting Attack Radar System (JSTARS).[35] And of course an Electromagnetic Pulse (EMP), the bogeyman of the information age, poses a general threat to many of the modern assets of information power.

As a general point, Major General W. J. P. Robins notes that no information is ever complete and up to date, and therefore it is important to be aware of its limitations.[36] There are times when of course information will be up to date and complete, but General Robins' point is well taken. It is also worth remembering that as both Sun Tzu and the history of strategy remind us, deception by the enemy will often degrade the utility of information. Again, being aware of these limitations of information is wise counsel.

An information power campaign is complicated by the civilian and shared nature of some of its assets. This produces a level of unpredictability which may make information power less controllable at times. Of course this complication can be an advantage depending upon the user and his objectives. An information warrior operating in cyberspace may welcome the complexity of interconnections to hide his presence and activities. Another problem of being deeply interconnected is the potential for cascading effects of an information attack. For example, an ill-conceived worm attack against enemy information systems may return to one's own systems over the global network. In this way, information power can be misused, and it can bite back.

THE CONTINUED ROLE OF PHYSICAL FORCES

There are more fundamental limitations to the strategic efficacy of information power. If the information revolution is to make physical geography and its relationships increasingly unimportant, then by implication it must make physically-based military forms of power irrelevant. Otherwise, if strategic objectives are still pursued through the use of traditional military forces, then physical geographical factors will still be relevant. Troops and equipment will need to be transported, in which case physical geography and distance matters. Also, the effects of terrain and the weather will still matter in the conduct of operations.

There are two main ways in which the information revolution may render traditional forms of military power and geography obsolete. First, information may become the dominant factor in warfare, to the point at which information dominance may be the defining war-winning characteristic. Martin Libicki postulates that information assets will create such visibility that offensive operations cease to be practicable.[37] In this way information power attains such dominance as to make physical expressions of power all but obsolete. Alternatively, one belligerent in a conflict may have such obvious information dominance allied to precision guided munitions, that victory becomes inevitable. It is not inconceivable, in permissive conditions, for a conflict to end once information dominance has been achieved. Even Clausewitz, who was a great believer in the deciding battle, recognised that there could be times when the odds prior to battle were so decisive that one side would capitulate.[38]

However, more often than not information power will act in concert with the other expressions of strategic power. Information power still needs air, land, or sea forces to destroy the targets it has identified, or physically to move supplies and troop deployments. Although, as an aside, it is important to note that the technique of 'chipping' can disable an enemy system or vehicle without the intervention of the other forms of strategic power.[39] In the Gulf War of 1991 it took the physical destruction and removal of ground forces to achieve the coalition's objectives. Iraq's forces did not capitulate in the face of the coalition's obvious information dominance. Also, the attainment of information dominance may require the destruction of enemy information assets. This will more often than not require the utilisation of physically-based forces.

In response to Michael Vlahos' article 'The War After Byte City', Ryan Henry and C. Edward Peartree correctly point out that even if Byte City becomes a reality, countries like the United States are still going to be required to fight in physical places like Mogadishu.[40] This only serves to emphasise the point that information power will exist alongside its physical cousins, not replace them. Echoing this, Robert O. Keohane and Joseph S. Nye Jr note that 'soft power', for which information power is ideally suited, may at times require the application of 'hard power'. The example they use is that of military force being required to seize a radio station from which soft power can be generated.[41] This is not to underestimate the utility of information power, but merely to note that it is but one instrument of strategy alongside the others. Often the best results will come from a combination of these instruments.

The requirement to combine information power with the other instruments of strategy is nowhere better illustrated than in holding the high ground. The exploitation of the third and fourth dimensions this century leaves the high ground most potently composed of the air and space environments. Richard Szafranski and Martin C. Libicki make a strong case that the infosphere must now be regarded as the high ground.[42] It may be more appropriate for the fifth dimension to be seen as the third part of the high ground equation. As a consequence, ensuring command of the high ground is an increasingly complicated task, which involves a synergistic relationship between these three dimensions. In this way, what might be called a 'high ground trinity' has developed in strategy.

Within the context of a military campaign, these three dimensions of warfare (infosphere, air, and space) are so inextricably linked, that command or control must be ensured in all of them simultaneously. Joint operations have a long history in warfare, but the relationship among these three dimensions is almost symbiotic. To lose command or control of space would seriously compromise information power, due to the inability to utilise space-based information assets. Losing command of the air would create a similar situation, due to the inability safely to deploy air-based information assets, such as JSTARS, AWACS, and Unmanned Aerial Vehicles (UAVs). Likewise, to lose information control to the enemy would undermine space and air power. An adversary with some degree of information control could interfere with satellites and their communications, or simply challenge the integrity of information across the board. Losing information control to the enemy also increases the vulnerability of space and air assets. From these thoughts we see how the trinity develops, requiring protection for all three of its dimensions. This protection demands simultaneous operations in all three dimensions to ensure some form of command or control in each of them. Therefore information power relies on more traditional forms of military power just as much as they rely on it.

The second means by which information power may render physically-based forces and environments obsolete, is through strategically successful attacks against the National Information Infrastructure (NII) of an opponent.

This form of attack is often referred to as Strategic Information Warfare (SIW). The adjective 'strategic' implies a direct cause and effect relationship between the attack and strategic victory. This form of semantics is akin to that employed in the theory of strategic bombing. In order to fulfil the promise of making geography and other forces irrelevant, SIW would have to be an independent war-winner. If this were the case, then indeed wars could well be waged solely through the infosphere, and in that respect distance and geography would begin to take more of a back seat in strategy.

Because there have been no examples of a comprehensive SIW campaign, we have no direct history upon which to draw. In which case we can look to the history of strategic bombing. The theories of these two war-forms have some significant similarities. They can both rest their hopes of victory either upon attacking the will of the enemy through massive destruction or disruption, or by attacking key nodes in order to paralyse the enemy's ability to continue the fight. As noted earlier in reference to Douhet, strategic bombing has thus far failed in its attempts to be an independent war-winning instrument of strategy.

The history of strategic bombing suggests several factors that could similarly limit the strategic efficacy of SIW. First, the context in which a campaign is conducted is critical to how effective it will prove. Some enemies may be less vulnerable to SIW than others. In the same manner in which the North Vietnamese, who were pursuing an insurgency strategy for much of the war, and had a predominately rural based economy, did not present an ideal target for the US air campaign, there will undoubtedly be enemies in the future whose lack of informational infrastructure will prove equally irksome for SIW. Context can of course also refer to political considerations. The political nature of the enemy may make them less vulnerable to coercion. Alternatively, political considerations on the part of the side conducting the SIW campaign may impose limits on the scale of the effort. In the Vietnam War, President Johnson restricted the 'Rolling Thunder' bombing campaign for two principal political reasons. First, in the early stages of the campaign Johnson wanted to limit the profile of the war so as not to detract attention from his 'Great Society' domestic programme. Second, he limited the campaign to prevent aggravating the Chinese and Soviets and thereby avert an escalation of the war.[43]

Any SIW campaign will undoubtedly suffer from what Clausewitz termed 'friction'.[44] Put simply, things will go wrong, with the result that the outcome will be somewhat short of that intended. Strategic bombing has also revealed that rather than destroying the morale of the target population, attacks have often strengthened the resolve of the society under attack. Industrial age economies have also proved to be far more resilient than the theorists assumed. There is no reason to believe that these observations should not prove the same for information age economies and societies. The early airpower theorists also underestimated the potential for those under attack to develop effective defences and countermeasures, which once again helped limit the success of bombing campaigns. What Edward Luttwak describes as the 'paradoxical logic of strategy' dictates that an effective weapon or war-form will eventually be countered.[45] To believe that this logic will not apply to information power activities is naive. In short, it is unlikely that SIW will generally be converted into an independent theory of victory. Within the SIW literature there is often reference to a potential electronic Pearl Harbor. In response, it is worth remembering that the United States recovered from the real physical Japanese attack in 1941, and went on to win the Pacific War.

From the above discussion it has been suggested that information power is unlikely to provide an independently successful tool of strategy. In which case the more traditional physically-based instruments of strategy will still play an important role. However, it has also been shown that by utilising the infosphere a wide variety of actors, both big and small, can project power globally without reference to established geographic realities. So what does this all mean for geopolitics?

GEOPOLITICS AND THE FIFTH DIMENSION

As noted in the introduction, several writers foresee revolutionary implications for geopolitics. Walter B. Wriston unequivocally states that 'Information technology has demolished time and distance.'[46] Likewise, Jessica T. Mathews argues that the information revolution is bringing a novel redistribution of power, which reduces the importance of proximity and endows non-state actors with unprecedented levels of power.[47] Some of these observations seem to have some basis. For example, information power is extremely accessible, and to reiterate, *a little information power goes a long way.* In relation to acts of SIW, interdiction, economic warfare, and political warfare, small actors and even individuals have seldom had such readily available capabilities. Overall it seems credible to suggest that these characteristics of information power will have geopolitical implications. The important questions are how much influence, and how will it manifest itself? What follows is a speculative assessment of why, and in what ways, the information age may or may not affect geopolitics.

Geopolitically the information age may create somewhat of a paradox. On the one hand it may encourage states to become involved more readily in issues and crises regardless of their relative geographic position.

Alternatively it may lead to a more isolationist stance. Back in 1968 Albert Wohlstetter noted that technological advances in transportation and telecommunications results in an extension of the neighbourhood, which brings increased chances for both cooperation and conflict. A state's interests become more global as cultural, capital, and economic exchanges increase.[48] Alongside the fact that a state may have greater interest in events which are not geographically contiguous to it, information power may also present an actor with a greater capacity to become involved in external matters. Sending military forces into a crisis zone is often an expensive and risky undertaking, and can prove politically controversial. Information power presents the opportunity to influence events without direct presence and in a more discreet manner.

In contrast, being vulnerable to certain information power activities may make states more wary of becoming involved. The vulnerability of a state's NII to information attack, or the prospect of widespread political warfare campaigns against the involvement of the state in an external matter, could propel foreign policy towards an isolationist mode. Of course such considerations are heavily influenced by the context in which they take place. The issue involved may be of such import that a state is willing to accept the adverse effects of an information power campaign. Also, a state may have developed effective countermeasures or counter-information campaigns in order to limit the damage.

Ultimately, when considering the broad implications of technological developments on geopolitics, it is crucial to remember Luttwak's theory that countermeasures will be developed which limit the long-term influence of any successful strategy or instrument. Desmond Ball regards the development of these countermeasures as inevitable, in which case the conclusions of any technological development have only passing relevance.[49] Martin Libicki has suggested that each new medium brings with it a new geographical logic which dominates and transforms the old media. He cites the exploitation of the air environment as an example of this. Libicki suggests that the significance of this lies in the fact that the British Isles could be attacked regardless of the fleet, which had traditionally acted as the ultimate protector against homeland attacks.[50] In response to this, it is important to remember the previous discussion regarding the failure of airpower to effect an independent strategic victory. Also, it should be noted that the fleet still played a critical role in that it prevented the Germans from mounting an invasion of Britain during World War II, in which case the logic of the old medium (the sea) still mattered. Finally, the British development of a countermeasure, in the form of an integrated air defence system, helped limit the ability of the air environment to change the geopolitical logic of Europe fundamentally.

Historically, even technologies which might at first appear to change the prevailing geopolitical logic quite dramatically, have not ultimately rendered physical geography, and consequently the established geopolitical environment, irrelevant. Even under the potentially geopolitically-ambivalent nuclear shadow, traditional geographic concerns still played their part. Again this reveals that although certain technological developments can affect the geopolitical world they do not necessarily make all aspects of the previous environment obsolete. For example, Desmond Ball reminds us that geography still pervades nuclear matters. One particular case is the lack of suitable bases for the Soviets' ballistic missile nuclear submarines (SSBN) force. The absence of these bases meant that Soviet SSBNs had to pass through chokepoints en route to the open seas, which made them easier to track for NATO.[51] Therefore, physical geography can influence even nuclear matters.

Geography pervades the nuclear field in another related manner. Where an enemy missile is launched from has significant implications for the command and control of nuclear forces. Shorter flight times for delivery systems can make quite a difference. As Ashton B. Carter has noted, Soviet SLBMs reduced the time-scale for nuclear operations to 15 minutes or less. This increased the likelihood of US nuclear forces, especially its bombers, being caught on the ground in a Soviet first strike. In these examples, although ICBMs and SLBMs made geographical distance less of an obstacle to the projection of force, they did not make distance nor geography irrelevant. Far from it, these factors were critical in nuclear operations.

During the Cold War, geopolitical concerns which could trace their origins to a time before nuclear-armed ICBMs, still held sway. The American involvement in Vietnam was an expression of a containment policy which owed much to Mackinder's theories on the heartland. In this sense, some conflicts are fought for reasons unrelated to the dominant technology of the period. Although the shadow of nuclear weapons influenced how the United States conducted the war, the conflict was not fought over issues relating to nuclear weapons, *à la* Cuba in 1962. The point being made is that Vietnam was fought because of a logic which owed nothing to nuclear concerns. Also, the forces used were conventional and physically-based, and therefore physical geopolitics still mattered, as did geographic issues such as terrain and weather.

It is also important to bear in mind the broader strategic limitations of any particular dimension of strategy. The maritime environment is certainly critically important to many countries, and plays a central role in the world's transportation and trading activities. But Colin Gray is undoubtedly right when he notes that sea power is only relevant to how it affects the main area of human dwelling, the land.[53] Gray extends this logic to the information age, and in response to Martin Libicki's claim that cyberspace is placeless, Gray claims that humans are not placeless because they exist in a geographic reality.[54] The same can of course also be said for the natural resources humans rely upon. To produce strategic leverage, information power must significantly influence the physical world. As has been argued here, to achieve such influence will more often than not require the aid of physically-based forms of power.

Finally, it is important not to become deterministic with regards to geopolitics and technology. Albert Wohlstetter is right when he points out that being able to project power to a certain area or actor, does not mean you have to do so.[55] When thinking about geopolitics we should not forget the 'politics' side of the equation. There has to be some policy rationale for utilising information power against, or in support of, someone. Simply being able to project power in real-time and on a global scale, does not mean that you will do so.

CONCLUSIONS

Although not wholly recognisable as a physical environment, the infosphere does constitute a fifth dimension of strategy. Ultimately, a form of strategic power can be projected within and through it. Information power is an extremely flexible instrument. It is also certainly true that the information age empowers non-state actors in ways we have not seen before. As a consequence of its flexibility, ubiquity, and accessibility, it is hard to imagine a strategic actor performing well in the twenty-first century without understanding and taking account of information power. The broader geopolitical implications of the fifth dimension are directly dependent on how effective information power can be in the means-ends world of strategy. At times, and in certain cases, information power may prove to be independently sufficient to achieve policy objectives. This may be the case in the transfer of reconnaissance information to an ally. But in many instances information power will have to act in concert with the other physical instruments of power. This results primarily from the fact that humans exist and operate in the physical world. As a result, physical geography continues to matter both in military and geopolitical terms. Because geography matters, distance and proximity will also continue to play an important role. In addition it is worth remembering that the infosphere and information are being territorialised. Rather than being an environment which is ambivalent to the traditional geopolitical reality, the infosphere will partially reflect it.

Also, as Keohane and Nye remind us, the information revolution can enhance the potency of a state's conventional military power. In fact Keohane and Nye go further, and correctly note that the geographically-based nation states will continue to structure politics in the information age. They may be less accurate however when they suggest that the nation states will rely more on information and less on material resources.[56] It is a mistake to raise the significance of information above the other instruments of power. States in general will base their power in all the dimensions of strategy as befits their particular situation and the circumstances of the time.

Ultimately, strategy is a complex beast. The twenty-first century strategic and geopolitical environments will not be solely determined by any one dimension or form of power. The only one which could make such a claim is the physical land environment on which humans live. In the end, the expressions of power in the other dimensions must be able to exert leverage into this most basic of environments.

But the geopolitical landscape will change, because a form of strategic power (information power) can be projected globally without recourse to physical geography. However, the limitations of information power, allied to the basic dominance of physical geography, suggests that the new geopolitical reality will reflect physical geography at least as much as it will reflect the infosphere.

NOTES

1. Walter B. Wriston, 'Bits, Bytes, and Diplomacy', *Foreign Affairs* 76/5 (Sept./Oct. 1997) p.172 of pp.172–82.
2. The following works variously include some of these ideas: Martin Libicki, 'The Emerging Primacy of Information', *Orbis* 40/2 (Spring 1996) pp.261–76; Michael Vlahos, 'The War after Byte City', *The Washington Quarterly* 20/2 (Spring 1997) pp.39–72; Jessica T. Mathews, 'Power Shift', *Foreign Affairs* 76/1 (Jan./Feb. 1997) pp.50–66.
3. Halford J. Mackinder, *Democratic Ideals and Reality* [1919] (NY: Norton 1962). Ciro Zoppo also notes that geography, technology and power politics are intrinsically related. See Ciro E. Zoppo, 'Classical Geopolitics and Beyond', in idem and Charles Zorgbibe (eds.) *On Geopolitics: Classical and Nuclear* (NATO ASI Series, Dordrect: Nijhoff 1985).
4. The Midland Ocean was to comprise a strategic reserve in North America, an aerodrome in Britain, and a beachhead in France. The similarity of this concept to NATO is interesting.
5. Giulio Douhet, *The Command of the Air* [1921] (London: Faber 1943).
6. For an exploration into the means-ends relationship, good places to start are, Carl von Clausewitz, *On War* (London: David Campbell 1993), and also Colin S. Gray, *War, Peace, and Victory: Strategy and Statecraft for the Next Century* (NY: Simon & Schuster 1990).
7. Laurie Brettingham, *Royal Air Force Beam Benders No.80 (Signals) Wing 1940–1945* (Leicester: Midland Publishing 1997).
8. Alvin and Heidi Toffler, *War and Anti-war: Survival at the Dawn of the 21st Century* (London: Little, Brown 1994). .
9. Libicki, 'Emerging Primacy' (note 2) p.274.
10. Robert O. Keohane and Joseph S. Nye Jr, 'Power and Interdependence in the Information Age', *Foreign Affairs* 77/5 (Sept./Oct. 1998) pp.81–94.

11. History reveals a number of cases in which the other dimensions have been expanded or contracted. To take land as an example, cases can be found which show limited examples of both expansion and contraction of this dimension. During the siege of the island city Tyre in 333–332 BC, Alexander the Great constructed a 200-foot wide mole between the coast and the city. This enabled Alexander's land forces to attack the city directly. See Arther Ferrill, *The Origins of War: From the Stone Age to Alexander the Great* (London: Thames & Hudson 1985) pp.204–5. In 1672, the Dutch responded to the French invasion by opening the dikes to flood the land, and thereby hold back the invaders. See Russell F. Weigley, *The Age of Battles: The Quest for Decisive Warfare from Breitenfeld to Waterloo* (London: Pimlico 1991) p.59. These two examples show an expansion and contraction of the land environment respectively. In a less direct sense, the submarine environment could be expanded – in a strategically useful manner – through the development of vessels which can withstand higher hull pressures. This of course is not an expansion of the environment itself, it is rather an expansion of man's exploitation of it. Nevertheless, it is an expansion.
12. As Georgetown University computer science professor Dorothy Denning notes, '*The problem is that the technology leaps ahead of the security, and that's going to be with us forever*'. See John Carlin, 'The Netizen: A Farewell to Arms', *Wired* 5/5 (May 1997).
13. Libicki, 'Emerging Primacy' (note 2).
14. David Chandler, *The Campaigns of Napoleon* (London: Weidenfeld & Nicolson 1966) p.165.
15. Max Hastings and Simon Jenkins, *The Battle for the Falklands* [1983] (London: Pan Books 1997) pp.300–1.
16. See Stephen Hawking, *A Brief History of Time: From the Big Bang to Black Holes* (London: Bantam Books 1995).
17. Robert B. Asprey, *War in the Shadows*, 2nd ed. (London: Little, Brown 1994) p.419. For a full account of the campaign in Burma, see Slim's excellent account: Field-Marshal the Viscount Slim, *Defeat into Victory* (London: Cassell 1956).
18. Sun Tzu, *The Art of War* (trans. by Samuel B. Griffith) (London: OUP 1971).
19. See Martin C. Libicki, 'Technology and Warfare', in Patrick M. Cronin (ed.) *2015: Power and Progress*, http://www.ndu.edu/ndu/inss/books/2015/chap4.html See also Stacey Evers, 'US Navy Seeks Fast Track to Revolution', *Jane's Defence Weekly*, 26 Nov. 1997, pp.55–9.
20. Douhet (note 5) p.83.
21. Ibid. p.34.
22. Julian S. Corbett, *Some Principles of Maritime Strategy*, 2nd ed. (London: Longmans, Green 1919) p.77.
23. Ibid. p.89, and Col. John A. Warden III, *The Air Campaign: Planning for Combat*, Future Warfare Series, Vol.3, (Washington DC: Pergamon-Brasseys 1989) p.130. A good analysis regarding the refinement of the command of the sea concept can be found in Eric Grove, *The Future of Sea Power* (Annapolis, MO: Naval Institute Press 1990) esp. pp.12–13.
24. A useful distinction between the Global Information Environment (GIE) and the Military Information Environment (MIE) is outlined in *FM 100-6: Information Operations*. See Col. M.D. Starry and Lt. Col. C.W. Arneson Jr, 'FM 100-6: Information Operations', *Military Review* 76/6 (Nov./Dec. 1996) pp.3–15.
25. George I. Seffers, 'Army War Game Reveals Power of Commercial Data', *Defense News*, 22–28 Sept. 1997, p.44. See also Starry and Arneson (note 24).
26. Joseph S. Nye Jr and William A. Owens, 'America's Information Edge', *Foreign Affairs* 75/2 (March/April 1996) p.24 of pp.20–36.
27. See Rick Atkinson, *Crusade: The Untold Story of the Persian Gulf War* (Boston: Houghton Mifflin 1993) p.439.
28. This last point is not designed to suggest that information was the decisive factor in the conflict. Although it was an important element of the victory, other factors played their part. War is a very complex activity, and to succeed in war requires competence in many areas.
29. Colin S. Gray, *The Leverage of Sea Power: The Strategic Advantage of Navies in War* (NY: Free Press 1992) p.12.
30. This exploitation of sea power by the Tamil separatists has led Sri Lankan President Chandrika Kumaratunga to announce an upgrade of the Sri Lankan Navy. See 'Sri Lanka says navy will be upgraded to combat Tigers', *Jane's Defence Weekly*, 12 Nov. 1997, p.5.

31. Chris O'Malley, 'Information Warriors of the 609th: Air Force's 609th Information Warfare Squadron', http://www.infowar.com/mil_c4i/mil_c4i_100397a.html-ssi.
32. See Bill Gertz, 'Pentagon Fortifying Computer Networks to Block Hackers', http://www.washtimes.com/nation/nation/.html. 17 April 1998.
33. For a discussion of counter-insurgency in the information age, see A.J. Baddeley, 'Insurgency and Counter Insurgency in the Information Age', paper prepared for the BISA Annual Conference, 15–17 Dec. 1997, Univ. of Leeds. Martin Libicki also discusses the potential of providing allies with information as a means of intervention. See Libicki, 'Emerging Primacy of Information' (note 2) esp. pp.266–8. Post-heroic warfare is discussed in Edward N. Luttwak, 'A Post-Heroic Military Policy', *Foreign Affairs* 75/4 (July/Aug.1996) pp.33–44.
34. Barbara Starr, 'Wargames highlight US vulnerability in space', *Jane's Defence Weekly*, 8 Oct. 1997, p.17.
35. Libicki, 'Emerging Primacy' (note 2) p.268.
36. W.J.P. Robins, 'Information Age Operations', *RUSI Journal* 142/3 (June 1997) p.40 of pp.37-41.
37. Libicki, 'Emerging Primacy' (note 2).
38. In Book 1, Ch.1, Clausewitz states that to force the enemy to do your will, you must: '*either make him literally defenseless or at least put him in a position that makes this danger probable*'. An acknowledged information dominance is one way to make such a situation probable. Clausewitz (note 6) p.85.
39. See Winn Schwartau, *Information Warfare: Cyberterrorism: Protecting Your Personal Security in the Electronic Age*, 2nd ed. (NY: Thunder's Mouth Press 1996) esp. Ch.9, 'Chipping: Silicon-Based Malicious Software'.
40. Ryan Henry and C. Edward Peartree, 'Assessing 'Byte City': An Insightful or Misleading Vision?', *Washington Quarterly* 20/2 (Spring 1997) p.77 of pp.73–8.
41. Keohane and Nye (note 10) p.90.
42. This is a point stressed in Richard Szafranski and Martin C. Libicki, '... Or Go Down in Flame? Toward an Airpower Manifesto for the Twenty-first Century', *Airpower Journal* 10/3 (Fall 1996) pp.65–77.
43. See Mark Clodfelter, *The Limits of Air Power: The American Bombing of North Vietnam* (NY: Free Press 1989).
44. See Clausewitz (note 6) Book 1, Ch.7.
45. Edward N. Luttwak, *Strategy: The Logic of War and Peace* (Cambridge, MA: The Belknap Press of Harvard UP 1987).
46. Wriston (note 1) p.172.
47. See Mathews.
48. Albert Wohlstetter, 'Illusions of Distance', *Foreign Affairs* 46/2 (Jan. 1968) pp.242–55.
49. Desmond Ball, 'Modern Technology and Geopolitics', in Zoppo and Zorgbibe, *On Geopolitics* (note 3) p.175.
50. Libicki, 'Emerging Primacy' (note 2) p.261.
51. Ball (note 49) p.187.
52. See Ashton B. Carter, 'Assessing Command System Vulnerability', and 'Sources of Error and Uncertainty', in Carter, John D. Steinbruner, and Charles A. Zraket (eds.) *Managing Nuclear Operations* (Washington DC: Brookings 1987) pp.555–610, 611–39.
53. Gray, *Leverage of Sea Power* (note 29) p.4.
54. See Colin S. Gray, 'A Rejoinder by Colin S. Gray', *Orbis* 40/2 (Spring 1996) pp.274–76.
55. Wohlstetter (note48) p.246.
56. See Keohane and Nye (note 10) pp.88 and 94.

PART II

GEOGRAPHY AND STRATEGY: GEOPOLITICS IN ACTION

9

Inescapable Geography

COLIN S. GRAY

What does geography mean for strategy and the strategist? More manageably, perhaps, how should one think about geography in order to understand better both the permanent nature, and the ever changing character, of politics and strategy? This essay seeks answers to those questions.

We know that geography is important. Virtually every scholar and practitioner of strategy tells us so. Furthermore, if such universal and recurrent testimony were not quite sufficient, commonsense plausibility also argues for geography's salience. But, if geography matters, as all concede, how does it matter? – and, to hazard a perilously post-modern thought, what is the nature of this 'geography'? Is geography, for example, the physical reality of the hilly Ardennes forest, or is it a substantially mythical Ardennes forest of the strategic imagination, impossible of *rapid* transit by armoured forces?[1] Or, is it both? On 8 September 1914, Colonel General Alexander von Kluck expressed a renewed optimism over the prospect for a successful denouement to the invasion on the next day. John Keegan comments emphatically, if a little opaquely, '[g]eography spoke otherwise'.[2] Keegan's 'geography' is the physical geography of marshes and wooded defiles. But 'geography' can speak to mind and imagination, as well as to eye and limb. For example, a study of the German soldier in Russia in World War II emphasizes 'the foreignness of it all'.

> The history of Panzer Corps *Grossdeutschland* ... records how very early in the first campaign [1941] many men of the regiment, as it then was, were overcome with depression at the immensity of the task involved in subduing the Soviet Union and of the war which they were committed to fighting.

> The same thought occurred to many: that extending from the German front line and reaching as far as Vladivostock there existed a vast area of enemy territory wherein their regiments, indeed the whole German Army, could vanish without trace.[3]

Plainly there is the geography of space, distance, time, terrain, and weather[4] – and there is the geography of the imagination. The two are related, but frequently they are far from synonymous. Physical geography, and accepted conventions of political geography, place the British Isles unambiguously in the column of European terrain and European polities. Within those British Isles, however, 'Europe' is a continental phenomenon 'over there' beyond the moat.

To allow some social construction to 'geography', is to risk opening the flood-gates to those whose truly liberal appetite for cultural relativism encourages a most unsatisfactory tolerance for illiberal triumphs of the will (and imagination). Emphatically, this essay is not an exercise in applied critical theory.[5] Nonetheless, the meaning of geography for strategy and the strategist is both physical and psychological. Of course, physical geography matters. An exceptionally important reason why that should be so is because the often, and always partially, mythical geography of the imagination can blind us to an appreciation of what is, and what is not, practicable in the conduct of war.[6]

So habituated are we to affirmations of the importance of geography for strategy, and so unarguable are those claims, that the theory explaining why and how geography really counts is, in effect, missing in action. Interesting, let alone plausibly convincing, theory about the meaning of geography for strategy, sadly is absent. There is much geopolitical theory about grand spatial relations, and there is even more geographical writing about the conditions which must constrain strategic behaviour. There is extant, however, next to no general theory which helps us understand the several ways in which the geographical dimension to strategy actually plays. This essay is crafted to contribute to construction of such a theory.

This discussion explains why *all politics is geopolitics*, and why *all strategy is geostrategy*. To risk exercising the pathetic fallacy, geography is interested in you, whether or not you are interested in geography. The essay proceeds to explore some distinctive meanings of geography. Most particularly, we will consider geography (1) as physical environment, or 'terrain' (of all kinds), (2) as the driver of technology for tactics, logistics, and organization, and (3) as the spatial and temporal relations that inspire rival grand theories of geopolitics. Finally, the analysis explains how geography 'plays' in what T. E. Lawrence called 'the whole house of war, in its structural aspect which was strategy'.[7]

GEOGRAPHY IS ON THE TEAM

Scholars are repelled by what seems unduly obvious. Unfortunately, much of that which truly is obvious, also is pervasive and important. 'Geography', in its many meanings, is one such obvious dimension of strategy whose very pervasiveness can thwart careful treatment. If there is a sense in which everything strategic is 'geographical', then, logically, geographical influence is both everywhere yet discernibly nowhere.

Readers may favour this or that grand geopolitical theory, or possibly no such theory at all, but whether they like it or not geography matters. Physical geography literally is inescapable. In John Collins' words, '[l]and forms constitute the stage whereon military pageants play ashore'.[8] Moreover, given that human geography must function in particular cultural space, even the geography of the imagination is inescapable. Our imaginations are, after all, 'encultured' by the civilization that dominates the geographical coordinates of our location.[9]

The argument in this essay rests upon four working propositions.

1. All politics is geopolitics.
2. All strategy is geostrategy.
3. Geography is 'out there' objectively as environment or 'terrain'.
4. Geography also is 'within us', in here, as imagined spatial relationships.

Gearóid Ó Tuathail is right when he claims that '[a]ll concepts have histories and geographies and the term "geopolitics" is no exception'.[10] I suggest that the historical baggage that is the colourful past of geopolitics should be treated with respect for both its contextual and inherent interest, but it should not be regarded with fear or awe. Fear of a presumption of guilt by association, or an awestruck inability to think anew about the subject, are equally ennervating of intellectual enquiry. Ecumenical definition of geopolitics is necessary. In that regard, Geoffrey Parker provides a definition that is usefully bland and inclusive and hits some of the mark well enough. He recommends 'geopolitics as the spatial study of international relations'.[11] The problem with Parker's definition is the telling one that it confines geopolitics to the efforts of the scholar. By contrast, I prefer to define 'geopolitics as the spatial study *and practice* of international relations'. Politics and strategy can, of course, be studies. However, they happen to be quintessentially practical endeavours that are 'done' by people and institutions.[12] In this essay, at least, I am more interested in the practice of geopolitics than in its intellectual history.

The claim that all politics is geopolitics, though perhaps perilously imperial, on reflection is little more than a necessary truth. All political life has geographical referents, and all international political life is played out on a game board displaying spatial relationships which lend themselves to assertion and argument concerning alleged patterns. This is not to say that politics is *about* geography, save in the obvious sense that there is usually some geographical meaning to 'who gets what, when, and how', and neither is it to insist that politics is about spatial relations. The point in need of the clearest recognition simply is that all political matters occur within a particular geographical context; in short, they have a geopolitical dimension.

A parallel argument must be recorded for the relationship between strategy and geography. All strategy is geostrategy. Strategy is not only geostrategy, any more than politics is only geopolitics. There is a sense in which strategy is beyond particular geography. Viewed properly as effect, strategy can find its fuel provided by any instrument operating in any kind of 'terrain'. Nonetheless, strategy is always 'done' tactically by what Carl von Clausewitz called war's 'grammar', in specific geographical contexts.[13] Everyone and every organization that generates strategic effect does so on land, at sea, in the air, in space, or through cyberspace. It follows that all strategy is geostrategy. Geography cannot be an optional extra for consideration by the strategic theorist or planner, because it drives the character and the potential contemporary reach of tactical, hence operational, prowess.

The geography of the imagination is important, as this discussion already has claimed. But, social and psychological construction is ever apt to be trumped by what needs recognition as 'objective geography'. 'Constructed' views of geography will be deconstructed and, if viewholders are fortunate, reconstructed for the survivors by physical reality. In addition to the ideas about 'geography' that express hopes, fears, and ambitions, there is also the physical geography of brute distance, weather, and terrain. Of course, those geophysical matters must vary with technology in their significance for politics and strategy. However, mountains are mountains, and mud is mud. Thinking warm thoughts of home could not protect thinly-clad German soldiers in Russia against frostbite.

Finally, to repeat, as well as the 'objective geography' 'out there', one has to acknowledge the profound, though less than all-conquering, significance of the geography that we imagine or otherwise are persuaded to believe. It is useful to frame the point thus: the human mind proposes, but geography disposes. Security communities will decide and attempt missions based on their beliefs; for example, are there wells in the Sinai desert? However, objective geography will have the last word if one seeks to cross Sinai – 'a true desert' – in the mistaken belief that water can be found.[14]

The four working propositions outlined constitute the basis of my thesis that geography is inescapable. The thesis cannot be evaded by atmospheric or orbital overflight. Neither can it be retired by the growing importance of an allegedly 'placeless' cyberspace,[15] or by acts of will and journeys of the imagination. Now we must turn to the question of how geography 'works' for (and against) strategy.

THREE VIEWS OF GEOGRAPHY

Geography works for, perhaps more accurately on, strategy in at least three ways. First, it is the physical playing field for those who design and execute strategy. Both objectively providing a more or less resistant medium for strategic behaviour, and subjectively appreciated with greater or lesser accuracy, geography provides the stage for the historical drama of strategic experience. Second, as physical parameters unique to each environment, geography drives, certainly shapes, the technological choices that dominate tactics, logistics, institutions, and military cultures. Third, geography works as inspiration for the grand narrative of high theory that appears as the common understanding of geopolitics. As Parker explains:

> The principal tool of geopolitics is the political map, and its methodological approach consists in the examination of its characteristics with a view to understanding the phenomena which it reveals and the processes which have produced its morphology. The component parts of the world political scene are considered as spatial objects and their interactions as producing spatial phenomena.[16]

By making the distinctions among these three views, it is possible to recognize the true pervasiveness of geographical influence for the whole realm of strategy. Such recognition needs accomplishment, though, without surrendering precision of understanding in the face of undifferentiated evidence. The evidence of the influence of geography, therefore, can be located in the physical environments within which all strategy must be 'done'; in the machines for tactics adapted to unique physical conditions; and in the ideas, which may inspire strategic behaviour, invented to explain spatial relationships (for example, heartland, midland ocean, rimland).[17]

These three views of geography reduce to seeing geography as physical environment, as requirements for mechanical and electronic performance mandated by the tactical demands of environments, and as fuel for high theory. No-one had difficulty appreciating geography as, for example, the air we breathe, let alone as the hills that can impede military movement or hide warriors who dare not engage in regular forms of war. But, geography as physical environment and indeed probably as the principal source of distinctive military cultures, is a connection less commonly grasped. Not for nothing did Williamson Murray write that

> [T]he four [US military] services, reflecting their differing historical antecedents and the differences in the environments in which they operate, have evolved cultures that are extraordinarily different. The environmental influences are particularly important to any understanding of the peculiar cultures that the services have developed.[18]

Murray proceeds to theorize about the environmental influences which, he argues, drive the air force and the navy respectively to a 'mechanistic approach' and ' towards a technological, engineering approach to warfare'. He suggests that as agents for land combat, the army and marine corps 'will be driven to a more Clausewitzian view of war' (which is to say, a view properly respectful of the play of friction, chance, risk, and uncertainty). A powerful argument tangential to Murray's was provided a generation ago by Rear Admiral J.C. Wylie.

> [T]he connotation of the word 'strategy' is not the same to the soldier as to the sailor or airman. The reason for this is elusive but very real. It has to do with the environment in which the concept is set.
>
> Where the sailor or airman think in terms of an entire world, the soldier at work thinks in terms of theaters, in terms of campaigns, or in terms of battles. And the three concepts are not too markedly different from each other.
>
> This state of mind in which the soldier derives his conception of the strategic scene is brought about primarily by the matter of geography. Prominent and direct in its effect is the fundamental fact of terrain. 'Terrain' as a word does not have deep meaning to the nonsoldier, but to the soldier it is everything. It is the fixed field within which he operates.[19]

Wylie and Murray tell us different things. What they have in common is sensitivity to distinctions among service-based military cultures, and suitable appreciation of the fundamental significance of geography, or geographies, for those distinctions. To function at sea and to defy gravity in the air, the sailor and the airman have to ride on, or in, environmentally unique machines. Those machines - ships and aircraft – and the distinctive geographies to which they are restricted, have inescapable tactical and operational signatures. Thus are two of our views of geography connected.

Is it true, as Murray appears to suggest, that the extreme machine dependency of air and naval forces literally mandates a 'mechanistic' and a 'technological, engineering' approach to war? He argues that the inherent complexity of land warfare allows for 'a more Clausewitzian view of war'. But, where does the balance of responsibility lie for style in war-making between an environmental fundamentalism that focuses upon the machines adapted to specific geographies, and national (including military-cultural) preferences?[20] There is a sense in which to the air strategist the whole world is a dartboard.[21] Given what can and cannot be done from altitude, the strategic effect of air war tends to reduce to the consequences of bombardment. As Giulio Douhet remarked, in aerial warfare targeting 'may be defined as aerial strategy'.[22]

Wylie and Murray complement each other wonderfully. The latter emphasizes persuasively the way in which geography influences combat style; the former stresses the physically and psychologically confining effect of 'terrain' upon the capabilities and operational ambitions of the soldier. Neither author should be taken too literally; at least, too much should not be read into the quotations offered here. Murray is not, perhaps not quite, suggesting that the *art* of war in the air and at sea has to fall victim to inescapable engineering impulses. Since his broadside of an article is levelled at the sins of the US military establishment today, plainly he has hopes that American airmen and sailors, though restricted by their technologies, can become better warriors in the future. As for Rear Admiral Wylie, in common with Murray he is deeply persuasive on the matter of the geography behind military cultures. But, just as Murray writes in hope of US military improvement – even though air and naval forces are tied to their particular high-technology chariots – so Wylie knows that soldiers *can* elevate their eyes and minds to strategic ambition further distant than the nearest hedgerow or ditch.

Wylie and Murray need to be read together. Wylie points to the global character of geographical domain entirely natural to sea, air – and now sea, air, space and cyberspace – minded people, and to the constraining pressure of a landward focus. In contrast, Murray alerts us to the geographically-derived technological character of air and naval forces, and to the engineering mindset that that technological character can encourage at the expense of appreciation of war as operational art. Each view is correct, but because it is not wholly correct, each needs balance with the other. It is the view of this essay that there is significant, though admittedly fundamentally limited, scope for warriors' discretion, even in a military world apparently dominated by feats of engineering.

Geopolitics and geopolitical theory are as inescapable as is the geography to which they must relate (however debateable the connection). Governments and individuals reason, at least think, geopolitically. We exist in geography, specifically on 'terrain', and we order our particular variant of understanding of the world with geographical references, accurate and otherwise. Geopolitical theory, provided one detaches therefrom the idea of scholarly rigour (or pretension), is as inalienable as ethics. It is human to seek a code of behaviour and to make moral judgments. It is no less human to relate our plot of terrain to other plots according to grand or modest theories. Those theories will purport to explain the strategic meaning of the apparent relations among the various plots of land and usually contiguous water.

The physical size, shapes, and distances among, politically organized 'spaces', in short *the map*, is nourishment for the breeding of geopolitical ideas or theory. The theory is indeed socially constructed, as critical theorists remind us, but so what? In the social sciences, what else could such theory be? The point is that geopolitics is not *a theory* of spatial relations, rather it comprises *theories*, certainly ideas, about those relations. To denounce a particular geopolitical grand theory – for example, the theory that strategic history is condemned to, or blessed by, a recurrence of bipolar rivalry between leading land power and leading sea power[23] – is not, *ipso facto*, to denounce geopolitics. One theory does not 'own' geopolitics. Modern social scientists do not subscribe to the scientistic Scholar's Fallacy which holds that sufficient study and applied intellect must generate the correct theory (in this case, of geopolitics). Human behaviour and misbehaviour, even when constrained by geography and enabled by technology, is much too rich in its range of possibilities to lend itself to final resolution by *the* geopolitical theory.

The impulse to theorize geopolitically stems from recognition that geography and the spatial (and by implication the temporal) relations thereto associated matter for security. Historical experience and an all but infinite cultural common sense feed us with ideas about the meaning of geography. Of course, distance is both spatial and cultural. Differences of race, religion, civilization, and history, may well count for more than does mere mileage. For example, 'the whole of the Balkans', which Otto von Bismarck once famously claimed were 'not worth the healthy bones of a single Pomeranian grenadier',[24] is both a somewhat uncertain region on the map and, at least to Britons, a legendary terrain with mythical properties of exceptional 'foreignness' and general beastliness.

When geopolitical theory severs its connection with some strictly physical geographical principle – for example, when Sir Halford Mackinder's 1904 'geographical pivot of history' keyed to landlocked or to Arctic drainage systems, evolved into the 1919 'heartland'[25] – then one is, of course, in the realm of the (strategic) imagination. It should be needless to add, perhaps, that the objective physical basis of, say, a geopolitical theory tied to drainage patterns, does not, as a result of that objective footing, bear any necessary political or strategic merit. Physical geography is always important for strategy, on occasion it may even be critically important. But geography does not necessarily, indeed does not often, literally determine strategy's course and outcome.

THE NATURE OF STRATEGY

Strategy is the product of dialogue between policy and military power. In reconciling political objectives with military objectives, the strategist must deal with a realm of great complexity and uncertainty. Policy, in a sense, must be more important than strategy, just as strategy must be superordinate to operations and tactics. Strategy would be literally senseless in the absence of policy, and no less literally it would be all vanity if operations and tactics could not 'do' it. Those relationships granted, the fact remains that strategy is both more difficult to effect competently and is more complex, than either policy or tactics. So, what is strategy 'made of' and how does geography fit in that composition?

Strategy has several, or many – as one prefers, the exact number does not matter – elements or dimensions. Clausewitz advises that there are five 'elements of strategy'. He cites 'moral, physical, mathematical, geographical, and statistical'.[26] Michael Howard located four 'dimensions of strategy', the operational, logistical, social, and technological. He contended quite plausibly in the American debate over nuclear strategy in the 1970s that the first, second, and third of those dimensions were 'forgotten'.[27] I find it useful to identify many more dimensions than did

Clausewitz and Howard; 17, no less.[28] There are, however, no substantive differences among us. Analytical purpose and convenience must determine how finely the theorist elects to wield Occam's Razor. My 17 dimensions sub-divide into three clusters: 'people and politics', 'preparation for war', and 'war proper'. (The distinction between cluster two and three is, of course, lifted gratefully from Clausewitz).[29] My third cluster of strategy's dimensions, 'war proper', includes military operations, command (political and military), geography, friction (including chance and uncertainty), the adversary, and time.

Geography is an integral element or dimension of strategy, along with society, culture, ethics, organization (defence and force planning), information and intelligence, technology, and the rest. Although 'geography' is a distinguishable dimension, it manifests itself in, and helps shape, strategy in every dimension. Two analogies illustrate the point. First, geography can be likened to just one component in the complex person-machine 'system' that performs as a car driven on the road. Just as a notable change in one of the motor system's elements – tyres, brakes, engine power, driver skill – *must* have implications for the others, so the geography specific to each individual historical conflict *must* influence the requirements placed on the other elements. The second analogy, this time of a culinary kind, makes the same point differently. Geography can be thought of as one ingredient in a complex dish (a curry, for example). We know that 'geography' is in the dish, indeed obvious 'pieces' of it may be easily identified (e.g., we can see the geography in strategy plainly in the physical environments in which the military agents contend). But, 'geography' will flavour variably every other ingredient with which it interacts.

The point is that geography is a pervasive dimension of the whole phenomenon of strategy. For a particular conflict one can enquire as to the relative significance of geography, or technology, or (quality of) command. But, the basis for such specific study has to be the dual recognition that each of strategy's dimensions (including geography) always 'plays', though not to consistent effect, and has to influence every other dimension. To discuss geography and strategy narrowly, would be akin to analyzing engine power and the motor 'system' in isolation, or the individual effect of a particular spice on a curry dish. It can be done, but it makes little sense. Readers might care to recall that a principal glory of the 'grand narrative' that is geopolitical theory (actually narratives and theories) is the generic capacity – admittedly, actual performance can fall short – of that theory to tie apparently disparate phenomena together in meaningful ways. One need hardly add that it is exactly the hugely meaningful character of geopolitical theory that has rendered it so controversial. Geopolitical theory lends itself to the telling of stories with a political message.

Geography does not determine strategy, any more than does ethics, economics, technology, or any other preferred dimension or element. The reason why this should be so is implicit in the analysis above. Geography is a team player. If each of strategy's dimensions is a 'player' in conflict, how much can it matter if the relevant geography privileges one side rather than another? In 1940, the *Wehrmacht* secured a geographical position in France and Norway for the conduct of naval war, of which German naval theorists of the interwar period could only dream.[30] Success in military operations in April–June 1940 yielded the *Kriegsmarine* U-boat bases in Norway and on the Biscay coast of France. Truly, this was maritime 'strategic geography' with a vengeance. Unfortunately for Nazi Germany, even a hugely advantageous strategic geography (as compared with 1917–18), could not compensate persistently and reliably for appalling incompetence in communications security, amateurish staff work, lack of aerial reconnaissance, and too few U-boats.

The geographical dimension to the maritime dimension to World War II mattered deeply. The changes in political geography enforced by the *Wehrmacht* in April–June 1940 secured changes in operational military geography pregnant with the possibility of decision for a submarine *guerre de course*. Alas for simplicity in theory and ease of researchability, each dimension of strategy plays upon, and through, all of the others. If one poses the elemental question, 'where is the geography in strategy?', the following is an illustrative – not intended definitive – answer:

> The geography in strategy can be found in:
>
> - The very identity of belligerents, whose status as belligerents stems noticeably from the relative location and scope of their politically organized 'space' (which has shaped their strategic history)
> - The strategic and military-cultural characteristics of polities, influenced by the variably continental, or insular, situation of their homelands.
> - The armed forces, organized largely by environment for combat (land, sea, air, space), with equipment specialized for tactical performance in unique geographies.
> - The logistic enabler which is about supply and movement through geographically different kinds of 'space'.

- The temporal dimension which always is liable to pace events through the powers of resistance of the various geographies within which armed forces must act.

Thus can we see that strategy is inherently geographical, and that even when other dimensions are examined each is subject to the influence of what fairly can be termed geographical influence. In no sense is this a claim for geography as the 'master dimension' of strategy.[31] Rather is my argument simply that geography always matters for strategic experience, and on occasion it will matter hugely. Commandant Jean Colin spoke truly for all time when he wrote:

> There is no hierarchy among the elements of war; one cannot pretend that one is more important than another. One day Napoleon said, 'Victory is to the big battalions; the next day he declared that in an army the men don't count', that 'one man is everything'. Genius triumphed over numbers at Dresden, and succumbed at Leipzig.[32]

The political geography of Central Europe enabled Prussia, then Germany, to exploit its economic geography (in the form of the *Reichsbahn*) for the purpose of waging a structure of war that it should have striven much harder to avoid: war on two (or more) fronts. Germany's excellent rail network allowed its geostrategically central location to translate as the conduct of war on those interior lines which Jomini recommended so strongly.[33] Sadly for Germany, however, the geostrategic blessings of interior lines were insufficient to compensate for inept statecraft, incompetent intelligence, and a lethal disdain for logistics, to mention but a few of Germany's recurring sins against sound strategic conduct.

Net advantage or disadvantage can attach to each of strategy's dimensions. Even if 'geography' in its several forms should yield a signal net benefit, for example for Britain in maritime competition and war, still the other dimensions could cancel the strategic effect of that benefit. British insular geography (once the Scottish 'backdoor' complication was formally neutralized by cooption in 1707) was a strong plus for British security, but that geography did require exploitation by a navy.[34]

CONCLUSION: IS THERE AN ESCAPE FROM GEOGRAPHY?

It has been said of emigrants to Canada that they fled Europe to escape history, only to find themselves overwhelmed by geography. This essay does not argue even that geography must dominate, let alone in an adversarial sense overwhelm, the labours of the strategist. It does suggest, however, that the possible constraints and frictions of space and time always must command the strategist's respect. It would not be useful to seek to expand the strategic domain of Major-General Charles E. Callwell's insightful observation that 'it is perhaps the most distinguishing characteristic of small wars [defined as wars wherein regular troops fight irregulars] as compared with regular hostilities conducted between modern armies, that they are in the main campaigns against nature'.[35] However, the limiting element in the observation lies not in the basic idea, but rather only in the qualifier, 'in the main'. If two neighbouring city states elect to settle a dispute the old fashioned way by rolling the iron dice of battle, then geography is unlikely significantly to shape the course, or noticeably to influence the outcome, of the combat. But for how many of the conflicts in strategic history can that be claimed with high confidence? The answer is not many, and that is probably an exaggeration.

The geographical element or dimension is always a 'player' in strategic history. The title of a popular British memoir of World War II by Spencer Chapman, *The Jungle is Neutral*, is both strictly accurate geographically, yet profoundly misleading geostrategically.[36] Of course, physical geography is politically 'neutral'. But, the combatant who adapts best to the terms and conditions of life and warfare in the jungle, will count that particular terrain as an ally rather than as a 'neutral' geographical stage. Geography is neutral among contending polities, but – for another example – those polities able to launch spacecraft East-about (with the Earth's rotation) from spaceports close to the equator, assuredly will enjoy a 1,600 kph kick-start towards the gravity-escape velocity needed to achieve orbit (28,000 kph), and hence must be privileged in the payload they can send aloft.

Three points conclude this discussion of the working proposition of an 'inescapable geography'.[37]

1. Clausewitz wrote all too briefly about the relationship between a logic of policy and a grammar of war. His 'grammar of war' means a grammar to strategy comprising the terms and conditions of the tactical 'doing' of the strategist's art, science, or trade. The grammar of strategy literally and inalienably is dictated by the distinctive requirements of physical geography. No matter how 'jointly' military people reason, act, and organize themselves for war, combat has to be waged on land, at sea, in the air, in space, and along and through the electromagnetic spectrum. Tactics are not wholly determined by technology; the 'art of war' allows for some discretion in how armed forces are used. But technology, at the least, is the greatest of enabling agents for tactical ideas and prowess.

Technology drives tactics, and it cannot help but be driven by the demands of particular physical conditions. The military and civil technology behind the conduct of war is a technology created for, and characteristic to, specific physical environments. It is true that the airy realm of the high strategist transcends particular geographies and, following the master, uses 'engagements [in any environment] for the object of the war'.[38] Nonetheless, what the strategist is using are the outcomes to a (tactical) grammar of war that is thoroughly shaped by the influence of geography.

2. Some possible forms of modern war appear to challenge the proposition that there is an enduring significance to strategy for geography. If a great nuclear war could be conducted in a matter of hours in large part by missiles that shrink time and space to the status of minor management details, who cares about distance and 'terrain'? For a similar thought, if cyberwar in cyberspace can be conducted instantly and globally, it may be at least apparently geographically placeless as well as mocking of time and distance.[39]

   A claim that nuclear strategy effectively occupies a region 'beyond geography' is false on at least two principal counts. First, the tactical 'doing' of nuclear strategy (for deterrence) is anything but beyond geography. Indeed, the strategic logic of the nuclear forces' 'triad' maintained by the United States and the USSR/Russia, has rested wholly on a grammar of strategy driven by the relevant operational properties of land, sea, and air.[40] Second, even if large-scale intercontinental nuclear war would take strategy in some sense 'beyond geography', it is scarcely a revelation to note that such a form of 'war' would be entirely pointless as an example of the strategist's art.

   The argument that cyberspace, and hence cyberwar, is beyond geography, suffers from one major and one minor existential flaw. The major flaw is that no matter how global and instant information combat may become, that action must connect cyberwarriors and their cyber-victims at distinct geographic reference points and with the physical 'kit' of 'combat' hardware and software. Admittedly, cyberwar in cyberspace is not war as we have known it, but it would certainly be war within geography. The minor existential flaw in the case for a geographically placeless cyberspace, is the strong probability that cyber-combat is likely to be more of an enabling adjunct to a somewhat traditional (bombs and bullets, albeit ever smarter bombs and bullets) character of war, than itself to be an independently decisive 'strategic' agent.[41]

3. Finally, critics of the relative significance of geography among strategy's many dimensions, make a valid point when they emphasize the extent to which modern technology has shrunk distance, and therefore time. Furthermore, the 'terrain' whose contours, extent, weather, and vegetation used to frustrate some of the genius of operational artistry, today can be overflown within and beyond the atmosphere in minutes, certainly in hours. Moreover, if judged expedient, terrain can be reconfigured by fuel-air and other forms of instant forceful environmental modification.

   However, to register facts of technological, and largely consequential tactical, change, is trivial in comparison with the persisting validity of the central premise to this essay. The essential error in equating speed with the 'death of geography' as a significant element in strategy, is demonstrated most readily by inviting geography's critics to cast their eyes and minds skywards. Consider the spatial, temporal, and mathematical metric of the 'light-year'. As strategic agents and as the objects of strategy, humans and their institutions are inherently geographical and geopolitical in thought and deed. Geography as space remains such, no matter how speedily we can move across it.

   To think, plan, and act globally, rather than regionally or locally, is not to transcend geography, let alone geopolitics, quite the reverse, in fact. A global (and beyond) focus is simply to conceptualize and behave for a more extensive domain. Humans may not think accurately about geography, but even geographically inaccurate thought is still geographical. Strategy and politics must be done within geography. They cannot help but be influenced by ideas, and physical constraints, that reasonably are termed geographical. Geography is inescapable.

NOTES

1. See Robert Allan Doughty, *The Breaking Point: Sedan and the Fall of France, 1940* (Hamden, CT: Archon 1990) pp.11–12.
2. John Keegan, *The First World War* (London: Hutchinson 1998) p.128.
3. James Lucas, *War on the Eastern Front, 1941–1945: The German Soldier in Russia* (London: Jane's 1979) p.33. Dept. of the Army, *Effects of Climate on Combat in European Russia*, Pamphlet No.20-291, Restricted (Washington DC: Dept. of the Army, Feb.1952); Omer Bartov, *The Eastern Front, 1941–45: German Troops and the Barbarisation of Warfare* (NY: St Martin's Press 1986); idem, *Hitler's Army: Soldiers, Nazis, and War in the Third Reich* (NY: OUP 1991); and Stephen G. Fritz, *Frontsoldaten: The German Soldier in World War II* (Lexington: UP of Kentucky 1995), are useful.
4. See John M. Collins, *Military Geography for Professionals and the Public* (Washington DC:

National Defense UP 1998), and Harold A. Winters, *Battling the Elements: Weather and Terrain in the Conduct of War* (Baltimore: Johns Hopkins UP 1998).

5. See the contribution to this special issue by Gearóid Ó Tuathail. Also idem, *Critical Geopolitics: The Politics of Writing Global Space* (Minneapolis: U. of Minnesota Press 1996). Further enlightenment can be sought from idem, Simon Dalby, and Paul Routledge (eds.) *The Geopolitics Reader* (London: Routledge 1998); Gertjan Dijkink, *National Identity and Geopolitical Visions* (ibid. 1996); and John Agnew, *Geopolitics: Re-visioning World Politics* (ibid. 1998).
6. On the importance of 'what the French call le sens du praticable' see Gen. Sir Archibald Wavell, *Generals and Generalship* (NY: Macmillan 1943) p.10.
7. T.E. Lawrence, *Seven Pillars of Wisdom: A Triumph* [1926] (NY: Anchor Books 1991) p.191.
8. Collins, *Military Geography* (note 4) p.3.
9. See Colin S. Gray, 'Strategic Culture as Context: The First Generation of Theory Strikes Back', *Review of International Studies* 25/1 (Jan.1999) pp.49–69.
10. Gearóid Ó Tuathail, 'Introduction' to idem, Dalby and Routledge, *Geopolitics Reader* (note 5) p.1.
11. Geoffrey Parker, *Geopolitics: Past, Present and Future* (London: Pinter 1998) p.7.
12. Andre Beaufré, *An Introduction to Strategy* (London: Faber 1965) p.14; Bernard Brodie, *War and Politics* (NY: Macmillan 1973) pp.452–3.
13. Carl von Clausewitz, *On War*, trans. Michael Howard and Peter Paret (Princeton UP 1976) p.605. Also see Colin S. Gray, *Modern Strategy* (Oxford: OUP 1999) Ch.1.
14. For the strategic significance of this particular example, see John Gooch, *The Plans of War: The General Staff and British Military Strategy c.1900–1916* (London: RKP 1974) pp.248–9.
15. Martin C. Libicki, 'The Emerging Primacy of Information', *Orbis* 40/2 (Spring 1996) pp.261–74.
16. Parker, *Geopolitics* (note 11) p.16.
17. Halford J. Mackinder, *Democratic Ideals and Reality* [1919] (NY: Norton 1962); Nicholas J. Spykman, *The Geography of the Peace* (NY: Harcourt, Brace 1944).
18. Williamson Murray, 'Does Military Culture Matter?' *Orbis* 43/1 (Winter 1999) p.36.
19. J.C. Wylie, *Military Strategy: A General Theory of Power Control*, (ed.) John B. Hattendorf (Annapolis, MD: Naval Institute Press 1989; repr. of 1967 ed.) pp.41–2. Collins makes the same point when he claims that '[h]igh-level strategists, airmen and astronauts see mountains and valleys, plateaus and lowland plains. Frontline soldiers, who deal with details instead of big pictures, have vastly different viewpoints – hummocks, gullies, river banks and bottoms loom large from their foreshortened perspectives'. *Military Geography* (note 4) pp.3–4.
20. For example, at the turn of the century, was the 'goose step' of the Royal Navy's deployment manoeuvres strictly mandated by the nature of ships and the sea, or was a goodly measure of military-cultural preference exercised? Much, if not all, is revealed in Andrew Gordon, *The Rules of the Game: Jutland and British Naval Command* (London: John Murray 1996).
21. See the presentation of 'the five ring system' in John A Warden III, 'Success in Modern War: A Response to Robert Pape's *Bombing to Win', Security Studies 7/2* (Winter 1997/98) esp. pp.174–85.
22. Giulio Douhet, The Command of the Air, trans. Dino Ferrari (New York: Arno Press 1972; reprint of 1942 edn.) p.50.
23. Mackinder's affection for recurring bipolar oppositions (*Democratic Ideals and Reality*) is emphasized usefully in W.H. Parker, *Mackinder: Geography as an Aid to Statecraft* (Oxford: Clarendon Press 1982) p.175. Parker, *Geopolitics* (note 11), is exceptionally clear on the point that bipolarity is only one of the organizing principles that can drive geopolitical grand theory.
24. Otto von Bismarck quoted in Gordon A. Craig, *Germany, 1866–1945* (NY: OUP 1978) p.110.
25. Compare 'The Geographical Pivot of History' with the strategic idea of the 'heartland' in the title work in Mackinder, *Democratic Ideals and Reality* (note 17).
26. Clausewitz, *On War* (note 13) p.183.
27. Michael Howard, 'The Forgotten Dimensions of Strategy', *Foreign Affairs* 57/5 (Summer 1979) pp.975-86.

28. Gray, *Modern Strategy* (note 13) Ch.1.
29. Clausewitz, *On War* (note 13) p.131.
30. See Vice Adm. Wolfgang Wegener, *The Naval Strategy of the World War* [1929], trans. Holger H. Herwig (Annapolis, MD: Naval Institute Press 1989).
31. The title to Colin S. Gray, 'The Continued Primacy of Geography', *Orbis* 40/2 (Spring 1996) pp.247–59, overreaches, though the content of the essay does not.
32. J. Colin, *France and the Next War: A French View of Modern War* (London: Hodder 1912) p.300.
33. Antoine Henri de Jomini, *The Art of War* (London: Greenhill Books 1992, repr. of 1862 ed.) pp.102, 104, 127.
34. It is worth noting that Alfred Thayer Mahan lays far more emphasis upon the need for a persistence of sound government policy, than he does upon geographical parameters. *The Influence of Sea Power upon History, 1660–1783* (Boston: Little, Brown 1890) Ch.1. 'Geography', unaided, does not bequeath naval power. N.A.M. Rodger, *The Safeguard of the Sea, A Naval History of Great Britain: Vol.1, 660–1649* (London: HarperCollins 1997) tells the same story.
35. Charles E. Callwell, *Small Wars: A Tactical Textbook for Imperial Soldiers* (London: Greenhill Books 1990, repr. of 1906 ed.) p.44.
36. F. Spencer Chapman, *The Jungle is Neutral* (London: Chatto 1949). See J.P. Cross, *Jungle Warfare: Experiences and Encounters* (London: Guild 1989).
37. On the geography of space questions, see Michael J. Muolo, *Space Handbook : An Analyst's Guide, AU-18* (Maxwell AFB, AL: Air University Press Dec. 1993).
38. Clausewitz, *On War* (note 13) p.129.
39. Libicki, 'Emerging Primacy of Information' (note 15) p.274.
40. David Miller, *The Cold War: A Military History* (London: John Murray 1998), Part II, presents the basics, while for an explicitly environmental thesis *contra* nuclear war, see Carl Sagan and Richard Turco, *A Path Where No Man Thought: Nuclear Winter and the End of the Arms Race* (London: Century 1990).
41. See the discussion in Lawrence Freedman, *The Revolution in Strategic Affairs*, Adelphi Paper 318 (London: IISS April 1998) Ch.4.

10

Weather, Geography and Naval Power in the Age of Sail

N. A. M. RODGER

The tyranny of lines on a map distorts historians' understanding of the realities of warfare in the age of sail. Half-remembered school atlases marking steamer tracks and air routes as straight lines across the empty oceans persuade modern scholars that distances can be measured simply by laying a ruler across a map. Maps themselves commonly mark the sea as an unbroken expanse of blue stretching from coast to coast, as indeed it seems when viewed from a cliff or an aeroplane, revealing nothing of the shoals and tides which in reality constrain the movements of ships in coastal waters.

Shoals and tides are with us yet, but in the age of sail there were two more equally fundamental factors which limited the free movements of sailing vessels. The first of these was the extreme difficulty of making progress against the wind. For practical purposes no ship[1] could point higher than six points (67½°) off the wind, to which must be added at least another point of leeway to arrive at distance made good. This meant that it was always difficult and often impossible to win any ground to windward without a favourable tide or current. Added to the strain on crew and gear of constant beating, this meant that ships did not normally attempt to work to windward for any considerable distance except in emergency. Usually they awaited a fair wind; one on or abaft the beam was best for most ships, but a following wind was perfectly satisfactory. This gave an enormous strategic importance to those anchorages, safely and easily entered, and cleared when the wind shifted, in which shipping might anchor to await a fair wind.

By the far the most important of these in the British Isles was the Downs off Sandwich (see Map 1, p.180), the focal anchorage used by the shipping of London, East Coast ports and most of the North Sea ports when waiting for an easterly wind; control of this anchorage alone helped England to control the deep-sea commerce of the Netherlands, Denmark and other countries to the eastward. In the words of James II, 'our situation proper to command all trades going through our seas to and from the northern parts of the world, and the plenty and quality of our ports, are the principal real advantages above our neighbours'.[2] In a dead calm or light airs, ships might make progress by working the tides: drifting with the favourable stream and anchoring at the turn of the tide. This was often done during the Anglo-Dutch Wars (1652–74), mostly fought in summer in the Narrow Seas (the upper part of the Channel and the south-western corner of the North Sea), and it was the means by which the Allied fleet withdrew after the defeat of Beachy Head in 1690, but the time and effort required to weigh anchor by manpower ruled it out in deeper water.

The great difficulty of beating to windward not only imposed numerous delays, and forced ships to make passages by roundabout routes in search of fair winds, but made all approaches to the land, or shoal water, inherently dangerous. The nightmare of every seaman under sail was the lee shore, for if the wind blew towards the land there were many circumstances in which there was grave danger of shipwreck. At night or in thick weather a ship might be on or very near the coast before being aware of it, and unable to claw off. It was easy to become 'embayed'; trapped between two headlands neither of which the ship could weather. Then the anchors were the only hope, but in an onshore gale they were not likely to hold. Even if the wind were blowing offshore and the coast could be closed in relative safety, the wind might shift much faster than the ship could gain an offing. For all these reasons seamen constantly sought sea room, and regarded any approach to the land as their most dangerous moment. Unfortunately it is impossible to make port without approaching the land, and all sorts of naval operations repeatedly called for warships to put themselves in harm's way by working close inshore.

Navigational conditions, interacting with national traditions of warship design, had a large effect on the course of the Dutch Wars. The Straits of Dover, the Thames Estuary and the south-western quarter of the North Sea are shoal everywhere and much of the area is occupied by sands which dry or break at low water, and could not be crossed even at high water by the larger ships of the English fleet. Very few of these shoals were marked, and in wartime those buoys which existed might be removed or misplaced. Even if the sky were clear, observations accurate to 20 or 30 miles were useless in an area where the pilot often needed to know his whereabouts to within a few cables.[3] In any case it was pointless attempting to plot positions on charts which were grossly unreliable. In 1673 Sir John Narborough found the Dogger Bank laid down between 24 and 36 miles too far south and the charted soundings everywhere erroneous.[4] With the exception of the cliffs of Kent and the Blackness and Whiteness (Capes Gris Nez and Blanc Nez) east of Calais, the coasts surrounding the southern North Sea are low-lying, and the best seamarks are windmills and church steeples visible no more than ten miles off at best.

In these waters local knowledge and constant sounding were the pilots' only recourse, and out of sight of land they were frequently mistaken. English ships often ran aground through mistaking their positions in familiar waters. At the Battle of the Kentish Knock in 1652 two of Admiral Robert Blake's ships went aground on that shoal. The *Prince Royal* was lost on 3 June 1666, during the Four Days' Battle, when she ran on the Galloper. In 1682 on his passage to Scotland the Duke of York nearly lost his life when the *Gloucester* was wrecked on the Leman Bank off Yarmouth.[5]

MAP 1
THE THAMES ESTUARY

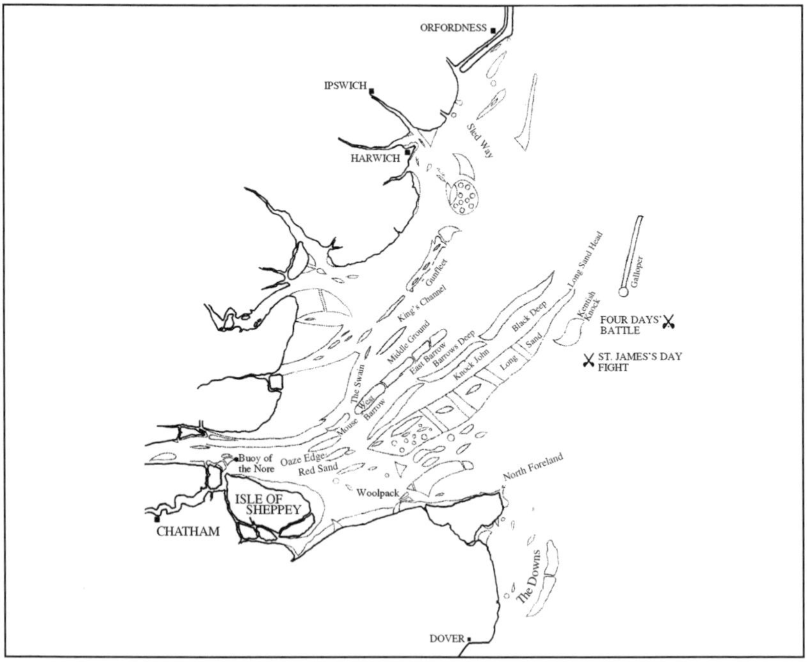

Source: J.R. Powell and E.K. Timings (eds.) *The Rupert and Monck Letter Book, 1666* (London: Navy Records Society Vol.112, 1969) facing p.288.

For both sides the strategic situation was dominated by the navigation of their coasts, and the approaches to their ports. The Thames Estuary, which looks like a large expanse of open water on a land map, is actually open only to small craft at high water in good weather. Most of the estuary is filled with sands which form a pattern of ridges separated by narrow channels, lying roughly parallel with the Essex shore. The King's Channel, the nearest to that coast, was until modern times the usual deep-water channel. It extends roughly north-east and south-west, from the Nore at the junction of Thames and Medway, to the anchorage north of the Gunfleet shoal and east of the Naze. The outer anchorage of a fleet sailing from the Thames was the Gunfleet. From here it could sail northward, keeping to seaward of the Shipwash; or southward, rounding the Long Sand Head and keeping outside the Kentish Knock; or eastward, towards the Dutch coast, avoiding the Inner Gabbard and the Galloper which partially block that course. Here too the resources of the small naval yard at Harwich were available. The Gunfleet was safe in most weather conditions, and covered the mouth of the Thames, but the shoals to the north and south-east made it difficult to clear the anchorage on an easterly wind.

The Barrows Deep, parallel to the King's Channel and just to the south, was surveyed in 1666 and occasionally used[6] (for which reason the Dutch plan in 1673 to bottle up the English fleet in the Thames by sinking blockships in the narrowest part of the King's Channel would probably not have worked)[7] but the only other common entrance to the Thames was parallel to the Kentish shore, through Queen Elizabeth's Channel and over the Kentish Flats. This was practicable for small and medium-sized ships, including all but the largest merchantmen, and was the obvious choice for ships bound to the westward down-Channel. Ships of the line, however, could only take this passage in charge of an expert pilot who was confident of finding one of the 'holes' where a big ship could anchor at low water, or with a leading wind, in charge of one who would risk making the whole distance between the Nore and the North Foreland on a single tide. Prince Rupert, the boldest navigator of all the admirals of his day, took the *Royal Sovereign* over the Kentish Flats in 1673. Sir Phineas Pett, asked what Trinity House would make of such rashness, 'answered that he believed they would say his Highness was mad, whereto the Prince replied, "I believe so too"'.[8] It was out of the question to take a whole fleet that way.

For English fleets of the period, the first strategic question which presented itself was usually whether to stay at the Gunfleet or to move. Southwold Bay 25 miles north was completely open to the eastward, so that a fleet could conveniently sail for the Dutch coast with any suitable wind. It was equally open to Dutch attack, as the Anglo-French fleet discovered in May 1672. The major dilemma, however, was usually whether to shift to the Downs, the only position from which the Straits of Dover could be covered. The strategic danger of using the Downs was that the mouth of the Thames was left open. The tactical danger was that the anchorage itself was a trap. The Downs is formed by the Kentish coast to the west, and the Goodwin Sands to the east. Its southern entrance is easy, but the Gull Stream to the north is narrow and big ships can only pass it in single file, so that no squadron could escape that way in a hurry. With a southerly or south-westerly wind a squadron lying in the Downs might be trapped by an enemy entering from the southward. This was exactly how Admiral Maarten Tromp gained his crushing victory over the Spaniards in 1639, and neither the Dutch who had won the battle nor the English who had witnessed it ever forgot the lesson.

Tromp spent much of the First Dutch War vainly attempting to repeat his triumph, but the English were extremely wary of risking large squadrons in the Downs. The same considerations recurred in 1688, when the Downs would have been the perfect anchorage from which to watch the Straits of Dover and intercept William III's fleet, whether he chose to go down Channel, as in the event he did, or if he had gone north, as he was expected to do. No 'Protestant Wind' could have prevented the English fleet from sailing from there. Its great disadvantage was that it would have exposed the fleet to being trapped by a surprise attack, which was no doubt why Sir Roger Strickland and his Council of War chose the Gunfleet. James II initially preferred a position midway between the two, just south of the Kentish Knock, and it would have been well for him if he had kept to that resolution and not allowed the fleet to return to the Gunfleet.[9]

The Dutch were equally constrained by geography. Political history and commercial logic dispersed their naval resources among widely separated ports, whereas the four principal English dockyards were all on the Thames or Medway. Ships from the Zuider Zee ports of Amsterdam, Hoorn and Enkhuizen (also Harlingen in Friesland) had a long and tricky passage to their advance anchorage of the Marsdiep, inshore of the island of Texel. Amsterdam, moreover, was a bar harbour, and big ships could not cross the bar (the Pampus), which limited the size of warships which could be contributed by the richest of the provincial admiralties. Rotterdam, the other major naval port of Holland, could float bigger ships, but its tortuous channels to the open sea issued either by the Goereese Gat between the islands of Goeree and Voorn, or by the Brouwersgat north of Schouwen.[10] That is to say that though Amsterdam and Rotterdam are only 30 miles apart by land, their respective harbours were about 300 miles apart by sea, and their advance anchorages on the North Sea 100 miles apart. The last major naval port, Flushing in Zealand, had deep water and easy access to the open sea, but was further south still. This meant that the first problem of the Dutch admirals was to unite the scattered units of their fleet before the enemy could attack them in detail.

Most often they tried to do so off the southern ports. Partly this was because they lay nearer to England there, partly it was because several of the greatest Dutch admirals (notably Michiel De Ruyter and the Evertsen family) were Zealanders themselves who knew these waters best,[11] but chiefly it was because the coast here is screened by a considerable number of scattered offshore banks which make the movement of any fleet hazardous unless it is perfectly familiar with the waters. This was the key to De Ruyter's brilliant handling of the 1673 campaign, when his fleet operated in and around the area known as the Schoonvelt off the mouth of the Western Scheldt, which covered the coast on which the allies threatened a landing. This is sufficiently open water to allow free movement of the Dutch fleet, near enough to the Scheldt and the Brouwersgat for easy escape if necessary, but surrounded by scattered shoals which made the English and French extremely cautious of approaching.[12] By contrast the coast of North Holland is open, and an enemy fleet might have trapped the Dutch against the land, as Admiral Adam Duncan did at Camperdown in 1797.

When everything depended on expert pilotage, fleets of warships were remarkably cautious in enemy waters, even though on both sides during the Dutch Wars there were numerous seamen who had been accustomed in peacetime to trade there. Partly this was because warships, especially English warships, were so much bigger and deeper than merchantmen that an ordinary pilot's experience was not very useful. There must have been hundreds of Dutch pilots who knew the Thames intimately, but the great majority were no doubt accustomed to using the Kentish Flats. In 1653 the Dutch admirals refused to consider entering the Thames, and when Jan De Witt, Grand Pensionary of Holland, sent the Dutch fleet into the Thames in 1667 De Ruyter and his colleagues were extremely reluctant to risk their ships in the unknown waters of the King's Channel. Only political authority overrode the seamen's professional objections and made possible the Medway attack.[13]

The Glorious Revolution overturned the strategic situation as completely as the political. England's geographical and strategic situation in the Dutch Wars was highly favourable,

> when (like an eagle's wings extended over her body) our coast surrounded theirs for 120 leagues from Scilly to the Maas in Holland one way, and as many from the Orcades thither the other way; and the wind blowing above three-quarters of the year westerly on the coast of England, made all our cape-lands and bays very good roads for ships to anchor at …[14]

War with France forced the Royal Navy to operate down Channel and to the westward, in waters with which it was not so familiar, and where it lacked bases. English ships, especially the bigger ships of the line, had been designed to carry the maximum broadside into battle in shallow, enclosed waters with no considerable fetch, where most gales could be ridden out at anchor. In the deep and open waters of the lower Channel and the Western Approaches they had to face onshore storms and seas sweeping off the open Atlantic which they could not beat into. Dutch ships were still less adapted for these waters. Instead of the friendly weather shores the English had enjoyed during the Dutch Wars, all the coasts were dangerous lee shores. In these circumstances it was considered 'a mighty boldness to advance with the Grand Fleet further westward of the Isle of Wight than the *Soveraigne* had been knowne to have been, since the time of her built'.[15] Commanding the Allied fleet after the victory of La Hogue (Barfleur) in 1692, in summer weather 'fitting only for Laplanders to be at sea with', Admiral Edward Russell felt that

> no fleet of ships, being so many in number, nor of this bigness, ought to be ventured at sea but where they may have room enough to drive any way for eight and forty hours, or where they may let go an anchor and ride. In the Channel six hours with a change of wind, makes either side a lee shore …[16]

In order to appreciate the real difficulties of operating down-Channel, or anywhere across the open oceans, from bases on the Thames and Medway, it is necessary to understand the weather system of the British Isles, where the prevailing winds are westerly or south-westerly throughout the year. This means that ships sailing from ports in the English Channel, or coming down the Channel from the North Sea, are likely to face long delays while waiting for a favourable wind. The same is generally true of ports in the Bristol Channel and Irish Sea, though it is rather easier to clear Scottish ports on a north-westerly course. Easterly or north-easterly winds are commonest in the spring, between January and May, which was an important reason why major military expeditions, and those foreign trades which followed an annual cycle, usually planned to sail during these months.[17] At the cost of preparing in mid-winter, often in hard frosts produced by the same high pressure which generated the easterly winds, this gave the best prospects of getting clear of the British Isles without undue delay, of reaching the Caribbean or North America early in the campaigning season, and in the case of the West Indies, of achieving some success before the onset of the hurricane months of September and October made those waters deadly for men and ships. For ships bound to the East Indies a departure early in the year was essential in order to reach the Indian Ocean during the season of the South-West Monsoon, May to October. At all seasons, but especially in winter, a succession of depressions blows in from the Atlantic over the British Isles or to the north. These cause the prevailing wind to veer northerly as they pass, which gives other opportunities for ships to work down Channel. It seems also to have been the case that winter easterlies were relatively more common (and the winters harder) at periods in the late seventeenth and late eighteenth centuries.[18]

Nevertheless, in every age the prevailing westerlies severely disadvantaged English ports, and none more so than London, which is almost the furthest from the open Atlantic of any major British seaport. What was worse, the axis of the Thames Estuary and that of the English Channel are almost the same, so that ships sailing from London and bound down Channel needed first a westerly and then an easterly wind, or the reverse for the homeward passage. No steady wind would serve. Indeed the Thames itself twists so much that 'there is only one point of the compass that the wind can be at, which will carry a ship from Sea-Reach into the Pool without making a board'.[19] It was this which made the anchorage of the Downs so important, for it could be entered from the Thames Estuary round the North Foreland, and from the Channel round the South Foreland, while the anchorage itself was large enough to shelter hundreds of sail, protected from westerlies by the land, and from easterlies by the Goodwin Sands. It was the great focal point for much of the trade of London and many North Sea ports in the age of sail, for in westerly winds ships lay here, sometimes for weeks, waiting their chance to get up the Thames or down the Channel. If the wind shifted easterly, many hundreds of ships would make sail at once and the great anchorage would empty in a few hours.

As soon as the main fleets began to operate down-Channel, they left the pilotage waters of the Narrow Seas and faced the other great challenge to the navigator under sail: the impossibility, before the mid-eighteenth century, of fixing longitude. In principle it had been possible from the late

Middle Ages to fix a ship's latitude by observation of the altitude of a heavy body – usually the the Pole Star at dawn or the sun at noon – and most English navigators could do so in practice by the late sixteenth century. By the mid-eighteenth century a good observer with a good instrument could fix his latitude to within about ten miles, but this was an ideal figure. Errors of scores or even hundreds of miles were still common, and of course no observations were possible when the sky was overcast or the horizon obscured, that is, on the majority of days in the year around thc British Isles.[20]

Moreover the best latitude position without longitude only answers half the navigator's question. Since the earth is symmetrical about its polar axis and in constant rotation, the problem of fixing the longitude of any point on the earth's surface relative to any other is the same as determining the difference of local time between the two. Several methods of doing so were theoretically available, and in the 1750s two became practicable more or less at the same time. The Göttingen astronomer Tobias Mayer published in 1755 tables which for the first time described the complex and irregular motions of the moon with sufficient accuracy to permit the calculation of longitude by lunar distances; that is, by inferring the rotation of the earth by measuring the movement of the moon against fixed stars. This called only for three straightforward observations with standard instruments, but the calculations were extremely lengthy and difficult. The Reverend Neville Maskelyn, the Astronomer Royal, reduced the time needed from about four hours to only half an hour with the publication of the *British Mariner's Guide* of 1763, followed by the first *Nautical Almanac* in 1767. The mathematics remained demanding, but they were immediately adopted into the curriculum of the schools which trained boys for careers at sea, and 'lunars' became the standard method of determining longitude well into the nineteenth century. The method allowed a good navigator to fix his longitude to better than one degree.[21] Even so, large errors of longitude remained normal. Vice-Admiral Lord Howe's squadron crossing the Atlantic in 1776 got 300 miles out of their reckoning in spite of taking a lunar halfway across.[22]

The rival method was the chronometer, perfected by John Harrison in the 1760s after 30 years of work, and soon imitated by other watchmakers in England and abroad. An instrument which can keep accurate time at sea over long periods permits an easy comparison between local sun time (so long as the sun can be observed) and the fixed or mean time of some datum meridian of longitude, the difference between the two representing the observer's easting or westing from the datum. For British navigators, and eventually for the whole world, the longitude of Greenwich Observatory was this datum. The accuracy required is considerable; to fix longitude to half a degree after a six-week voyage (a fast transatlantic passage) the chronometer must lose or gain no more than three seconds a day.[23] Before Harrison no-one had been able to make a clock which would keep accurate time in a constantly moving ship, subject to damp and rapid changes of temperature. The chronometer is a simple method of fixing longitude, and eventually it became the normal method, but initially chronometers were too expensive for many masters to buy them; 60 guineas in the 1780s, or between two and four months' salary for a master in the Navy. Even the Royal Navy did not begin to issue official chronometers until early in the nineteenth century, and ships in home waters did not receive them until the 1840s.[24]

Before the 'discovery of the longitude', all ocean navigation was a combination of observation of the latitude component, and dead-reackoning for the longitude. When the sky was obscured and observations impossible, dead-reckoning had to serve for both, until the development of radio aids to navigation in the twentieth century. Dead-reckoning is simply an estimation of the ship's progress from a given point of departure whose position is known, measuring speed by casting the log, recording courses steered by the compass, and adding a guess for leeway and drift. In the best circumstances it cannot be relied on for more than a few days. Admiral Lord Dartmouth's squadron sailed from Plymouth for Tangier on 23 August 1683 and on 10 September sighted the Burlings, a group of islands on the coast of Portugal. Of 12 officers of the flagship who were keeping a reckoning, the best was 75 miles out of his reckoning, and some were over 200 miles out. Moreover the different charts aboard the flagship disagreed widely on the position of Portugal, there being over 50 miles between the longitudes given for Cape Finisterre (see Map 2, p.188).[25]

The impossibility of fixing longitude made it a matter of great uncertainty when any ship making a passage involving much easting or westing – which in practice means any ocean passage – would actually make the land. One aspect of this uncertainty was question of fixing the length of a degree of longitude. The diameter of the earth, and hence the length of a degree of latitute and the length of the nautical mile (one minute of arc of latitude, conventionally reckoned as 6,080 feet) was measured with good accuracy in 1669–70.[26] Since the meridians of latitude converge at the poles, the length of a degree of longitude varies from nothing at the poles to 60 nautical miles at the Equator. For accuracy the navigator has to recalculate the length of the degree of longitude continuously. In practice

MAP 2

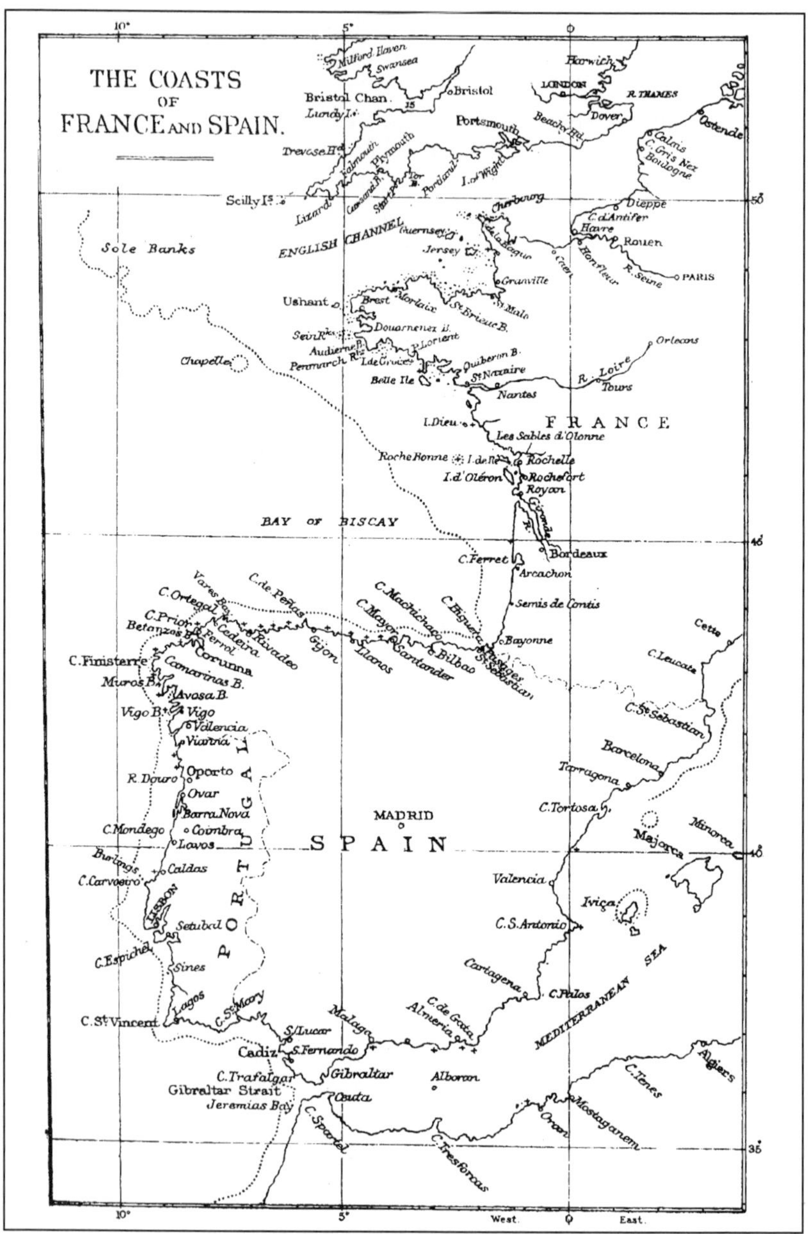

Source: J. Leyland (ed.) *The Blockade of Brest* (London: Navy Records Society Vols.14–15, 1899) pp.1 and 176.

English navigators preferred approximation. For convenience they kept 60 miles to the degree, but reduced the mile to some conventional figure, most often 5,000 feet.[27] This is roughly correct for Lat. 35°, but progressively too small as the ship approaches the Equator. On transatlantic voyages from England to America a ship would make virtually all her westing south of 35°N.

Even when the traditional measures were known to be inaccurate, navigators preferred to 'sight land after they sought it', in order to be forewarned of danger.[28] They had additional reason to do so since the longitude even of entire continents was laid down wrongly on the charts until the late eighteenth century (nor could the average navigator afford to replace his expensive charts with the latest editions at frequent intervals), and it would have been dangerously misleading to plot the ship's position accurately on a chart which misplaced the land. Thus in 1755 HMS *Winchester* on passage to Barbados, 'by allowing only forty-two feet to a glass of thirty seconds, overrun her reckoning by near a hundred leagues between Madeira and this island'.[29] Moreover the same log-line was used on all courses, so this deliberate inaccuracy was liable to affect dead-reckoning of latitude as well unless the navigator remembered to apply a correction.

Uncertain of their own longitude and that of the land, mariners making an ocean passage, say across the Atlantic, would usually try and make the land by getting into the latitude of a good landfall and running their easting or westing down (cautiously, at night or in thick weather) until they made landfall. The ideal port for oceanic trade in the pre-longitude era was one lying roughly midway along a coast trending north and south, with high land inshore and deep water offshore, the entry to the port itself marked by a prominent peak visible at a great distance – in a word, Lisbon. No other European seaport was as easy to find after a long ocean passage, but the ports on the Atlantic coast of Andalusia are nearly as satisfactory, for Cape St Vincent is a good landfall from which it is easy to make Seville, Cadiz and the rest. This alone is a powerful explanation for the lead taken by the Portuguese and then the Spaniards in oceanic navigation. By contrast, English ports in general, and London in particular, are exceptionally difficult to reach under sail from the open sea.

In wartime, the desirability of closing the coast along a parallel of latitude was an important strategic factor, because it made the course of friendly or hostile shipping predictable. In the sixteenth century French and English pirates cruised off Cape St Vincent waiting to surprise inward-bound Spanish ships from the West Indies, knowing that the 'Indies trade' was a legal monopoly of the port of Seville, and the 'Cape of Surprises', as

Spanish seamen nicknamed it, was their only likely landfall.[30] Others lay in the Azores to catch the same ships earlier in their voyages. In eighteenth-century wars French privateers from Martinique or Guadaloupe would cruise in the latitude of Barbados, 50 or 100 miles to windward, waiting for British ships bound into the Caribbean to swim into their jaws. More difficult landfalls like the French Atlantic or the English Channel ports, which could not safely be approached on a parallel of latitude, were more dangerous to make but less vulnerable to enemy interception.

There was a particular problem in finding islands in the open sea, for having got into their latitude, the navigator might not know which way to turn. This was the situation of Commodore George Anson's squadron in 1741. Having struggled round the Horn, in a desperate condition with men dying daily of scurvy, they made the latitude of their intended landfall in the Juan Fernández Islands, guessed that they were west of the island, and did not discover their mistake until they sighted the coast of Chile. This error cost them 11 days in finding the island, and the lives of between 70 and 80 men.[31] The easiest island landfalls were those in the trade wind latitudes, where the weather is reliably clear for much of the year, and a stationary cloud hangs over the islands which may be visible 100 miles or even more. Hence for example St Helena, though small and very remote, was relatively easy to find, and early established itself as a popular way-station on the long passage home from the East Indies (though in 1696 Commodore Thomas Warren spent weeks vainly searching for it and eventually had to put back to Rio de Janeiro with 77 men dead of scurvy).[32] For British ships, Madeira and the Canary Islands served the same function on westward transatlantic voyages, the high peaks of Madeira and Teneriffe being especially easy to find. In the same way Spanish ships homeward bound from the Caribbean often called in the Azores.

In both cases the islands lay more or less directly on the usual sailing routes, for the wind and current systems of the North Atlantic are broadly circular. With only minor variations over the year, the winds blow from the north on the coast of Portugal, north-easterly around Madeira and the Canaries, and thence easterly across the southern part of the North Atlantic (roughly between 30°S and 10°S) and into the Caribbean basin (see Map 3, p.192). Off the Bahamas they blow south-easterly then southerly and south-westerly along the coast of North America, and so westerly back across the North Atlantic and across the British Isles. The currents, generated by the winds, follow the same pattern, the northerly drift of the Gulf Stream flowing at two or three knots out of the Florida Strait and up the American coast being especially powerful.[33] For this reason the natural and normal route from European ports to North America traced a great arc to the southward, sometimes as far south as the Cape Verde Islands (15–16°N), and thence across the Atlantic and up the coast.

Modern writers often speak of the Atlantic as being 3,000 miles wide, because that is the actual distance on a great circle course from the Bishop's Rock to Nantucket Light, such as a modern ocean liner might follow. The real distance for a sailing vessel following the usual course to New York is at least 1,000 miles longer, and the Scillies are 400 miles by sea from London.[34] The total distance under sail is 50 per cent greater, and the real difficulties of the passage are completely overlooked.

The strategic importance of the West Indies is likewise obscured. To the modern eye the Caribbean appears to be marginal to the American War of Independence, whereas in the real terms of sailing passages, the islands lay on the easiest direct route from Europe to North America. Hence the strategic importance, but also the navigational danger, of the Bahamas, a great area of low-lying reefs and islands lying on the western edge of the normal route. Further north many ships bound for the middle or northern colonies were lost on the Carolina Banks, for they had to pass not far off this most dangerous coast, unmarked and invisible from a distance, with no good idea of their longitude.

The Atlantic wind system gave the Spaniards a huge advantage in settling the Caribbean basin, for the transatlantic passage from Seville and back is swift and easy. Since both winds and currents set westward across the Caribbean, all shipping entered through the Windward Islands. Spanish ships generally gathered at Havana and left through the Florida Strait, continuing up the coast past Cape Hatteras before picking up the westerlies to blow them home across the central North Atlantic to the Azores and so on, due east for Cape St Vincent. The navigation was simple, predictable, and consequently dangerous in wartime. The early English colonies in Roanoke and Virginia were partly inspired by the hope of establishing privateer bases within easy reach of homeward-bound Spanish shipping.[35] In the seventeenth century Spain conceded a much more serious strategic advantage in permitting the French and English to settle the Windward Islands, and hence in due course to control the entrance to the Caribbean. This was the strategic function of the British Leeward Islands squadron (which in spite of its name covered the Windward Islands as well), as established in the 1740s. It was necessarily a distinct force from the Jamaica squadron to leeward, for though all ships bound for Jamaica passed through the Lesser Antilles, the reverse passage was impossible. Ships leaving Jamaica beat through the Mona Passage into the Atlantic, or ran to leeward,

MAP 3
THE CARIBBEAN

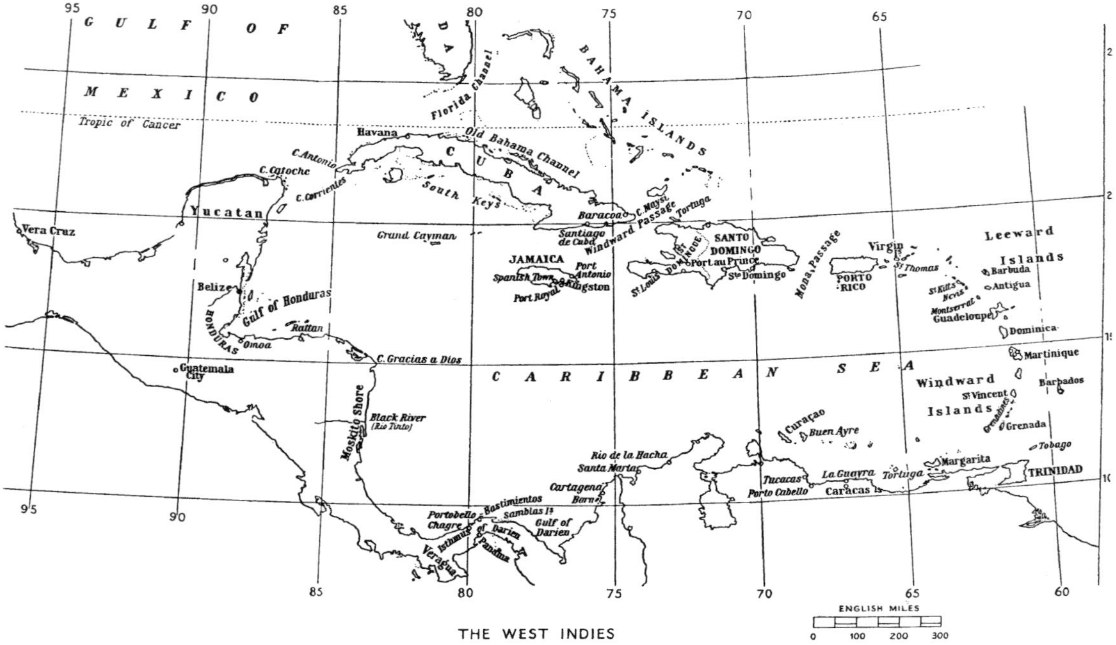

Source: Bryan Ranft (ed.), *The Vernon Papers* (London: Navy Records Society 1958) endpaper.

rounded Cape Corrientes and beat up the north coast of Cuba (where the current is favourable though the wind is not) and so through the Florida Strait. In the eighteenth century the quickest passage normally available from Jamaica to Barbados (a distance of just over 1,000 miles by steamer) was via London or New York.

Just as the wind and current systems favoured the Spaniards in the Caribbean, they favoured the Portuguese in the South Atlantic. The early Portuguese explorers found favourable winds and currents to work down the coast of Africa and into the Bight of Benin. To return they had to learn to make the 'leap' out into the open Atlantic and so north to the Azores or thereabouts to pick up the westerlies to carry them home. This was not so easy, but it was the essential school of deep-sea navigation which made possible all subsequent oceanic voyaging. From the Bight of Benin along the African coast southwards both wind and currents were adverse, but there was another and better way, by crossing the Atlantic and striking south-westward, across the belt of calms around the Equator, and so down the coast of Brazil. Portuguese settlement of Brazil (and Dutch rivalry for it) followed naturally from the fact that it was on the way to the Far East. On the coast of Brazil, as over most of the South Atlantic, the South-East trades blow throughout the year, providing an easy passage down to the latitude of Rio de Janeiro or even the River Plate, where a ship may pick up the westerlies which blow all round the world in high southern latitudes, often with great force. These blew a ship easily down to the Cape of Good Hope, though it was a surprisingly difficult landfall to make. A small error of latitude to the north would put a ship ashore, or drive her northward up the coast; too far to the south and she missed the Cape altogether, without being aware of the fact in the absence of a precise longitude.

Some ships voyaging to the East deliberately risked scurvy and passed well south of the Cape to continue across the Indian Ocean. Others took the trouble to heave-to and take a sounding with a deep-sea lead, a process which took several hours, but gave the most reliable indication of the proximity of land: 'This sounding served the purpose of correcting our reckoning as much as though we had seen the land.'[36] Returning from the East, ships rounding the Cape had an easy run up the South Atlantic before the South-East Trades before rejoining the North Atlantic wind system north of the Equator.

For British ships inward bound from the Atlantic, the prevailing westerlies obviously served very well, but from the navigational point of view the approaches of the Channel were difficult. There are no safe landfalls which might be approached by a vessel unsure of her longitude.

The Scillies are protected by a screen of reefs to the west and south-west, unmarked and unlit before the nineteenth century, on which any ship approaching them risks being wrecked before having the chance to verify her position. Until well into the eighteenth century, the islands were laid down 15 miles or more to the north of their true position on English charts.[37] Moreover there is a variable northerly set, the Rennell Current, across the mouth of the Channel after south-westerly gales, which was not described until 1793 and cannot be predicted without good knowledge of the weather in the area over the previous month – unavailable to inward-bound shipping in the days before wireless.[38] It was this current which drove Admiral Sir Cloudesley Shovell's squadron onto the Scillies in 1707.[39] It is impossible to run into the Channel on a parallel of latitude, for a course due east clearing the Scillies by ten miles (an exceedingly small margin even with a good observation) leads straight onto the Casquets reef off Alderney.[40] Ushant at the southern mouth of the Channel is a rather less dangerous landfall than the Scillies, but only so long as the navigator approaches in daylight with a good idea of his position. For anyone unsure of his whereabouts western Brittany is one of the most perilous coasts in the world.

The only possible entry to the Channel is on a NW or WNW course aiming initially, not for a landfall which might be identified, but for the right area of open water. In these circumstances, and every circumstance 'in soundings' (within the 100-fathom line, on the Continental shelf), the navigator placed great reliance on the lead. Armed with tallow, it not only gave him the depth but a sample of the bottom, and a line of soundings might give him a good idea of his whereabouts. Precise knowledge of the composition and smell of the bottom was one of the most precious skills of the pilot, and often the key to the survival of a ship running into the Channel, unsure of her position after weeks at sea.[41] Captain Richard Rooth of the *Bear*, homeward bound from Jamaica in 1655, hove to on 29 August to sound with the deep-sea lead, getting 70 fathoms, 'sandy with cockle shells and small dark grains like mustard seeds'. Next morning early he sounded again and found 63 fathoms with small pebbles and 'brandy sand', which he interpreted as putting him 15 leagues SW of the Lizard. At 8 o'clock he sounded again, and reckoned himself 7 leagues SW; one hour later he raised the Lizard 5 leagues to the north-east. With luck and judgement, the lead might yield a perfect landfall like this; yet even a careful seamen like Rear-Admiral Sir John Narborough in 1673 might very easily mistake:

> the soundings also deceived men in their depth and ground, for the same depth is 5 leagues SW from Scilly as is 5 leagues W from Scilly,

> and the ground fine white sand in many places; also, heave the lead three times one after another as fast as you can, and you will find the ground to differ every cast; sometimes sand and sometimes sand and stones &c will come up in the tallow, which deceiveth men.[43]

Narborough was lucky to disentangle himself from the Bishop and Clerks. Ten years later Lord Dartmouth on his passage home from Tangier found himself in similar uncertainty:

> Strange the disagreement in so fair weather with so fair a wind immediately upon a fair observation and clear sounding at 65 fathoms and 49°34′ latitude, among our navigators about the entrance into our Channel, my lord and Mr Phillips being very positive we were shot to the Eastward of Scilly, while Sir W. Booth with the master and mates were of opinion we were yet to the westward, and one part of them apprehensive of our running upon the French coast, and the other upon the English …[44]

The intention of the English navigator would be to make a landfall somewhere along the South Coast of England. In many ways this was relatively easy, for there is a succession of prominent headlands: the Lizard, the Dodman, Rame Head, Bolt Head or Tail, the Start, Portland Bill, St Alban's Head, Anvil Point and finally St Catherine's Point on the Isle of Wight, each of which is fairly easy to identify in clear weather and safe to approach from the south-west. Many of them, moreover, have practicable anchorages on their eastern side, sheltered from the prevailing westerlies.[45] The danger in making this coast by night or in poor visibility, however, was in becoming embayed on the windward side of one of these headlands. This was how HMS *Ramillies* was wrecked in Hope Cove in 1760 when the master mistook his landfall in thick weather and she was unable to weather Bolt Tail.[46] There was also a danger to ships sheltering in one of the anchorages on the south-easterly side of these headlands if the wind backed (unusual but always possible), for all of them are exposed to easterly or south-easterly winds. Torbay, throughout the eighteenth century the usual advance anchorage of the Channel Fleet, was capacious and safe in most circumstances, but notoriously a deathtrap if the wind blew up and backed suddenly easterly. Lord Howe very nearly lost the entire fleet when this happened on 13 February 1795.[47]

Having once made a landfall on the English coast, the ship bound up Channel had a relatively simple task of working along the coast. For French navigators the situation was more difficult, especially in wartime when they could not safely hug the English coast. No ship having made landfall at

Ushant and bound up-Channel, would choose to coast the north coast of Brittany, for not only is the coast itself dangerous, with numerous offshore reefs and islands, and a dead lee shore if the wind veers northerly (as it regularly does), but it also leads straight into the great bight enclosed by the Côtentin Peninsula and occupied by the Channel Isles and their numerous outlying reefs and shoals.[48] To add to their dangers the bight collects the flood tide coming up Channel, leading to a large tidal range (nearly 40 feet in places) and violent tidal streams (up to eight knots in the Race of Alderney). Combined with frequent fog, these dangers provided an effective defence for St Malo, the great privateer base of the late seventeenth-century wars, which enemy warships were reluctant even to approach, but they forced ships bound for Norman ports over towards the English shore of the Channel. Ships bound to the westward from Dieppe or Le Havre were likewise forced north towards the English shore by the Côtentin Peninsula.

Naval historians have often remarked how French fleets entered the Channel reluctantly and seldom, and how strangely ignorant French sea officers were of these neighbouring waters.[49] Much of the explanation lies in navigational conditions which tended to force ships into English waters. This was compounded by the French tradition of building warships of very deep draught, so that French ships of the line were unable to enter any French Channel ports, until the artificial harbour of Cherbourg, begun by Louis XIV, was finally completed by Napoleon III.

Nevertheless the French began their naval wars against England in 1689 with the enormous advantage of a major naval base directly to windward at the mouth of the Channel. They could and should have used the advantage of Brest to dominate the Western Approaches, cut off British and Dutch trade, and support James II in Ireland. The British were slow to appreciate their new position, and it was not primarily their efforts which prevented the French from exploiting their situation. It took the British nearly 60 years before they learned to make best use of the prevailing winds and the geography of the English Channel. It is not going too far to say that the Western Squadron, as developed in the years 1746 and 1747, was the key to British naval supremacy for over a century. Its essential principle was to keep the main fleet cruising for much or even all of the year in the Western Approaches to the Channel. Far enough in the offing to avoid the worst navigational dangers of lee shores, the fleet was placed to answer all Britain's most essential strategic requirements at once.

If France or Spain mounted an invasion attempt, the fleet to cover it would have to sail from Brest or some port to the southward, and pass directly to leeward of the Western Squadron. Transports might sail from ports in Brittany or Normandy, but without a fleet to escort them they could safely be left to local forces in the Channel. The Western Squadron was well placed to blockade, or at least watch, all the French Atlantic ports, and to intercept warships and merchantmen clearing or entering the Bay of Biscay. Its cruising ground equally covered the passage of most important British overseas trades, excepting those to the Baltic.[50]

All this was made possible by the intelligent exploitation of the prevailing westerlies, plus the fact that Britain's naval and colonial rivals, France and Spain, lay near at hand. Success in dominating the waters of Western Europe translated progressively into dominance of the whole world, as the enemy was cut off from his forces overseas. Only once did the system fail, during the American War, when the British forgot what had given them victory in two previous wars and sent their main fleets overseas, beyond the reach of effective direction or proper maintenance, where campaigns were reduced to aimless blunderings and their results to chance. They never made the same mistake again, and the Western Squadron (under various names) remained the basis of British naval superiority until the rise of major naval powers outside Europe in the later nineteenth century finally undermined its foundations.[51]

This was not in the least inevitable. The hard facts of geography favoured England in its wars against the Netherlands, but against France the British had few natural advantages. The western winds were available to all, and might have served France or Spain as well as they did Britain if these nations had seized their potential. France was better placed to exploit them, and the Spaniards actually planned to establish a western squadron to dominate the Channel in 1574, though circumstances frustrated the attempt.[52]

As a base for oceanic trade and expansion across the world, English ports were for the most part ill placed, and London especially so. Easy access to the Atlantic wind systems goes far to explain how Portugal and Spain took an early lead in oceanic voyaging; but the French, especially Normans from the Channel ports, were not far behind them in spite of substantial disadvantages, and they in turn were followed by the English and Dutch from a still worse position. Naval strategy was necessarily dominated by weather and geography, but it was not in the least predetermined. Britain's eventual success can be explained in terms of a prolonged process of learning how to exploit the favourable, and overcome the unfavourable, aspects of the situation. None of this was inevitable, and not much of it is intelligible to the historian who ignores the real world of winds and currents, navigation and pilotage.

NOTES

1. Virtually all men of war of any size, and all merchantmen engaged in deep-sea trade, were ship-rigged, and it is in any case something of a myth that fore and aft rigged vessels can point higher.
2. J.R. Tanner (ed.) *Samuel Pepys's Naval Minutes*, Navy Records Society [hereafter NRS] Vol.60 (London: NRS 1925) p.38.
3. The cable is one-tenth of a nautical mile, conventionally reckoned equal to 100 fathoms or 200 yards.
4. R.C. Anderson (ed.) *Journals and Narratives of the Third Dutch War*, Navy Records Society Vol.86 (London: NRS 1946) pp.122 and 132.
5. P.M. Cowburn, 'Christopher Gunman and the Wreck of the *Gloucester*', *Mariner's Mirror* 42 (1956) pp.113–26 and 219–29.
6. J.R. Powell and E.K. Timings (eds.) *The Rupert and Monck Letter Book, 1666*, Navy Records Society Vol.112 (London: NRS 1969) pp.41–2 and 90.
7. J.C.M. Warnsinck, *Admiraal De Ruyter: De Zeeslag op Schooneveld Juni 1673* (The Hague: Nijhoff 1930) pp.3–6.
8. Tanner, *Pepys's Naval Minutes* (note 2) p.112.
9. Clyve Jones, 'The Protestant Wind of 1688: Myth and Reality', *European Studies Review* 3 (1973) pp.201–21; Brian Tunstall (ed.) *The Byng Papers*, NRS Vols.67, 68 and 70 (London, 1930–32) Vol.I, p.xxxii. Charles II also preferred to avoid the Downs in 1666: Powell and Timings, *Rupert and Monck Letter Book* (note 6) p.55.
10. G. Asaert *et al.* (eds.) *Maritieme Geschiedenis der Nederlanden* (Bussum: De Boer 1976–78, 4 vols) II, pp.83–4 and III, pp.69–72.
11. Contrast the opinion of the Hollander Witte de With, in Johan Elias, *Schetsen uit de Geschiedenis van ons Zeewezen* (The Hague: Nijhoff, 1916–30, 6 vols) Vol.III, p.51.
12. Anderson, *Third Dutch War* (note 4) pp.29–44. Warnsinck, *Admiraal De Ruyter* (note 7) pp.32–42.
13. S.R. Gardiner and C.T. Atkinson (eds.) *Letters and Papers relating to the First Dutch War, 1652–1654* , NRS Vols.13, 17, 30, 37, 41 and 66 (London: NRS 1899–1930) Vol.III, p.236. Johanna K. Oudendijk, *Johan de Witt en de Zeemacht* (Amsterdam: Noord-Hollandsche, 1944) pp.181–5. C.A. van Waning and A. van der Moer, *Dese Aengenaeme Tocht: Chatham 1667* (Zutphen: De Walburg 1981) pp.25–30.
14. Gardiner and Atkinson, *First Dutch War* (note 13) Vol.I, pp.31–2.
15. Michael Duffy, 'Devon and the Naval Strategy of the French Wars 1689–1815', in idem *et al.* (eds.) *The New Maritime History of Devon* (London: Conway Maritime Press 1992–94, 2 vols) Vol.I, pp.182–91, at p.182.
16. Philip Aubrey, *The Defeat of James Stuart's Armada, 1692* (Leicester UP 1969) p.140. Duffy, 'Devon and the Naval Strategy of the French Wars' (note 15) p.182.
17. Peter Allington *et al.*, 'Shiphandling and Hazards on the Devon Coast', in *New Maritime History of Devon* (note 15) II, pp.14–24, at p.14.
18. J.L. Anderson, 'Climatic Change, Sea-Power and Historical Discontinuity: The Spanish Armada and the Glorious Revolution of 1688', *The Great Circle* 5 (1983) pp.13–23; H.H. Lamb, *Climate, History and the Modern World* (London: Methuen 1982) pp.50–1.
19. William Spavens, *The Narrative of William Spavens, a Chatham Pensioner* (London: Chatham 1998) p.97.
20. N.A.M. Rodger, *The Wooden World, An Anatomy of the Georgian Navy* (London: Collins 1986) p.47; E.G.R. Taylor, *The Haven-Finding Art: A History of Navigation from Odysseus to Captain Cook* (London: Hollis & Carter 1956) pp.216–17. C.J. Sölver and G.J. Marcus, 'Dead Reckoning and the Ocean Voyages of the Past', *Mariner's Mirror* 44 (1958) pp.18–34.
21. Derek Howse, *Greenwich Time and the Longitude* (London: Philip Wilson 1988); this is the 2nd ed. of *Greenwich Time and the Discovery of the Longitude* (London: OUP 1980) pp.57–71.
22. Edward H. Tatum Jr (ed.) *The American Journal of Ambrose Serle, Secretary to Lord Howe 1776–1778* (San Marino, CA: Huntington Library 1940) pp.26–7.
23. Howse, *Greenwich Time* (note 21) pp.71–8. David W. Waters, *The Art of Navigation in*

England in Elizabethan and Early Stuart Times (London: Hollis & Carter 1958) p.58.

24. Howse, *Greenwich Time* (note 1) pp.71–8.
25. Edwin Chappell (ed.) *The Tangier Papers of Samuel Pepys*, NRS Vol.73 (London: NRS 1935) pp.126–7.
26. Taylor, *Haven-Finding Art* (note 20) pp.236–7.
27. Waters, *Art of Navigation* (note 23) pp.58–66; G.B.P. Naish, 'The "Dyoll" and the Bearing-Dial', *Journal of the Institute of Navigation* 7 (1954) pp.205–8; see particularly the comment by W.E. May on p.208. Taylor, *Haven-Finding Art* (note 20) pp.224–30.
28. Waters, *Art of Navigation* (note 23) pp.64–6; Spavens, *Narrative* (note 19) p.103.
29. Rodger, *Wooden World* (note 20) p.53. This equates to a mile of 5,040 ft. or a degree of just under 50 nautical miles, about right for Madeira in 33°N, but eight miles too short for the parallel of Barbados in 13°N. A 51ft knot to a 30-sec. glass equates to a true nautical mile.
30. Huguette and Pierre Chaunu, *Séville et l'Atlantique, (1504–1650)* (Paris: Colin 1955–59, 8 vols in 11) Vol.VIII, i, p.267.
31. Glyndwr Williams (ed.) *A Voyage Around the World by George Anson* (London: OUP 1974) pp.109–10.
32. Robert C.Ritchie, *Captain Kidd and the War against the Pirates* (Cambridge, MA : Harvard UP 1986) p.77.
33. Boyle T. Somerville (ed.) *Ocean Passages for the World* (London: Admiralty 1923 ed.); James Clarke, *Atlantic Pilot Atlas* (London: Adlard Coles 2nd ed. 1996). Note that winds are described by the direction from which they blow, currents by the direction to which they set, so a southerly wind goes with a northerly current.
34. Somerville, *Ocean Passages* (note 33) pp.80 and 347.
35. John C.Appleby, 'War, Politics, and Colonization, 1558–1625', in Nicholas Canny (ed.) *The Oxford History of the British Empire Vol.I: The Origins of Empire, British Overseas Enterprise to the Close of the Seventeenth Century* (Oxford: OUP 1998), pp.55–78, at p.64.
36. Spavens, *Narrative* (note 19) p.41.
37. D.W. Waters, 'The English Pilot: English Sailing Directions and Charts and the Rise of English Shipping, 16th to 18th Centuries', *Journal of Navigation* 42 (1989) pp.317–54, at p.342.
38. Waters, *Art of Navigation* (note 23) pp.267–8. Allington, 'Shiphandling' (note 17) p.15.
39. G.J. Marcus, 'Sir Clowdisley Shovel's Last Passage', *Journal of the Royal United Service Institution* 102 (1957) pp.540–8; W.E. May, 'The Last Voyage of Sir Clowdisley Shovell', *Journal of the Institute of Navigation* 13 (1960) pp.324–32.
40. The Bishop Rock is in 49°52′ N, the Casquets in 49°43′N.
41. Allington, 'Shiphandling' (note 17) pp.15–16.
42. John F. Battick (ed.), 'Richard Rooth's Sea Journal of the Western Design, 1654–55', *Jamaica Journal* 5/4 (1971) pp.3–22, at p.21.
43. Anderson, *Third Dutch War* (note 4) p.287.
44. Chappell, *Tangier Papers* (note 25) p.248.
45. Carrick Roads in the lee of the Lizard, Mevagissey Bay in the lee of the Dodman, Cawsand Bay in the lee of Rame Head, Start Bay and Torbay in the lee of the Start, Portland Bay in the lee of the Bill, Swanage Bay in the lee of Anvil Point, and the Solent behind the Isle of Wight.
46. Rodger, *Wooden World* (note 20) p.46.
47. Duffy, 'Devon and the Naval Strategy of the French Wars' (note 15) p.186.
48. Allington, 'Shiphandling' (note 17) p.16.
49. E.g. A.Temple Patterson, *The Other Armada: The Franco-Spanish Attempt to Invade Britain in 1779* (Manchester UP 1960) p.28.
50. Michael Duffy, 'The Establishment of the Western Squadron as the Linchpin of British Naval Strategy', in idem (ed.) *Parameters of British Naval Power, 1650–1850* (Exeter UP 1992) pp.60–81; H.W. Richmond, *The Navy in the War of 1739–48* (Cambridge UP 1920, 3 vols) Vol.III, pp.6–8, 20–3, 82–4, 226–9; B.McL. Ranft (ed.) *The Vernon Papers*, NRS Vol.99 (London: NRS 1958) pp.436–7, 441, 451–2, 459; A.N. Ryan, 'The Royal Navy and the Blockade of Brest, 1689–1805: Theory and Practice', iu Martine Acerra, José Merino and Jean Meyer (eds.) *Les marines de guerre européennes, XVII-XVIIIe siècles* (Paris: Presses

de l'Université de Paris-Sorbonne 1985) pp.175–93; Daniel A. Baugh, 'Great Britain's "Blue-Water" Policy, 1689–1815', *International History Review* 10 (1988) pp.33–58.

51. N.A.M. Rodger, 'Sea-power and Empire, 1688–1793', in P.J. Marshall (ed.) *The Oxford History of the British Empire Vol.II, The Eighteenth Century* (Oxford: OUP 1998) pp.169–83.
52. Magdalena de Pazzis Pi Corrales, *La otra Invencible, 1574: España y las potencias nórdicas* (Madrid: San Martin 1983).

11

Some Thoughts on War and Geography

WILLIAMSON MURRAY

At present there is substantial worry in the United States as the discipline of history disappears into the study of social, gender, and racial issues. Of course, the corruption of the academic world is nothing new. It was only a few decades ago American universities regarded the study of geography as a serious area with its own departments and scholarly examination of the world. But those who determined the direction of academic life in the 1960s and 1970s in the United States decided that geography did not deserve such status. At the same time, geography disappeared from the curricula of American grade schools and secondary schools. What little remained of the discipline lay buried within environmental studies and departments, which not only had little interest in the study of geography or geopolitics, but undoubtedly regarded such efforts as completely unenlightened.

Part of the explanation has to do with the shrinkage of the world in an age of jet travel and superhighways. The elites of the first world now zip across continents in a matter of hours – distances that as recently as two centuries ago took months to cover. And on the great superhighways crisscrossing the spaces of the first world, those making the journey gain little sense of the land or the people they so rapidly pass. The result of their intellectual framework and the physical experience of travel is that Americans have become increasingly ignorant of the geography of the world in which they live. This may well have a crucial impact on America's capacity to understand and adapt to the challenges of the next century. The tortured theories of the early 1960s that posited the defense of South Vietnam as the first of a series of dominoes that would fall in Southeast Asia should only serve to underline the price that Americans have paid in the past for their ignorance of geography and history.[1]

Were this simply a matter of the less-well educated possessing little sense of geography, one might dismiss the issue as not being of great significance, even for a great democracy. The problem is that this ignorance of geopolitics and geography has become an increasing mark of the American elites. This author recently sat through a briefing in which one of the briefers identified the world's chokepoints for the benefit of the National Security Study Group. The briefing slide unfortunately placed the Straits of Malacca 500 miles to the east of their geographic location – in the middle of Indonesia. One may have been dealing with an oversight by harried planners confronting one more briefing, but then again the mistake may well reflect the actual geographic sense of those making the briefing. Such ignorance is exceedingly worrying, when one understands the profound importance geography has played in military history as well as in the strategic framework within which world politics have played themselves out over the past four centuries. This essay aims to suggest some of the ways that geography has framed the international and strategic as well as military environments..

GEOGRAPHY AND WAR: THE TACTICAL FRAMEWORK

Because, in fact, geography possesses such a pervasive influence on human affairs in both a direct and indirect sense, this piece will begin by examining its impact on military events at the tactical level and move to the operational and strategic levels. At the tactical level one is talking about geography largely as terrain, a crucial component in war.

Philip Caputo in his classic memoir of the Vietnam War mentions that his view of terrain underwent a fundamental change when he attended Marine Corps officer candidate school and Basic School at Quantico, Virginia, in the early 1960s.

> A year earlier [before Caputo became an officer], I would have seen the rolling Virginia countryside through the eyes of an English-major who enjoyed reading the Romantic poets. Now I had the clearer, more pragmatic vision of an infantry officer. Landscape was no longer scenery to me, it was *terrain*, and I judged it for tactical rather than aesthetic value. Having been drilled constantly to look for cover and concealment, I could see dips and folds in a stretch of ground that would have appeared utterly flat to a civilian. If I saw a hill – `high ground' – I automatically began planning how to attack or defend it, my eyes searching for avenues of approach and fields of fire.[2]

Soldiers and marines – at least those requiring a sense of tactics (particularly infantry and artillery officers) – gain an instinctive sense of the impact that minute changes in terrain have on the course of military events.

Unfortunately, military historians have had a tendency to downplay or even ignore the impact of terrain at the tactical level. Historians have often referred derisively to an incident where Field Marshal Graf Alfred von Schlieffen replied to the comment of an aide about the beauty of the Pregnitz River in the dawn sun with the remark 'an unimportant obstacle'.[3] In fact, Schlieffen was simply voicing an opinion that any competent infantry officer would have made in similar circumstances. The German government was paying him for his ability to consider military rather than the artistic factors – a job that he fulfilled with some degree of competence.

A few examples should suffice to underline the crucial role terrain has had on the success or failure of military operations. One of the more obscure questions dealing with the American Civil War Battle of Antietam (17 September 1862) has to do with the question of why Major General John Sedgwick's division of Major General Edwin Sumner's Corps ended up advancing almost due east to smash directly into positions in the northern end of the Confederate line, while the other two divisions swung to the left, so much so that they ended up advancing almost due south, attacking the center of the Confederate line. The answer is obvious in walking the terrain. There is a ridge line on the far side of Antietam Creek. It is sufficiently high so that which shoulder one followed would determine which direction one took, especially without direction from above (there was none, either from the corps commander or Major General George McClellan, commander of the Army of the Potomac). The result was two radically different lines of approach that had a direct, if incalculable, impact on the battle.[4]

There are, of course, any number of other incidents in military history where the unseen hand of terrain has taken the control of events out of the hands of generals. Competent generals, not surprisingly, have consistently taken into account terrain and, where possible, used it to advantage. The Duke of Wellington's consistent use of reverse slope position, behind which his British regulars could shelter from French artillery and then rise to destroy French columns as they came over the top of the rise, presaged a fundamental principle of German tactics through two world wars.[5]

On the other hand, bad generals have displayed an astonishing capacity to place their armies in dreadful positions and then watch their forces disintegrate. Generals Baron Levin Bennigsen at Friedland in 1807 and Ludwig Benedek at Könnigratz (1866) are only two examples of the fact that generals as well as lieutenants can display a general ignorance of terrain. Lieutenant General Mark Clark's obdurate refusal to recognize the advantages that the terrain on the far side of the Rapido River gave the Germans in January 1944 resulted in heavy losses for the US 36th (Texas) Division (over a thousand dead or missing and 600 wounded); astonishingly Clark made 36th Division attempt the crossing not just once (which was bad enough), but twice.[6]

In war as in geography, the obvious is rarely obvious until it enters the history books. Those who have walked the battlefields of Flanders know how little rise there is in the terrain. Nevertheless, that gradient provided the Germans a considerable advantage in the terrible battles that swirled around the Ypres salient and Passchendaele – an advantage they took full advantage of throughout those battles. Yet, what is obvious to us today with the benefit of hindsight may not have been obvious to those in the military organizations of the time. Nevertheless, one of the most astonishing comments on British tactical proficiency in World War II is the admission that British attackers were consistently surprised to find that the Germans had sited their positions on reverse slope positions throughout the Normandy battles. The Royal Scots Fusiliers found it most disconcerting to come over the top of hills to discover 'the Germans dug in on the reverse slope, 'something we had never envisaged'.[7]

In an operational sense, Normandy represented the ideal solution to the Allied problem of achieving a lodgment on the European Continent. Flanked to the east by swamps and the River Seine, and to the west by the Atlantic, Normandy offered the Germans only one avenue of approach – from the south. The other major possibility, Pas de Calais, while it was closer to Germany, offered the Germans three different axes of operation to attack a bridgehead. Moreover, since it was further west, Normandy also allowed the Allies the protection by its greater distance from German centers of power. On the other hand, Normandy's terrain presented considerable tactical difficulties. The *bocage* country represented a nightmare to Allied armies trying to fight their way out into more open terrain. The massive hedgerows and stone farmhouses offered the Germans ideal terrain to conduct a defense in depth and an almost infinite number of defensive positions.

Thus, by the end of July 1944 Allied armies remained hemmed in within Normandy, far from the objectives Allied planners assumed they would reach. A major factor in this dismal situation was that the one Allied commander who understood Normandy terrain was Lieutenant General George S. Patton, who had toured the area in the 1920s. But in June and July 1944 Patton was in the doghouse and cast in the role of acting as leader of an imaginary army preparing to land at Pas de Calais. However, one can argue the Allies gained a long-term advantage in the sustained battle in Normandy. The lengthy circumstances of the campaign allowed General Sir Bernard Montgomery to fight a long-term battle of attrition by a series of battles that played to Allied strengths. After two months of exhausting fighting the Wehrmacht finally broke and the Allies took advantage of the situation to exploit the collapse all the way to the German frontier. Moreover, the regional geography in the path of the American breakthrough at Avranches provided the defensive terrain (in terms of the town as well as Hill 317 to the east) that protected the long narrow neck of the breakthrough from the inevitable German counterattack.

Soldiers and marines obviously find themselves intimately entwined with the harsh realities of tactical geography. How about sailors and airmen? A facile answer might be not at all. In fact, the former have found themselves intimately connected with terrain, largely, but not exclusively, in terms of avoiding direct contact with the land (such as running one's ship aground). Yet, on occasion sailors have taken extraordinary risks with terrain, such as when Admiral Sir Edward Hawke took his ships in full course after the fleeing French fleet into the uncharted Biscay waters of Quiberon Bay in November 1759 (uncharted at least from the British point of view) and won one of the great victories in Royal Navy history. Here too, for sailors the terrain of the sea can represent the difference between victory and defeat. US Navy and Marine commanders at Tarawa in 1943 miscalculated Central Pacific rip tides to the extent that landing craft had to drop the marines far from the beaches. The long walk in against a hail of Japanese small arms fire gave the marines one of the grimmest days in their history.

One of the more astonishing aspects of military history has been the willingness of military historians to believe that the defeat of Fighter Command in the Battle of Britain would have inevitably led to a successful German landing on the British Isles, 'Operation Sealion'. However, considering the harsh terrain of the English Channel in terms of weather at all times of year, it is astonishing the Germans actually considered Rhine River barges for transporting and supplying an army across the Channel. But consider the idea they did. After all, that great expert on military affairs, Field Marshal Wilhelm Keitel, argued that a cross-Channel invasion represented nothing more than a 'large river crossing'.[8]

Airmen have always (at least since the 1920s) claimed that their great advantage lies in the fact they are not prisoners of terrain, as are the other services. However, tactical geography has tied them as closely to the earth as do the realities of manned flight. Air bases are the tactical framework within which air forces wage campaigns. Possession of Henderson Field in the SW Pacific Guadalcanal campaign of 1942–43 allowed a small group of US Marine aviators to dominate the skies over the southern Solomons and thereby play a crucial role in the victory of the first American counterstroke against the Japanese.

But the tactical framework within which airmen work is also one where the terrain of the skies, weather, has dominated virtually every aspect of air war from the Western Front in winter 1914/15 through to the 1991 Gulf War. Even as it acquired its massive technological capabilities, the RAF's Bomber Command discovered that attacking Berlin over the winter of 1943/44 was an extraordinarily difficult proposition, largely because of the appalling weather that impacted on its night-time operations. So bad was the weather in December that defending Luftwaffe fighters were hardly able to take off – which contributed to the Command's relatively low losses that month, but hardly to the accuracy of its bombing.

A casual look at the geography of the North Pacific might suggest that the US Army Air Forces might have considered using the Aleutian chain. But again the weather in the area was so appalling that after their grim experiences in 1942 and 1943 at Attu and Kiska, both the Americans and the Japanese simply never bothered with the area for the remainder of the Pacific War. The 1991 Gulf War, that most technological of all wars, also underlines the impact of weather on air operations. And it has certainly suggested that weather has not, and will not for the foreseeable future, cease to be a major factor in air operations. During the last nights of 'Desert Storm' bombing, with critical political nodes of the Iraqi government targeted for destruction, bad weather prevented the F-117s from attacking anything over the night of 25–26 February and relatively few targets the next night, the last one of the war.[9]

GEOGRAPHY AND WAR: THE OPERATIONAL FRAMEWORK

The operational context of war has traditionally represented the aspect of geography that most intrigues military historians. Yet, it is also an area where it is all too easy to confuse the possible with the theoretical. Part of the problem is that military historians, following the lead of military organizations themselves, tend to emphasize the combat aspects of operations as opposed to the less appealing, but equally important contributions of logistics and intelligence. Nothing underlines this point better than Matthew Cooper's suggestion that the mechanized and motorized divisions in the German Army should have driven straight on to Moscow without pausing to sweep up the Soviet concentrations in the great encirclement battles that characterized the fighting in 1941.[10] The fact that most of these units would be down to less than 25 per cent of their fuel reserves by the time they reached Smolensk (and almost out of ammunition) suggests that a further advance in August would have almost immediately come to a complete halt within 50 miles of the Dnepr – hardly offering the possibility for anything other than catastrophic military defeat.[11] Ironically, the German logistic experts warned in November 1940 that there would be severe limits to what the German supply system could support in the Soviet Union – a warning that those concerned with the operational side of the invasion planning entirely ignored.[12]

The Ardennes has offered one of the prime real estate locations for the conduct of operations in the twentieth century. In 1914 that mountainous forested region provided the avenue for the inner wing of the Schlieffen Plan to close with French forces. Moreover, a substantial portion of the French offensive in 1914, the infamous Plan XVII, attacked through the southern portions of the Ardennes. Thus, the idea that somehow the French completely discounted the possibility the Germans might move through the Ardennes in May 1940 is nonsense.[13] The French knew that there were good secondary roads through the area, running in an east–west direction, and that a major German drive might occur through the region. However, they believed German forces would take at least ten days to come up on the Meuse in sufficient strength to make a major river crossing.

Ironically, they were in agreement with the *Oberkommando des Heeres* (*OKH*), the German Army High Command, which also believed it would take at least ten days to make a successful breakthrough on the Meuse. The real cause of the French disaster lay in three areas: an unwillingness to prepare themselves mentally or physically for the test that came; appalling mistakes by the French High Command which removed the army's operational reserves from the area of Rheims to the far west of the Allied line; and a belief that it would not be necessary to undertake delaying actions in the Ardennes to hamper a German drive – the forces on the Meuse would suffice to hold the door closed until reinforcements arrived.

The performance of US troops in thwarting the second major German offensive through the Ardennes in World War II, the Battle of the Bulge in December 1944, suggests what the French might have achieved in 1940 had they sought to delay the Germans in the Ardennes itself. Despite the breaking of the US front in several places, scattered groups of US infantry, combat engineers, and rear area personnel, carried out extensive rearguard actions and demolitions, actions sufficient to hold German forces long enough for Allied reinforcements to flow into the region. The fact that two small companies of Belgian reservists from the 1st Regiment *Chasseurs Ardennais* was able to hold 1st Panzer Division up for an entire day at the town of Bodange underlines the possibilities that were open to the French.[14] But for the most part, they refused to take advantage of geography to slow and hinder what was to prove the decisive operational blow of the 1940 campaign.

Operation 'Barbarossa' underlines in even more graphic fashion the penalty geography imposes on those who ignore its frictions at the operational level. Three things were clear in the early stages of the *OKH*'s planning for the proposed invasion of the Soviet Union. First, the funnel shaped nature of the theater would result in a rapid decline in the force-to-space ratio in the campaign. The second was that German logistic capabilities could only reach three-quarters of the way to Leningrad, barely to Smolensk, and only into the central portions of the Ukraine, before the supply situation for spearhead divisions became critical. Third, geography experts in the *OKH* indicated early in the planning process that a major shift in the location of Russian industry had occurred as a result of the Five Year Plans: now nearly 40 per cent of that industry lay in the Urals or to the east of that mountain range.[15] Thus, conquest of much of the European portions of the Soviet Union would not necessarily lead to the economic and military collapse of Soviet resistance.

And what was the German response to these geographic factors? In the first case the *OKH*'s planning finessed the problem by suggesting the Wehrmacht would destroy the bulk of the Red Army and Air Force in the border areas, hence making the force to space ratio issue of no significance. Dismissal of the second geographic problem followed along similar lines: the destruction of Soviet military forces in the border areas would remove much of the logistic problem, although, of course, logistics represented no great hurdle, as the French campaign had suggested.

Finally, the Germans solved the third problem with the assumption Hitler clearly enunciated and with which the generals happily agreed: Germany would only have to kick in the door, and the whole rotten structure of the Soviet Union would collapse like a house of cards. The mixture of a bland dismissal of geographic factors with racist assumptions about Jewish/Slav subhumans explains much about why the Germans miscalculated so extensively in their plans to invade the Soviet Union in June 1941. Not surprisingly, the Germans did not improve in their judgement as the campaign proceeded. In November 1941 in a conference with the chiefs of staffs of the various armies in Russia, the Chief of the General Staff, Colonel General Franz Halder suggested that the next two months might bring cold weather – thus freezing the mud – but that it might not snow.[16] He got it 50 per cent right.

Man-made geography can be as important in the conduct of operations as the physical geography. The advance after the 1944 breakout from Normandy at Avranches liberated all of France in a campaign that carried Allied forces all the way to the German frontier. But at that point, the drive came to an abrupt halt. Squabbling among Allied commanders at the time – and historians since – over where to place the main emphasis of the campaign into Germany has obscured the unintended effects that their own air campaign had in bringing the advance to a screeching halt. The air offensive against the French transportation network (rail and ground) in spring and early summer 1944 in effect isolated the Normandy battlefield from German reinforcements and resupply. Thus, the Allies had won the crucial battle of the buildup and had worn the ill-supplied Wehrmacht troops to breaking point. But now in September 1944 the logistical desert created by their air forces lay behind the Allied armies.

Perhaps the finest understanding of the role of geography in military operations came in the US Navy's drive through the Central Pacific in 1943 and 1944. Twenty years of wargames and study at the Naval War College in Newport, Rhode Island, had inculcated a grasp of the physical realities of geography and distance in the Central Pacific into a whole generation of naval and marine officers. The innovations in both carrier war and amphibious war, in which the Americans led the rest of the world, created military forces that could reach out over the immense distances of the Pacific and by carrying independent air and land components seize the advance bases from which to launch the next great jump. This island hopping campaign carried US forces from the first costly experience at Tarawa in the Gilberts in November 1943, to the Marshalls, and on to the Marianas, and eventually to the Philippines all in under a year.

There is a larger point to be made about the 'American Way of War'. In the late 1970s and early 1980s there was a host of books that criticized the overemphasis on logistics and production at the expense of the tactical and operational levels of war that has supposedly characterized the conduct of war by American military forces.[17] Unfortunately, these critics were unwilling to recognize the fact that the geographic isolation of the United States from its battlefields (except in the Revolutionary and Civil Wars) forced American military commanders to think about getting to the war as the first step in the equation of military power. After all, the finest military organization in the world is not worth a damn, if it cannot get to the theater of operations and then supply its forces. As Clausewitz has suggested, '[t]he end for which a soldier is recruited, clothed, armed, and trained, the whole object of his sleeping, eating, drinking, and marching *is simply that he should fight at the right place and the right time*'.[18] Getting military forces to 'the right place and right time' is what logistics is all about, and American commanders, to their credit, solved that portion of the equation with true distinction in World War II.

What made that campaign so devastating against Japanese hopes in the Pacific that they could defend island barriers was the fact that the US fleet remained at sea for the entire period, while only individual ships returned to US bases for rest and refit. The creation of the fleet train of logistic ships to support the effort resulted from an American understanding of distances in the Pacific that even their Japanese opponents never fully grasped. The net result was that the American wolf consistently appeared at the Japanese door earlier than expected and at least until Okinawa and Iwo Jima, American casualties remained considerably under what might have been expected.

Geography has also exercised a major influence on how military organizations have shaped their doctrinal and warfighting conceptions. In the 1920s and 1930s, British and American airmen articulated a dogmatic thesis that air power could achieve decisively results independently of ground and naval forces. They argued that by reaching across the front lines of combatant armies and navies air forces could attack the enemy's homeland directly and bring wars in the future to a quick and decisive end. Thus, armies and navies would no longer be needed. Such doctrinal principles largely reflected the geographic reality that as island nations, neither Britain nor the United States could be attacked directly. Whatever defeats happened on the ground would happen to armies drawn from the Allies. This simplified, technological approach, came a cropper with the catastrophe of May–June 1940. Moreover, the British and Americans soon discovered that, while air power could be a crucial component in damaging the German war economy, political reasons demanded that Anglo-American ground forces seize a substantial portion of the European continent before the Soviets.

It is useful to contrast the Anglo-American approach to air power with that of the Germans.[19] German airmen never dismissed the idea of 'strategic bombing' in a misbegotten belief that air forces should remain tied to 'the coat tails of armies'. Rather, unlike their Anglo-American contemporaries, they had to contend with the real threat of land invasion. American and British airmen could rhapsodize about leaping over the battle lines to batter the enemy nation, but German airmen had to deal with the more prosaic threat that they might lose their airfields to an enemy invader. Bombing factories and sowing terror in Prague, Warsaw, and Paris was all very well, but such exploits would avail the Reich little, if the German Army lost the Rhineland and Silesia. Luftwaffe planners did recognize the possibility of strategic bombing, but because of Germany's geographic position, they could not view it as the sole role for air power. For geographic reasons, German airmen had to think about supporting the ground war.[20] For the British and Americans the loss of Belgium, Holland, or even France would not preclude the possibility of fighting on.

GEOGRAPHY AND WAR: STRATEGY AND POLITICS

It is in the realm of strategy and politics that geography has seemingly exercised its greatest influence. Germany's bad behavior in two world wars has given the term geopolitics a bad reputation. But that reputation in turn has led all too many commentators on strategic and international relations issues to ignore what might reasonably be said about the influence of geography on human affairs, at least in a macro sense. In fact, the size and location of a nation are crucial determinants in the way its statesmen and military leaders think about strategy. The importance of these factors is seemingly obvious. However, their influence is often subtle. In the case of Israel the realities of geography have, not surprisingly, produced an obsession with national security. In combination with historical memories, geography has pushed the Israelis into aggressive responses to perceived threats that have not always been in the best interests of the state. On the other hand, the location and size of the United States, far removed from any serious threat, historically created an unwillingness to participate in the world's strategic equation that at times bordered on the pathological.

The geographic position of the British Isles offers a convenient case to explore some of the ramifications of geography's influence on the strategy and policy of a state. Britain's position has allowed it to participate fully in the economic, political, and military life of the European Continent. But its position as an island has also allowed the British almost entirely to escape the scourge of war that proved so damaging to continental powers. A mere comparison of the state of Britain's medieval buildings with those across the Channel underlines the point. The North Sea and the English Channel have provided shields that have successfully barred successful invasions since 1066 – although William and Mary's relatively bloodless invasion in 1688 forms a partial exception to the rule.

Nevertheless, while Britain escaped the consequences of military operations on its home soil, the possibility of a foreign invasion has remained at the center of British strategic concerns. That fear spurred the development of the Royal Navy. It also guided British policies towards the Low Countries, and Holland in particular. Thus, since the days of Elizabeth I the Low Countries have been a major focus of British strategic policies that aimed at keeping the region out of the hands of a major power. Whether it was Philip II, Louis XIV, the French Republic, Napoleon, Kaiser Wilhelm's Germany, or the Third Reich, the British have expended their national treasure and blood to preserve the independence of the region. Britain's response to the plight of Czechoslovakia in 1938 ('How horrible, fantastic, incredible it is that we should be digging trenches and trying on gas masks because of a quarrel in a far away country between people of whom we know nothing'[21]) underlines that Britain's persistent interest in the security of the Low Countries has little to do with a moral desire to protect the rights of the weak against the aggressions of the strong.

But Britain's relative security, at least compared to its European neighbors,inevitably led to the development of specious but attractive conceptions of the 'British way in war'. Liddell Hart argued the idea with great eloquence in the 1930s (and even greater bias). But Jonathan Swift's biting essay, on *The Conduct of the Allies* (1711), fits into a similar pattern of strategic thought 200 years earlier. That approach, conditioned very much by Britain's geographic position as an island power off the shores of Europe, argued that over the centuries Britain had been most successful when it eschewed heavy land commitments in favor of a strategy utilizing the Royal Navy to project military power against the enemy's weak points.

Of course, Liddell Hart's strategy of 'limited liability' represented an effort to prevent the replication of Britain's experiences in the First World War, which had cost the island nation over 700,000 deaths. But Liddell Hart was at times more a propagandist than a military historian. Most obviously, history indicated that at times Britain had had to commit great armies to the continent. Louis XIV's defeat in the War of Spanish Succession was simply inconceivable without the Duke of Marlborough's British Army and generalship. Similarly, Wellington's forces in Spain, while never quite equal to the forces mobilized by the European allies in the last years of the Napoleonic Wars, were of considerable size and required great financial and manpower expenditures.

But there were other factors that made the realities of geography and strategy quite different from Liddell Hart's analysis. Britain's success in the eighteenth and nineteenth centuries had to a great extent depended upon the ability of its continental allies to maintain pressure on its enemies. Britain's enormous success in the Seven Years War, the conquest of Canada and India, rested to a great extent on the dogged resistance put up by Frederick the Great's outnumbered Prussians. Without that resistance, it is doubtful whether the British would have come out of the war quite so successfully. The extent to which Britain had been able to limit its forces on the European mainland depended primarily upon whether it had major continental allies capable of maintaining considerable pressure on the enemy.

Britain's peripheral strategy also owed much to the exposed position of valuable enemy colonies, which had provided the Royal Navy with easy targets and the Foreign Office bargaining chips in negotiations. In the first half of the twentieth century, however, this situation no longer held. Germany's central position on the continent and its lack of major offshore interests made a peripheral strategy irrelevant. As Sir Michael Howard has suggested:

> It was…precisely the failure of German power to find an outlet and its consequent concentration in Europe, its lack of possessions overseas, that made it so particularly menacing to the sprawling British Empire in two world wars and which make so misleading all arguments about 'traditional' British strategy drawn from earlier conflicts against the Spanish and French Empires, with all the colonial hostages they had offered to fortune and the Royal Navy.[22]

If over the centuries Britain's geographical position as an island power has had a decisive influence over its strategic policies, one can say much the same about the United States. Removed by great distance from the affairs of Europe, the Americans almost fanatically resisted the allure of great power politics until the early 1940s (except in their own sphere of interest in the Americas). Even the outbreak of the Second World War and the complete breakdown of the European system in 1940 failed to persuade the American public to come into the war. Only a completely insane attack by the Japanese on Pearl Harbor provided President Franklin D. Roosevelt with the political clout to wage two great wars at the same time in the European Theater of Operations and the Pacific Theater of Operations. Then, after the war, it was not until exceedingly bad behavior on the part of the Soviets in the late 1940s – to include the North Korean attack on South Korea – that the United States shouldered its international responsibilities for the long term. How long that state of affairs will continue in the post-Cold War world is at present, it is worth noting, a matter of considerable debate among American academics.

The British and American cases stand in stark contrast to the experiences of most of the rest of the world. The waves of invasions, beginning with the damage inflicted by Mongol hordes in the thirteenth century, that have washed over Russia have influenced Russian society and culture in a fashion that is difficult for outsiders to understand. Charles XII and Napoleon only added to a paranoia that the Germans reinforced twice more in the twentieth century. Open in both directions, with great rivers that provide rather than deny access, Russia has had only time, distance, and weather to block the depredations of its invaders.

If geography has laid Russia open to invasion, it placed Germany in the middle of everything that was happening in Europe. While German frontiers at least offered some measure of protection, geography has dictated that almost invariably when war occurred in Europe that it was going either to begin in or spread to Germany. The Thirty Years War (1618–48) started with a religious explosion, but quickly turned into a war of geography. In the seventeenth and eighteenth centuries the very weakness of the German states, resulting from the influences of geography as well as history, insured that almost all European wars ended up in being fought over German territory. In the early eighteenth century, the Germanies found themselves providing the territory for two great simultaneous European Wars: the War of Spanish Succession and the Great Northern War. A hundred years later Napoleon conducted the majority of his greatest battles on German or Austrian territory: Ulm, Jena/Auerstädt, Friedland, Wagram, Bautzen, Dresden, Leipzig underline the price the Germanies paid for their location. The catastrophe of Jena/Auerstädt in 1806 set the Prussian Army on its single minded pursuit of offensive warfare to the exclusion of strategy and politics, a course that culminated in the catastrophes of World War I and World War II. The successors of Moltke and Schlieffen aimed at insuring they would fight the next war on someone else's territory. At least in the early stages of the wars Prussia/Germany waged between 1815 and 1945, they were successful.

The influences – or constraints – of geography can place severe limits on the achievement of national strategic aims.[23] Philip II of Spain (reigned 1556–98) aimed at achieving a hegemonic position in Europe. Yet, his far flung domains exposed Spanish power and military forces to pressures from so many directions that it often seemed that Spain was a beleaguered power rather than an aggressive one. In the Mediterranean, the Ottoman Turks were a constant and powerful threat. In the north the Dutch Revolt presented an economic and religious (ideological) threat the English delighted in exacerbating. In the center the French, despite internal fractures, represented a latent threat. Finally, as Drake's voyage around the world underlined, the wealth of the Americas, on which so much of Spain's economic and strategic position in Europe depended, was vulnerable to attack. Admittedly, many of Philip's problems stemmed from his inability or unwillingness to make concessions in the diplomatic sphere which might have reduced the number of his enemies. Unfortunately for Spanish strategy, the merest survey of a map (not to mention any knowledge of the realities of communications and travel in sixteenth century Europe) suggests the severe limitations that geography exercised on Spain's strategic choices.

As with much in human affairs, size does matter. In fact, it can be a central element in how statesmen and generals evaluate the strategic and political situation. As suggested above, Israel's compactness and lack of territorial depth, particularly in the face of immediate neighbors who have enthusiastically proclaimed until recently their desire to destroy utterly the Jewish state, has made a preemptive strategy almost imperative. Conversely, Russia's sprawling expanse has made possible its historical strategy of trading space for time in a protracted defense. Tragically for those living under Stalin's tyranny in 1941, the tyrant spent much of the summer and fall refusing to trade space for time. The results were catastrophic losses for the Red Army (over 3½ million) as well as the loss of much of the territory of the western Soviet Union (including some of the most important industrial areas). That the Soviet Union survived the war as a victorious power did little to mitigate the effects of the price that was paid.

But geography has had an impact beyond mere physical distance. In its war against the rebellious American colonies, Lord North's government found it impossible to control the military forces that it had dispatched across the North Atlantic. Admittedly the political preconceptions with which the British had embarked on the conflict made it a dubious prospect from the beginning. Nevertheless, of Secretary of State for the Colonies Lord George Germain's approximately 63 letters of instruction to Lieutenant-General Sir Henry Clinton from 1778 to 1781, 6 took less than two months to arrive in North America, 12 took about two months, 28 took two to five months, and 2 took five to seven months.[24]

While the wonders of modern technology have removed some of the difficulties involved in communicating orders and projecting power, time, distance, and weather still impose considerable constraints on the strategic options and capabilities of states.

CONCLUSION

In the current atmosphere within the Washington Beltway and throughout all too much of the American defense establishment, it has become all too easy to dismiss geography and history from the calculations of the 'revolution in military affairs'. Yet, both history and geography will have their revenge on US military forces, strategy, and policy in the next century. The harsh reality of the post-Cold War world is that America's military forces are coming home and that the great base structure spread across the face of the globe is also rapidly disappearing.

The result is that the United States confronts the harsh geographic reality that the two oceans, that provide it with great security, are once again imposing limits on the ability to project military forces out into the world where needed. Again, the United States must emphasize that delicate balance between logistical capabilities on one side and tactical and operational capabilities on the other side. Unfortunately, there is little sign within the Pentagon that much of the US military leadership is paying the slightest attention to the constraints that geography and history have placed and will always place on the conduct of American strategic policy.

NOTES

1. For the contribution made an ignorance of geography as well as history to the disastrous decision of the US government to embark on the Vietnam War in 1965, see H.R. McMaster, *Dereliction of Duty: Lyndon Johnson, Robert McNamara, The Joint Chiefs of Staff, and the Lies that Led to Vietnam* (NY: HarperCollins 1997).
2. Philip Caputo, *A Rumor of War* (NY: 1977) pp.21–2.
3. Quoted in Barbara Tuchman, *The Guns of August* [1964] (NY: Macmillan 1988) pp.17–18. Tuchman gets the river wrong.
4. For the most thorough examination of the battle see Stephen W. Sears, *The Landscape Turned Red, The Battle of Antietam* (NY: Ticknor & Fields 1983).
5. See the extensive discussions on the development of the German defense-in-depth, reverse-slope tactics in Capt. G.C. Wynne, *If Germany Attacks, The Battle in Depth in the West* (London: Faber 1940).
6. Dominick Graham and Shelford Bidwell, *Tug of War: The Battle for Italy, 1943–1945* (London: Hodder 1986) p.147–9.
7. Max Hastings, *Overlord: D-Day and the Battle for Normandy* (London/NY: M. Joseph/Simon & Schuster 1984) p.141.
8. Air Ministry, *The Rise and Fall of the German Air Force, 1933–1945* (London: HMSO 1948) p.75.
9. Williamson Murray, *The Air War in the Persian Gulf* (Baltimore, MD: Nautical & Aviation 1995) pp.226–7. Also see Barry Watts, *Clausewitzian Friction and Future War* (Washington DC: NDU Press 1996) p.40.
10. Matthew Cooper, *The German Army, 1933–1945* (London/NY: Macdonald & Jane's/Scarborough House 1978) pp.272–3.

11. Martin Van Creveld, *Supplying War: Logistics from Wallenstein to Patton* (Cambridge, UP 1977) is particularly good on the constraints surrounding 'Barbarossa'.
12. Horst Boog, *et al.*, *Das Deutsche Reich und der zweite Weltkrieg*, Vol.4, *Der Angriff auf die Sowjetunion* (Stuttgart: Deutsche-Verlags-Anstalt 1983) p.117.
13. On the French campaign see Robert Doughty, *The Breaking Point: Sedan and the Fall of France, 1940* (Hamden, CT: Archon 1990) and Telford Taylor, *The March of Conquest, The German Victories in Western Europe, 1940* (NY: Simon & Schuster 1958).
14. Doughty, *Breaking Point* (note 13) pp.46–53.
15. Boog, *Der Angriff auf die Sowetunion*, p.114.
16. Klaus Reinhardt, *Die Wende vor Moskau: Das Scheitern der Strategie Hitlers im Winter 1941/1942* (Stuttgart: Deutsche Verlags-Anstalt 1972) p.140.
17. See in particular Martin van Creveld, *Fighting Power* (Westport, CT: Greenwood Press 1982) and Russell F. Weigley, *The American Way of War: A History of United States Military Strategy and Policy* (Bloomington: Indiana UP 1973).
18. Carl von Clausewitz, *On War* (eds.) Michael Howard and Peter Paret (Princeton UP 1976) p.95.
19. See Williamson Murray, *Luftwaffe: Strategy for Defeat 1933–45* (Baltimore, MD: Nautical & Aviation 1985) Ch.1.
20. Williamson Murray, 'The Luftwaffe before the Second World War: A Mission, A Strategy?' *Journal of Strategic Studies* 4/3 (Sept. 1981) pp.261–70.
21. Telford Taylor, *Munich: The Price of Peace* (Garden City, NY: Doubleday 1979) p.884.
22. Michael Howard, *The Continental Commitment* (London: Temple Smith 1972) p.32.
23. See Geoffrey Parker, 'The Making of Strategy in Hapsburg Spain: Philip II's 'Bid for Mastery,' in Williamson Murray and MacGregor Knox and Alvin Bernstein (eds.) *The Making of Strategy: Rulers, States, and War* (Cambridge UP 1994).
24. Piers Macksey, *The War for America, 1775–1783* (Cambridge, MA: Harvard UP 1964) p.73.

12

Geopolitik: Haushofer, Hitler and Lebensraum

HOLGER H. HERWIG

> *Haushofer was Hitler's intellectual godfather. It was Haushofer, rather than Hess, who wrote* Mein Kampf ... *Geopolitics was not merely academic theory. It was a driving, dynamic plan for the conquest of the heartland of Eurasia and for domination of the world by the conquest of that heartland ... Really, Hitler was largely only a symbol and a rabble-rousing mouthpiece. The intellectual content of which he was the symbol was the doctrine of Haushofer.*
>
> Office of US Chief of Counsel
> 7 September 1945

Generalmajor Prof. Dr. Karl Haushofer (1869–1946) and his influence on the geopolitical conceptions of Adolf Hitler and the National Socialist regime remain controversial. For much of the non-German world, interpretations have been largely negative, as scholars and statesmen shared the opinions raised in the popular press. *The New Statesman and Nation* on 26 August 1939 depicted the Nazi-Soviet Non-Aggression Pact as Haushofer's intellectual work. Four months later, the *Daily Express* trumpeted that Haushofer was the 'man who stood behind Hitler's war aims', and claimed that the attack on Poland on 1 September constituted the start of 'Haushofer's war'. The German exile publication *Neue Weltbühne* proclaimed from Paris in January 1940: 'Everything that Hitler has accomplished or wishes to accomplish in the future ... is the program of the geopolitician Karl Haushofer; he thinks, plans and recommends; Hitler repeats and obeys'. In the United States, *Reader's Digest* in November 1941 claimed that Haushofer at Munich maintained an 'Institute for Geopolitics' with a staff of 1,000 to 'dictate' Hitler's program. *Harpers' Magazine* suggested that the world would never return to 'normalcy' until these 'academics, journalists, and spies' were safely behind bars.[1]

Haushofer and his defenders adamantly rejected these charges.[2] The Professor of Geography, they countered, was simply an academic engaged in wedding geography to history, demography to political science. Haushofer pointed to the fact that he and his family had spent almost three years in incarceration at the hands of the Hitler regime, that his journal *Zeitschrift für Geopolitik* had been closed down by the Nazis, and that his eldest son Albrecht had been murdered by the Gestapo in April 1945.[3] Above all, Haushofer informed his American interlocutors in 1945 that his readership had embraced men of moderation and intellect: Weimar Foreign Minister Gustav Stresemann, Austrian Chancellor Ignaz Seipel, French Foreign Minister Aristide Briand, Czechoslovakian President Tomás Masaryk, and countless other statesmen and intellectuals.[4]

In 1962 the German political scientist Karl Dietrich Bracher in his classic study, *Die nationalsozialistische Machtergreifung*, first attempted to tack a middle course. While pointing out the close relationship between Haushofer, Deputy Führer Rudolf Hess and National Socialist expansionism, Bracher nevertheless rejected as overly simplistic the notion of Haushofer's direct line of influence to Hitler.[5] And he argued that the topic needed closer scrutiny – beyond the wartime polemics of Robert Strausz-Hupé, Johannes Mattern, Derwent Whittlesey, Andreas Dorpalen, and Sigmund Neumann.[6]

GENESIS OF GEOPOLITICS

Where does the truth lie? The first order of business is to define geopolitics. Haushofer struggled unsuccessfully to come up with a cogent definition; his son Albrecht denied its validity as an academic discipline. The term was first used in its modern sense by the Swedish political scientist Rudolf Kjellén (*Der Staat als Lebensform*[7]), who based his theories in large measure on the German geographer Friedrich Ratzel's *Politische Geographie*.[8] In 1928 Haushofer posited his 'official' definition of *Geopolitik*: 'the doctrine of the earth relations of political developments … based on the broad foundations of geography, particularly political geography, as the doctrine of political space organisms and their structure'.[9] Such offerings tend merely to buttress Mark Twain's pithy comments regarding 'The Awful German Language'. For our purposes, a simple

Webster's dictionary definition will suffice: 'a study of the influence of such factors as geography, economics, and demography on the politics and esp. the foreign policy of a state'.

The basic contours of Haushofer's geopolitics were hardly original. From Ratzel he adopted the notion of space, which Ratzel by 1897 had already defined as Lebensraum. A colleague of Karl Haushofer's father, Max, at Munich Polytechnical University, Ratzel tested his theories during long walks with both Haushofers along the banks of the Isar River. He strove to develop political geography as a discipline designed to trace man's evolution over time as it related to his physical geography. Ratzel viewed the state basically as a 'form of the distribution of life on the earth's surface'. The state was 'part man, part soil', given shape and form by the idea of the state. For Ratzel, Charles Darwin's widely misunderstood concept of the 'struggle for survival' came down to 'a struggle for space'. And space was reserved for the victor: 'It is not like the case of the oak, which permits a good deal of weed and grass to grow under its crown. The state cannot tolerate a second or third [state] on its territory if it does not wish to weaken itself.'[10] What Ratzel termed 'bio-geography' fit well into the 1880s and 1890s, when Imperial Germany set out on a course of overseas expansion (*Weltpolitik*) – a 'natural biological development'.

From Kjellén, Haushofer borrowed the term Autarky, or national self-sufficiency. For the Swedish Professor at Uppsala, 'state' and 'power' were synonymous. States rose because they were powerful; they maintained their status only if they remained powerful. The state was 'a biological revelation, a living being'. States, especially 'vigorous, vital states with limited space' – read, Germany – were held together by neither laws nor constitutions, but rather by 'the categorical imperative of expanding their space by colonization, amalgamation, or conquest'. Haushofer embraced this social Darwinism, and as early as 1924 developed the notion of 'social aristocracy', that is, rule by the fittest on the basis of natural selection without class or racial exclusivity.[11]

From Sir Halford Mackinder,[12] Haushofer seized upon the concept of the 'heartland' (a term first used by the British geographer in 1919), whereby the nations of the world were arrayed into two camps – the land power of inner Euro-Asia and the sea power of the maritime states peripheral to the 'heartland'; categorized as 'robbers of the steppe' and 'sea robbers'. Mackinder described the 'heartland' (Russia) thus: 'a continuous land, ice-girt to the north, water-girt elsewhere, measuring 21 million square miles, or more than three times the area of North America'. The periphery consisted of Britain, Canada, the United States, South Africa, Australia, and

Japan. The two spheres eternally were at loggerheads – in Haushofer's view, a continuance in new form of 'the ancient opposition between Roman and Greek'. The real danger to the 'over-sea powers', Mackinder warned his countrymen in 1904, was that Germany might ally itself with the 'pivot state, Russia'. Mackinder defined political power as the product of 'geographical conditions, both economic and strategic', and the 'relative number, virility, equipment, and organization of the competing peoples'.

Finally, from the Pan-German (*Alldeutsch*) movement, Haushofer adopted the idea of 'panregions', beginning with the concept of 'Mitteleuropa' and moving from there to 'Eurafrica' – two visions central to Chancellor Theobald von Bethmann Hollweg's controversial war-aims program of September 1914. Ratzel had been one of the founders of the Pan-German League and instrumental in formulating its demand that the new Germany acquire 'elbow room'.[13]

Haushofer in his writings after 1919– no fewer than 40 books and about 400 articles, lectures, and reviews – amalgamated the general theories of geopolitics as espoused by Ratzel, Kjellén, and Mackinder, among others. His major contribution was the notion of 'borders' – political boundaries that marked nothing more than the temporary halt of the nation-at-arms en route to territorial expansion. In Haushofer's view, boundaries were living organisms and thus the object of eternal struggles; battle zones in the interplay of greater and lesser powers. 'Everywhere we encounter the frontier as battlefield.' He had no understanding for the static concept of the 'exact border line'; instead, he called for a new sense of a dynamic and ever-changing 'border region'. The latter concept embodied fluidity, uncertainty, instability – the conditions upon which growth and struggle, permanent war and revolution nourished.[14]

But were Haushofer's anti-positivist concepts mere academic musings designed to reveal the nature of events past; or were they intended to guide the nation, once liberated from the Versailles *Diktat* of 1919, to a renewed struggle for hegemony? Haushofer's writings were full of contradictions and ambiguity, steeped in nineteenth-century German philosophy and mysticism, nebulosity instead of the rational scientific discipline that he aspired to create. They almost overwhelm by sheer bulk and verbosity.

HAUSHOFER'S CAREER

To understand Haushofer as theorist and activist, officer and professor, journalist and politician, it is necessary to delve into his multifaceted career.

For, Haushofer was formed as much by his environment and activities as by his education and reading. His career spanned German history from the birth of the Second Reich to the Götterdämmerung of the Third. Born at Munich on 27 August 1869, Haushofer died on 10 March 1946. On 8 August 1896 he had married Martha Mayer-Doss, daughter of Georg Ludwig Mayer, a baptized Sephardic Jew.

The military phase of Haushofer's life began in 1887. Frustrated in his ambition to become an artist or architect, Haushofer joined the Royal Bavarian Army. He graduated third in his class at the Prussian War Academy, in 1900 penning a critical analysis of the Battle of Tannenberg (1410) for the then General Count Alfred von Schlieffen, Chief of the General Staff.[15] Seven years later, Haushofer left the Catholic Church when a priest refused to bury his father for the latter's 'earlier liberal political activity'.[16] From 1908 to 1910, Haushofer served as military observer in Japan. He was so impressed by that island nation's rise to great power status that, once back at Munich in 1913, he completed and published a book, *Dai Nihon*[17] (Greater Japan), analyzing early twentieth-century Japan's 'military power potential and future'. The keys to success lay in Japan's 'noble race' (*Edelrasse*), its appreciation of iron leaders, its veneration of the samurai warrior class, and its willingness to use 'just wars' to attain its goals (especially the annexation of Korea in 1910). The book was intended as a counterpoint to Norman Angell's *The Great Illusion* (1909). It lead to a major *Leitmotif*: the creation of a grand alliance of Japan, Russia, and Germany to counterbalance the Anglo-Saxon maritime powers.

In 1914 Haushofer penned a second project, 'The German Share in the Geographical Opening-Up of Japan and the Sub-Japanese Earth Space, and its Advancement through the Influence of War and Defence Politics',[18] which he submitted to Munich University for his PhD degree (*summa cum laude*).

A second major influence – indeed, caesura – was the First World War, during which Haushofer served with the Bavarian artillery, rising in rank from major to colonel and taking part in the fighting on both the Eastern and Western Fronts. Haushofer, like Ernst Jünger, another veteran of the Somme, found the 'steel bath' of war to be an uplifting experience, one that substituted comraderie, duty, self-sacrifice, service, and discipline for the chaos of western liberal politics.[19] He attributed the outbreak of the war to 'Slavic arrogance', 'French revanchism', 'British lust for power and wealth' – and 'Austrian half-wittedness' as well as 'neo-German parvenu sins'.[20] Haushofer expected the war to last at least three years. He pestered his wife with platitudinal anti-Semitic letters from the front and calls for a German

FIGURE 1

Karl Haushofer, aged 69, entering Eger (Cheb), Bohemia (Czechoslovakia), Sept. 1938 after the Munich Agreement, 'a happy day in the history of geopolitics'.
Bundesarchivr, Koblenz

'Caesar'. Haushofer blamed the Reich's defeat on pacifists, socialists, liberals, and capitalists – thereby following closely the infamous 'stab-in-the-back' legend. As early as 1916, Haushofer determined to dedicate his life to the pursuit of four great ideals: military geography, military history, political geography, and ethnological psychology (*Völkerpsychologie*).[21] He ended the war in command of 30th Bavarian Reserve Division and quit military service in 1919 with the brevet rank of major general.

Haushofer began his academic career in July 1919 as unsalaried university lecturer in geography at Munich University after having completed an inaugural dissertation (*Habilitationsschrift*) dealing with the 'Basic Contours of the Geographical Development of the Japanese Empire 1854–1919'.[22] He was promoted to the rank of honorary professor in March 1921, and full professor in July 1933; on 13 February 1939 he gave his last lecture.

But there was also a darker side to Haushofer's Munich existence: beginning in June 1919, he served in a local anti-republican civil guard (*Einwohnerwehr*) headed by Georg Escherich, and later in the paramilitary organization 'Oberland'. In 1923 Haushofer joined – and a year later became president of – the League for the Preservation of Germandom Abroad (*Verein für die Erhaltung des Deutschtums im Ausland*, or VDA). In this capacity, he maintained close contact with the leaders of the 10 million Germans of the former Austro-Hungarian and German empires living beyond the then borders of their successor states. Politically, Haushofer belonged to the German Peoples' Party until 1925, when he supported Field Marshal Paul von Hindenburg for president of the Weimar Republic.

It was through these non-academic ties that Haushofer on 4 April 1919 was introduced to Rudolf Hess. The latter had last served with Fighter Squadron 35 during the Great War. Within a year, Hess became a devoted Haushofer student, attended teas at the Haushofer residence, spent Easter there, and came to be on intimate Christian-name terms (*duzen*) with the professor. Under Haushofer's guidance, Hess – whom the geographer later described as 'a very attentive student' with great 'heart and character' but 'not very intelligent' – in 1922 penned a Munich University prize-winning essay detailing the rise of a new 'Caesar'.[23] In November 1923, after the ill-fated Beer Hall putsch, the Haushofers hid Hess in their Munich residence. When Hess married Inge Pröhl in December 1927, Haushofer and Hitler served as best men. The close ties between Hess and Haushofer would last until the Deputy Führer's bizarre flight to Scotland in May 1941. It was through Hess that Haushofer met Hitler, probably sometime in 1919.

HAUSHOFER AND HITLER

Haushofer's influence on Hitler is difficult to pin down. The two had less than a dozen, mostly public, meetings. Contrary to popular belief, Haushofer did not contribute a word to *Mein Kampf*; he declined to review it in his *Zeitschrift für Geopolitik* as it had 'little to do with geopolitics'.[24] Yet the general introduced Hitler to the cream of Munich society, steered Reichswehr personnel to his fledgling movement, and assisted in securing Swiss financial support for Hitler.[25] For reasons of 'camouflage', as Haushofer put it in a confidential letter to the Dean of the Faculty of Science at Munich University in December 1938, he had declined to join the National Socialist German Workers' Party (NSDAP) – while nevertheless since 1919 engaged in 'active work' on behalf of the Nazi leadership (Hess, Bormann, Ribbentrop, Rosenberg, Schirach, Todt, etc.).[26] Of course, he did have a traceable conduit to the Führer: Hess.

Starting on 24 June and ending with 12 November 1924, Haushofer visited Hess and Hitler in prison at Landsberg on the Lech. The geographer saw the inmates over eight weeks; each visit came on a Wednesday, once in the morning and again in the afternoon.[27] Haushofer never commented on why a university professor would take so much time out of a busy schedule to 'educate' what he termed the 'young lions' at Landsberg. Did he perhaps see them already as future practitioners of his geopolitical musings? All we know is that Haushofer regarded Hitler as a potential 'fisher of men'.[28]

During these 22 hours of mentoring, Haushofer tried to make terms such as Lebensraum, heartland, geopolitics, and especially Ratzel's *Politische Geographie* intelligible to the two men. The general introduced them to Carl von Clausewitz's patriotic writings of February 1812 and his opus *Vom Kriege*. And he had Hitler read *Dai Nihon*, especially Chapter XV detailing a future Japan-Russia-Germany alliance.[29] The loss or destruction after 1945 of Hess' notes of these Landsberg sessions precludes a definitive answer to the critical question of how much of Ratzel's and Haushofer's 'bio-geography' and social Darwinism Hess' 'tribune' soaked up.[30]

Once more, the historical evidence is ambiguous and contradictory. Hitler throughout his life refused to acknowledge any intellectual indebtedness to the Munich geographer; neither the name 'Haushofer' nor the term 'geopolitics' is indexed in his most important writings and monologues.[31] For Joseph Goebbels and many Nazi insiders, Haushofer remained an obscure 'occulter' and 'subtilizer' (*Spinstisierer*).[32] Still, as late as 1940–41 – that is, after he had fallen out of favour with Hitler and leading National Socialists – Haushofer resolutely maintained that Ratzel's opus had constituted one of the most prized possessions in the inmates' library at Landsberg.[33] Thus, there is no question that Hitler was exposed to the views of Ratzel-Kjellén-Haushofer at Landsberg, and that his amanuensis, Hess, compiled them in *Mein Kampf*. 'These ideas came to Hitler from Hess', Haushofer later stated.[34] Hence, they deserve closer scrutiny.

Haushofer's theories, when stripped of all their nuances and philosophical rhetoric, ambiguities and contradictions, can be summarized under five major headings. Two of these stem from geographic theory; two are proposals for global (re)organization; and the last is a facilitating device.[35]

Haushofer defined *Lebensraum* in practical terms as the right and duty of a nation to provide ample space and resources for its people. Differential increases in population growth among nations guaranteed constant friction in the international power structure; it was thus the duty of the stronger state to expand at the cost of the weaker. This idea was postulated perhaps most graphically in Hans Grimm's wildly popular 1926 novel, *Volk ohne Raum* (265,000 copies sold by 1933). Additionally, Haushofer saw the state as an organism subject not to international but rather to biological laws. Combined, these two concepts encapsulated Ratzel's term 'bio-geography'. To obtain the requisite Lebensraum, a state could resort to empire (direct or indirect), peaceful expansion, or, most obviously, 'just wars'. Thus, while in theory the term Lebensraum may be geographic and academic, in practice it constituted an operational political-military device. Above all, the attractiveness of the concept – for both its inventors and its practitioners – is that it lent pseudo-scientific character to outright greed and conquest. The term Lebensraum appeared twice in the second volume of *Mein Kampf* and 11 times in Hitler's unpublished 'Zweites Buch' of 1928. Haushofer used it already in the first volume of his *Zeitschrift für Geopolitik*, which appeared at the time of Hitler's Munich trial (February–March 1924).[36]

A second geographical construct, *Autarky*, refers to economic national self-sufficiency. Put differently, a great power has the requirement to produce everything that it needs, leaving the state in economic balance and independent of imports. Certainly, the Allied 'hunger blockade' of Germany in 1914–18 gave credence to the term. Combined, the two geographic theories devolved to Mackinder's notion of the heartland, for without the vast lands of Ukraine and European Russia, and the mineral resources of the Donets basin, the Caucasus, and the Urals-Siberia region, no European power could achieve a state of self-sufficiency.[37]

In terms of global (re)organization, Haushofer touted the concept of *Panregions* (see Figure 2).[38] Put simply: no nation is a region unto itself;

FIGURE 2

HAUSHOFER'S PANREGIONS

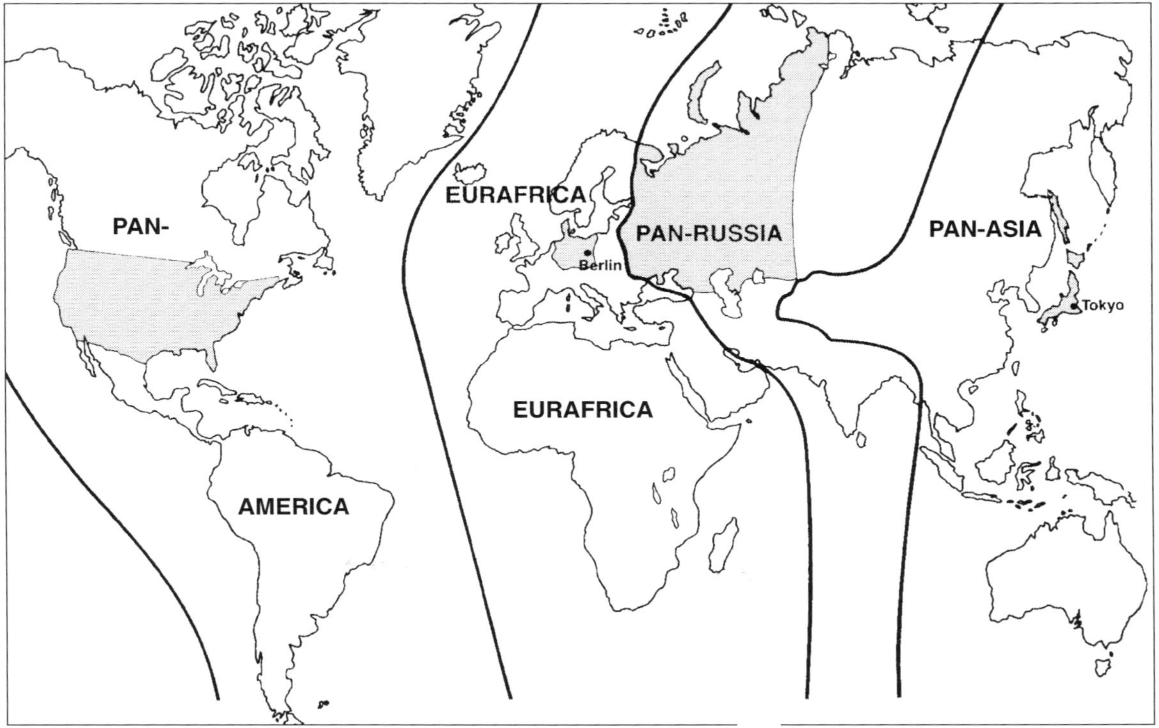

Source: Karl Haushofer, *Geopolitik der Pan-Ideen* (Berlin: Zentral 1931).

hence the necessity to extend its area (space) to include first, people of similar speech and culture, and second, people of related speech and culture. The Pan-Germans of the Second Empire spoke long and loud about nature-given German 'cultural' and 'trade' domains. Scattered German settlements of earlier ages had created enclaves of *Deutschtum*, while earlier German traders (Hanseatic League) had established their language as the *lingua franca* in parts of the East. German notions of 'Mitteleuropa' and 'Eurafrica', expounded during the Great War, were manifestations of these demands. But the geopoliticians went further, dividing the globe into three major 'panregions', each combining middle and low latitudes: Pan-America centred around the United States, Pan-Asia with Japan as master, and 'Eurafrica' under eventual German tutelage. A possible fourth 'panregion', the Russia-India combination, awaited future resolution.

Next, Haushofer posited Mackinder's notion of *Land Power vs. Sea Power*. The land mass Eurasia-Africa – by far the largest, most populous, and richest of all possible land combinations – was depicted as the 'pivot' or centre of gravity of all human existence. This heartland alone provided the base sufficient for dominant land power and Autarky. On its western, southern, and eastern fringes lay a crescent of sea powers – marginal lands with ready access to the oceans. The British Isles and the Japanese Archipelago for Haushofer constituted the two greatest sea powers; he would later add to the list what he termed the 'sluggish' American 'eagle'. The lesser Americas, Black Africa, and Australia-New Zealand formed an outer crescent of 'continental islands' to this global geopolitical configuration. Still under the domination of the sea powers, the 'continental islands' could over time come under the mastery of a heartland state with sufficient sea power to overwhelm the inner crescent. In Haushofer's view, a German-Russian combination – the 'pivotal heartland' – might be able, in conjunction with Japan, to control first the inner crescent of British sea power and finally the outer crescent of 'continental islands'.

Haushofer's own contribution to global (re)organization was his concept of fluid and dynamic *Frontiers*. He rejected his era's faith in legal guarantees of borders as well as the concept of 'natural' physical borders and even that of 'biologically correct borders'. Boundaries, Haushofer argued, were mere temporary halts, breathing spells, for a nation on the march to expansion, Lebensraum, and Autarky. History was full of examples of nation states that used existing borders as political devices to expand their spheres of influence. Europe, with the most numerous and longest frontiers, historically has been the classic continent of conquest – from ancient Rome to modern Russia.

Embittered over the loss of the First World War, the Versailles *Diktat* ('Volk in Chains'), and Germany's isolation in the 1920s, Haushofer posited these five concepts – Lebensraum, Autarky, Panregions, Land Power vs. Sea Power, and Frontiers – as academic constructs to overcome the Reich's plight. There is no question that many of these constructs, undoubtedly inculcated by the general into the minds of Hitler and Hess in 1924, found their way into Hitler's *Mein Kampf.* A few examples must suffice.

In the section of the first volume of *Mein Kampf,* dictated to Hess at Landsberg in 1924 and entitled 'The Four Ways of German Politics', Hitler drew the lessons of the First World War. Central to these was an understanding of the term 'space' in the nation's future. 'The size of a peoples' living area'. Hitler argued, 'already constitutes an essential factor in determining its external security'. The greater that area, the greater the nation's 'natural protection'. Conversely, the smaller the state, the easier its conquest, 'effectively and more completely'. Thus, the nation's 'liberty and independence' were factors of its political geography.[39] Pure Ratzel and Haushofer.

In the section of the second volume, conceptualized with Hess at the Obersalzberg in 1925–26 and entitled 'Eastern Orientation or Eastern Policy', Hitler dealt at length with what he termed the 'geo-military' consequences of this line of reasoning: *'The foreign policy of a* völkisch *state has to guarantee the existence of the race brought together by the state ... by establishing a viable, natural relationship between the size and growth of the Volk on the one hand, and the expanse and value of the soil and territory on the other.'* Pure Haushofer. Hitler went on: *'A sufficiently extensive area on this globe alone guarantees a Volk its freedom to exist.'* But this area can not be calculated simply on the basis of the present population or immediate needs of a people; rather, *'in addition to that area* [being] *a source of nourishment for the Volk, there is also its significance in the military-political sphere*'. Thus, apart from guaranteeing its people 'self-sufficiency', the state also must 'secure the territory in hand'.[40] Pure Kjellén.

In quintessential Haushoferian terminology, Hitler rejected as '*political nonsense*' and a '*crime*' all demands simply to restore Germany to the '*borders of 1914*'. Instead, the future state had the duty to acquire additional '*right to soil and territory*' through conjoint application '*of the plow and the sword*'. In a radicalization of Haushofer's concept of 'borders' as future 'battlefields', Hitler resorted to General Friedrich von Bernhardi's catch word from before the Great War: '*Germany will either become a world power or it will cease to exist.*'[41] Obviously, Hess' 'tribune' had learned his lessons well.

But Haushofer managed to bring his views to a much larger audience than the Landsberg inmates. Beginning in 1919, his geopolitical theories found their way regularly into the *Süddeutsche Monatshefte* – along with articles on the monthly magazines (and Haushofer's) obsession with the 'stab-in-the-back' legend.[42] By the late 1920s, Haushofer's own *Zeitschrift für Geopolitik* was doing well at the newsstands, selling between 300,000 and 500,000 copies annually, and thus spreading his message of national mass claustrophobia.[43] Additionally, the general's comments reverberated throughout the land in other national and regional newspapers such as the *Deutsche Rundschau, Deutsche Allgemeine Zeitung, Frankfurter Zeitung, Schwäbische Merkur*, and a host of regional papers. At another level, Haushofer's arguments concerning Germany's 'just' claims to Lebensraum as well as his 'blood and soil' terminology found their way into elementary and middle-school geography and history textbooks for students and into handbooks for teachers.[44] In 1929 German university students, at their annual meeting at Hanover, with the support of faculty petitioned the Ministry of Culture to establish university chairs in Popular National Studies (*Volkstumskunde*) and Geopolitics.[45]

Haushofer's greatest influence perhaps came through his clever use of the radio: beginning in 1924, the geographer reached at least a portion of the three million German homes with radios by means of his monthly broadcasts on the Deutsche Welle and the Bayerischer Rundfunk, among other senders, on politics and geopolitics.[46] His message was consistent and constant: Germans could only begin to work towards national revival if they taught themselves to think 'geopolitically' and to insist upon Germany's 'eternal and indestructible geopolitical power base'.[47] Through these activities, Haushofer's private income from 1927 to 1933 amounted to between 30,000 and 60,000 Marks per annum; after Hitler's accession to power, that amount soared to between 120,000 and 200,000 Marks – at a time when a skilled railroad worker earned 2,000 Marks a year.[48]

The Nazis would avail themselves of his cabalistic catchwords in the 1930s with regard to expansionism: 'Volk renewal', 'rule by the fit', 'goals of expansionism', 'soil mastery', 'organic frontiers', 'struggle for power', 'space struggle', 'willingness to sacrifice with thousands of martyrs', and the like. Thus, while it may not be possible to trace a direct link between Haushofer's theories and the general staff, the foreign office, or the government, it is nevertheless incontrovertible that his geopolitical theories were in wide circulation throughout the 1920s. With regard to Hitler, Haushofer played a clever game: publicly he kept his distance from the radical 'tribune'; privately, via Hess he fed Hitler his peculiar world view (*Weltbild*) on space, race, and 'just wars'.

HAUSHOFER AND NATIONAL SOCIALISM

The political phase of Haushofer's career began with the Nazi accession to power in 1933. In truth, the geographer shared – indeed, helped create – many of the beliefs espoused by Hitler. In his published 'Monthly Reports' of the 1920s, Haushofer had stated that Germany once again was 'encircled' by a ring of hostile powers, by a new 'entente' consisting of France, Poland, and Czechoslovakia. He had opposed all attempts by Weimar statesmen to break out of this isolation and to ameliorate by negotiation the Versailles *Diktat*. Specifically, Haushofer had rejected the 'spirit of Locarno', the Dawes Plan, and the League of Nations as further manifestations of Germany's ongoing subjugation. He had no qualms about the first three points of the NSDAP (Nazi Party) program of 24 February 1920: union of all Germans into a Greater Germany under the motto of self-determination; equality of Germans with other peoples and revocation of the treaties of Versailles and St Germain; and 'territory and soil' for the feeding of the German nation and the settlement of its excess population. Haushofer proved quite willing to couch his views in racial terms familiar to any Nazi.

It is fair to place Haushofer squarely within the camp of the anti-democratic, anti-republican, anti-socialist, and anti-Semitic neo-conservatives such as Moller van den Bruck, Ernst Jünger, Carl Schmitt, and Oswald Spengler – men who laid the intellectual foundations for National Socialism. But unlike many of his fellow travelers, who rejected what they perceived to be the vulgar, herd-like mentality of the Nazis, Haushofer after 1933 lauded Hitler and Hess as men of peace and common sense. And he placed his journalistic abilities at the service of the new order, preaching the gospel of geopolitics to the German public through countless newspaper articles and radio broadcasts.

Haushofer's *Zeitschrift für Geopolitik* was in vogue after 1933, reaching an annual circulation of almost 700,000 copies. And the general found new venues to spread his message. When the giant Ullstein publishing empire was bought by the NSDAP's press chief, Max Amann, in 1934, Haushofer was appointed to the firm's new editorial board. Therewith, he had direct and insider access to more than six influential newspapers, including the *Berliner Morgenpost* (500,000 circulation), *B-Z am Mittag* (200,000), *Berliner Illustrierte* (2 million), the venerable *Vossische Zeitung* (500,000), and the weeklies *Montagspost* (500,000) and *Grüne Post* (1 million).[49] Obviously, Haushofer was well placed to influence both the public and the party with his views; the NSDAP hailed him as the 'educator of the Volk'.

But Haushofer, then 65 years old, also played a more direct and official role in the Third Reich – his later 'Apologia' that he had done everything after 1933 'under pressure'[50] notwithstanding. In October 1933 he accepted Hess' invitation to head the Volksdeutscher Rat, an advisory council designed to promote the cause of Germans abroad – thereby formalizing his former role as president of the VDA. In May 1934, again on Hess' initiative, Haushofer was appointed to the Deputy Führer's staff to help plan the so-called 'Reichsreform', whereby the division of Germany into historic *Gaue* was to be accelerated and expanded. While most reformers thought only in terms of traditional 'cultural' or 'economic' divisions, Haushofer immediately seized upon 'Reichsreform' to realize his pet scheme of using political borders as a vehicle to attract and eventually to incorporate former German lands into the Reich.

Specifically, Haushofer, deploying the language of his military career, argued that the state should create as many border *Gaue* as possible; and to use these 'security districts' (*Abwehrgaue*), supported in-depth by 'core districts' (*Kerngaue*), as 'permanent warlike troublemakers' against especially Poland and Czechoslovakia.[51] From 1934 to 1937, Haushofer served as President of the German Academy (for the preservation and protection of German history and language), a pale copy of the Académie française. Therewith, he operated within some of the leading organizations of the Third Reich – in effect partly attaining his ambition of quietly operating as 'king maker'. After 1945, Haushofer would deny that he ever played such a role.

Yet again, the question: where does the truth lie? And yet again: the answer is both ambiguous and contradictory. On the surface, there were numerous indications that Haushofer belonged to the favoured few in the new order.[52] In August 1933 he received from Hess a special letter of protection (*Schutzbrief*) to permit his '1/4 Jewish sons' to pursue their state careers. The following month, Haushofer became a 'patron' of the SS-Sturmbann I, 1. SS-Standarte Munich. In 1935 Hess again came to the rescue of his former mentor. First, he issued Haushofer a letter of protection to exempt the general's 'non-Aryan' wife from the infamous Nürnberg Racial Laws; and then he exempted Haushofer from having to sign a 'racial purity form' with Radio Munich, arguing that the broadcasts were 'in Germany's national interest'.[53]

In return, Haushofer that same year placed his intimate contacts to the

Japanese (Ambassador Kintomo Mushakoji, Military Attaché Major General Hiroshi Oshima, and Prince Tsunenori Kaya) at Hitler's service to bring about the formation of the Anti-Comintern Pact. As well, Haushofer had joined the Academy of German Law, the NS Union of Teachers, and the NS Union of Professors; had taught at the NS Union of Students and the NSDAP Commission of Examiners; and had spoken regularly to Strength Through Joy and German Labour Front groups as well as to army cadres.[54]

In truth, Haushofer basked in the glory of Hitler's early triumphs. He supported Hitler leaving the League of Nations, remilitarizing the Rhineland, introducing rearmament and conscription, and secretly testing weapons systems in the Soviet Union (the 'Black Reichswehr'). In March 1936 Haushofer in the *Zeitschrift für Geopolitik* reminded Germans of their 'duty to race and Volk' and called on them to 'trust the Führer' and to aspire to Lebensraum ('continents and oceans') 'by way of the Führer'.[55] In September 1938 the general met with Hitler and Hermann Göring during the Munich Conference, at which his son Albrecht served as an expert on geography – a clear indication that both Haushofers on occasion had direct access to Hitler's decision-making process. Karl Haushofer celebrated the Munich Agreement as 'a happy day in the history of geopolitics', the result of the Führer's 'geopolitical mastery'.[56] He could not help but revel in the fact that Hitler thereby laid the groundwork for 'the Central European solution in its Germanic form': the eventual return of the 'ancient imperial lands of Bohemia and Moravia into the heart of the Reich'.[57] In the wake of the Crystal Night pogrom in November 1938, Hess for a third time issued the Haushofers a *Schutzbrief*. Meetings with Hitler and his inner circle took place in March 1933, September and November 1937, April and November 1938, and finally February 1939. In the words of his official biographer, Hans-Adolf Jacobsen, Haushofer had become the 'cultured advertising executive for the Third Reich'.[58]

Throughout 1933 to 1941, Haushofer met almost monthly with Hess. The Deputy Führer was always able to 'clear up' Haushofer's concerns with the less savoury side of the new order. At other times, Haushofer merely suppressed such concerns or rationalized their obviously 'fleeting' existence. In July 1934, for example, Haushofer congratulated Hess on the mass murders of Ernst Röhm and 89 others in the so-called 'night of the long knives'.[59] Above all, Haushofer was awestruck by the military might and pageantry of the Hitler state as well as by its ability to rally the masses in an organized and disciplined manner. On 20 April 1939, Hitler's 50th birthday, Haushofer celebrated the Führer as a 'statesman' who combined in his person 'Clausewitz's blood and Ratzel's space and soil'.[60] The following month, Haushofer reveled about his work 'behind the scenes' over the past two years with regard to 'the events of 1938/39', that is, the breakup of the Czechoslovakian state and the Austrian *Anschluss*.[61] As late as the summer of 1940, the general still raved about Hitler and Hess as men guided by the 'highest human principles' – at a time when Haushofer already knew of the Nazi policy of murder and extermination in Poland as well as of the first transports of west European Jews to points east.

In 1945 Haushofer assured his American interrogators that he had played no role in Hitler's road to war; indeed, that Hitler had operated specifically in contradiction to his *Weltbild*. The record suggests otherwise. Haushofer celebrated the Nazi-Soviet Non-Aggression Pact of August 1939 as a blow against the 'anaconda policy' of the 'western Jewish plutocracy'.[62] The general's dream, as first enunciated in *Dai Nihon* in 1913, of a Japan-Russia-Germany alliance against the Anglo-Saxon sea powers was at last reality. He rushed to print with a new book lauding Hitler's brilliant 'Eurasian' vision. 'The creation of a powerful continental block embracing Europe, North and East Asia, undoubtedly is the greatest and most important world-political turning-point of our time.'[63] The dreams of Landsberg 1924 had been translated into flesh and blood.

Haushofer interpreted Hitler's destruction of Poland in September 1939 – 'a heroic stroke of seldom attained greatness' – as the conquest of hitherto '*dead space*' by way of a new symbiosis of ancient 'blood and soil' in the 'Vistula region'.[64] In a personal letter to Hess, Haushofer waxed nostalgic. 'Now the axis from the North Sea to the Pacific has been created ... How many times did we in our most audacious dreams conjure up world-political visages of space as have now been realized! It is a shame to be 70 years old and to be able to serve only as a cultural-political umbrella from behind the scenes.' In the wake of the Poland campaign, Haushofer sent Hess a detailed plan for the 'resettling of Baltic Germans'.[65] And the veteran of the Great War was mesmerized by Hitler's crushing defeat of France. On 22 June 1940 Haushofer in a personal letter to Hess reiterated Hitler's claim that German history had been radically altered for the next thousand years, and that 'the world holds its breath as once during the coronation of Charlemagne'.

Then Haushofer added his own laudation: the 'staging in the forest of Compiègne' had taken the world 'by storm'; the time was already at hand to plan 'yours and the Führer's place in Valhalla'. All that remained was to implement Haushofer's own version of the doctrine of 'freedom of the seas': 'racial enhancement', 'disarmament of the blacks', and 'return of our colonies', all by way of 'Europe's war of liberation against the piracy and domination of Anglo chains'.[66] Unbeknown to Haushofer, Hitler in September 1940 for a brief moment toyed with the general's grand design – a firm 'tripartite pact' among Japan, Russia, and Germany – by combining the Hitler-Stalin pact of August 1939 with the Three-Power Pact of September 1940 into a grand geopolitical constellation.[67] When the Führer opted for Japan and against the Soviet Union, Haushofer saw that tie to Tokyo as the direct result of 'thirty years of work on my part'.[68]

On the other side of the coin, Haushofer's relations with the new order were beset with problems. As early as March 1933, party officials had searched his residence in Munich, allegedly for 'concealed weapons'. The need for three special letters of protection from Hess attests to Haushofer's constant fears of state reprisals against his 'non-Aryan' wife. By 1939, Haushofer's book on borders (*Grenzen*) was banned in Germany as a result of Benito Mussolini's protest against the general's support of 'Germandom abroad', in the South Tyrol. In November 1940 the Hitler regime obstructed Haushofer's plans for a new book on Japan, seeing therein an infringement upon official policy. With Hess's flight to Scotland, Haushofer was left without a patron: he was arrested and questioned by the Gestapo in May 1941; Hitler railed against what he called the 'Jewish' professor and regretted that he had not earlier 'silenced' the entire 'Munich brood'.[69] Albrecht Haushofer's knowledge about the attempt on Hitler's life in July 1944 brought about for his father first a house search and then arrest and incarceration at Dachau Concentration Camp from 28 July to 31 August. In October 1944 Haushofer's Munich residence was again searched by Gestapo agents. In the final analysis, Haushofer had misjudged the revolutionary and criminal nature of Hess' 'tribune' – as well as the power of his patron. It never occurred to Haushofer to join the small circle of opposition to Hitler.

To be sure, there were significant differences of opinion between Haushofer and Hitler. First, and most obviously, there was the issue of racism. At the personal level, Haushofer could never quite trust the Nazis with regard to what he termed 'the only really great piece of good fortune of my life',[70] his wife Martha, due to her 'Jewish blood'. Thus he feared point four of the 1920 NSDAP program, which stated that only a person of 'undiluted German blood' could become a *Volksgenosse*. As well, he rejected race as the major determinant of history; to have done so would have been a negation of his life's work in political geography. Conversely, for the Nazis, Haushofer's 'space' concepts left too little room for their insistence on the decisive influence of biological-racial factors upon history. In the end, while Haushofer clamoured for the construction of a Greater

Germany that included all ethnic Germans as well as former German 'cultural' lands and 'trade' domains, and did so using the vocabulary of the Nazis, the latter saw such a 'Greater German Reich' as but a stage on the road to a more radical 'reordering of the European continent' along racial-biological lines.

And there was the matter of the Soviet Union. While Haushofer later claimed that Hitler's invasion of the Russian heartland on 22 June 1941 had constituted a radical break with his *Weltbild*,[71] the general's published comments on Operation 'Barbarossa' do not support that claim. In July 1941 he informed his readers that 'Barbarossa' constituted 'the greatest task of geopolitics, the rejuvenation of space in the Old World'. Haushofer saw the invasion of the Soviet Union as the Führer's bold attempt 'positively and creatively' to turn the task of forging 'Eurasia and Eurafrica into reality'. Already looking beyond the anticipated victory of the NS-ideology over Communism, the general gave his geopolitical emotions free rein: 'Thereafter, a veritable cornucopia of space-related, economic and geopolitical tasks will be showered down on Eurasia', one whose vast dimensions not even the guardians of the new order 'can fully fathom'.[72]

Thus, Hitler's invasion of the 'pivot' of history was not at all in violation of all that the general had preached since his *Dai Nihon* book of 1913. Only the means of creating a Japan-Russia-Germany heartland poised to tackle the sea power of the inner crescent had changed – from alliance to conquest. To be sure, by 1941 Haushofer's theoretical geopolitical constructs had long been drowned out by Hitler's ever-escalating pace of diplomatic crises, war, and extermination. But the general remained true to his convictions to the bitter end: after the Battle of Stalingrad, he penned for Hitler a shopping list of German war aims that included the annexation of Poland, Bohemia, Moravia, Slovenia, Alsace-Lorraine, Eupen-Malmédy, North Schleswig, South Tyrol, Togoland, and the Cameroons; 'friendly' regimes in Finland, the Baltic states, Slovakia, Croatia, Serbia, Greece, Belorussia, and the Ukraine; and a German-dominated 'economic union' with Denmark, Norway, Sweden, Switzerland, and Italy.[73] Geopolitics 'Through the Looking Glass'.

NEMESIS

At war's end, Karl Haushofer feared arrest by the Americans or murder by the Russians. In November 1945 American occupation authorities rescinded Haushofer's university lectureship as well as honorary professorship and confiscated his library. On 10 March 1946 Heinz Haushofer, the younger son, arrived at the family estate near Pähl, Bavaria, to pick up his mother. He discovered her body hanging from a tree, and that of his father beneath another tree; both had taken arsenic. In a terse suicide note, Karl Haushofer decreed that he wished 'no form of state or church funeral, no obituary, epitaph, or identification of my grave'. He closed more than half a century of service as officer, academic, publicist, and political adviser with the words: 'I want to be forgotten and forgotten.'[74]

Haushofer never issued an order to go to war, never killed a Jew, never transported a slave labourer, never arrested a fellow citizen. Near the end of his life, he maintained that he had always acted in good faith according to the maxim of two of his peers, Sir Thomas Holditch and Sir Halford Mackinder: 'Let us educate our masters.'[75] His major regret was that the Nazis – with the 'half-educated' Hitler and Hess at their head – had never understood his geopolitical theories.[76]

Haushofer's cardinal sin – beyond that shared by so many German academics, of openly opposing the democratic, parliamentary Weimar Republic – was that he paved the way intellectually for much of the Nazi terminology of expansionism. From the Olympian heights of Munich University as well as through hundreds of newspaper articles and countless hours of radio broadcasts, he first provided their slogans and then popularized these under the guise of 'scientific research'. By way of his august standing as a former Great War veteran and academic mandarin, Haushofer gave credence and respect to what in Hitler's mind and from his pen became the vulgar doctrines of Lebensraum, 'bio-geography', Autarky, eternal struggle, and permanent revolution. In a sense obviously not appreciated by Haushofer, the general had, indeed, 'educated' his 'masters'.

Haushofer's biographer, Jacobsen, concluded that the geopolitician had made National Socialist expansionism palatable to the broad public, indirectly blessed its course of aggression and conquest, and directly contributed to 'the moral seduction of the German Volk'.[77] Albrecht Haushofer from Moabit prison shortly before his murder in March 1945 acknowledged Karl's critical role under the Nazi regime in a sonnet entitled 'My Father': 'But my father broke away the seal ... He let the daemon soar into the world.' Albrecht concluded in another sonnet, 'My father was blinded still by the dream of power.'[78] With the accuracy of historical hindsight, geopolitics may well have been 'the greatest hoax of the century',[79] yet it was serious business first for Karl Haushofer, and then in Nazi Germany.

The historian Dennis E. Showalter has argued with regard to the influence of Julius Streicher and his racist-pornographic publication, *Der Stürmer*, that popular writers must be judged by their paper's circulation and influence. Publication means recognition and influence. It mobilizes frustrations and hostilities. It can play a direct instrumental role in shaping the future. And it can translate into acceptance of the author's views and the implied possibility of solutions to real or imagined problems within the framework of a new order.[80] Streicher was tried at Nürnberg and hanged for these sins.

In the final analysis, Haushofer provides a fascinating study of a central character of modern German history as defined by the novelist Thomas Mann: *General Dr. von Staat*. For, Haushofer combined in his person three pivotal careers: military officer (1887–1919), university professor (1921–39), and advisor and confidante to Deputy Führer Rudolf Hess (1920–41). In many ways, the general's suicide in 1946 personified the end of a particularly complex and tragic phase of his nation's history.

NOTES

1. Hans-Adolf Jacobsen, *Karl Haushofer. Leben und Werk* [Schriften des Bundesarchivs 24] (2 vols., Boppard: Harald Boldt 1979) Vol.1, pp.409–12, 568–69. All original Haushofer documents stem from the Nachlass (N 122) at the Bundesarchiv (BA), Koblenz; the latter also contains copies of the Haushofer materials (T 253) at the National Archives, Washington DC, as well as of the Institut für Zeitgeschichte, Munich, as ED 98 Nachlass Haushofer, MA-162, MA 618-19, MA 1190, and MA 1464-66. Jacobsen culled from the Haushofer Nachlass all materials that he used in his two-volume biography and hence much of this is in the Nachlass Jacobsen (N 413) rather than N 122 at Koblenz. Finally, there is a private Haushofer family archive at the Hartschimmelhof near Pähl, Bavaria. My various attempts to see this material were met with silence, my letters returned unopened.
2. For a most recent apologia, see Frank Ebeling, 'Karl Haushofer und die deutsche Geopolitik 1919–1945', unpub. diss., Hanover 1992.
3. See Haushofer's Nov. 1945 'Apologie der deutschen Geopolitik' in BA, N 413, Vol.2.
4. Statement of 2 Nov. 1945. BA, N 413, Vol.6.
5. Karl Dietrich Bracher, *et al.*, *Die nationalsozialistische Machtergreifung. Studien zur Errichtung des totalitären Herrschaftssystems in Deutschland 1933/34* (Cologne and Opladen: Westdeutscher 1962) p.226.
6. Robert Srausz-Hupé, *Geopolitics: The Struggle for Space and Power* (NY: Putnam's 1942); Johannes Mattern, *Geopolitik: Doctrine of National Self-Sufficiency and Empire* (Baltimore: Johns Hopkins Press 1942); Derwent Whittlesey, *German Strategy of World Conquest* (NY and Toronto: Farrar & Rinehart 1942); Andreas Dorpalen, *The World of General Haushofer: Geopolitics in Action* (Port Washington, NY: Kennikat 1942); and Sigmund Neumann, *Permanent Revolution: The Total State in a World at War* (NY and London: Harper 1941).
7. Rudolf Kjellén, *Der Staat als Lebensform*, German ed. (Leipzig: S. Hirzel 1917); in Swedish, *Staten som Lifsform* (Stockholm 1916). Kjellén lived 1864–1922.
8. Friedrich Ratzel, *Politische Geographie* (Munich and Leipzig: R. Oldenbourg 1897). Ratzel lived 1844–1904.
9. Karl Haushofer *et al.*, *Bausteine zur Geopolitik* (Berlin: K. Vowinckel 1928) pp.23–4. Already in the summer of 1916, after his first reading of Kjellén, Haushofer vowed to find a

German term for geopolitics; he failed, rejecting even his own best effort, *Erdmachtkunde*.
10. Ratzel (note 8) p.7.
11. Karl Haushofer, 'Nationaler Sozialismus und soziale Aristokratie', *Zeitschrift für Geopolitik* 1 (1924) pp.127ff.
12. Halford J. Mackinder, 'The Geographical Pivot of History', *The Geographical Journal* 23 (April 1904) pp.421–44. See also Paul M. Kennedy, 'Mahan versus Mackinder: Two Interpretations of British Sea Power', *Militärgeschichtliche Mitteilungen* (1974) pp.39–66.
13. *Alldeutsche Blätter* 4, 7 Jan. 1894.
14. Karl Haushofer, *Grenzen in ihrer geographischen und politischen Bedeutung* (Berlin and Heidelberg: K. Vowinckel 1927 and 1939).
15. BA, N 413, Vol.1.
16. Ibid.
17. Karl Haushofer, *Dai Nihon. Betrachtungen über Groß-Japans Wehrkraft und Zukunft* (Berlin: E.S. Mittler 1913).
18. Karl Haushofer, 'Der deutsche Anteil an der geographischen Erschließung Japans und des subjapanischen Erdraums und deren Förderung durch den Einfluß von Krieg und Wehrpolitik', Munich Univ. diss. 1914.
19. Letter to his wife, 4 Feb. 1915; Jacobsen (note 1) Vol.1, p.121.
20. Letter to his wife, 6 July 1917; ibid. p.128.
21. Letter to his wife, 8 May 1916; ibid. p.124.
22. Karl Haushofer, *Grundrichtungen in der geographischen Entwicklung des Japanischen Reiches 1854–1919*, special *Habilitationsschrift* publication (Munich: Bieler 1919).
23. The essay is reproduced in Bruno Hipler, *Hitlers Lehrmeister. Karl Haushofer als Vater der NS-Ideologie* (Erzabtei St Ottilien: EOS 1996) pp.221–6. Haushofer's description of Hess is from the 5 Oct. 1945 interrogation by the US Army. BA, N 413, Vol.1.
24. See the Nov. 1945 'Apologie' in BA, N 413, Vol.2.
25. See Willi Gautschi's report in the *Neue Zürcher Zeitung*, Vol.199, Fernausgabe Nr. 302, 30 Dec. 1978, pp.23–4.
26. Letter of 24 Dec. 1938. BA, N 413, Vol.5.
27. Strangely, the dates of these visits have been scissored out of the letter, Justice Department Landsberg to Jacobsen, 24 Aug. 1971. BA, N 413, vol. 2.
28. Statement of 1925. BA, N 122, Vol.955b.
29. Haushofer deposition of 22 Sept. 1945, US Third Army Intelligence Center. BA, N 413, Vol.2. See also Wolf Rüdiger Hess (ed.) *Rudolf Hess. Briefe 1908–1933* (Munich and Vienna: Langen Müller 1987) p.328. 'He [Hitler] is at the moment reading the general's Japan books ...'.
30. Jacobsen (note 1) Vol.1, p.241. The notes were last known to be deposited with the Bayerische Hypotheken- und Wechselbank at Munich in 1945.
31. See Adolf Hitler, *Mein Kampf* (Munich: Zentralverlag der NSDAP, Frz. Eher Nachf. 1939); Werner Jochmann (ed.) *Adolf Hitler. Monologe im Führer-Hauptquartier 1941–1944* (Munich: Wilhelm Heyne 1980); and Gerhard L. Weinberg (ed.) *Hitlers Zweites Buch. Ein Dokument aus dem Jahr 1928* (Stuttgart: Deutsche Verlags-Anstalt 1961). Hermann Rauschning, *Hitler Speaks: A Series of Political Conversations with Adolf Hitler on his Real Aims* (London: Thornton Butterworth 1939) p.226, states simply: 'Hitler recognised no predecessors – with one exception: Richard Wagner.'
32. Elke Fröhlich (ed.) *Die Tagebücher Joseph Goebbels. Sämtliche Fragmente* 4 (Munich: K. G. Saur 1987) p.727.
33. See Friedrich Ratzel, *Erdenmacht und Völkerschicksal. Eine Auswahl aus seinen Werken* (ed.) Karl Haushofer (Stuttgart: A. Kröner 1940) p.xxvi.
34. Deposition of 22 Sept. 1945. BA, N 413, Vol.2.
35. See Derwent Whittlesey, 'Haushofer: The Geopoliticians', in Edward Mead Earle (ed.) *Makers of Modern Strategy: Military Thought from Machiavelli to Hitler* (Princeton UP 1943) pp.398–406. The article was dropped from the major rewrite of the volume by Peter Paret in 1986.
36. Karl Lange, 'Der Terminus "Lebensraum" in Hitlers "Mein Kampf"', *Vierteljahrshefte für Zeitgeschichte* 13 (Oct. 1965) pp.427, 431.

37. Haushofer consistently acknowledged his intellectual debt to Mackinder. See James Trapier Lowe, *Geopolitics and War: Mackinder's Philosophy of Power* (Washington DC: UP of America 1981) pp.86–7.
38. Karl Haushofer, *Geopolitik der Pan-Ideen* (Berlin: Zentral 1931).
39. Hitler, *Mein Kampf* (note 31) p.142.
40. Ibid. pp.638–9. Italics in the original.
41. Ibid. pp.645, 650, 651–2. Italics in the original. The Haushoferian view on borders in general and especially against merely reconstituting those of 1914 was also repeated by Hitler in the *Zweites Buch*, p.114. Yet it would overstretch the evidence to suggest that *Dai Nihon* and *Mein Kampf* were cast from the same mould: Hitler (note 31) pp.178ff.
42. Harry Pross, *Literatur und Politik. Geschichte und Programme der politisch-literarischen Zeitschriften im deutschen Sprachgebiet seit 1870* (Olten and Freiburg: Walter 1963) p.113.
43. See Karl-Heinz Harbeck, 'Die "Zeitschrift für Geopolitik" 1924–1944', unpubl. diss., Kiel University 1963, pp.257–64.
44. David Thomas Murphy, *The Heroic Earth: Geopolitical Thought in Weimar Germany 1918–1933* (Kent, OH and London: Kent State UP 1997) p.242.
45. Kurt Sontheimer, *Antidemokratisches Denken in der Weimarer Republik. Die politischen Ideen des deutschen Nationalismus zwischen 1918 und 1933* (Munich: Nymphenburger Verlagshandlung 1962) p.312.
46. Murphy (note 44) pp.106–8.
47. Cited in ibid. p.28.
48. BA, N 413, Vol.1. 'Finanzen'; Gerhard Bry, *Wages in Germany 1871–1945* (Princeton UP 1960), pp.439 ff.
49. Oron J. Hale, *The Captive Press in the Third Reich* (Princeton UP 1964) pp.131–2.
50. Haushofer's statement of 2 Nov. 1945. BA, N 413, vol. 6.
51. Bracher (note 5) pp.609–11.
52. The following is compiled from Jacobsen (note 1) Vol.1. See also Donald Hawley Norton, 'Karl Haushofer and His Influence on Nazi Ideology and German Foreign Policy, 1919–1945', unpubl. diss., Clark Univ., Worcester, MA, USA 1965.
53. Hess to Radio Munich, 9 Feb. 1935. BA, N 413, Vol.5.
54. Rainer Matern, 'Karl Haushofer und seine Geopolitik in den Jahren der Weimarer Republik und des Dritten Reiches. Ein Beitrag zum Verständnis seiner Ideen und seines Wirkens', unpubl. diss., Karlsruhe Univ. 1978, pp.143–4.
55. 'Stimme der Geopolitik zum 29. März 1936', *Zeitschrift für Geopolitik* 13 (1936) p.247.
56. 'Geopolitischer Erntedank 1938!', ibid. 15 (Oct. 1938) p.782.
57. Jacobsen (note 31) Vol.1, p.372.
58. Hipler (note 23), p.173.
59. Haushofer to Hess, 1 July 1934, in Jacobsen (note 1) Vol.1, pp.377–8.
60. Ibid. pp.370–71.
61. Haushofer to Hess' staff, 17 May 1939. BA, N 122, Vol.23.
62. 'Herbsten?', *Zeitschrift für Geopolitik* 16 (Oct. 1939) p.741.
63. Karl Haushofer, *Der Kontinentalblock. Mitteleuropa-Eurasien-Japan* (Munich: F. Eher Nachf. 1941).
64. Haushofer to Hess, 20 Oct. 1939. BA, N 122, Vol.15; and 'Geopolitische Gundlagen', *Die Verwaltungs-Akademie. Ein Handbuch für den Beamten im nationalsozialistischen Staat* (Berlin and Vienna: Deutscher n.d. [1940]) Vol.1, p.40.
65. BA, N 122, Vol.15, Jan. 1940; Jacobsen (note 1) Vol. 1, p.394.
66. Haushofer to Hess, 22 June 1940. BA, N 122, Vol.15.
67. See Andreas Hillgruber, *Hitlers Strategie. Politik und Kriegführung 1940–1941* (Frankfurt: Bernard & Graefe 1965) p.241.
68. Haushofer to Hess, 27 Sept. 1940. BA, N 122, Vol.23.
69. Gerhard Engel, *Heeresadjutant bei Hitler 1938–1943. Aufzeichnungen des Majors Engel* (ed.) Hildegard v. Kotze (Stuttgart: Deutsche Verlags-Anstalt 1974) p.105.
70. Suicide note cited in Jacobsen (note 1) Vol.1, p.447.
71. Ibid. pp.460–61.
72. Karl Haushofer, 'Die größte Aufgabe', *Zeitschrift für Geopolitik* 18 (July 1941) pp.369–70.

73. 'Gedanken zur Friedensordnung', BA, N 122, Vol.832.
74. Cited in Jacobsen (note 1) Vol.I, p.447.
75. Ibid. p.343.
76. Edmund A. Walsh, 'Die Tragödie Karl Haushofers', *Neue Auslese aus dem Schrifttum der Gegenwart* 2 (March 1947) p.22.
77. Jacobsen (note 1) Vol.I, p.389.
78. Albrecht Haushofer, *Moabit Sonnets* (London and NY: Norton 1978) pp.49, 77.
79. Edmund A. Walsh, *Total Power: A Footnote to History* (Garden City, NY: Doubleday 1948) p.7.
80. Dennis E. Showalter, *Little Man, What Now?* Der Stürmer *in the Weimar Republic* (Hamden, CT: Archon Books 1982) p.236.

13

'Russia Will Not be Trifled With': Geopolitical Facts and Fantasies

JOHN ERICKSON

Geopolitics, persistently demonised during the days of the Soviet Union, has returned with a vengeance to haunt post-Soviet Russia. Gone are the denunciations of geopolitics as a pseudo-science, nothing more than a heinous capitalist ideological device to promote both militarism and chauvinism among the masses. Worse, it had become the instrument of 'military adventurers', among them West German revanchists, Maoists, Zionists, vilified by L. A. Modzhoryan in *Geopolitika na sluzhbe voennykh avantyur,* 'Geopolitics in the service of military adventurisms', published in 1974. Gone are the anti-Western diatribes published in the *Soviet Military Encyclopaedia* under the rubric of 'geopolitical theories of war' excoriating Friedrich Ratzel (1844–1904) and Rudolf Kjellén (1864–1922) for their anti- scientific, reactionary concepts, culminating in post-1945 anti-Communism and anti-Sovietism, witness NATO, CENTO and SEATO.[1] These 'anti-scientific theories' including 'geosociology' (*geosotsiologiya*) spawned yet more 'reactionary ideas'. For the truth the reader was directed to the entry under 'Military policy' (*Politika voennaya*) which reiterated the canons of the Marxist-Leninist party, emphasised the 'class character' of 'military policy', contrasting the 'Leninist defence of the socialist Motherland' with the military policy in the service of monopoly-capitalism.[2] The *Military Encyclopaedia* minus its Soviet imprimatur published in 1994 repeated the formula 'Geopolitics: see Military Policy', the entry 'Geopolitical theories of war' refers the reader to 'Concepts of war'. 'Geostrategy' is similarly re-aligned to 'Military-political strategy'.[3]

Both the term itself and the basic concept of geopolitics have been fully returned to the public domain, refurbished with a rush, together with the restoration to prominence of Alfred Thayer Mahan, Halford Mackinder,

Karl Haushofer himself, coupled with the contributions of more recent practitioners including those prominent during the days of Cold War 'Anglo-American geopolitics': Colin Gray (*K. Grei*), Henry Kissinger *(G. Kissindzher),* Ray Cline (*R. Klein*). The reason for the current obsessive preoccupation with geopolitics, its attendant analysis of global power configurations and its relevance to key issues of Russian national security, is not hard to determine. With the collapse of communism Russia has suffered a huge crisis of identity and a challenge to its security requirements of truly historic dimension. The result has been a combination of despair and defiance. Of the latter, the title of the book by Gennadii Zyuganov, leader of Russia's post-Soviet Communist Party, speaks for itself: *Geografiya pobedy*, 'The Geography of Victory', sub-titled 'The Foundations of Russian Geopolitics'. He patently discounts any ideological *lèse-majesté* by prefacing his book with a quotation from none other than Rudolf Kjellén.[4]

None dispute the visible diminution of Russia's geostrategic space in the aftermath of the disintegration of the Soviet empire. Geopolitical axioms affirm that control of space (*prostranstvo*) is the critical issue, a problem now hideously complicated by the distortions and discrepancies in the 'space' remaining to Russia and the serious deterioration of Russia's strategic posture. The disappearance of the Warsaw Pact violently disrupted Russia's previous geostrategic surety in the west, followed by a strategic withdrawal on an almost unprecedented scale (and one largely unacknowledged). Withdrawal from the centre of Europe, from Prague to Smolensk, has forced Russia back in Dr Alexei Arbatov's view to a peacetime position which last pertained three centuries ago, transforming the Moscow Military District from 'the deep rear into Russia's advanced western defence line' . This was not the sole consequence. The unstable, unpredictable 'geopolitical conglomerate of East European states and former Soviet republics' has contributed to, if it did not actually contrive, the erection of 'a barrier effectively isolating Russian from European security affairs', while these same conditions promise to advance the presence of 'a not clearly friendly military alliance', namely NATO, now in its first stage of enlargement, bringing Moscow within uncomfortably close range of missiles and aircraft.[5]

Further afield the geostrategic horizon continued to darken, increasing Russian vulnerabilities and complicating security requirements. Russia faced the emergence of a novel security environment, former union republics of the Soviet Union to the west, southwest and south, recognised as foreign countries in their own right but also distinctively identified as

Russia's 'Near Abroad' (*Blizhnoe zarubezhe'e*).[6] No less than 26 million Russians are settled in the 'Near Abroad' coupled with an appreciable Russian military presence implanted from Moldova and Georgia to Tajikistan. What was initially simply an impersonal term of demarcation, distinguishing the 'near abroad' from the 'far abroad', quickly assumed unwelcome political overtones, not least suspicions of Russian neo-imperialism. The term 'Near Abroad' can also be misleading by conveying a sense of a unified region much belied by the reality of the rise of 'multiple military and security environments', nothing less than a 'new Eurasian security geography'.[7]

Dr Arbatov also exposes a twin dilemma for Russia, the first: the manner in which Russia must straddle the problem of treating the former Soviet republics as independent states even as it cultivates a 'special relationship' with them, the second: encouraging the elimination of the distinction between the 'Near Abroad' and the 'Far Abroad', the wider world yonder.[8] His own stance on this question is that these two entities are effectively indivisible, the one affecting the other. Both are enmeshed in what he espies as the basic security challenge to Russia: finding 'a new Russian place' in the international environment, one neither resembling a 'scaled down version of Soviet geopolitical expansion' nor one mired in isolationism. The former would not only antagonise the 'Near Abroad' but also propel the 'Far Abroad' towards a revival of former containment policies. The latter, isolationism, would be self-defeating, depriving Russia of any benefit from co-operation with the West, while simultaneously condemning other post-Soviet states to 'disintegrate in violence and chaos'.[9]

But how should this 'Russia' seeking 'a new Russian place' be first identified and then defined? Yurii Afanas'ev argued that Russia must first find the answer for itself: 'A unitarian state? A multinational empire?' For him 'modern Russia is pre-modern', the end-product of Russian history, geopolitics, centuries of absolutism and 75 years of Soviet totalitarianism'. Russia knocks on the door of the modern world only to sell 'what sows anxiety, unbalance and death – weapons, missiles and military consultation'.[10] Less rancorous but in similarly pessimistic vein was the extensive 'geopolitical prognostication' assembled by several senior military and political Russian specialists from the 'Section for Geopolitics and Security' in the Russian Academy of Natural Sciences.[11] In a pert phrase Russia was described as having been transformed from a 'geopolitical extrovert' into a 'geopolitical introvert'. Geopolitical change at large has worked to the serious detriment of Russia, which can no longer be regarded 'functionally as a great power'.[12] The disdain with which Russian diplomats

FIGURE 1
THE EXPANSION OF RUSSIA c.1450–1914

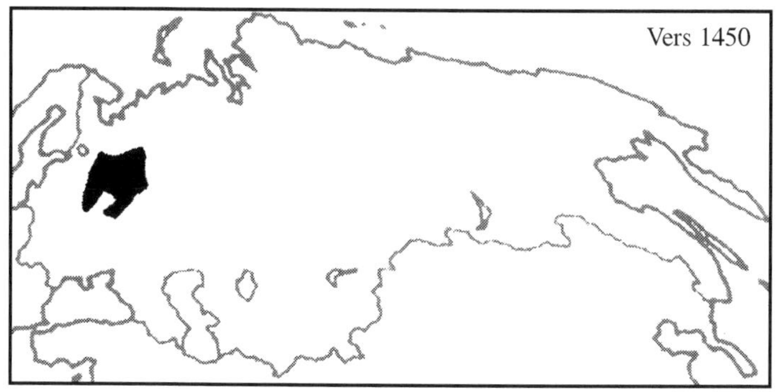

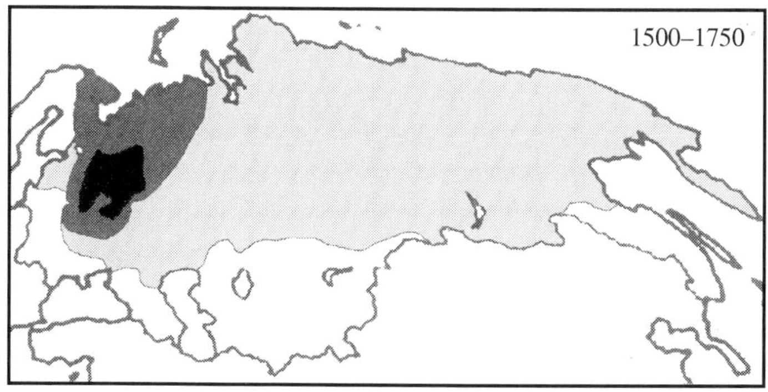

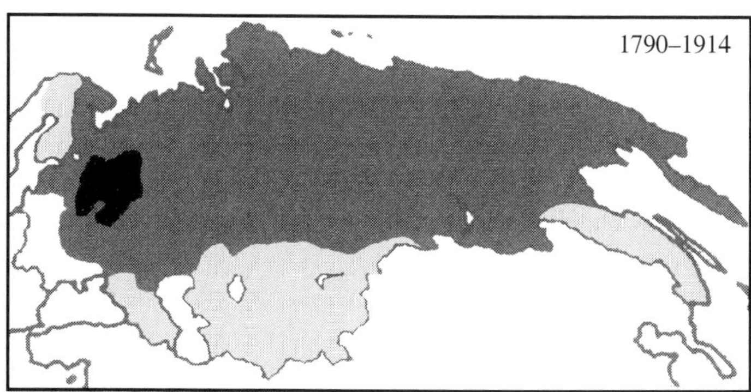

Source: See endnote 4.

are treated speaks for itself. A shrunken Russia lost heavily in the geostrategic and geo-economic stakes: reduced access to the sea, loss of port facilities, shut off as a 'northern-continental country' like some obscure corner of Europe. Russia was deprived of key elements of its strategic early warning system and air defence capabilities, vulnerability magnified by the reduction in the number of airfields available. The security of lengthy land and maritime frontiers fell to a shrinking military force. If the much-vaunted 'mobile forces' had materialised, which so far they had not, such forces would have had to rely upon a poorly-developed transport infrastructure. The demographic factor further exacerbated Russia's unfavourable geopolitical situation, rising mortality outstripping the birth rate with consequences for the immediate future.[13]

A dubious, dramatic, wildly melodramatic contrast with this type of elaborate academic analysis was provided by Vladimir Zhirinovskii who entered the geopolitical fray with his brash, demagogic political biography, *The Last Thrust South*, *Poslednii brosok na yug*. In the search for what constitutes 'Russia', Zhirinovskii asserted that national self-perception will evolve side by side with international perceptions of the nation, elevating all, Russians and non-Russians alike, to equality across Eurasia. 'To be Russian' is simply to speak and think in Russian. On the other hand the imperialist stamp was pronounced in his geopolitical Armageddon, nothing less than the elimination of that well-spring of war, pestilence and turbulence, the 'south' of his title, an agglomerate of Transcaucasia, Iran, Afghanistan, Turkey, all brought to heel by Russia. The price of peace throughout Eurasia was nothing less than Russia's pacification of and imperial dominion over these fissiparous malcontents. In a grand megalomaniacal geopolitical fantasy Zhirinovskii also invited America, Europe, China and Japan to emulate Russia, to 'thrust south', thereby creating a world of co-prosperity spheres running this time along a north-south divide. Ever a dedicated follower of fashion Zhirinovskii garbed himself as a serious geopolitical analyst in *Ocherki po geopolitike* in 1997, published courtesy of his 'Liberal-Democratic Party of Russia', neither liberal nor democratic. To add gravitas to a pedantic tone the brochure includes a multi-lingual bibliography, in places as bizarre as it is irrelevant.[14]

The aftermath of the dissolution of the Soviet Union not only generated neo-imperialist geopolitical phantasmagorias exemplified in Zhirinovskii's earlier writings but also prompted serious if tentative attempts to connect the 'geopolitical approach' with the issue of Russia's national security (see Figure 2).[15] Increasingly aspects of 'security', *bezopasnost"* (literally 'absence of danger') have been associated with the 'geopolitical approach',

FIGURE 2

BASIC ELEMENTS AND COMPONENTS OF NATIONAL SECURITY

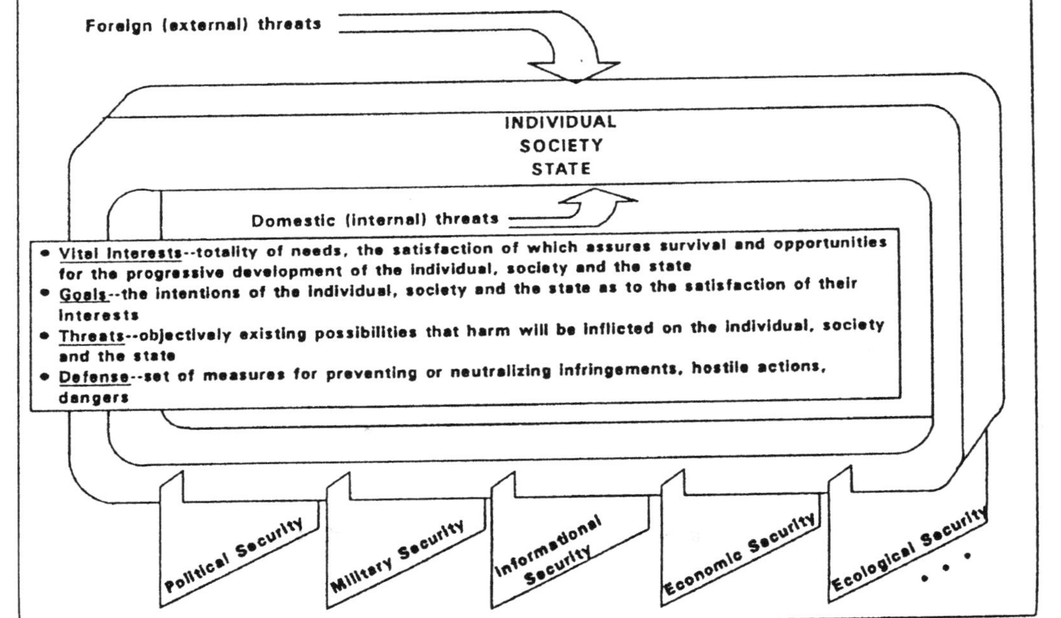

Source: See endnote 11.

the latter undergoing elaboration to the point of prescribing 'methodological principles' for a 'general theory of geopolitics and security' (*obshchaya teoriya geopolitiki i bezopasnosti*).[16] While that has yet to materialise, a tangible result of these explorations has been to expand the concept of 'security', in particular 'national security' and coincidentally to amplify the nature of 'threat'. Here geopolitics acts to synthesise several disciplines: strategic theory, economics, geography, military affairs, sociology, demographic and ecological studies. Accordingly the response to a complex 'threat spectrum', whether externally or internally generated, involves a diversity of political, military, 'informational', economic and ecological reactions.[17] To formulate the elements of Russia's 'national security' without admitting a 'systematic analysis of geopolitical factors' (see Figure 3) relevant to it, embracing the properties of the geostrategic and geopolitical regions which constitute the overall 'geopolitical situation', (*geopoliticheskaya obstanovka*) is essentially pointless.[18]

Coming as it did from retired Rear Admiral V. S. Pirumov, Vice-President of the Russian Federation Academy of Natural Sciences, head of the Academy's section on Geopolitics and Security, member of the Russian Federation Security Council, this insistence on the relevance of geopolitics to considerations of national security could hardly be dismissed as mere academicism. Here were two significant innovations: the revival, the restitution of the 'geopolitical approach' coupled with recourse to the term 'national security', *natsional'naya bezopasnost'*, usage which Admiral Pirumov points out was never part of the Soviet political lexicon. The introduction of the wide-ranging concept of 'national security' thus marks a radical departure from the ideologically-driven Stalinist model of state socialism which placed the state above the individual and the nation. 'National security' embraces the idea of the state as a tool assuring 'the best possible conditions' for the individual, for society and for the state itself '*as conditioned by the entire spectrum of active geopolitical factors*' [emphasis added].[19]

This commitment to a concept of 'national security' raises two questions: what vital interests in the context of 'active geopolitical factors' are involved and what threats will they encounter? The immediate point is the contraction within 'geopolitical space' of Russia's 'vital interests' when compared with those of the former Soviet Union. Soviet geopolitical space was 'directly contiguous' to that space where both the United States and China were dominant. That 'geopolitical space' has been transformed for Russia, consisting, save for China and Japan, of 'a mixed and unstable conglomerate of states', former Soviet republics or the neighbouring 'Far

FIGURE 3
BASIC GEOPOLITICAL FACTORS

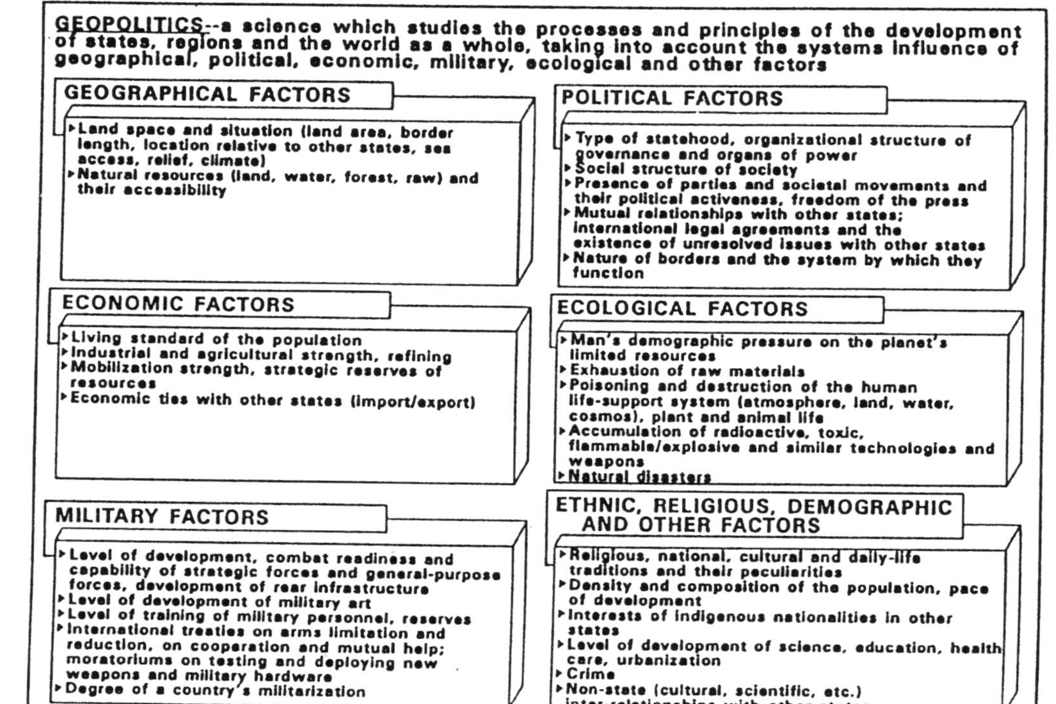

Source: See endnote 11.

FIGURE 4

STRUCTURE AND INTER-LINK OF BASIC GEOPOLITICAL FACTORS AND ELEMENTS OF NATIONAL SECURITY

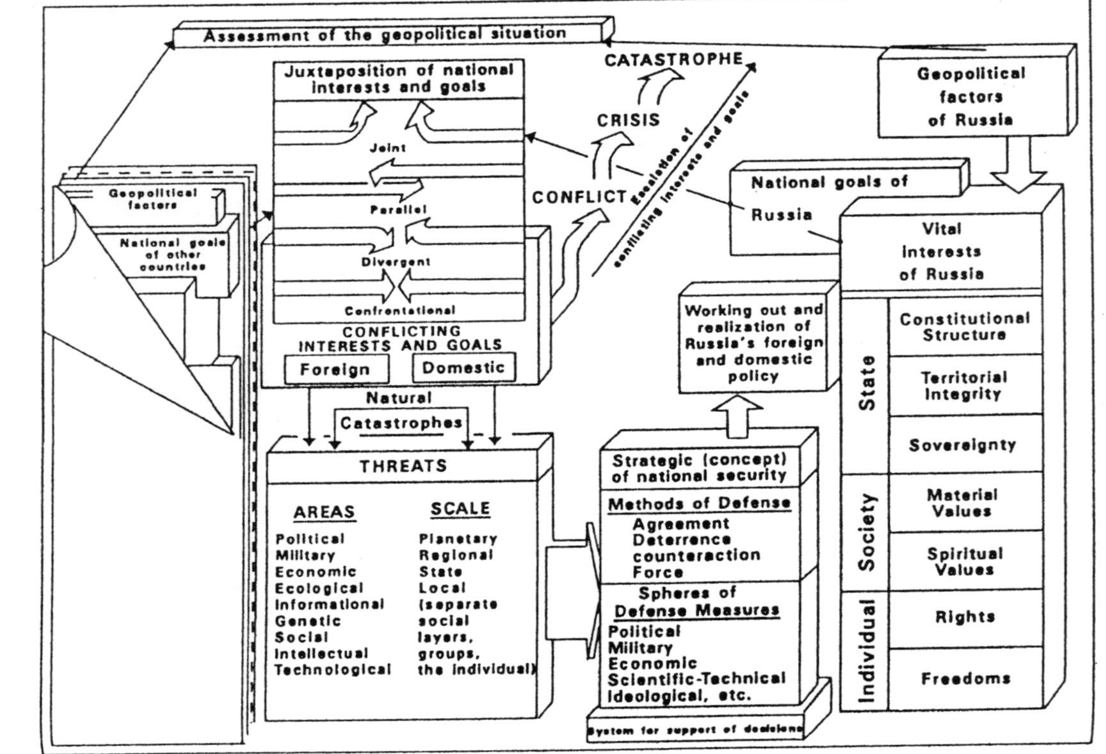

Source: See endnote 11.

FIGURE 5

GENERAL SCHEMATIC OF A DECISION SUPPORT SYSTEM FOUNDED ON THE STRATEGY (CONCEPT) OF NATIONAL SECURITY

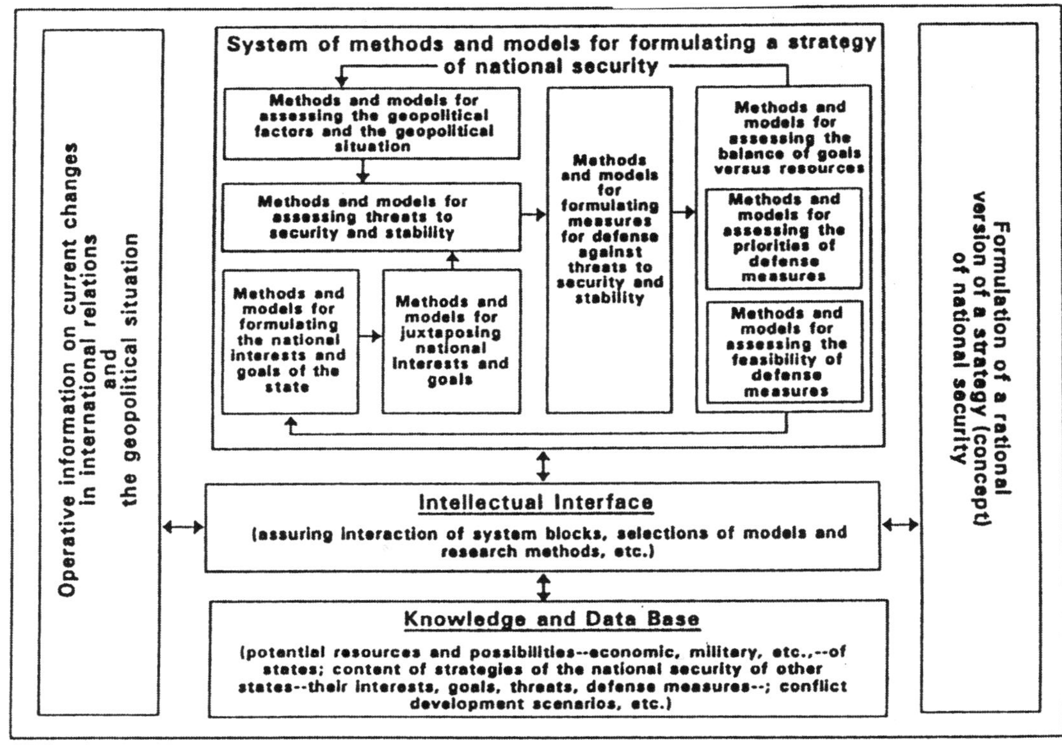

Source: See endnote 11.

Abroad'. Thus the 'zone of Russia's vital interests' will be confined to this 'geopolitical space' until the year 2010. Admiral Pirumov presented a threat profile against a background of increasing ambiguity. It coupled threats to Russia's security at large and to the 'vital interests' of the citizen in particular. The *political threat* occupied first place namely, those actions inimical to maintaining the integrity of the Russian Federation or directed to weakening the 'integrative processes of the Commonwealth of Independent States' (CIS), violation of human rights, conflicts in adjoining states. No less important were threats to the international position and status of Russia.

Military threats persist: conflicts and the danger of conflict on Russia's own doorstep, the proliferation of weapons of mass destruction and delivery means, 'huge nuclear arsenals' in the possession of other states (?) and risks to strategic stability from violations of arms limitation agreements. The environmental/ecological threat is set out in very dramatic terms: land area eroded or water-logged, high environmental toxicity, poor food and suspect water quality, damage to the gene pool through disease.[20]

It took many months for the 'geopolitical approach' to suffuse through the system, particularly into the senior military echelons and the General Staff. In 1992 security was conceived and promulgated in essentially stark military terms. *Draft 1992* of Russia's official military doctrine identified the 'main threat' as that which emanated from 'some states and coalitions' bent on world domination or regions within it, relying on force to resolve disputes. What was implicit in this Draft produced by the General Staff was that the United States and NATO, patently 'some states and coalitions', still constituted the 'main threat' to Russia and its security.[21] What was singularly absent in *Draft 92* was any recognition of internal threat to the Russian Federation. On the contrary the Commonwealth of Independent States (CIS) was construed as a working military entity in its own right even though warning signs of disassociation from Ukraine made this a very dubious assumption. Nevertheless it was impossible for the military to escape the consequences of the 'great debate' concerning Russia's perception of itself and its role in the world, a world undergoing nothing short of a geostrategic and geopolitical transformation. An initial recognition of the nature of this change came with the promulgation of a revised military doctrine with Presidential Decree No. 1833, 2 November 1993.[22]

While the new doctrine announced itself representing a period of transition, one encompassing the implementation of statehood, the process of democratic reform and the emergence of a new system of international relations, in spite of this disclaimer Air Marshal Yevgenii Shaposhnikov took the view that the time was not yet ripe for the promulgation of a new military doctrine. What he had in mind was a concept of 'national security, a definition of national interests', in which military doctrine would play a part but only a part (see Figure 3). Nevertheless the Cold War paradigm had been removed, though there was a residual refrain warning against a return to Cold War practices with dire consequences for strategic stability, a resumption of the arms race and an expansion of NATO. More space was allotted to the threat posed by the proliferation of weapons of mass destruction and terrorism, though the threat of large-scale foreign aggression aimed directly at Russia substantially downgraded. What was momentarily eye-catching was the formal abandonment of Moscow's long-standing declaratory policy of no-first-use of nuclear weapons. This implied reliance upon nuclear weapons expressly as a political deterrent rather than a war-fighting capability, a deterrent capability designed to forestall nuclear or conventional aggression. It was also an overt recognition of Russia's diminishing conventional capabilities, but no sign of a waning geopolitical appetite.

A realistic 'geopolitical approach' seems largely to have eluded those who formulated the 1993 military doctrine, though the Russian Ministry of Defence evidently attempted to curb the rigid orthodoxies of the General Staff. Equally the turbulent politics of the day precluded the Security Council advancing its own 'geopoliticised' version. What the 1993 military document demonstrated unequivocally was that the Russian military lacked the necessary authority, possibly the competence, to present Russia with 'blueprint for national security'. There was a recognition of growing instability in the regions bordering on the Russian Federation, the product of 'aggressive nationalism' coupled with 'religious intolerance', though this 'threat analysis' extended beyond the confines of the Russian Federation itself into what appeared to resemble the previous Soviet sphere of influence. Former non-Soviet members of the Warsaw Pact were pointedly and peremptorily advised not to become over-familiar with NATO. In the military doctrine itself there was little concession to the reality of Russia's shrinking geostrategic space.

It fell to Foreign Minister Andrei Kozyrev in advance of the promulgation of the new doctrine to enlarge on the implications of a pronounced switch from a pro-Western stance to one of the defence of Russia's 'vital interests' even if this ran counter to Western interests or those of the CIS itself. Among those 'vital interests' were Russia's 'special rights and responsibilities' in the geopolitical space of the former Soviet Union.

Moreover, it was imperative to prepare to conduct 'military actions' designed not only to support peace but to '*establish peace*' within '*the zones of our traditional geopolitical interests*'.[23]

Combining as it did contradictions with conceits, the 1993 military doctrine achieved little and signified even less, dismissed within the Russian Defence Ministry as simply 'toilet paper'.[24] Nevertheless the implications were disquieting, particularly as Kozyrev in 1994, doubtless prodded by Zhirinovskii's dramatic electoral success, conflated an assertion of Russia's 'great power' status with an aggressive affirmation of Russia's interests and its rights. This inevitably ignited a controversy over what precisely constituted 'Russia', its status, capabilities and 'vital interests'. In the aftermath of the 1993 military doctrine Dr Aleksei Arbatov, Director of the Moscow Centre for Geopolitical Military Forecasts, required of Russian policy-makers a studied assessment of 'reasonably formulated national interests', simultaneously presenting the case for implementing the 'neutral and non-nuclear status' of the independent states of Eastern Europe and the western republics of the former Soviet Union. This would automatically close off a military advance upon Russia from either east or west but equally it made NATO's eastward enlargement contrary to 'Russia's interests'.[25]

Which was to come first: a litany of Russia's interests or a geostrategic and geopolitical identification of 'Russia' and its inherent 'vital interests? What 'geopolitical configuration' within the global scene does Russia represent or should represent? In an interview with Lieutenant General Aleksandr Lebed and Grigorii Yavlinskii, the latter stated somewhat delphically that 'Russia has neither permanent friends nor permanent enemies. Russia has *interests*', immutable interests, to be defended at all costs. A Russian Army, one maintaining nuclear parity, sustaining nuclear deterrence, preventing an attempted nuclear strike on its territory, is an 'extremely important factor' in its own right in world politics (26 October 1994). Given Russia's size and situation, given that 'so much in the world depends on Russia', the Russian Army will always be 'the army of a great power'. Yavlinskii finally turned his back on 'Western alliances and unions', including the European Union: 'We have other dimensions and other tasks.'[26]

In a not dissimilar vein Vladislav Chernov from the Foreign Ministry argued that a 'strategy of partnership' between the West and Russia rested on uneasy foundations, given what he described as a questionable Western policy of 'double containment'. The positive side was financial assistance, the negative aimed at limiting Russian influence and reducing Russia's status to that of merely one nation state among many in the global order.

'Russia is simply too big' for that, never reconciled to considering itself 'a minor state in the world'. Better that Russia should go its own way, following historical precedent, recognising that Russia has never been a part of Western society nor ever been considered a Western democracy.[27]

The debate on Russia's role in the world and the status of post-Soviet Russia which developed in the wake of the demise of the Soviet Union has never been fully resolved. If anything it has intensified. That Russia is no longer a superpower, save with respect to its large if deteriorating nuclear arsenal, is generally accepted. The abandonment of superpower pretension was discreetly signalled in the 1993 military doctrine which expressed concern for the maintenance of *strategic stability* (*strategicheskaya stabilnost'*) rather than sustaining strategic parity with the United States. That concept of 'stability' was also extended to those regions and territories adjacent to Russia's borders.

Speaking in geopolitical terms Russia has found itself 'at the epicentre' of a massive global transformation, but it would be a serious mistake to think that Russia had been side-lined on the world scene, that it had been reduced to the level of a second-rate or third-rate power. There are those who see Russia's status in terms of a 'natural highway' for trade and communications between Europe, Asia and Africa or a 'Eurasian bridge' furnishing the shortest trade route between Asia and Europe. Interpreting Russia's place in the world primarily as a 'Christian outpost' confronting the Islamic world is plainly preposterous. Russia faces the wider world along three fronts, to the west (Euro-American), to the south (the Islamic world) and to the east (Asia and the Asia-Pacific region).[28] This said, the most important factors in Russia's 'geopolitical security' (*geopoliticheskaya bezopasnost'*) are internal conditions rather than external parameters.

As early as April 1992 President Yeltsin had declared publicly that 'Russia is rightfully a great power by virtue of its history, of its place in the world, and of its material and spiritual potential', amplified a little later into Russia as a 'great world power', one not afraid to defend its own interests. Henceforth priority would lie with the countries of the CIS, the area of Russia's vital interests and immediate security concerns. Yeltsin's recital of Russia's past, present and future characteristics befitting a great power, *velikaya derzhava*, have been repeated quite consciously and largely accepted within an assortment of political circles.

The same might be said with respect to the general agreement on Russia's national security interests. On his appointment as foreign minister in January 1996, Yevgenii Primakov insisted that 'Russia was and is a great power', committed to a foreign policy suited to this status. However, for many Russia is affirmatively not a superpower: 'It [Russia] knows better than anyone other the fearful price of superpower status and does not aspire to it.'[29] Such an assessment is reflected in a revision of Russian strategic capabilities, replacing previous parity with the United States by an emphasis on strategic stability, already foreshadowed in the 1993 military doctrine.

A similar general understanding of Russia's status affects the view of Russia's vital interests, expressed as a conglomerate in the 'National Security Concept' (*Kontseptsiya natsional'noi bezopasnosti*) approved on 17 December 1997 and published on 26 December.[30] In *Voennaya bezopasnost' Otechestva* published in 1996 Major General V. A. Zolotarev had emphasised the close link between 'security' and geopolitics.[31] However, the 1997 'Concept' goes very much further. 'Security' must not only embrace the geopolitical but also the geo-economic, the geo-environmental, the geo-ecological, the geo-technological, even the spiritual (national values).[32] Much of this had already been subsumed by Admiral Pirumov and his associates in 1993. It now appeared in the guise of 'officially accepted views regarding goals and state strategy' to ensure security for the individual, society and state from internal and external threat. The Concept dramatically downgraded the geostrategic threat: '... *the threat of large-scale aggression against Russia is virtually absent for the foreseeable future*', simultaneously emphasising that 'the main threats to Russia's national security come from internal political, economic, and social spheres and are *predominantly non-military*' [emphasis added].[33]

In addition to representing the interests of several institutions, the Defence Ministry, Internal Affairs, Federal Security (FSB), Foreign Intelligence Service (SVR), Border Service and Federal Government Communications and Information (FAPSI), the Concept is a combination (if not an actual fusion) of the geopolitical with the geo-economic plus an injection of 'the spiritual'. Under the last it is Russian 'national values', culture, language and faith which are specifically identified, sitting oddly with professed support for multi-ethnicity. In much the same contradictory vein the suggested restriction on foreign financial houses runs counter to commitments of economic co- operation.[34]

Of threats and interests, the Concept reiterates Russian opposition to NATO's expansion eastwards, posing nothing less than a threat to Russia's national security. Less explicit but none too thinly veiled are the references to 'a number of states' bent on deliberately weakening Russia or yet again pointing to foreign intelligence activity malevolently directed towards undermining the territorial integrity of Russia. Describing Russia as 'an influential Europe-Asian state' the Concept finds isolation from the Asia-Pacific region unacceptable especially when Russian national interests extend to it, as they do to Europe, the Balkans, the Near East, Central, Southwestern and Southeastern Asia. Globally it has to be admitted that Russian influence has waned. Institutions such as the United Nations, Organization for Security and Cooperation in Europe (OSCE), even the CIS itself lacked effectiveness, offering no real assurance of Russian prominence in a multipolar world, presenting no real obstacle to Primakov's fundamental aversion, the advent of a unipolar world responsive only to the will of 'one national capital'.[35]

According to Gennadii Zyuganov in *Geografiya pobedy* all Russian geopolitical concepts from 'Moscow – the Third Rome' to the 'Brezhnev doctrine' have embraced two basic aims which guarantee the nation's security. The first involves Russia as a state attaining ease within itself, the second establishing around itself an independent 'Great space' (*Bol'shoe prostranstvo*).[36] In this respect the Concept conforms to established Russian 'geopolitical precepts', recognising the primacy of economic well-being and social stability as the guarantor of national security. The same factors also contribute to the preservation of territorial integrity and the substance of a geopolitical force, distinguished from the West, which defines its interests within contiguous 'Great space'.

In some respects the recourse to and preoccupation with geopolitics could be regarded as a deliberate flight from political reality, in Zyuganov's case a rhetorical substitute for urgent decisions in day-to-day Russian politics. The abysmal state of the Russian economy induces incomparably more anguish than ease for Russia, bringing in its wake unemployment, flourishing organised crime, ethnic dissent, ecological ravages, brutal, regressive 'de-modernisation'. In purely territorial terms the desperate economic situation encourages 'centrifugal aspirations' among the 89 regions of the Russian Federation itself, to which General Zolotarev adds the further threat emanating from 'uncontrolled disintegrative processes in the territories of the former Soviet Union'.[37]

Zyuganov asks rather tendentiously what the 'geopolitical interests' of the Russian state actually are. The Russian government and elites have provided their answer, regularly citing central/east Europe, the Near East, Asia-Pacific but high, if not the highest on the list must be the CIS regions, described as a strategic geopolitical interest. The situation is, however, somewhat more complex than Zyuganov's artful leading question, designed to affirm the most inflated and revisionist interpretation of those interests, would suggest. Geostrategically on the defensive, Russia is engaged in complex geopolitical manoeuvres and enmeshed in geoeconomic competition in its contiguous 'Great space'. It is demonstrably within the CIS regions that all three features involving 'control of space' converge, utilising variants of military, political and economic power, a 'knot of problems around Russia and the CIS' which according to General Makhmut Gareev now presents long-term complications.[38]

That a geostrategic crisis of some magnitude is upon Russia, destined to last at least a decade or more is a view shared by several Russian analysts. This timespan also coincides with a period of increasing military weakness, not least the steady encroachment of block obsolescence in the current Russian weapons inventories, the bulk of it built during the 1970s and 1980s. Given the severely curtailed procurement, the shortfall in inventories will become even more pronounced, particularly with respect to modern weapons and critically for weapons requiring long lead times to produce and introduce into service. General Yakovlev reports that 62 per cent of the Russian strategic missile force is already beyond guaranteed service life. The most pessimistic assessment projects a drastically shrunken strategic capability by 2015, as low as 700 warheads, even a capability only marginally greater than that of China, Russian ballistic missile submarines (SSBNs) by then an extinct species. Obsolescence may well be outpacing arms control measures. Given that the National Security Concept pronounced the existing military organisation a burden on the state, the emphasis on military reform, cutting manpower and reducing the defence budget, was a logical concomitant, but one in the context of an army reduced to penury and consequently demoralised. What sounds admirably positive and progressive is virtually cancelled out when the Chief of the Russian Staff General Anatolii Kvashnin observes that it could well take until 2025 to complete these reforms.[39] What price 'strategic stability'?

In the western strategic theatre NATO's proposed expansion eastwards, accompanied by sustained Russian protest and vigorous objection, exposed a deepening geostrategic fissure between Russia and the West. Contrary to Russian wishes and expectations NATO did not vanish in a puff of smoke. The Russian design for a pan-European security system, long a Soviet objective, failed to materialise. Similarly the idea of the Organization for Security and Co-operation in Europe (OSCE) acting as a 'security agency' for Europe, or for a wider 'military-political association' stretching from the Atlantic to the Urals, was still-born.[40] The subsequent negotiations between NATO and the Russian Federation resulted in an acknowledgement, in principle at least, of Russia's international importance and its significant role in European security affairs at large but in no wise modified or qualified

NATO's adamantine refusal to forego expansion, mocked by General Lebed as the equivalent of carrying out ' brain surgery with a chisel' if this was the intended answer to Europe's new security needs.[41]

From the Russian side not only enlargement but NATO in its entirety was interpreted as an instrument of American hegemony in Europe and the world at large, 'global military control over international space'. NATO was unequivocally identified by Lieutenant General Leonid Ivashov as the external threat in the West to Russia's security in the West, along with Iran and Turkey in the Caucasus, Islamic extremism in Central Asia, uncertainties surrounding China in the East where Chinese military power increases and where demographic and economic change accelerates.

The first wave of NATO expansion into central and eastern Europe does not, in spite of the rhetoric, present a *direct* military challenge to Russia, though it is denounced as an encroachment upon a traditional Russian 'sphere of influence' which formerly included Ukraine and as a means of isolating and weakening Russia. That latter charge was levelled by Anton Surikov from the Institute for Defence Research in a virulent attack on both NATO and the United States, seeking their formal designation as hostile powers, while the World Bank and the International Monetary Fund are also committed to a strategy of reducing Russia to Third World status. The deadliest thrust is aimed at Russia's military-industrial complex, thus depleting the nation's scientific and technological potential.[42] In practice during the first stage of NATO's enlargement deployed NATO and Russian forces will remain geographically separated, without the previous military confrontational line.

It is, however, a situation which has marked potential for change dependent on the degree and depth of the security association of Belarus with Russia. The 'forward frontier' of Russia is substantially advanced westwards together with closer links with Russia's westerly outpost at Kaliningrad. Russo-Belarusian bilateral agreements on military co-operation were signed in 1996, coupled with vague talk about joint 'countermeasures' in the event of NATO's expansion. In addition to a possible military bonus in this burgeoning integration, geo-economics and geostrategy appear to share a mutually advantageous relationship. Two of the five major Russian oil and gas pipelines run through Belarus to the West and greater investment in Belarus might ultimately enable Russia to bypass Ukraine's pipelines for Russian energy exports.[43]

NATO and Russia walked a swaying tight-rope over the first stage of NATO enlargement. Moscow 'grudgingly' agreed to join the Permanent Joint Council, designed to facilitate a co-operative relationship between

Russia and NATO, in the expectation of exercising substantial influence within and over NATO. This proved not to be the case. Russia now faces thc implications of further enlargement under NATO's 'open door' policy, a process 'well studied and geopolitically based', bearing directly on several dimensions of Russia's perceived national security interests.[44] NATO expansion into the Baltic states would face Russia with serious strategic problems, though it is the blustering content and crude conduct of Russia's own policies in the Baltic region which have contributed substantially to furnishing a specific rationale, even conceivably a certain legitimacy for NATO enlargement here.

However, NATO enlargement is not the 'only game in town' with respect to the Baltic states and indeed European security issues at large. The advance of the European Union (EU) to Russia's border has both significant geoeconomic and geopolitical consequences, diverting trade from Russia, raising trade barriers against Russia, finally 'sealing off' the Baltic states from Russia.[45] The implications of this 'moving to the West' are consequently dire for those who insist doggedly that post-Soviet 'space' in its entirety, encompassing the former states of the former Soviet Union, is and must remain a closed Russian geopolitical preserve.

That notional preserve has now been violated quite spectacularly in the 'war of the Caspian pipe-line', where economics have been deliberately subordinated to an unabashed geopolitical confrontation. The Russians are bent on frustrating *strategic* access to Russia's 'space' by external powers and commercial agencies, but the Americans have expressly declared through Energy Secretary Bill Richardson the converse, an intention to prevent '*strategic* inroads by those who don't share our values' into the hugely energy-rich Caspian region; 'the pipeline map and politics' must 'come out right'.[46] Earlier there had been a vigorous, not to say hostile reaction to American involvement in the TransCaucasus, clearly impinging on Russia's hold over the region already weakened in the North Caucasus after the military debacle in Chechnya.[47]

Russia meanwhile manoeuvres within its 'geopolitical space', entrenching itself in Armenia via the Russo-Armenian Treaty, supplying a counter-weight to balance American and Turkish support lent to Azerbaijan, installing its bases in Georgia and throughout the CIS.[48] Foreign support has nevertheless played a significant role enabling both Azerbaijan and Georgia to slip that final tightening of the Russian noose, both having signed up to NATO's Partnership for Peace (PfP), thus allowing the West to extend a long probing finger into TransCaucasian security affairs.[49] If the Russian objective is re-integration of former Soviet republics, here it faces not only a burgeoning Western military-political and economic presence but also a 'defensive association' within the CIS which ranges Georgia and Azerbaijan with Ukraine and distant Kazakhstan, not least to ensure some diversity in the matter of routing pipelines.

A Trojan horse could not assume a guise perhaps more incongruous than pipelines, normally innocuous commercial installations, but in this form it has intruded into the TransCaspian region, a critically important region of Russia's national interests, where the question of siting pipelines for the export of oil and gas from Baku has the potential not only to work major geopolitical change but is being deliberately designed to do so.[50] Russia and Iran press pipeline routes of their choosing, the former favouring the northward route to the Russian port of Novorossiisk on the Black Sea, the latter southwards through Iran to the Persian Gulf. Turkey at an early stage pointed to the disadvantages of the Baku–Novorossiisk pipeline, the possibility of sabotage by Chechen separatists, the limitations of the port of Novorossiisk itself, congestion in the Bosphorus, the potential risk to Istanbul.

Amid this entanglement of Russia, Iran, Turkey and China, the United States has committed itself in earnest to pipeline geopolitics, challenging Russia's claims to an energy monopoly to sustain 'energy security' and implanting a presence in defence of its oil interests in Kazakhstan. Pursuing a policy designed to draw the Caspian region westwards and wean it away from overweening Russian influence, the United States supports the proposed Baku–Ceyhan pipeline transiting Georgia and Turkey with its outlet on the Mediterranean. Given the additional cost involved, this places geopolitical priorities ahead of economics to bypass Russia and Iran, simultaneously exploiting the territory of pro-American states Azerbaijan, Georgia and Turkey, shifting the balance of power across the entire Caspian region and even further .

Nor surprisingly Zhirinovskii describes the situation in near-apocalyptic terms, pointing to the 'geopolitical reality' of Russia encircled by the 'most economically powerful leading states – the USA (from the north), integrated Western Europe (from the west), Japan (from the east) and also China and the Islamic states (from the south)'. Should the 'energy and raw material resource economy' become a fully globalised market dominated only by those major countries already mentioned, this could well presage the 'economic and hence the political disintegration of Russia'.[51] What Zhirinovskii describes in somewhat lurid language does nevertheless reflect the serious tone of a report by the Russian Security Council, emphasising that by 2005 Russian dependence on CIS 'energy and raw materials resources' will increase, making Russian access to these reserves and to markets a 'vital interest'.[52] Put bluntly, this means that Russia must strive to retain as much as possible of CIS energy resources for its own purposes, with a particular commitment to exploration of Caspian fields and Russian ownership of sizeable sections of pipelines traversing several CIS states.

Putting Zhirinovskii's declamation on the implications of the global economy in a more rational setting, serious Russian attention is directed towards control of trade, transcontinental transportation networks and information channels, all regarded as vital elements in Russia's future economic progress at large, including also those of Russian private corporations. The incentives to pursue 're-integration', the restoration by stages of 'common economic space', the implications of 'defence space', represent a variety of interests which overlap but which are by no means uniform, indeed at times they are contradictory and conflicting. What precisely is to be 're-integrated' from within 'post- Soviet space' and even more importantly, in what manner is it to be designed to implement Russia's security?

In general terms what Dr Henry Kissinger has called Russia's 'dominant geopolitical thrust' remains essentially the assertion of 'great power' status designed to restore Moscow's pre-eminence in territories formerly under its control. In unabashed neo-Mackinderian style Zyuganov insists that the 'main geopolitical aim' is to ensure control of the 'heartland' ('*hartlend*'): '*only the attainment of this objective will guarantee the basic national security of our state*'. This 'control', vital for Russia's security, can at best be accomplished not through Zhirinovskii's 'lunges' to the south or anywhere else but rather through 'inter-state union', at least a confederation, in which the prime candidates are Russia, Belarus, Kazakhstan, Kyrgyzstan, Tajikistan and Armenia: less promising are Ukraine, Uzbekistan, Georgia and Moldova. Not surprisingly Latvia is rated a remote possibility.[53]

It is the Russian military, however, which practises the pragmatism Zyuganov advocates, eschewing the idea of simply restoring the Soviet Union, rather pushing a form of integration within the CIS on its own terms, relying on military presence together with Russian style 'peace-keeping'. Russian military presence in the CIS is considered paramount, its ultimate aim the establishment of a 'unified defence space', possibly the precursor of a collective security arrangement embodying a 'unified military space' to replace or supplement bilateral military agreements. At the conference on CIS military co-operation in 1994 Lieutenant General Leonid Ivashov outlined ' a possible version' of a collective security arrangement involving four regions, Caucasus (N. Caucasus area of the Russian Federation,

Azerbaijan, Armenia, Georgia), Central Asia subdivided into western and eastern zone (west Tajikistan, Uzbekistan, eastern Urals-Siberia area of Russia, Kazakhstan, Kyrgyzstan), Far Eastern (eastern area of Russia, eastern *oblast* Kazakhstan).[54] Meanwhile, reverting to Zyuganov's terminology, the Russian military has ringed its 'heartland' with a glacis of client or compliant states stretching to the south, east and west, in the Caucasus, Kazakhstan and Belarus respectively, of which the 25-year agreements with Kazakhstan and Belarus are of major strategic significance, the latter substantially extending Russia's 'defence space' .[55]

Quite patently Russian military interests and security priorities are an highly significant 'locomotive' driving a specific form of integration, carving out defined geostrategic and geopolitical 'space'. Equally the conclusion in March 1996 of the quadripartite agreement between Russia, Belarus, Kazakhstan and Kyrgyzstan also suggests that 're-integration' might not inevitably follow the existing framework of the present CIS . Rather the aim is to fuse geostrategic and geopolitical priorities with geoeconomic interests to structure a 'neo-imperial space' in which Russia maintains military, economic and financial pre-eminence.

The use of 'neo-imperial' here is neither pejorative nor instance of ineradicable predatoriness. It is merely formal recognition of the persistence of 'geostrategic or geopolitical explanation' for certain Russian behaviour. This is best characterised by Professor William Fuller in *Strategy and Power in Russia:1600–1914*, asserting that Russia's eighteenth century statesmen were by no means collectively or individually master-minds working to long-range plans for dominion. They worked within an environment uncommonly like that of the present, 'the cacophony of faction, the whispers of private avarice, and the bleating of idiots' but when viewing Russia's position in Europe and in the world, 'we must conclude that generally they thought in strategic terms'.[56] The 'geopolitical thrust' is long-lived, the permanent consciousness of Russia's strategic location, bent not only on protecting but also enhancing Russia's status as a 'great power', warding off isolation and frustrating encirclement, above all facilitating 'pre-eminence'.

Given this pre-disposition it is readily understandable why Gennadii Zyuganov should exuberantly repeat the claim that a form of 'geopolitics', *geopoliticheskie problematiki*, was first conceived during the 1720s in Russia's Academy of Sciences and should then posture as heir to part if not all of a somewhat questionable inheritance whenever rhetoric takes precedence over reality.[57]

While this may be dismissed as overblown pretentiousness, Professor

Fuller's admonition that Russians have an ingrained historical proclivity to think in strategic terms has been strikingly borne out by events connected with Operation 'Desert Fox', the Anglo-American air strikes directed against Iraq in December 1998. That situation was described by Marshal Sergeev, Russian Defence Minister, as one which demanded 'careful analysis and a correction to our approaches to the problems of international security'. Ignoring Russia's opinion put a question mark over supposed 'co-operation and partnership' a reference presumably to American-Russian relations. Yevgenii Primakov, who with characteristic bluntness asserted that 'the entire system of international security relations' had been prejudiced, had already headed off in search of a new strategic partnership, pursuing the geostrategic imperative of a Moscow–New Delhi–Beijing axis. During his visit to India in late December 1998 Primakov entered into a draft strategic agreement with India, the formal signing of which waits on a summit meeting later in 1999. Extensive military aid for India, including 300 T-90 main battle tanks, was agreed between Colonel General Yurii Bukreev and Indian Chief of Staff General Malik. The Indian Navy also agreed to purchase the Russian aircraft carrier *Admiral Gorshkov* plus aircraft. No mention was made of China in the draft Russo-Indian strategic agreement though it was proposed by Primakov.

The grand Eurasian geostrategic design remains incomplete, nevertheless its proportions were projected in the reference not only to India and to Russia but also to 'other major countries of Asia and the Pacific region' contributing to the cause of 'stability and security'. Japan, notably 'odd man out' in refusing to join the Asian chorus of condemnation of Operation 'Desert Fox', is most unlikely to be one of the 'other major countries of Asia' to associate itself with such a compact. Russia and China are joined in a strategic partnership recently lauded by President Jiang Zemin, both sharing a common detestation of a unipolar world dominated by 'hegemonism and power politics'. It remains to be seen how far Primakov's geostrategic design will fit with China's review of its security policies in a world of increased multipolarity. Nevertheless, even a tenuous Russo-Indian-Chinese combination could present itself as an encouragement to further global diversity, all without presenting an outright challenge to the 'hegemonism' of the United States, rather outflanking it.

As if to forestall any presumption of a strategic challenge Foreign Minister Igor Ivanov published a singular article in *Nezavisimaya Gazeta* on 16 December 1998, the timing as significant as the content. Russia and America have strategic aims in common which, not for the first time, coincide. For proof Minister Ivanov cited one of his Tsarist predecessors,

Prince Alexander M. Gorchakov, Tsar Alexander II's Foreign Minister who espied 'a natural solidarity of interests and sympathy' between both nations, evinced in particular by the co-operation between Russia and America during the American Civil War. Ivanov may simply be taking out a form of diplomatic insurance, shutting no door to the Americans, or merely emphasising that in an interdependent world Russia's present dependence on others is greater than the influence it can itself exert. Now is not the time to challenge American supremacy whatever the siren call of geopolitics and the lure of geostrategy. But that is not to deny or foreswear the potential geostrategic shape of things to come.

NOTES

1. See *Sovetskaya voennaya entsiklopediya* (Moscow: Voenizdat 1976) Vol.2, pp.521–3 under 'Geopoliticheskie teorii voiny'.
2. See *Sovetskaya voennaya entsiklopediya* (Moscow: Voenizdat 1978) pp.413–14.
3. See *Voennaya entsiklopediya* (Moscow: Voenizdat 1994) Vol.2, pp.387.
4. Gennadii Zyuganov, *Geografiya pobedy. Osnovy rossiiskoi geopolitike* (Moscow: no publisher 1997) 10,000 copies, 303pp., with a photographic supplement of Zyuganov on his world travels. In his introduction on what constitutes 'geopolitics' he intimates that the subject has now gained academic respectability, citing two 'major geopolitical dictionaries', Y. Lacoste, *Dictionnaire de geopolitique* (Paris 1993) and J. O'Loughlin, *Dictionary of Geopolitics* (Westport, CT: London 1994).
5. See Alexei Arbatov, 'Russian Security Interests and Dilemmas: An Agenda for the Future' in idem, Abram Chayes, Antonia Handler Chayes and Lara Olson (eds.) *Managing Conflict in the Former Soviet Union.* Russian and American Perspectives *CSIA* Studies in International Security. (Cambridge, MA and London: MIT Press 1997) pp.411–58, here p.418
6. See Sherman W. Garnett, 'Russia and its Borderlands: A Geography of Violence', *Parameters* 27/1 (US Army War College Quarterly) (Spring 1997) here p.5 outlining 'five key aspects of the new Eurasian security geography' the 'hodgepodge of Russia's commitments in Central Asia, Russian force pockets in the western regions of the former USSR, the rise of the Ukrainian Armed Forces and the future of Russian military forces in Belarus'; also 'The Revolution in Eurasian Military Affairs' in *The Future of the Russian Military: Managing Geopolitical Change and Institutional Decline* (Washington DC: Heritage Fdn 12 Dec. 1996).
7. Arbatov 'Russian Security Interests' (note 5) p.415.
8. Ibid. p.420.
9. Yuri N. Afanasyev, 'Seems Like Old Times? Russia's Place in the World', *Current History* 93/585 (Oct. 1994) pp.307–8.
10. The 'Section of Geopolitics and Security' of the Russian Academy of Natural Sciences was established for all practical purposes by the Russian General Staff on 22 Nov. 1991, its membership composed of senior Russian officers associated with the General Staff. The details of the new Section, plus a list of 'specialties' together with vacancies available, were published under 'Military-Scientific Information' in *Voennaya mysl'* No.2 (1992) pp.94–6. The Russian General Staff was also instrumental in establishing another 'think-tank', Institute for Defence Research (*Institut oboronnykh issledovanii*).
11. See V.G. Lebed'ko *et al.*, 'Prognoznaya otsenka sostoyaniya izmeneniya geopoliticheskoi kartiny mira v raionakh "dal'nego zarubezh'ya' in *Geopolitika i bezopasnost'* (Moscow: 'ARBIZO' 1993) No.1, here p.37. Academician Rear Adm. V.S. Pirumov's important

introductory article 'Nekotorye aspekty metodologii issledovaniya problem natsional'noi bezospasnosti Rossii v sovremennykh usloviyakh', pp.7–16 has been translated (complete with 4 figures) as 'Methodical Aspects in the Research of Russia's National Security Problems under Contemporary Conditions' by Robert R. Love in *Journal of Slavic Military Studies* 7/3 (Sept. 1994) pp.367–82.
12. See Lebed'ko *et al.* (note 11) pp.38–9.
13. For very perceptive comments on Zhirinovskii, Mark Yoffe, 'Vladimir Zhirinovsky, the Unholy Fool', *Current History* 93/585 (Oct. 1994) pp.324–6; also *Ocherki po geopolitike*, (Moscow 1997)
14. An early example of the relationship between geopolitics and the 'national security of Russia' was presented albeit somewhat diffusely by Col. A.S. Sinaiskii in *Voennaya mysl'*, No.10 (1992) pp.2–10 (English language ed.).
15. See V.P. Luyanin,'Geopolitika i voennaya bezopasnost' Rossii' in *Geopolitika i bezopasnost'*, p.81 with a diagram of 'Structure of the methodological concept of a general theory of geopolitics and security' p.77, also diagram on 'stability indicators', p.80.
16. See Figure 2 which is also in Rear Adm. V.S. Pirumov, *Geopolitika i bezopasnost'*, p.11 (p. 372 in Robert R. Love trans. note 11).
17. Pirumov (note 11) p.8.
18. Ibid.
19. Ibid. p.12.
20. Ibid.: 'In ecological terms Russia belongs to the most polluted group of nations'.
21. The text of the draft doctrine was published in a special edition of *Voennaya Mysl'*, May 1992, the draft circulated to the conference on Collective Security for Russia and the CIS held in June 1992; see Col. Gen. (Ret.) A. A. Danilovich, 'On New Military Doctrine of the CIS and Russia', also Charles J. Dick, 'Initial Thoughts on Russia's Draft Military Doctrine', *Journal of Soviet Military Studies* 5/4 (Dec. 1992) pp.517–38 and 552–65 respectively.
22. See 'Osnovnye polozheniya voennoi doktriny Rossiiskoi Federatsii (Izlozhenie)', *Krasnaya Zvezda* (19 Nov. 1993) 8pp.; also East View Publications text, 21pp. Col. Gen. V. Manilov, Deputy Secretary of the Security Council, stated that the full text of the new doctrine would not be published, only 21 of 23 pages; see also S. M. Rogov on the 1993 military doctrine, 'SshA: Ekonomika, politika, ideologiya' (1994 No.4) pp.3–10 and No.5, pp.3–11, emphasising the danger of 'the divergence between military doctrine and state policy'.
23. See Charles S. Dick, 'The Military Doctrines of the Russian Federation and Ukraine', *Journal of Slavic Military Studies* 7/3 (Sept. 1994), Kozyrev speech to the UN, 2 Sept. 1993, *Izvestiya* interview, 8 Oct. 1993, also Radio Moscow 14 Oct. 1993. Charles Dick points to Kozyrev specifying that the 'others' who might fill any vacuum left by Russia are 'Islamic fundamentalist "intruders"'.
24. Pavel Felgengauer, 'Military Reform: Ten Years of Failure', p.25 quoted in Stuart D. Goldman, *Russian Conventional Armed Forces: On the Verge of Collapse?* (Washington DC: Congressional Research Service, Library of Congress 4 Sept. 1997) CRS-39.
25. Paper presented to the Friedrich Ebert Stiftung, Oct. 1994; see also 'A NATO that creeps eastwards is bad for Russian democrats', *International Herald Tribune,* 27 Aug. 1997.
26. Comments on US National Strategy and Hearings in the Defence Committee of the Duma, *Moskovskii Komsomolets*, 26 Oct. 1994.
27. Vladislav Chernov, 'Significance of the Russian Military Doctrine', *Comparative Strategy* 13/2 (1994) pp.161–6.
28. See K. S. Gadzhiev, *Geopolitika* (Moscow: Mezh. Otnosheniya 1997) Ch.8, pp.331–2, 'Problemy natsional'nykh interesov i natsional'noi bezopasnosti Rossii'.
29. See M.A. Khaldin, 'Geopoliticheskie gorizonty Rossii' in Yu. N. Afanas'ev (ed.), '*Sovetskoe obshchestvo: Voznikovenie, razvitie, istoricheskii final*', Tom 2 (Moscow: Russian State Humanitarian Univ. 1997) pp.617–32, here p.622.
30. Text 'Kontsept natsional'noi bezopasnosti Rossiiskoi Federatsii', *Rossiiskaya Gazeta* (26 Dec. 1997) pp. 4-5.
31. Maj. Gen. V.A. Zolotarev, *Voennaya bezopasnost' Otechestva* (Moscow: IPO'AVTOR' 1996) Pt. 1 'Rossiya v sovremennom mire', p.7ff.

32. See, for example, 'Formirovanie dukhovnykh tsennostei naroda' in *Natsional'naya doktrina Rossii* (Moscow: Obozrevatel 1994) Pt.6, pp.419–90.
33. Ivan Rybkin, head of the Security Council, *Rossiiskie Vesti*, 13 May, 1997.
34. See Dr Mark Galeotti's analysis, 'Russia's National Security Concept', *Jane's Defence Review* 10/5 (May 1998) pp.3–4.
35. Galeotti (note 34) p.4 see his summary 'A surrogate for real activity?'
36. Zyuganov, *Geografiya pobedy* (note 4) p.130.
37. See Zolotarev, *Voennaya bezopasnost Otechestva* (note 31) pp.12–13: among the 'new dangers' Gen. Zolotarev includes 'international criminality (mafia, drug trafficking, terrorism, present day slave trade, *rabotorgovlya;* in this context see also Dr Mark Galeotti, 'The Russian Wild East: a complex criminal threat', *Jane's Intelligence Review* 10/9 (Sept. 1998) pp.3–4, also his *JIR* Special Report No.10, 'MAFIYA: organised crime in Russia' (June 1996).
38. Gen. M.A. Gareev, *If War Comes Tomorrow?: The Contours of Future Armed Conflict* (London and Portland, OR: Frank Cass 1998) p.34 argues that this 'long term problem' is due to the West not infrequently ignoring the key issue, 'the preservation of Russia's unity', which in any event is also in the West's interests.
39. The literature on the Russian military's degeneration is extensive. On the conventional forces, see CRS Report for Congress, *Russian Conventional Armed Forces* (note 24), also Dr Mark Galeotti, 'Russia's grafting generals', and 'Crisis continues for Russia's army', *Jane's Defence Review* 10/4 (April 1998) pp.3–4 and 10/6 (June 1998) pp.3–4 resp.: also Robert W. Duggleby, 'The Disintegration of the Russian Armed Forces', *Journal of Slavic Military Studies* 11/2 (June 1998) pp.1–24, without drastic measures to deal with basic issues 'far reaching reforms from on high' will never take hold. Also a bleak recent study is Dale R. Herspring, 'Russia's Crumbling Military', *Current History* 97/621 (Oct. 1998) pp.325–8.
40. See Peter Truscott, *RUSSIA FIRST Breaking with the West* (London: I.B. Tauris 1997): Duma Speaker Ivan Rybkin's suggested 'peace belt'. Personal exchange with Truscott, March 1995, p.46.
41. Benjamin S. Lambeth, *The Warrior Who would Rule Russia* (Santa Monica, CA: RAND 1996) p.49. Lebed was equally distrustful of the Partnership for Peace: 'I don't believe one word of it.'
42. See *Kontseptualnye polozheniya strategii protivodeistviya osnovnym vneshnim ugrozam natsional'noi bezopasnosti Rossiiskoi Federatsii'* (Moscow: INOBIS Oct. 1995). Surikov's claim that the MIC is threatened by exclusion from world markets is somewhat belied by Russian arms sales of advanced military technology to China: see Stephen J. Blank, 'Sino-Russian Ties: Implications for the West?', *Aviation Week and Space Technology* (18 Aug. 1997) pp.71–2; this situation is made more intriguing by President Jiang Zemin's visit to Science City, Novosibirsk (New Siberia) 24 Nov. 1998, praising 'Russia's huge potential for development' based upon 'strong scientific and technological capabilities', difficulties are 'temporary', 'broad prospects' open for Sino-Russian scientific and technological co-operation: see *People's Daily*, 25 Nov. 1998.
43. See under Prospects for the Russo-Belarusian Agreement in Olga Alexandrova, BIOS Cologne, 'Mutually Beneficial Re-integration or Restoration of Empire' in Lars B. Wallin (ed.), *Lectures and Contributions to East European Studies at FOA* (Stockholm 1996) here pp.53–6. On Russian, Belarusian attitudes to NATO enlargement Marc Nordberg, 'Limiting a larger NATO: diverging views from Russia and Belarus', *Jane's Intelligence Review* 9/8 (Aug. 1997) pp.342–5. See also a modern study on Belarus, 'the country collaborating most closely with Russia, E. Kozhokin (ed.), *Belorussiya: put' k novymn gorizontam* (Moscow: Inst. of Strategic Studies 1996) p.384.
44. See John Hillen and Michael P. Noonan, 'The Geopolitics of NATO Enlargement', *Parameters* 27/3 (Autumn 1998) here p.32 on a 'geopolitically informed and enlarged NATO', quoting the Chairman of the Senate Foreign Relations Committee to the effect that well-studied and geopolitically based enlargement 'will make constructive relations with Russia easier, because a stronger NATO will shut off Russia's avenues to destructive patterns of behaviour'. Senator Jesse Helms, *Wall Street Journal*, 23 March 1998.

45. On NATO enlargement and 'the Baltics', see Pavel K. Baev's important article 'Boris woos the Baltics, but are the Russians for real?', *Jane's' Intelligence Review* 10/2 (Feb. 1998) pp.9–12; also 'EU Moves Forward on Expansion Plan', *International Herald Tribune*, 10 Nov. 1998.
46. See ibid. 9 Nov. 1998, p.10 on 'Caspian Pipeline Tug-of-War', Washington favouring geopolitics over economics, Energy Secretary Richardson on America's 'energy security'; by way of comparison on 'energy security', see Dr Elaine Holoboff, 'Russia's draft energy security doctrine', *Jane's Intelligence Review* 9/1 (Jan. 1997) pp.19–22.
47. For the background see a valuable survey by Svante E. Cornell, 'The Unruly Caucasus', *Current History* 96/612 (Oct. 1997) pp.341–7, inserted passage Robert E. Ebel on oil, TransCaucasus and pipeline politics, pp.344-5: on Chechnya, the acclaimed study by Anatol Lieven, *Chechnya: Tombstone of Russian Power* (New Haven, CT: Yale UP 1998).
48. For a tabulation of 'Agreed Russian Military Presence in the CIS' see Frank Umbach, 'The Role and Influence of the Military Establishment in Russia's Foreign and Security Policies in the Yeltsin Era', *Journal of Slavic Military Studies* 9/3 (Sept. 1996) here p.483, full text of this excellent survey, pp.467–500.
49. See Professor Stephen Blank's two-part study, 'Instability in the Caucasus: new trends, old traits', *Jane's Intelligence Review* 10/4 (April 1998) pp.14–17 and 10/5 (May 1998) pp.18–21 for Pts. 1 and 2 resp.
50. Trojan horses begin to crowd the scene. One possibly working in Russia's favour of Russia's interests is identified by Dr Elaine Holoboff in an illuminating study, 'The FSU energy debt: Russia's Trojan Horse?', *Jane's Intelligence Review* 9/8 (Aug. 1997) pp.351–4.
51. Zhirinovskii, *Ocherki po geopolitike* (note 13) p.64 on the economic and political threat.
52. Cited by Dr Irina Isakova, 'The NATO-Russian relationship one year after: Next steps after First Enlargement?', *RUSI Journal* 143/5 (Oct. 1998) p.17 'Vital Interests', also 'Vulnerability factors' pp.17–18 citing *Armeiskii sbornik No. 10 (1997)* 'Geostrategicheskie ugrozy'.
53. Estonia and Latvia are totally excluded. See Zyuganov, *Geografiya pobedy* (note 4) p.255 quoting *Vozroditsya li Soyuz? Buduschee postsovetskogo prostranstva. Tezisy Soveta po vneshnei i oboronnoi politike.* (NG-stsenarii May 1996).
54. Undated speech (July 1994), of Gen. Ivashov, *Nezavisimaya gazeta*, 6 July 1994, pp.1 and 3.
55. On Kazakhstan in particular, see Dmitri Vertkin, *Kazakhstan Security and the New Asian Landscape*, Lancaster University, CDISS, Bailrigg Paper No.26 (1997) pp.34.
56. William C. Fuller Jr, *Strategy and Power in Russia 1600–1914* (NY and Toronto: The Free Press 1992) p.132.
57. Zyuganov (note 4) p.44 under 'Russkie geopoliticheskie idei', quoting from V.N. Kaledin's essay in *Geopoliticheskie i geoekonimicheskie problemy Rossii (Materialy nauchnoi konferentsii v RGO, oktyabr' 1994)*, (SPb: 1995) p.85.

Abstracts

Sir Halford Mackinder: The Heartland Theory Then and Now

GEOFFREY SLOAN

One of the aims of geopolitics is to emphasise that political predominance is a question not just of having power in the sense of human or material resources, but also of the geographical context within which that power is exercised. States do not find themselves in a geographical strait-jacket; instead, geography or geographical configuration present opportunities for policy-makers and politicians. This was recognised by Sir Halford Mackinder (1861–1947) one of the founders of modern geopolitical theory. The three versions of the heartland theory: 1904, 1919, and 1943 are explained in the unique historical periods of their formation. Attention is then focused on the proposition which can be reduced to suggest the future release for Mackinder's ideas. Mackinder's view of geography is interpreted as a combination of a geographical *longue durée* and a theatre of military action.

Alfred Thayer Mahan, Geopolitician

JON SUMIDA

The present essay advances four major revisionist propositions about Mahan and geopolitics. First, Mahan believed that good political and naval leadership was no less important than geography when it came to the development of sea power. Second, his unit of political analysis in so far as sea power was concerned was a trans-national consortium rather than the single nation state. Third, his economic ideal was free trade rather than autarchy. And fourth, his recognition of the influence of geography on strategy was tempered by a strong appreciation of the power of contingency to affect outcomes.

Air Power, Space Power and Geography

BENJAMIN S. LAMBETH

Success in major wars continues to require the involvement of all combat elements in appropriately integrated fashion. However, new air and space capabilities now permit joint force commanders to conduct operations against organized enemy forces more quickly and effectively than ever before. Properly applied, those capabilities enable the achievement of strategic effects directly, by offering commanders the prospect of engaging and destroying or neutralizing enemy ground forces from stand-off ranges with virtual impunity, thus reducing a threat to friendly troops who might otherwise have to engage undegraded enemy ground forces in direct contact and risk sustaining high casualties as a result.

Geography in the Space Age: An Astropolitical Analysis

EVERETT C. DOLMAN

The line of geopolitical theory known as grand geostrategy includes assessments for land, sea, and air operations. Space power is here advocated as the next logical step in a coherent evolution of geostrategic thought. In this brief essay, I extend the classical geostrategic theories of Mackinder, Mahan, and Douhet into outer space. If these broad concepts can be proven transferable to the new realm, then arguments for the revivial of geopolitical theory as a useful avenue for academic inquiry are strengthened. By identifying salient and hopefully heuristic concepts in what should become the next arena for geopolitical analysis, I hope to add a still vital component to the rapidly growing literature on space power.

Understanding Critical Geopolitics: Geopolitics and Risk Society

GEARÓID Ó TUATHAIL

Critical geopolitics is a perspective within contemporary political geography that investigates the politics of geographical knowledge in international relations. It has four different dimensions: formal, practical, popular and structural geopolitics. All four dimensions are introduced and briefly illustrated with reference to Sir Halford Mackinder, the discourse of 'Balkanism', and the processes shaping the contemporary geopolitical condition. These processes, globalization, informationalization and proliferating techno-scientific risks, force a re-thinking of geopolitics in what Ulrich Beck terms a 'risk society'. Three critical geopolitical arguments about the dilemmas of geopolitics in risk society comprise the conclusion.

Geopolitics: International Boundaries as Fighting Places

EWAN ANDERSON

The importance of international boundaries in relation to sovereignty, state security and global flashpoints is identified. Boundary settlement requires geographical evidence, political will and international law support. Key recent concerns have been: maritime boundaries, transboundary issues, macropolitical problems and a post-modern approach to the subject. Examples of the main categories of boundary classification are given. The acquisition of territory and boundaries is discussed in detail with a focus upon the types of evidence used, the various settlement procedures and the stages of achieving agreement. The arguments are summarised in a discussion on boundaries as the environment for conflict.

Information Power: Strategy, Geopolitics and the Fifth Dimension

DAVID J. LONSDALE

In response to some of the current literature, this analysis argues that the information age will not invalidate the importance of physical geography in geopolitics and strategy. Although recognising that the infosphere represents a fifth dimension of strategy, the author contends that the strategic limitations of information power signify that physical expressions of military power will continue to dominate the practice of strategy. However, the infosphere is perhaps attaining greater significance. Consequently, this essay explores the nature of the fifth dimension, and outlines 'control of the infosphere' as a useful strategic concept for the twenty-first century.

Inescapable Geography

COLIN S. GRAY

A comprehensive analysis of geography and strategy which argues that the former vitally influences tactical and then operational prowess. Strategy comes from the dialogue between policy and military power, but the grammar of strategy is dictated by the distinctive requirements of physical geography even in nuclear war. Geography as well as being physical also has its effect on the imagination, not least in geopolitical theory.

Weather, Geography and Naval Power in the Age of Sail

N. A. M. RODGER

The essay examines the constraints imposed on naval operations in the seventeenth and eighteenth centuries by wind systems and available navigational techniques. The course of the Anglo-Dutch Wars was largely dictated by the shoals and tides of the North Sea and Channel. War against France moved to the open Atlantic and beyond, where wind systems and the longitude problem governed the strategic possibilities. British command of the sea was finally achieved by exploiting the geography and wind system of European waters to defend against invasion and dominate the French and Spanish navies.

Some Thoughts on War and Geography

WILLIAMSON MURRAY

The focus of this study is military historical looking in turn at the tactical, operational and strategic levels of war and geography primarily in the twentieth century. Even air power is a prisoner of terrain because of its need for bases. Mistakes at tactical and operational levels can be corrected promptly but not at the strategic level. The 'American Way of War' is defended because it recognises that only plentiful logistics can overcome geography and get US forces to the theatre of war as happened in World War II. This lesson is in danger of having to be relearnt by the Pentagon.

Geopolitik: Haushofer, Hitler and Lebensraum

HOLGER H. HERWIG

Karl Haushofer crafted, taught, and disseminated geopolitical theories throughout the Weimar and early Nazi periods. His influence on the development of Nazi policy remains controversial. Closely connected to Hitler and Hess, Haushofer supported the development of the Nazi Party and unquestioningly laid the intellectual framework which underpinned the concept of *Lebensraum*. In the hands of the Nazi regime, geopolitical theory became, in the words of Karl's son Albrecht Haushofer, akin to a genie released from the bottle. In the end, Haushofer discovered that he was disposable to those whom he had helped to empower.

'Russia Will not be Trifled With': Geopolitical Facts and Fantasies

JOHN ERICKSON

Long reviled in the former Soviet Union, geopolitics has returned to haunt post-Soviet Russia. Russian vulnerabilities, complicated security arrangements, the identity crisis intensified discussion of Russia's vital interests and threat identification. Russia's shrunken geopolitical 'space' has transformed geopolitical extroversion into introversion. A major effort has gone into developing a general theory of geopolitics and security, generating a concept of national security which also embraces energy security where geopolitics and geo-economics increasingly coincide. Without directly challenging American supremacy, ideas of a Russo-Indian-Chinese Eurasian geostrategic combination aim to promote diversity, foster multipolarity and outflank the 'hegemonism' of unipolarity.

About the Contributors

Colin S. Gray is the Director of the Centre for Security Studies at the University of Hull. Professor Gray held a presidential appointment in the Reagan administration from 1982 to 1987, and served on the Panel of Experts on Britain's Strategic Defence Review in 1997/98. His recent books include *The Leverage of Sea Power* (1992), *Weapons Don't Make War* (1993), and *Explorations in Strategy* (1996). In 1999 he will publish books on *Modern Strategy*, and *The Second Nuclear Age*.

Geoffrey Sloan is Deputy Head of the Department of Strategic Studies and International Affairs, Britannia Royal Naval College, Dartmouth. His most recent book is *The Geopolitics of Anglo-Irish Relations in the Twentieth Century* (Leicester UP 1997).

Jon Sumida is an Associate Professor of History at the University of Maryland, College Park. He received his undergraduate degree from the University of California at Santa Cruz, and his doctorate from the University of Chicago. He is the author of *In Defence of Naval Supremacy: Finance, Technology and British Naval Policy, 1889–1914* (Unwin Hyman 1989), *Inventing Grand Strategy and Teaching Command: The Classic Works of Alfred Thayer Mahan Reconsidered* (Wilson Center 1997), and the Editor of *The Pollen Papers* (Navy Records Society 1984). He has received fellowships from the Wilson Center and Guggenheim Foundation.

Benjamin S. Lambeth is a senior staff member at RAND. He has written extensively on defence matters and is the author of *Russia's Air Power* *in Crisis* (Smithsonian Institution Press 1999) and *The Transformation of American Air Power* (Cornell UP, forthcoming). A civil-rated pilot, he has flown in more than 35 different combat aircraft types with six air forces worldwide. In December 1989 he became the first US citizen to fly the Soviet MiG-29 fighter.

Everett C. Dolman is Assistant Professor, Department of Political Science, Berry College, Rome, Georgia, USA. Dr Dolman graduated with distinction in History from Montana State University in 1981 and was awarded his PhD by the University of Pennsylvania. He was Space Systems Analyst/Satellite Reconnaissance Warning Officer and Joint Staff Senior Intelligence Analyst in US Space Command (1986–94) for whom and the US Army he wrote or co-wrote five space-related handbooks and reports. Dr Dolman has a book in progress entitled 'Astropolitics and *Astropolitik*: International Cooperation and Conflict in Outer Space'. He has also published six journal or edited volume articles and reviewed regularly since 1994.

Gearóid Ó Tuathail (Gerard Toal) is Associate Professor of Geography at Virginia Tech., Blacksburg, Virginia. He is the author of *Critical Geopolitics* (Routledge and University of Minnesota Press, 1996), and is a co-editor of *The Geopolitics Reader* (Routledge 1998), *An Unruly World? Globalization, Governance and Geography* (Routledge 1998) and *Re-Thinking Geopolitics* (Routledge 1998) as well as the author of numerous articles on geopolitics. He is currently working on a manuscript on the American foreign policy debate over Kosovo for Blackwell.

Ewan Anderson is Professor of Geopolitics at the Centre for Middle Eastern and Islamic Studies, University of Durham, England. In research and applied studies, he has focused upon international boundaries, refugee movements, development, strategic resources and transboundary problems, particularly of water. His other main area of geopolitical interest is defence and security. His books include *An Atlas of World Political Flashpoints* (London: Pinter 1993).

David J. Lonsdale is a final year doctoral candidate and Graduate Teaching Assistant at the Department of Politics and Asian Studies, University of Hull, England. He is currently researching classical strategic thought in the information age.

N. A. M. Rodger is Anderson Fellow of the National Maritime Museum. His most recent book is the acclaimed *The Safeguard of the Sea: A Naval History of Great Britain 660–1649* (HarperCollins 1997), the first of three volumes on this subject.

Williamson Murray is Harold K. Johnson Professor of Military History at the US Army War College. He is known for his books on Hitler's Luftwaffe and military effectiveness in the twentieth century.

Holger H. Herwig is Professor of History at the University of Calgary. His published work concentrates on the Central Powers in World War I. Since 1996 he has been Editor of the Naval Policy and History Series of Frank Cass Publishers in which six titles have been published with another six due by the end of next year.

John Erickson is Honorary Fellow in Defence Studies and Professor Emeritus, University of Edinburgh, Scotland. Among his books are *The Soviet High Command 1918–1941* (1962 and 1984); *Stalin's War with Germany* (Vol.1: *The Road to Stalingrad*, Vol.2 *The Road to Berlin* (1983 and 1998); *The Soviet Ground Forces: An Operational Assessment* (1986); with L. Erickson, *The Soviet Armed Forces 1918–1992: A Research Guide to Soviet Sources* (1996) and as Editor, *Barbarossa: The Axis and the Allies* (1994 and 1998). Professor Erickson also writes for journals and newspapers, broadcast and acts as consultant to the media.

Index

Note: Bold page numbers refer to Tables and Figures. Notes have been indexed only when they give substantial further information.